A Handbook for Catholic Preaching

Developed under the auspices of
The Catholic Academy of Liturgy

General Editor
Edward Foley

Associate Editors
Catherine Vincie
Richard Fragomeni

Cosponsored by
The Catholic Association of Teachers of Homiletics and
The Federation of Diocesan Liturgical Commissions

A PUEBLO BOOK

Liturgical Press   Collegeville, Minnesota

www.litpress.org

A Pueblo Book published by Liturgical Press

Cover design by Ann Blattner. Illustrations by Frank Kacmarcik, OblSB.

1   2   3   4   5   6   7   8   9

Library of Congress Cataloging-in-Publication Data

Names: Foley, Edward, editor.
Title: A handbook for Catholic preaching / general editor, Edward Foley ;
    associate editors, Catherine Vincie, Richard Fragomeni.
Description: Collegeville, Minnesota : Liturgical Press, 2016.
Identifiers: LCCN 2016012048 (print) | LCCN 2016025631 (ebook) | ISBN
    9780814663165 | ISBN 9780814663417 (ebook)
Subjects: LCSH: Catholic preaching.
Classification: LCC BX1795.P72 H36 2016 (print) | LCC BX1795.P72 (ebook) |
    DDC 251.0088/282—dc23
LC record available at https://lccn.loc.gov/2016012048

Contents

Preface   ix

Introduction   xi
  Timothy Radcliffe

List of Abbreviations   xxiii

Introductory Essays

Preaching as a Spiritual Exercise   3
  Robert F. Morneau

The Teaching of Preaching   14
  Richard N. Fragomeni and James A. Wallace

Roman Catholic Teaching on Preaching: A Postconciliar Survey   26
  Con Foley and Richard N. Fragomeni

Historical Perspectives

Preaching in the New Testament   41
  vanThanh Nguyen

Preaching in the Early Christian Church   51
  Alden Bass

Medieval Preaching   62
  Carolyn Muessig

Preaching from Trent to the Enlightenment   74
  Robert Bireley

Preaching before Vatican II   84
  Guerric DeBona

Preaching after Vatican II   95
  Guerric DeBona

Genres of Preaching

Evangelization and the Ministry of Preaching   105
  Frank DeSiano

Biblical Preaching   116
  Dianne Bergant

Doctrinal and Catechetical Preaching   124
  Michael E. Connors and Ann M. Garrido

Mystagogical Preaching   134
  Catherine Vincie

Liturgical and Sacramental Preaching   146
  John F. Baldovin

The Homily   156
  Edward Foley

Contemporary Perspectives on Preaching

Narrative Preaching and Narrative Reciprocity   169
  Herbert Anderson

Preaching as Public Theology   180
  William T. Ditewig

Imagination and Preaching   190
  David J. Lose

Rhetorical Approaches to Preaching   200
  Lucy Lind Hogan

Prophetic Preaching   210
  Jorge Presmanes

The "New Hermeneutics"   221
  Mary Margaret Pazdan

Contemporary Issues in Preaching

Contextual Preaching   233
  Stephen Bevans and Ricky Manalo

Ecumenical and Interfaith Preaching   244
  Barbara K. Lundblad and Margaret Moers Wenig

Preaching in a Digital Age   254
  Anthony Collamati, Richard Vosko, and Alex Zenthoefer

Charism and Order in Preaching   264
  Patricia Parachini and Patrick Lagges

Preaching and Catholic Social Teaching   275
  John Carr

The Ecumenical Contributions of Roman Catholic Preaching   287
  Craig Alan Satterlee and Gregory Heille

List of Contributors   297

Index   300

Preface

Since the onset of Vatican II (1962–1965), the global Roman Catholic community has given significantly more consideration to the emphasis many sixteenth-century reformers placed on the Word of God and preaching. In particular, liturgical preaching—especially the ancient tradition of the homily—has received serious attention over the past few decades, both in preaching ministries as well as in graduate programs preparing future preachers. It is partly this recognition of renewed vitality around the preaching arts that has spurred the conceiving, designing, birthing, and production of this volume.

This work has an admittedly Roman Catholic origin and trajectory: developing in the Catholic Academy of Liturgy and subsequently cosponsored by that organization, the Catholic Association of Teachers of Homiletics, and the Federation of Diocesan Liturgical Commissions. One of the reasons for this "Roman" underscoring is the unusual amount of law, rubrical directives, and official instruction about preaching in our tradition. These exhortations and prescriptions have a singular impact in our communities regarding who can preach, in what settings, and in what capacities. Related is the focal import of sacraments—especially the Eucharist—in the life of our church and the multiple ramifications this has for our particular slant on sacramental and homiletic preaching.

While admitting these particular parameters and priorities for Roman Catholic preachers, this volume was intentionally envisioned as a handbook for "catholic" preaching in the broadest sense of that term. The role of the Scriptures in preaching, the challenges of preaching in a digital age, sermonizing in an interfaith context, and the need for a liberative and prophetic word cut across denominations and even some faith traditions. Thus we have been honored to share this venture with multiple Episcopalian, Jewish, and Lutheran collaborators. At the same time, we hope to highlight some of the distinctive contributions of contemporary Roman Catholic preaching, e.g., its dialogue with Catholic social teaching. Part of our catholic path here has also been to broaden our palette of contributors and engage women and men, academics and practitioners, established scholars and emerging voices, and lay and ordained of different ethnicities and perspectives, as well as voices from outside of North America. We also believe that the collaborative spirit of this volume—explicitly symbolized in many coauthored entries and implicitly recognized in the rich dialogue between editors and authors who published here without remuneration—also speaks volumes about preaching in a catholic mode.

While this resource is intended to aid those who teach or direct the preaching arts, professors and bishops, working preachers, and pastoral supervisors, the design and writing style were particularly calibrated to graduate students in ministerial studies. Every article—each of approximately four thousand words—was meant to be a self-contained overview of a particular historical period, genre of preaching, homiletic theory, or contemporary issue. This more encyclopedic approach—largely devoid of footnotes yet supported by pertinent bibliography—is intended to provide a sufficiently rich yet thoroughly accessible gateway to major facets of the preaching arts at this stage of the twenty-first century. This approach also, by necessity, limits the number of essays that could be included in such a volume. Thus, there are no individual articles on the preaching of Augustine of Hippo (d. 430), relevant architectural considerations, the impact of Paul Ricoeur's (d. 2005) hermeneutical approaches, or the role of women through the preaching tradition. On the other hand, it is hoped that the extensive indices at the end of the volume, as well as internal cross-referencing, might enable the reader to trace key individuals, ideas, or movements across the broad landscapes sketched in this volume.

Besides our distinguished and generous collaborators, the editors express again our gratitude to our cosponsors of this project and their respective leadership: the Catholic Academy of Liturgy, the Catholic Association of Teachers of Homiletics, and the Federation of Diocesan Liturgical Commissions. Finally, we are deeply grateful to the Liturgical Press for supporting this project since its inception, especially Hans Christoffersen and Peter Dwyer.

Edward Foley, Capuchin
Feast of the Presentation, 2016

Introduction

Timothy Radcliffe

Yves Congar, OP (d. 1995), one of the fathers of the Second Vatican Council (1962–1965), asserted that a congregation with good preaching but deprived of the sacraments would, after forty years, be more flourishing than a congregation with the sacraments but no preaching. In case you think that this is a typically Dominican exaggeration, the famous fifteenth-century Franciscan preacher Bernardino of Siena (d. 1444) said that if one had to choose between listening to a sermon or going to church, the sermon was more important. Paul wrote to the Romans: "How are they to call on one in whom they have not believed? And how are they to believe in one of whom they have never heard? And how are they to hear without someone to proclaim him? And how are they to proclaim him unless they are sent?" (Rom 10:14).

If preaching is at the very heart of the Christian community, why is it the focus of so much angst? If we are all missionary disciples, as Pope Francis (b. 1936) often asserts, then how are the laity to preach? Where do we hear the voice of women in the patriarchal church? How can our preaching of the Gospel reach our secularized contemporaries? Then there is the vexed question of the homily during the Eucharist: Should it be entrusted only to the ordained? Why are most homilies so boring?

Our Forebears Faced These Questions Before!

This *Handbook for Catholic Preaching* shows us that these are questions that have been posed from the beginning. Preaching has never been easy. When the Lord asked Moses to return to Egypt to summon the Hebrews to freedom, he answered: "Oh, my LORD, I have never been eloquent, neither in the past nor even now that you have spoken to your servant; but I am slow of speech and slow of tongue" (Exod 4:10). Jeremiah tried to refuse the Lord's invitation to prophecy: "Ah, LORD God! Behold, I do not know how to speak, for I am only a youth" (Jer 1:6).

The question of preaching by women also surfaces from time to time. Already it was a live issue in Paul's churches (1 Cor 14:34). In the twelfth century, many laypeople claimed the right to preach. Carolyn Muessig (see 64 below) shows that the preaching of women was debated in the fourteenth century. Nuns often preached in their monasteries; Hildegard of Bingen (d. 1179) famously went on preaching tours. Other women preachers approved by bishops include Rose of Viterbo (d. 1252) and Humility of Faenza (d. 1310). Contrary to the common impression that prior to Vatican II preaching was exclusively performed by male priests, Guerric De Bona (see 86 below) shows that before the Second World War women were actively involved in the street preaching of the Catholic Evidence Guilds, especially from Rosary College (now Dominican University) in River Forest, Illinois.

Most of us would sympathize with Anthony Trollope (d. 1882) who, in *Barchester Towers*, laments: "There is, perhaps, no greater hardship at present inflicted on mankind in civilized and free countries, than the necessity of listening to sermons. No one but a preaching clergyman has, in these realms, the power of compelling an audience to sit silent and be tormented" (Trollope 1857, 49). From the beginning of Christianity, listening to preachers has been a trial for the people of God. Paul preached so long once that a young lad, Eutychus, fell to his death (Acts 20:9). I console myself that never, to my knowledge, has my preaching caused anyone's death! We may lament the magnetic attraction of the new means of communication, but our forebears have also contended with more lively entertainments. Alden Bass (see 55 below) informs us that fourth-century preachers competed against the excitement of the hippodrome, the circus, civic festivals, and the theater. They employed claques to applaud them and encouraged fans to jump up and down "as occurred in the theater." Even Augustine (d. 430) enjoyed acclaim!

In Syria, another approach was adopted to combat boredom. Sermons were put to music and verse. Ephrem of Nisbis (d. 373), one of the most famous preachers of all times, taught his congregations to sing refrains to keep them awake. Jacob of Serug (d. 521) composed almost eight hundred homiletic poems and was known charmingly as "the flute of the Holy Spirit and the harp of the orthodox church."

In the Middle Ages, preachers employed all sorts of theatrical devices to draw in the crowds. Carolyn Muessig tells us about a Franciscan friar who constructed a sort of chapel near the pulpit from which emerged suitable noise—hammering nails and blowing trumpets—to enliven his description of the crucifixion (see 66 below). In the last century, Guerric DeBona (see 90–92 below) shows how Roman Catholics used radio and television to reach new audiences, especially the "golden voiced" Fulton Sheen, as *Time* magazine called him in 1946.

It is encouraging to discover that our forebears have faced similar challenges in the proclamation of the Gospel, used the new means of communication of their time, and struggled to prevent people from falling asleep!

Today's Challenges

Preaching in our time does face new challenges, even though they may be no more severe than those of former times. Paul VI (d. 1978), ten years after the closure of Vatican II, wrote in *Evangelii Nuntiandi*: "The split between the Gospel and culture is without a doubt the drama of our time, just as it was of other times. Therefore every effort must be made to ensure a full evangelization of culture, or more correctly of cultures. They have to be regenerated by an encounter with the Gospel" (*EN*, no. 20). Contemporary Western cultures are open to the Gospel in ways that some previous cultures have not been but closed to the Word in other ways.

We live in contexts in which endless images are diffused from tablets and laptops, in films and social media. The film about the death of the Trappist monks in Algeria, *Of Gods and Men* (2010), made an enormous impact when it was first shown in France because its images spoke immediately to generations attuned to the visual. Yet at the heart of our faith is the Word of God. It is a Word that is certainly filled with vivid images, but how can it engage cultures less nurtured by texts?

The twenty-first century is an era of immediate and compressed communication (see 257 below). A tweet is limited to 140 characters. The Word of God, however, is countercultural in ways that are difficult to grasp in a few seconds. God's Word opens up a world of gift and gratitude that radically contradicts our consumerist contexts. Yet how can we engage the attention of an impatient culture, which might not hang around long enough to get the message? Researchers claim that even goldfish have a longer attention span than twenty-first-century humans!

Like the late Roman Empire, many contemporary societies are hooked on entertainment. Education, sports, the news, and politics are under pressure to be entertaining in contexts whose worst condemnation is "boring!" Should we compete and make our worship and homilies entertaining or dare to explore issues in depth and risk being thought dull?

We prepare our preaching for particular congregations or gatherings. We choose words that will resonate with these people and suggest interpretations that will engage with their experiences. At any moment, however, what one has said may be snatched out of that context by the media and placed in a new context of another's choosing, often with the intention of dramatic effect and of arousing indignation! I once was asked to address an academic committee set up by the Church of England to consider the complex ethical issues raised by homosexuality, only to find the meaning of my words dragged out of context and distorted by furious campaigners who were eager to convict me of heresy!

Contemporary Western societies, as never before, are meeting places of strangers and yet fear difference. Zygmunt Bauman (b. 1920) maintains that the mobility of modern society encourages "the impulse to withdraw from risk-ridden complexity into the shelter of uniformity" (Bauman 2000, 179). Faced with the radically other, our inclination often is to retreat, to turn off, to hibernate. This is known as turtling. One retreats like a turtle into one's carapace. How can we facilitate a conversation between contemporary contexts and the alien worlds of the Babylonian exile or first-century Palestine? Might not a contemporary reaction be to say "weird!" and turn off?

We Christians—especially the ordained—suffer a crisis of authority. Fred Craddock (d. 2015) has called the preacher "as one without authority" (Craddock 2001). We have lost authority because faith is wrongly thought to be superseded by science, and rightly because of the sexual abuse crisis. Institutions are regarded with suspicion. How can we proclaim the Gospel with authority?

These challenges are probably no more daunting than those faced by the church many times before in her turbulent life, but they are *our* challenges today! In the essays of this handbook, you will find intelligent suggestions as to how we are to confront them. Perhaps I may be forgiven for offering a few brief suggestions of my own, all of which resonate with what is found in this volume.

Walking with the Lord

The disciples walking to Emmaus meet the Lord. Afterward they say: "'Were not our hearts burning within us while he was talking to us on the road, while he was opening the Scriptures to us?' That same hour they got up and returned to Jerusalem; and they found the eleven and their companions together" (Luke 24:32-33). That short verse encompasses much of the vocation of the preacher and homilist and even suggests how we may rise to the challenge of preaching in the twenty-first century.

"Were not our hearts burning within us?"

As many of the contributors to this handbook show, hearing the Word of God is not primarily receiving information about God. As Thomas Aquinas

(d. 1274) famously asserted, in this life we are joined to God as to the unknown. Hearing the Word is an explosive and ecstatic experience in which we are lifted out of ourselves and see the world anew.

It all begins with joy. Note that the disciples only refer to this joyful burning of their hearts *after* their eyes were opened in Emmaus. Before that, they had experienced a puzzling and intriguing joy of which they could make no sense and could not name. It is to be hoped that this is a joy we may, perhaps in a tiny way, embody. It is the beginning of our preaching; it is not a determined jollity: "Smile because Jesus loves you." Personally I find that sort of forced cheeriness deeply depressing! It is an often quiet joy that is large enough to carry sorrow.

This joy is described as burning within them. The encounter with God is being ignited by a fire that does not consume one—like the burning bush Moses came across in the wilderness (Exod 3:2) or the fire that engulfed the three young men in the furnace but did not burn them (Dan 3:27). Our burnt hearts are made tender.

Augustine says in *De catechizandis rudibus* that teachers should communicate with *hilaritas* (2:4) so as to provoke delight in their students. *Hilaritas* is usually translated as "cheerfulness," which suggests that we should liven up our homilies with a few jokes to stop the congregation from going to sleep. I suspect, however, that here *hilaritas* means something more like exuberance, mirth, an ecstatic joy. When preaching takes off, we are exhilarated. *Hilaritas* carries us out of ourselves.

Sometimes—maybe rarely—the Word of God erupts in our lives, liberating us from old assumptions. This was the effect of Jesus' parables. Van Thanh Nguyen writes: "More than just telling stories, however, Jesus spoke often in parables that were subversive and counterintuitive, grabbing the attention of those who heard them" (see 41 below). So in our preaching we hope and pray that we shall share with the people of God some tiny experience of how the Word of God bursts into our lives. This is the happening of grace, what my first tutor in the Dominican Order, Cornelius Ernst, OP, called the "genetic moment."

> Every genetic moment is a mystery. It is dawn, discovery, spring, new birth, coming to the light, awakening, transcendence, liberation, ecstasy, bridal consent, gift, forgiveness, reconciliation, revolution, faith, hope, love. It could be said that Christianity is the consecration of the genetic moment, the living center from which it reviews the indefinitely various and shifting perspectives of human experience in history. That, at least, is or ought to be its claim: that it is the power to transform and renew all things: "Behold, I make all things new." (Ernst 1974, 74)

This is the *hilaritas* that may—just sometimes—be detonated by our preaching.

Ultimately, no faith can be kept floating solely by experiences of emotion, however ecstatic. This is why so many converts to Pentecostalism drift away when religion seems dull and routine. This is why all preaching must reach toward the great doctrines of the church, which—as Michael Connors and Ann Garrido (see 124ff. below) show—keep alive a sense of the great mystery of our faith, even when the *hilaritas* is burning low. Contrary to popular belief, doctrine is not dry and dull but liberates the mind from the narrowness of any culture and enables us to glimpse the fullness of a truth beyond all words.

It would, however, be encouraging to see signs of delight on the faces of one's listeners from time to time. If we see only glazed eyes and furtive glances at wristwatches, we may be discouraged. Given the resistance of contemporary Western contexts to our preaching—perhaps even more in Europe than in the United States—it may be harder to penetrate that crust of indifference. The following words in that verse from the Emmaus narrative may offer us some clues as to how, with God's grace, to ignite a small fire in the hearts of our listeners.

"While he was talking to us"

Jesus joins in the conversation of the disciples as they flee from Jerusalem. He listens to their disappointment at the apparent failure of his mission: "We had hoped that he was the one to redeem Israel." The encounter with the Lord begins in conversation. Edward Foley points out that the Greek word *homilia* occurs only once in the New Testament (1 Cor 15:33), where it means communication or companionship (see 156 below).

Great preachers in the past often literally conversed with their hearers. Augustine's preaching included passionate interaction with the congregation. Peter Brown writes: "Brilliant, urgent at times, intransigent, his sermons are better described as 'dialogues with the crowd.' They are often inconclusive dialogues. One senses in them the constant presence of the unpersuaded, the indifferent and the downright disobedient" (Brown 2000, 446). If this was the reaction to the greatest preacher in Western Christianity, we should not be too abashed when our efforts seem to be fruitless!

Pedro di Cordoba (d. 1525), one of the Dominicans who arrived in the Americas with Columbus (d. 1506), astonished witnesses by refusing to preach to the indigenous people from the lofty height of a pulpit. Instead he sat on a bench, at their level, and talked to them as to friends. Robert

Bireley tells us that the seventeenth-century Jesuit Julian Maunoir, "the Apostle of Brittany," prepared the way for his missions by dialoguing with the crowd (see 79 below).

Recently the four Roman Catholic dioceses of Algeria had a yearlong exploration of the emerging identity and mission of the church in this Muslim land. As part of that process, the baptized were invited to describe what they were talking about "on the road." Hundreds reported what was on their mind and in their hearts: priests and religious, parish members, prisoners, students from other countries who had come to study in Algerian universities, migrants hoping to reach Europe. For months, the whole Roman Catholic Church in Algeria was talking on the road to Emmaus. We all listened.

Most of our preaching does not literally take the form of a dialogue. Even so, it should spring from our participation in the conversations of our communities, attending to what puzzles people, burdens them, inspires them, and gives them hope. The preacher should be listening in, learning about the things for which the sheep of this flock hunger. The homily does not just offer answers, which would be to halt the conversation. Rather, it facilitates its ongoing evolution, unsnagging it when it has become entangled, releasing the conversation from blind alleys, opening up new perspectives, and waiting to see how the conversation evolves. Our preaching serves the conversation of the community.

All preaching is at least implicitly conversational because God's revelation is. Benedict XVI (b. 1927) wrote in *Verbum Domini*, "[T]he novelty of biblical revelation consists in the fact that God becomes known through the dialogue which he desires to have with us" (*VD*, no. 6). The preacher's role is gently to facilitate the conversation between God and God's people as well as within the community. Revelation is dialogical because the very life of God is the eternal conversation of Father, Son, and Holy Spirit.

A contrast is sometimes made between proclamation of the Gospel and dialogue, with the implication that dialogue is less directly kerygmatic and tinged with relativism. The truths of our faith can only be proclaimed, however, through conversation, implying both the confidence to say what one holds most dear and the humility to listen. The earliest documents of the New Testament are Paul's letters, one-half of his passionate conversation with his churches. Reading them is like listening to someone talking on the phone and having to guess what the person at the other end of the line is saying. The Jesus of John's gospel is above all a man of conversation. Indeed, the canon of the New Testament is the eternal conversation of the gospels. Francis Watson observed: "A consensus slowly emerged that the four gospels are to be read alongside each other and that no other gospel is permitted to share in their intertextual conversation" (Watson 2013, 614).

If my preaching does not even slightly ignite my hearers, maybe I need to mingle in the crowd more, overhear what pains and puzzles them and what gives them joy. I learned what little I know about preaching when I was a university chaplain. I would go to the pub with some students after the Sunday evening Mass and discover what they really thought about my homilies! It was a painful experience, but I have never regretted it.

"On the road"

The disciples in the Emmaus story are, of course, walking in the wrong direction. They are fleeing Jerusalem, the place of revelation, where the Lord must make his ascension. They are, as it were, antidisciples. But Jesus does not bar their way or command them to return. He walks with them, respecting their freedom and sharing their journey.

It belongs to the vocation of a preacher to enter the skin of those whom he or she addresses and inhabit their doubts, knowing them from within. Even their failures are our own. Fr. Chuck Gallagher (d. 2013), the founder of Marriage Encounter, said of preaching: "You gotta start by saying, 'We lepers' and not 'You bums.'" Fr. Tony Philpot sees this identification with the congregation—even though it can tear you apart—as crucial to the vocation of the diocesan priest. One can relate what he says to any preacher. One of the most respected priests in England, he was spiritual director at the English College in Rome. In 1988 he attended a lecture in Cambridge given by the then-Cardinal Ratzinger. It was a wonderful, intelligent lecture, but it seemed vastly remote from what his parishioners were living. He felt torn apart. He wrote:

> It is uncomfortable, occupying the space between the rock and the hard place. It is uncomfortable to belong to the world of orthodoxy, and yet spend so much of my time and energy with the unorthodox, and indeed to belong to their world too. I would want to say to men preparing for diocesan priesthood that this divided heart is the characteristic pain of their vocation, and if they experience the pain, it is a sign that they will be good priests. (Philpot 1998, 88)

This is the pain of every preacher. Someone, I forget who, described preaching as swinging between the horns of a dilemma. Jesus was often confronted with dilemmas: should the woman caught in adultery be stoned? If he said yes, where was his mercy? If he said no, where was his obedience to the law? Should people pay tax to Caesar or not? Always he escaped the snare of the hunter and found a word that was both gracious and true, because he is indeed the Word of God "full of grace and truth" (John 1:14).

Because we are not the Word of God, we may swing awhile, only able to offer a tentative way forward or a partial response. Then our hearers will see us not as great masters, experts in theology and biblical study who have all the answers. We will be seen as being like them, disciples who are still learning and who may sometimes walk in the wrong direction. Then we might have true authority, because we only say what we believe to be true. William Hill wrote, "God cannot do without the stammering ways in which we strive to give utterance to that Word" (Hill 1992, 186). Paradoxically, such words may have more authority than those of preachers who are boiling over with conviction. Usually loud conviction is in inverse proportion to actual confidence. As Robert Morneau admits: "[P]eople easily spot a phony" (see 12 below).

By swinging between the horns of dilemmas, rejecting facile answers and living honestly with our doubts, preachers slowly discover their own voice. When I was a young friar, Blackfriars Hall at Oxford was blessed with several great preachers I admired enormously. When I began to preach, I usually imitated one or other of them, sometimes switching my model halfway through a homily, like a boy going through puberty, whose voice has not yet settled into maturity. Only slowly did my own voice emerge. I still lose it sometimes. Some patristic fathers taught that each of us is a Word of God, for we are spoken into existence. When we speak in our own voice, then somehow that Word of God which we *are* is heard and has a chance of convincing people. It will be a voice without pretention, maybe a quiet voice, but authentically our own and so God's too. Then it may have authority, though even Augustine, as we saw, often failed to persuade.

"While he was opening the Scriptures to us"

What are the Scriptures that we preachers are called to open, and how might this be a special challenge today? As many contributors to this book remind us, the preacher encounters the Word of God above all in the Lectionary. As far back as the mid-third century, there is evidence of the emergence of a lectionary. It was renewed at the Council of Trent (1545–1563), and Vatican II in *Sacrosanctum Concilium* called for its revision so that "a richer fare may be provided for the faithful at the Table of God's word" (*SC*, no. 51).

We treat the Lectionary with honor. It is usually solemnly carried in procession at the beginning of the Eucharist; it is incensed, accompanied by acolytes with candles, and kissed. This is the Word of God that summons each of us to come to the Lord. It gathers us in the community of the church. This is an especially Roman Catholic sense of the Word of God.

The Word of God, as found in the Lectionary (see 35 and 119 below), places us within the repeated story of the liturgical year, reaching from Advent to the feast of Christ the King. It challenges us to transcend the little stories we may tell about ourselves, the little triumphs and failures of our careers. We are summoned beyond all generational and ethnic and national stories, with their tales of aggression and competition. Our story is that of God's love of humanity, and of the whole of creation. At the beginning of the twenty-first century the global community does not always offer stories with much hope with the steady growth of terrorism and the threat of ecological catastrophe. The story of the liturgical year, embodied in the readings of the Lectionary, reaches forward to the kingdom and so is a story of hope.

This long story of salvation is embodied in the medieval cathedrals of Europe. To go to those great centers of prayer is to be embraced by a story of fall and redemption told in stone and stained glass. Every human life has its meaning inside this great adventure, in which our companions are the heroes of all ages.

The people of no previous era have had such a profound sense of the vast stretches of time of our universe's existence, created 13.5 billion years ago. And yet the people of no era have been so absorbed by the present moment, the immediacy of the "now generation." One challenge for the preacher today is to open the Scriptures so that people today sense the exhilaration of this great adventure, to be pilgrims with our hearts set on the kingdom. Martyrs truly witness to a faith that points to the kingdom, and there have never been so many martyrs as today. We need them!

The Scriptures, however, also come to us in another book, the Bible. We attend to the Word of God in this volume in a different way. It is illuminated not by candles carried by acolytes but by commentaries written by scholars. We are challenged to be obedient to the truth of the Word of God. This has been an especially Protestant perception.

Often we preachers may be tempted to scavenge the Word of God for texts that will support our agendas. God is right because God agrees with me! We seek proof texts to use in our campaigns for or against the ordination of women or as a justification for our governments to bomb or invade another territory. But this is to make the Scriptures serve me rather than humbly accepting the vocation to be the servant of the Word (*DV*, no. 10). Solid, patient biblical scholarship summons me back to the text, to its gritty otherness and challenging truth. We are reminded that it was written in a foreign language whose nuances must be respected. I cannot simply use it at my whim! The Lectionary and the Bible have their own authority and invite obedience in different ways. Both are necessary. Today we also encounter the Scriptures in a third form, on the web. This offers challenges and opportunities which are dealt with in other places in this volume (see 21 below), and which I explore elsewhere (Radcliffe 2016).

"That same hour they got up and returned to Jerusalem; and they found the eleven and their companions together"

Now they go home to Jerusalem. They will join the eleven and their companions who are gathered together. This is the church, the gathering of the people of God. The final goal of all our preaching is to invite people home to God. Pope Francis wrote, "The church is called to be the house of the Father, with doors always wide open . . . where there is a place for everyone, with all their problems" (*EG*, no. 47). This means being ministers and preachers willing to encounter and invite those who feel the need to take up again their path of faith.

We are called to accompany people—mentally, spiritually, and even sometimes physically—in their meandering journeys, with the hope of eventually helping them find a spiritual home. They cannot be driven home by threat or manipulation, for then it would not be truly their home. They must find their way there freely and with joy, their hearts burning within them. We walk with them.

Bibliography

Bauman, Zygmunt. *Liquid Modernity*. Cambridge, UK: Polity Press, 2000.

Brown, Peter. *Augustine of Hippo*. Rev. ed. London: Faber and Faber, 2000.

Craddock, Fred B. *As One without Authority*. 4th ed. St. Louis: Chalice Press, 2001 [1971].

Ernst, Cornelius. *The Theology of Grace*. Dublin: Fides, 1974.

Hill, William. "Preaching as a 'Moment' in Theology." In *Search for the Absent God: Tradition and Modernity in Religious Understanding*. Edited by Mary Catherine Hilkert. New York: Crossroad, 1992.

Philpot, Tony. *Priesthood in Reality: Living the Vocation of a Diocesan Priest in a Changing World*. Bury St. Edmunds, UK: Kevin Mahyew, 1998.

Radcliffe, Timothy. "Reading the Bible in the Twenty-First Century." *The Paulist Biblical Commentary*. Edited by José Enrique Aguilar Chiu, Richard Clifford, Carol J. Dempsey, Eileen M. Schuller, Thomas Stegman, and Ronald Witherup. New York: Paulist Press, forthcoming.

Trollope, Anthony. *Barchester Towers* (1857). https://books.google.com/.

Watson, Francis. *Gospel Writing: A Canonical Perspective*. Grand Rapids, MI: Eerdmans, 2013.

Abbreviations

AA	*Apostolicam Actuositate*, Vatican II, "Decree on the Apostolate of the Laity," 1965
AGD	*Ad Gentes Divinitus*, Vatican II, "Decree on the Church's Missionary Activity," 1965
b.	born
BCE	Before the Common Era
c., cc.	canon, canons
ca.	*circa*
CCC	Catechism of the Catholic Church, 1994
CE	Common Era
CELAM	*Consejo Episcopal Latinoamericano*, The Latin American Episcopal Conference of the Roman Catholic Church
CIC	*Codex Iuris Canonici*, The Code of Canon Law, 1917, 1983
CT	*Catechesi Tradendae*, John Paul II, "On Catechesis in Our Time," 1979
CUA	Catholic University of America
CVL	*Co-Workers in the Vineyard of the Lord: A Resource for Guiding the Development of Lay Ecclesial Ministry*, The United States Catholic Conference of Bishops, 2005
d.	died
DMC	"Directory for Masses with Children," Congregation for Divine Worship, 1973
DV	*Dei Verbum*, Vatican II, "Dogmatic Constitution on Divine Revelation," 1965

EG	*Evangelii Gaudium*, Francis, "The Joy of the Gospel," 2013
EN	*Evangelii Nuntiandi*, Paul VI, "On Evangelization in the Modern World," 1975
FIYH	*Fulfilled in Your Hearing: The Homily in the Sunday Assembly*. Bishops' Committee on Priestly Life and Ministry. Washington, DC: United States Catholic Conference, 1982. Numbering according to the text as it appears in *The Liturgy Documents, Volume One*. 5th ed. Chicago: Liturgy Training Publications, 2012. Pp. 527–55.
Gr.	Greek
GS	*Gaudium et Spes*, Vatican II, "Pastoral Constitution on the Church in the Modern World," 1965
HD	"Homiletic Directory," Congregation for Divine Worship and the Discipline of the Sacraments, 2014
ICEL	International Commission on English in the Liturgy
IGMR2002	*Institutio Generalis Missalis Romani*, the promulgated form of the 5th edition of the General Instruction of the Roman Missal, associated with *MR2002*, 2002
IO	*Inter Oecumenici*, Sacred Congregation of Rites, "First Instruction on the Orderly Carrying Out of the Constitution on the Liturgy," 1964
It.	Italian
Lat.	Latin
LG	*Lumen Gentium*, Vatican II, "Dogmatic Constitution on the Church," 1964
NCCB	National Conference of Catholic Bishops of the USA (1965–2001)
NCWC	National Catholic Welfare Conference of the Catholic Bishops of the USA (1919–1965)
No., nos.	number, numbers
OLM1981-Pr	Introduction (*Proemium*) of the *Ordo Lectionum Missae, editio typica altera*, 1981

PBC	Pontifical Biblical Commission
PO	*Presbyterorum Ordinis*, Vatican II, "Decree on the Ministry and Life of Priests," 1965
PTCM	"The Priest and the Third Christian Millennium: Teacher of the Word, Minister of the Sacraments and Leader of the Community," Congregation for the Clergy, 1999
PTMOF	*Preaching the Mystery of Faith: The Sunday Homily*, United States Catholic Conference of Bishops, 2012
RCIA	Rite of Christian Initiation of Adults
RM	*Redemptoris Missio*, John Paul II, "On the Permanent Validity of the Church's Missionary Mandate," 1990
RS	*Redemptionis Sacramentum*, Congregation for Divine Worship and the Discipline of the Sacraments, "On Certain Matters to Be Observed or to Be Avoided Regarding the Most Holy Eucharist," 2004
SC	*Sacrosanctum Concilium*, Vatican II, "Constitution on the Sacred Liturgy," 1963
SaCar	*Sacramentum Caritatis*, Benedict XVI, "Apostolic Exhortation on the Eucharist as the Source and Summit of the Church's Life and Mission," 2007
ST	*Summa Theologica*, Thomas Aquinas. Online at http://www.sacred-texts.com/chr/aquinas/summa/sum015.htm
Syr.	Syriac
Tanner	Norman Tanner, ed. *Decrees of the Ecumenical Councils*, 2 vols. London and Washington, DC: Sheed & Ward and Georgetown University Press, 1990.
USCCB	United States Catholic Conference of Bishops (from 2001)
VD	*Verbum Domini*, Benedict XVI, "On the Word of God in the Life and Mission of the Church," 2010

Introductory Essays

Preaching as a Spiritual Exercise

Robert F. Morneau

Preaching is a gift and a responsibility, a vocation and a duty, a delight and a sacrifice. As an art and a skill, it demands effortful discipline. When preaching is done well and is inspired by the Holy Spirit, it is one of the most powerful exercises leading to spiritual growth, namely, greater union with God and with the community. A key question is: what ingredients must be present for preaching to be a meaningful spiritual experience? I maintain that four ingredients are essential and nonnegotiable: prayer, study, creativity, and a love for language.

Before discussing each of these components of disciplined preaching, we might note what preachers are about, that is, the preacher's job description. In *Fulfilled in Your Hearing* (FIYH, no. 29) the Bishops' Committee on Priestly Life and Ministry articulated these objectives:

- provide the congregation with words to express faith,
- interpret life in relation to God,
- make connections between human existence and God's concerns,
- lead people to a greater unity of faith,
- face the ambiguities and challenges of the human journey, and
- share a vision of life that is faith filled.

What a demanding and challenging task! Yet, by God's grace and courageous commitment, preachers can meet these objectives in various ways at various times. It is possible when preaching is truly a spiritual exercise.

Preaching and Prayer

Before proclaiming and interpreting God's Word, preachers must never fail to spend sufficient time meditating on the Scriptures. *Lectio divina* is a proven discipline in preparing for the preaching ministry. This method employs the mind in discursive pondering, the heart in affective response, and offers an invitation to quiet the mind and heart so that the prayer of loving attention (contemplation) might be experienced. Preaching devoid of prayer might still impress the congregation with a show of intelligence and eloquence, but it will be lacking a Spirit-filled discourse.

George Herbert (d. 1633), the Anglican priest and poet, states well the relationship between preaching and praying in his verse "The Window":

> Lord, how can man preach thy eternal word?
> He is a brittle crazy glass:
> Yet in thy temple thou dost him afford
> This glorious and transcendent place,
> To be a window, through thy grace.
>
> But when thou dost anneal in glass thy story,
> Making thy life to shine within
> The holy Preacher's; then the light and glory
> More rev'rend grows, and more doth win:
> Which else shows wat'rish, bleak, and thin.
>
> Doctrine and life, colors and light, in one
> When they combine and mingle, bring
> A strong regard and awe: but speech alone
> Doth vanish like a flaring thing,
> And in the ear, not conscience, ring. (Herbert 1981, 183–84)

Transparency eventually wins out. Perceptive hearers will detect quite readily whether the preaching has the quality and tonality that only prayer can give: reverence for the Word, respect for the human condition, a deep sense of grace and sin, an authentic faith, and an epistemological humility precluding any trace of spiritual arrogance. Prayer purifies and purges preachers. It is no surprise that the prayer corner is often neglected.

Abraham Joshua Heschel (d. 1972) understood the power and necessity of prayer in the preaching ministry. He wrote: "If the vast amount of time and energy invested in the search of ideas and devices for preaching, if the fire spent on the altar of oratory were dedicated to the realm of prayer, we would not find it too difficult to convey to others what it means to utter a word in the presence of God" (Heschel 1954, 79). It is in prayer that the preacher's mind and heart lies open to divine inspiration in a special way. It is in that sacred "trembling silence" of which Augustine (d. 430) speaks that we are given access to divine wisdom that far exceeds our limited human intelligence. Unless this spiritual exercise of consistent and authentic prayer is undertaken, our preaching will be wanting.

There is yet another significant dimension of prayer and preaching. The preacher must not only ask for the guidance and inspiration of the Holy

Spirit in the task of preaching but also should also pray for the congregation that the Holy Spirit might make the people gathered for worship receptive to the wisdom and power of God's Word. The great Dominican theologian Yves Congar (d. 1995) put it this way: "The preacher has to beseech him [the Holy Spirit] earnestly to come both into his poor words and into the hearts of those who hear them" (Congar 1997, 1:x). To bring this level of intentionality to the preaching ministry is a sign of maturity and manifests a deep understanding of the human condition.

The preacher's prayer is talking things over with God. It is a mutual discourse between friends, a respectful listening and responding, a precious time of graced silence. The fundamental question that a preacher brings to the prayer corner is: "What is the message that you want me to deliver to your people today?" In his excellent book *Faith Maps: Ten Religious Explorers from Newman to Joseph Ratzinger*, Michael Paul Gallagher, SJ, writes: "Christian prayer means relaxing into the reality of being loved by God, in order to rise, each day, into the gritty realism of loving" (Gallagher 2010, 152). When preachers experience their being loved by a gracious God, their preaching will convene in some fashion the mystery that our God is Love itself.

Just as regular evaluation of our preaching is important, so too should we assess the quality of our prayer. In a conference given by Fr. Dan Felton, vicar-general of the Diocese of Green Bay, he challenged the ministers gathered to deal with three questions regarding our spiritual lives: what should we start doing, what should we stop doing, and what should we keep doing. These questions are relevant to our preaching and prayer life, for example:

> Is there anything we should START doing?
> read Augustine's *Confessions*, observe a daily personal devotion,
>   make a retreat?
>
> Is there anything we should STOP doing?
> speed-reading the Scriptures, multitasking while praying, daydreaming?
>
> Is there anything you should KEEP doing?
> pondering religious poetry, praying Psalm 23, singing great hymns?
>
> Start! Stop! Keep!
> Assess these imperatives each week.

Preaching and Study

The claim is often made that writing well demands reading broadly. The same claim might be made regarding the preaching ministry. Preachers who do not read and do not have a sustained, disciplined intellectual life will soon find themselves with little of any significance to say (but this does not mean that they may not have a lot of *insignificant* things to say). Though the reading of quality periodicals is commendable, more is required. Returning to the classics (Augustine's *Confessions*, the *Imitation of Christ*, the mystics) and exploring the writings of the great theologians (Karl Rahner [d. 1984], Yves Congar, Hans Urs von Balthasar [d. 1988]) provide insights and faith maps that enrich the preacher's theological horizons and eventually, it is hoped, the worldview of the congregation. Preachers would do well to read Michael Paul Gallagher's *Faith Maps*, mentioned above. Gallagher summarizes in a masterful way the faith insights of such scholars as Maurice Blondel (d. 1949), Karl Rahner, Bernard Lonergan (d. 1984), Charles Taylor (b. 1931), Dorothee Soelle (d. 2003), Flannery O'Connor (d. 1964), and Pierangelo Sequeri (b. 1944). Delving into the thoughts of these intellectuals and people of faith provides much material to share with the faith community.

Although a trend toward anti-intellectualism might be too strong an accusation against our times, certainly a high level of pragmatism reigns. The pastoral dimension of ministry over the intellectual is emphasized (and maybe rightly so). This is not, however, an either/or issue. Quality time must be devoted to ongoing theological formation lest the elements of truth and wisdom get shortchanged.

Besides reading the great classics and theological scholars, preachers would benefit by the reading of poetry (Gerard Manley Hopkins [d. 1889], Langston Hughes [d. 1967], Jessica Powers [d. 1988], Alice Walker [b. 1944]); the writings of social scientists (Robert Bellah [d. 2013], Peter Berger [b. 1929], Paul Gilroy [b. 1945]); the stories of excellent novelists (Georges Bernanos [d. 1948], Frederick Buechner [b. 1926], Willa Catha [d. 1947], Sandra Cisneros [b. 1954]). Add to these disciplines the great documents of the church that require constant rereading because of their clarity and vision: Pope Paul VI's (d. 1978) *Evangelii Nuntiandi* (*EN*), Vatican II's *Gaudium et Spes* (*GS*) and *Lumen Gentium* (*LG*), Pope Francis's (b. 1936) *Evangelii Gaudium* (*EG*).

There is great mobility in today's church as parishioners move easily from one parish to another. One reason for this migration: "People go where they are nourished." If the homily, Sunday after Sunday, fails to provide some insight into the relationship between life and faith, people will often move to where they can find that connection. In other words, people have appropriate expectations. Pope Paul VI captured some of these expectations when he wrote:

The faithful assembled as a Paschal Church, celebrating the feast of the Lord present in their midst, expect much from this preaching, and will greatly benefit from it provided that it is simple, clear, direct, well adapted, profoundly dependent on Gospel teaching and faithful to the Magisterium, animated by a balanced apostolic ardor coming from its own characteristic nature, full of hope, fostering belief, and productive of peace and unity. (*EN*, no. 43)

Unless there is serious study, there is little hope that the people will be fed. In her excellent work *Naming Grace*, Mary Catherine Hilkert (b. 1948) writes: "To take on the life of the preacher is to commit oneself to becoming a contemplative and to embrace ongoing study as part of one's vocation" (Hilkert 1997, 140). Study is a spiritual exercise that keeps the mind keen and alert. Preaching arising out of scholarship holds the promise of giving the congregation a perspective that makes life meaningful and faith intelligible, while filling the heart with hope.

We are all called to be lifelong learners. It is never too late to plunge into serious intellectual work. Our hunger for meaning, wisdom, and truth is never satiated.

Learning[1]

Is it too late to learn,
to learn to live in the dark,
to live in the light,
to live?

Like the art of loving,
the art of living is a *fine* art,
demanding risk and truth and hope.

The dark contains graces and dangers,
this "lunar" spirituality.
The dark holds its terrors too,
the great field of unknowing,
   lostness.

It's never too late to learn—
and we must remember
that it's the truth that sets us free.

—Robert Morneau

---

[1] Inspired by reading Taylor 2014.

Preaching and Creativity

Creativity doesn't just happen (except in rare geniuses). Similarly, effective preaching doesn't just happen (except when the Holy Spirit reigns in the heart of the preacher). Creative preaching, i.e., life-giving preaching, requires skillful use of the imagination and the ability to bring freshness and vitality to the age-old message of God's love and mercy revealed in Jesus. Creativity helps to relate the Good News to the unique circumstances of a particular context in an engaging, challenging, and captivating manner.

In *The Prelude*, William Wordsworth (d. 1850) offers a profound insight into the creative process that preachers undertake:

> The mind of Man is fram'd even like the breath
> And harmony of music. There is dark
> Invisible workmanship that reconciles
> Discordant elements, and makes them move
> In one society. (Wordsworth 1970, 10)

Jesus, *the* preacher, spent considerable time in the workshop of his imagination reconciling the mystery of life and death as he spoke about the grain of wheat having to die so as to live, or finding one's life only by losing it, or experiencing happiness in persecution. Disciples of Jesus are called into that same workshop to engage in that spiritual exercise known as creativity, an act whose conditions "are so intimate and secret that no one can penetrate into them from outside," as Simone Weil (d. 1943) claims (Weil 1951, 86). Only those who enter into that imaginative world can draw close to emulating Jesus' metaphors and similes.

The Emmy-winning "televangelist" Bishop Fulton Sheen (d. 1979) captured the imagination of millions of people in his televised preaching (see 89–92 below). His piercing eyes, his dramatic flair, his use of a chalkboard, his J.M.J. logo ("Jesus, Mary and Joseph") drew people into listening intently to the Gospel message he proclaimed. His creative, life-giving preaching led people to go forth and give life to others. Creativity is about life, life received and life shared. Made in the image and likeness of a creative God, we emulate God by being creative in a fresh, vital, and enthusiastic way.

One means to foster creativity is the "spiritual exercise" of keeping a journal, a journal not only of our daily encounters but also a journal that notes carefully the insights from the books we read, the plays we see, the art we view. Carefully and intentionally processing the inner and outer events of our life provides abundant material for the preaching ministry. The old adage contains so much truth: "Experiences unreflected upon dehumanize."

What does humanize our life and foster creativity is to take seriously the instances of joys and sorrows that God sends us. Preaching then will rely on "real" life, experienced and processed. The congregation will know that preachers have been out on the streets, as Pope Francis admonishes them to be (*EG*, no. 49). Such preaching has an authenticity that connects the preacher's life with the lives of the congregation.

Sacrifice is a spiritual exercise: giving up one thing for another. The creativity demanded in preaching also demands sacrifice and self-denial. When Jesus commanded the disciples to go and take up God's mission, they not only left their fishing nets or tax booth or Friday night get-togethers but also left family and friends to fulfill their mission of evangelization. Theirs was a sacrificial, creative, generative life. Alan Jones, in *Exploring Spiritual Direction*, makes it clear what creativity demands:

> The creation of the simplest thing requires sacrifice because, in order to create, something has to be given up: time, energy, and alternative possibilities. The creative artist has to make everything he does serve his artistic vision. Creativity, then, requires sacrificial single-mindedness. (Jones 1985, 113)

In writing to the Corinthians, Paul wanted that faith community to think of him as a servant of Christ and a steward of God's mysteries (1 Cor 4:1). Paul saw himself and the early followers of Jesus as coworkers with God. One of God's supreme gifts is creation. We are not only a part of the mystery of creation but are also invited to make that mystery present to others by being creative, by giving life in all circumstances of life. To do that well, preachers must invoke the Holy Spirit to empower them to be creative and imaginative.

Creativity also has another component: the moral life. It is not only the imagination that is involved here but also the conscience. Truly creative preachers, to be fully authentic, must live the Gospel message. The preacher's character is a significant factor in the communication process.

Character Preaching

Preachers, by necessity, must use words.
After all, a message there is to deliver.

But Monica, St. Augustine's mother,
preached to her husband by way of character.

It was her moral life,
her abiding affection,

9

her hidden, but visible faith
that won over her spouse.

Eloquence is not to be dismissed;
words have incredible power.
But in the end it is the preacher's character
that gives the message authenticity.

—Robert Morneau

Preaching and Language

Preaching is about communication; it is about using language effectively and wisely. A great deal of communication is nonverbal: facial expressions, posture, gestures, etc. Communication is also about words that link mind to mind, heart to heart. Finding the right words to convey the Gospel message is challenging; finding the right use of language is an art that calls for discipline.

As a spiritual exercise, preaching is intimately involved with expressing in words the truths of the faith, the moral imperatives by which we are to live, the stories and parables that have the power to shape our days. Preachers do not necessarily need an extensive vocabulary (though the range of one's lexicon is significant), but the words that are part of their lexicon should clarify and express forcefully the mystery of God's love and the Paschal Mystery. Paul, a noted preacher indeed, denied that he was gifted with eloquence. For him, eloquence was not the issue. Rather, his call was to proclaim Jesus as Lord and Redeemer.

Surveys regarding the quality of preaching have not been favorable. One major criticism of preachers is verbosity—simply too many words. To counter this criticism, preachers need to exercise an economy of language. A seven- or eight-minute homily, well-crafted and to the point, is greatly appreciated over a fifteen- to twenty-minute homily that simply rattles on and on and on. Succinctness is an admirable virtue in effective preaching.

Preachers who listen to great lyrics like those of Leonard Cohen (b. 1934), Paul Simon (b. 1941), and rapper Nasir Jones (b. 1973) or read a variety of literary genres—poetry, short stories, plays, novels, memoirs, and essays—have access not only to richness of vocabularies but also to the use of language at its finest. Reading and rereading the works of Cervantes (d. 1616) and Shakespeare (d. 1616), the poetry of Emily Dickinson (d. 1886) and Rainer Maria Rilke (d. 1926), and the essays of Ralph Waldo Emerson (d. 1882) and Mary Oliver (b. 1935) provide preachers with a treasury of syntax, grammar, and lexicons. Although this reading might not be labeled "spiritual" reading, it really is. Preachers are put in contact with truth and wisdom, insights and meaning systems, and the whole gamut of human affections.

Henry David Thoreau (d. 1862) would have us believe that words are "the choicest of relics." The implication here is that words are or can be holy, drawing us closer to God and to one another. But the opposite is also true: words can alienate and cripple relationships. A word once spoken is irreversible and, like an arrow flung from a bow, will have its effects come what may. Preachers are well advised to ponder the power of words— especially the Word of God, or *dabar* in Hebrew—and to realize both their ambiguity and the inability to control their effect. Words can heal or hurt, build up or tear down, bring life or death. Using words well is an art and discipline that needs the guidance of the Holy Spirit.

Paul saw himself as Christ's servant and God's steward. I am convinced that he would also maintain that preachers are servants of words, indeed servants of the Word of God. Christian preachers are to proclaim *the* Word, Jesus, who came to redeem the world. Sermons and homilies that drift from the central proclamation of Christ crucified and risen are to be questioned.

This brings us to the issue of the principle of limitation. Words are never totally adequate in expressing the mysteries of our faith. Language simply cannot capture the fullness of reality. Thomas Aquinas (d. 1274) understood this in his insistence that the only way to talk about God was through analogy, a type of speech that stresses both similarity and difference (*ST* I, q. 13, art. 5). Despite this bothersome fact, words are still filled with wonder and power. Wordsworth reminds us: "How wond'rous the power of words, how sweet they are / According to the meaning which they bring" (Wordsworth 1970, 108). Every vocation works within its limitations. Preachers will never be completely satisfied with their discourse (nor will their congregations). We need to come back time and time again to hear other dimensions of the sweet and wonderful power of words to ponder the multiple levels of meaning.

Sometimes a single word or a short phrase can hold us spellbound for hours on end. In order for that to happen, however, we must be receptive and available.

What's in a phrase?[2]
pausing doesn't stop time
but it does suspend activity

---

[2] Inspired by reading McEntyre 2014.

and enables the soul to catch its breath
to slow down and ponder
to consider carefully whatever is at hand

pausing over a phrase of God's word
and inviting that phrase to touch one's heart
brings about a gradual transformation
and reshapes one's interiority

there is much in a phrase—
buried truth, irritating challenges,
surprises galore

—Robert Morneau

Final Thoughts

A theme that is dear to Pope Francis is the need to cultivate a "culture of encounter." My sense is that he would want preachers to "encounter" their assemblies, their "hearers," seeking feedback again and again regarding their preaching ministry. Not only are preachers, according to Francis, to "take on the smell of the sheep" (*EG*, no. 24) but they are also to "contemplate" their people and keep "an ear to the people" (*EG*, no. 154). It may be that in such listening, with ears to the ground, preachers will be made aware of their own need for the other spiritual exercises we noted above: prayer, study, creative exercises, and the pursuit of a love of language. In the process, we might also learn that assemblies crave preachers who cultivate humility, simplicity, availability, and the gift of empathetic listening.

While writing this essay, I asked several members of the local worshiping community in which I serve as presider and preacher to comment on the ministry of preaching. Their insights and observations provide a basis for other "spiritual exercises" besides those mentioned above. Their comments are also an invitation to my future as a preacher, and maybe yours. They said:

- be genuine—people easily spot a phony
- assure the assembly by your preaching that you are a fellow pilgrim
- be humble
- talk about things people deal with in their daily lives
- form a "homily helper" group of parishioners who meet weekly with the preacher to break bread, pray, critique the previous week's homily, and offer ideas for the coming Sunday

- avoid theological abstractions
- focus on God's love, forgiveness, and compassion revealed in Jesus

This provides, at least for me, a preaching syllabus that will occupy me as long as God allows me to exercise the ministry of preaching. May each of you, in your own way, discover the syllabus that your own people reveal to you; may it not discourage you but only uplift you; and may all of us in our inadequacy in the face of this most amazing call submit ourselves in mind, heart, and soul to this highest of callings.

Bibliography

Congar, Yves. *I Believe in the Holy Spirit.* Translated by David Smith. New York: Crossroad, 1997.

Gallagher, Michael Paul. *Faith Maps: Ten Religious Explorers from Newman to Joseph Ratzinger.* New York: Paulist Press, 2010.

Herbert, George. *The Country Parson, The Temple.* Edited with introduction by John N. Wall, Jr. New York: Paulist Press, 1981.

Heschel, Abraham. *Man's Quest for God.* New York: Charles Scribner's Sons, 1954.

Hilkert, Mary Catherine. *Naming Grace: Preaching and the Sacramental Imagination.* New York: Continuum, 1997.

Jones, Alan. *Exploring Spiritual Direction: An Essay on Christian Friendship.* New York: Seabury Press, 1985.

McEntyre, Mary Chandler. *What's in a Phrase? Pausing Where Scripture Gives You Pause.* Grand Rapids, MI: Eerdmans, 2014.

Taylor, Barbara Brown. *Learning to Walk in the Dark.* New York: HarperOne, 2014.

Weil, Simone. *Waiting for God.* Translated by E. Craufurd. New York: Harper & Row, 1951.

Wordsworth, William. *The Prelude or, Growth of a Poet's Mind.* Edited by Ernest de Selincourt. New York: Oxford University Press, 1970.

The Teaching of Preaching

Richard N. Fragomeni and James A. Wallace

We know that Jesus called the twelve "to be with him and to be sent out to proclaim the message, and to have authority to cast out demons" (Mark 3:14-15). We also know that when he sent them out, his instructions focused mainly on traveling lightly—no staff, no bread, no bag, no money, allowing only for a pair of sandals and one tunic (Mark 6:7-9)—preaching the Good News of the kingdom and moving on. Unfortunately, we get no instructions on their training for preaching, other than the example of Jesus himself, his basic message, and his use of images and parables in getting it across. The gift of the Holy Spirit after his resurrection to fill their hearts and enlighten their minds must not be forgotten.

Centuries later, both John Chrysostom (d. 407, *Peri-Hierosynes)* and Augustine (d. 430, *De Doctrina Christiana*) offered instruction on the formation of preachers, defending the use of the art of rhetoric (see 200ff. below) against such respected figures as Cyprian of Carthage (d. 258) and Jerome (d. 420) who had less regard for it. Chrysostom called for preachers to work hard to gain the attention of their listeners, who too often came to be entertained rather than instructed (*Peri-Hierosynes,* 5.1*).* Recognizing human weakness, even in the face of God's revealed word, Chrysostom called on preachers to develop eloquence and cultivate their power through "constant application and exercise" (*Peri-Hierosynes,* 5.5*).* In a similar vein, Augustine's advice for preachers was rooted in the belief that since the Gospel provided them with the truth, indeed the Truth, what preachers must develop was a fitting style appropriate to what Cicero (d. 43 BCE) had identified as three ends of oratory: to teach, to delight, and to persuade (*De Oratore* 2.115).

The call to preach is rooted in baptism. All Christians are called to preach the Gospel, and the primary work of the church is preaching the Gospel to all. Francis of Assisi (d. 1226) is reputed to have said: "Preach often; sometimes use words." When the time comes to use words, preachers are called to use them well. From our perspective, the teaching of preaching today must concern itself with three goals: presenting a vision of preaching that includes its various purposes; encouraging certain attitudes within

14

the preacher; and cultivating homiletic habits in preaching preparation and performance.

A Multipurpose Vision of Preaching

Preaching is a multipurpose activity. Part of preaching formation is cultivating mindfulness about the various goals preaching can address. Preaching can take many forms, and it is helpful to introduce the neophyte preacher to the various ways of approaching this ministry, e.g., (1) evangelization (see 105ff. below) that introduces listeners to the Good News that is Jesus Christ: his life, ministry, suffering and death, resurrection and ascension, and continuing gift of presence "to the end of the age" (Matt 28:20) as he intercedes for us "at the right hand of God" (Rom 8:34); (2) catechetical preaching (see 124ff. below), which unfolds the mystery of Jesus Christ and what it means to continue living in Christ as a people who are prophetic, priestly, and ministerial to the world and its inhabitants (see *Catechism of the Catholic Church*, no. 783); (3) mystagogical preaching (see 134ff. below) that brings people more fully into the mystery initiated at baptism of life in the Trinity; and (4) liturgical preaching that draws listeners into the prayer life of the church, particularly during the celebration of the Eucharist (see 156ff. below) and other sacramental rites (see 146ff. below).

This vision also includes various ways in which preachers can imagine themselves in relation to the Gospel and communities to whom they speak, e.g., (1) as a herald who proclaims the Good News of what the Holy One has done, is doing, and will do for God's people; (2) as a teacher who leads us to a deeper understanding of the mysteries of our faith and a deeper commitment to the guiding principles of the Christian life; (3) as a witness, who embodies Gospel values in word and in deed; (4) as a hermeneut who interprets not only texts but also individual and communal lives through the lenses of Scripture; (5) as a mystagogue who shepherds a community into fuller participation in the mysteries being celebrated; or (6) as a prophet who speaks both a holy and disturbing truth that leads to deeper commitments to justice, peace, and reconciliation. Often, preaching will encompass a number of these tasks as preachers modulate their stance in the course of preaching in dialogue with the particular scriptural and liturgical texts of the day and the current local and global context (see 233ff. below) of this believing community.

Cultivating Appropriate Attitudes

No matter what the setting or visional stance, effective preaching is intrinsically connected to the interiority of the preacher (see 3–5 above), i.e., to the consistent pattern of attitudes—including presuppositions, prejudices, affective dispositions, and thinking—that manifest themselves in the preaching event. The appropriate alignment of such dispositions is, in our view, the most tangible intangible that requires continuous cultivation in the preacher. The ministers who diligently nurture these dispositions are inevitably a source of inspiration to their listeners.

A key aim of teaching the homiletic arts is to encourage the cultivation of these dispositions in the fledgling minister. Of the many attitudes appropriate for fostering in students, six will be emphasized here. Note, however, that such teaching is not simply passing on theory about the craft but rather an artistic apprenticeship, a gradual process of conversion and transformation. The homiletic mentor is more akin to a spiritual coach and artistic guide in these attitudes, rather than a mechanic offering techniques for some imagined oratorical toolbox.

Humility

An essential attitude for preachers is one of humility. The Christian spiritual tradition recognizes humility as a foundational virtue for communion with God. In her *Interior Castle* (Sp., *El Castillo Interior*), Teresa of Ávila (d. 1582) instructs that like bees in a honeycomb, humility must always be at work or it will be lost (2.9). At its root, humility is a truthfulness about reality. From this perspective, a student is encouraged to become truthful about several matters: first, about one's gifts and abilities. If a student is a gifted storyteller, for example, they are encouraged to refine this gift in their preaching. If a student is unable to narrate a tale or deliver a punch line effectively, humility acknowledges that reality. Such a student may learn some techniques of storytelling, recognize one's limits, and maybe employ this approach sparingly.

Humility is also the recognition that Christian preaching is about the proclamation of the Gospel. It is not a time for preachers to "undress in public," i.e., to work out personal issues in public confession or self-aggrandizement. Rather, in humility preachers recognize that their personal needs are more appropriately addressed in spiritual direction or therapy, not in the pulpit. Such humility resonates with the profound vulnerability that defines our very humanity as well as public ministry.

Another facet of humility touches the truthfulness about preaching itself. Announcing *godspel* (Old English for "good news") is heralding that all is a gift, all is grace (see Rom 4:16). Homiletic humility is an attitude of profound gratefulness both for the content of what is being preached and for the opportunity to preach such a gift in the midst of believers. Preaching is about grace, not duty. Any arrogance of purporting to have all the answers or any degree of moral superiority—often stemming from the insecurity of the preacher—has no place in preaching. Humility is an attitude of graciousness and lies at the heart of effective preaching.

Compassion

Another attitude important for effective preaching is compassion. Compassion implies empathetically engaging with the lives and struggles of others; it is an openness, particularly to the stranger and marginalized. In preaching, this is an exercise of pastoral care in light of the hopes, dreams, sufferings, and despairs of the listeners.

Compassion presumes a willingness to engage the lived reality of the local context. This is so essential that we contend that preaching without compassion for the listeners is not preaching at all. It may be brilliant oratory, but if the words do not resonate in the hearts of the listeners, they ring hollow—if they ring at all. Compassion for hearers occurs when the preacher puts his ear to the chest of the community to detect the rumblings and restlessness of human hearts. As *Fulfilled in Your Hearing* declares: the preacher must know what a community wants to hear, before a preacher can preach what a community needs to hear (FIYH, no. 4).

This is an especially difficult dimension of the craft for itinerant preachers. And yet, even the itinerant needs to cultivate an awareness of specific preaching contexts and nurture the habitus of reading such contexts—in all of their diversity and unfamiliarity. Creatively probing these contexts is essential for effective preaching.

Patience

In a digital context (see 254ff. below), where so much is immediately available at the touch of a screen, the virtue of patience needs cultivation. From many perspectives, patience is a disposition necessary for artistry—especially patience in service of insight.

The language of insight for preaching is poetic and imaginative. Such language simmers slowly. It is not a matter of finding abstract notions and theories that one can quote in a preaching event. Rather, it is a matter of allowing the metaphors and images to find their way into the preacher's imagination. This takes time. Teachers of preaching suggest patiently taking time with the readings of Scripture, with poetry, with a stroll in a museum, or with stillness itself. This disposition toward patience is one that waits for the event to arise, rather than attempting to manipulate or force insight into being.

Respect

For any pastoral minister to be effective, an attitude of respect in all its multidimensionality is obvious and necessary. For the homiletician, aside from respect for the hearers that we addressed above under the disposition of compassion, three further modes of respect are essential: respect for the tradition, for Scripture, and for the liturgy.

A preacher is one who appreciates and respects the importance of the church's doctrinal tradition (see 124ff. below). This respect is manifest in more than simple quotation. It is a matter of relishing the richness of the mystery to which the doctrine points, of honoring the mystery broached in church teachings and their implications for Christian life and service. Church teachings are not just tired, outdated dogmas. Rather, they are gems of proverbial wisdom and tested guides for encountering the presence of God.

Respect for Scripture—especially in its Lectionary configuration—is also foundational to a preacher's effectiveness. This attitude of scriptural regard honors the biblical stories, poetry, instructions, and parables as an irreplaceable wisdom heritage to be both interpreted and engaged in and outside the preaching event as a dynamic encounter with the God of Jesus Christ.

A third respectful disposition considers that treasury of prayers, antiphons, feasts and seasons, saints and popular devotions—which Roman Catholics esteem as the church's liturgy—as an authentic font and summit of ecclesial life (*SC*, no. 7). Fostering such respect imbues the liturgical preacher not only with an affection for this vast treasury as a preaching resource but also an essential treasury for the preacher's own spiritual development. Just as homileticians pray the Lectionary texts before the preaching event, so are we called to pray the liturgy in anticipation of preaching that liturgy with integrity.

Love

Love is one of the three theological virtues. These great virtues—faith, hope, and love—are considered theological virtues because they are godly gifts that cannot be attained without divine initiative. Love as a theological virtue is at the core of the habitus of preaching. A theological understanding of love is to be distinguished from a more ordinary understanding of the word. Frequently love is considered either a feeling or preferential desire, i.e., "I love you if," with the accent on "if." The latter could be deemed conditional loving as it places conditions on the desire.

Love as a theological virtue, however, is more intuitive: a sense of communion, of inter-being, that all are one. It is a deep knowing that in love there is no separation from others or God, as evoked in our eucharistic praying that we may be "one body, one spirit in Christ."

It is this profound sense of loving communion that spurs believers to a life of unbounded charity. Preachers as well are summoned to minister in service of this deep communion that God desires with us and among us. Accompanying fledgling preachers means not only inspiring them to "love" the preaching moment but also modeling this bond of charity with the triune God, the assembly of hearers, and the whole human family that should ultimately benefit from such preaching.

Joy

In his apostolic exhortation *Evangelii Gaudium* (*EG*) Pope Francis (b. 1936) offers an extensive meditation on joy. At the heart of the document is wise counsel on the homily. While admitting that preaching is often an experience of suffering both for assemblies and preachers (*EG*, no. 135), Francis encourages us to find gladness in this Word-event. Thus joy is another disposition to be nourished in the preaching habitus.

And what is joy according to Francis? It is not the fleeting experience of happiness arising when a thousand conditions or expectations have been met. Rather, it is the sustaining fruit of an authentic encounter with the living God (*EG*, no. 7). No matter what violence or pain engulfs us, the liberating presence of God can yet free us to abide in joy and in wonder at the divine gift. Thus joy—as with love—is not manufactured but received, and once it is received, it is to be shared (*EG*, no. 8). One unique form of this sharing is preaching. Nurturing fledgling preachers entails awakening them to this spirit of expectant joy that should pervade each minister and this ministry.

While tacitly understood, it should be emphasized here that teachers of preaching themselves have to model the dispositions of humility and compassion, patience and respect, love and joy: not only in their preaching but also in their mentoring of their students. Indeed, the preaching lab or classroom must be a crucible in which the teaching-learning is a virtuous encounter with the triune God and the communion of believers.

Preaching Preparation and Performance

The cultivation of the above-mentioned dispositions is a lifetime endeavor. The teaching of preaching must support and encourage such interior transformations. While these attitudes may be considered matters of the heart, there are also external habits in the preparation and performance of the homiletic arts that also require nourishing.

Prayerful Silence

Praying is sometimes described as the school for intimacy with God. Preachers are encouraged to pray daily, not only by the recitation of official prayer texts but also by cultivating a profound ease with silence (see 4 above).

Devoting oneself to the habitus of silence is an important phase in the contemplative journey of surrendering to the mystery of God. It humbles us before an ineffable presence, halts all vapid speech, and schools us in the face of the unspeakable. This habit of attentiveness to holy presence is not done in isolation, even when done alone. This wordless prayer habit connects us to a vast communion of saints: to Mary and the throng of hallowed ancestors who have preceded us into speechless transcendence. Moreover, the habit of prayerful silence becomes a portal for communion with the living who speak in languages beyond our comprehension and whose expanding diversity—like the very cosmos itself—renders us mute in appreciation and praise.

Looking and Listening

When discussing conversion and the process of gaining insight, Bernard Lonergan (d. 1984) suggested that the first essential habit for such transformation is paying attention (Lonergan 1972, 14–15). This is a skill often discarded in a context that rewards multitasking and perpetually shifting focus.

For the preacher, focus is an indispensable cognitive and spiritual praxis. Looking and listening with laser-like diligence—sometimes in silence—unlocks previously unanticipated pathways into divine wonders and life's mysteries. Such practiced diligence helps liberate the labyrinth of human consciousness and fosters sapience. There are multiple techniques available to the preaching novice for averting distraction and fostering spiritual alertness. These include *lectio divina* and its siblings *visio* and *audio divina*: not only the prayerful contemplation of a text but also parallel contemplations of images and music. Immersing oneself in a single scriptural passage, poem, painting, photograph, or musical composition rehearses the holy focus preachers need when engaging in the homiletic arts. These are enhanced when the preacher also engages in journaling about such practices of attentiveness.

Study

As previously noted (see 5–7 above) preachers must be lifelong learners. For this to happen, fledgling ministers need be intellectually persuaded and practically introduced to this cardinal habitus.

Three learning trajectories need particular encouragement in a preaching apprenticeship. First is the study of Scripture. This entails both honing classical exegetical skills while simultaneously staying current with contemporary biblical research. Happily there are high-quality internet resources that provide ample depth for this exploration. Many of these resources offer exegesis and analysis of the weekly Lectionary readings. Students may need guidance, however, in discerning the chaff from the wheat in this online universe. A second study habit of import for preaching is an ongoing engagement with theology. This, too, entails a praxis of befriending theological classics while concomitantly exploring how contemporary thinkers are interpreting the treasury of church teaching and emerging belief. Such study can also lead preachers into dialogue with other religious traditions and the eye-opening ways in which ultimate questions of meaning are addressed across the believing spectrum. Finally, it is critical for preachers to engage in serious study about the human condition. Breakthroughs in neuroscience, psychology, and political and contextual fields can offer the preacher a breadth of insight into the human family, the specific communities that are the locus for this ministry, and even the preacher's own self-awareness.

Imagining

Imagination is the gift of making connections, leaping in wonder, playfully creating something fresh (see 190ff. below). The habit of imagining is fostered by funding the imagination with regular contact with artists great and small: painters, playwrights, poets, novelists, dancers, filmmakers, songwriters and the like (see 10 above). Such contact allows for a collecting of stories and images, language and metaphors that can be woven into the preaching event both to illustrate as well as enliven the rhetorical arts. Yet there is more. The habitus of imagining comes alive in the leisure moments, in the rumination when the preacher allows herself to be affected and altered by some lyric, short story, or sculpture. This could appear to be a complete waste of time, leading to nothing tangible or productive. Yet, this is the very precondition that allows the imagining habitus to flourish: the willingness to waste time in openness to beauty. Such is necessary if we are to discover, as Rainer Maria Rilke (d. 1926) understood, that "beauty is nothing but the beginning of awesomeness which we can barely endure and we marvel at it so because it calmly disdains to destroy us" (Rilke 1975, 3). The habit of imagining is the willingness to allow the ordinary ways of perceiving to be calmly destroyed and to allow the freshness of beauty to appear in consciousness. This is a dangerous and exhilarating habit, not intended for the anxious.

Writing (and Rewriting) for the Ear

Preaching is primarily an oral-aural event, though in the case of the hearing impaired it is a visual event. As an oral-aural event, the preacher needs to grasp that there is a difference between writing for the ear and writing for the eye. This is challenging because formal education ordinarily trains us to write for the eye in a fashion of traditional literacy. While the preaching text is written, however, it is not for the eyes but for the ears of the hearers. Thus, it is necessary for neophyte preachers to engage in the praxis of writing and rewriting with an ear to orality. This requires attending to the dynamics of communication that are colloquial and respect contextual modes of speaking and hearing. It also means ceding the visual to the allurement of sound as a trusted guide into the heart of the hearers.

A classic text that effectively addresses this challenge is Richard Carl Hoefler's *Creative Preaching & Oral Writing* (1978). Like FIYH (no. 63), Hoefler emphasizes that preaching should possess the quality of an authentic conversation. He wisely elaborates that such a homiletician "gives the impression that he is thinking and uttering ideas for the first time even though he has carefully prepared and written them beforehand" (Hoefler 1978, 99). Those who wish to foster this habit would do well to study this wisdom-packed volume.

Incubation

Not unlike habits of prayer and imagining, a habitus of incubation is an intentional slowing down in *chronos* for the sake of experiencing *kairos*. When a text or outline for preaching has been crafted, the incubating muse cajoles us to let go and allow for the unconscious self to make connections and surprise the preacher with new insights and ideas (Ritter 2014). From a Christian context, this can best be understood as allowing the Holy Spirit to influence what we have done and move us to new revelations.

This maturing habit demands that we schedule time for such incubation. A weekly preparation schedule for preaching could be considered a subset of this habit. Clearing a space for such homiletic ripening is one essential moment in the process of spirit-filled preaching.

Practicing Aloud

Often overlooked, this praxis is an obvious necessity in service of the preaching arts. Like a pianist rehearsing a Chopin Étude for recital, or a ballet troupe practicing before a performance of *Swan Lake*, the preaching event requires practice. More pointedly, since this is an oral-aural event, the only way that such practice can effectively occur is when it is performed aloud.

Hearing the homily before others do is essential. With the proliferation of modern technologies, this is a simple undertaking: a smartphone, for example, is an accessible device for this task. The preacher should be listening for language that sounds conversational, connections within the piece, transitions between key moments, and a strong beginning and ending, as well as changes in vocal dynamics, the pace of the delivery, and clear enunciation. Such recordings also alert us to the actual rather than imagined length of the sermon. This ongoing exercise can be enormously contributory for the flourishing of a preaching art.

Seeking Feedback

This habitus, also obvious and self-explanatory, is nonetheless crucial. It seems inextricably connected with the concluding habitus below and can only be effectively learned and fostered in a community. This praxis strongly relies on the previously discussed virtue of humility and the parallel openness to receiving feedback and learning from it. Humility reminds us that no matter where we are on the homiletic trajectory, we can all get better; it is difficult to do so, however, without consistent feedback. Honest feedback can be cultivated through the consistent employment of some questionnaire that allows select hearers to respond. Some ask for online feedback by e-mailing a link to a survey website. Some do it more informally in conversation with trusted listeners. Others take regular refreshing courses on preaching at local seminaries or conferences.

Another model was developed by Bishop Kenneth Untener (d. 2004). He traveled around his Diocese of Saginaw, Michigan, and gathered with select clergy who together listened to audiotaped recordings of recent homilies. Criteria were established and critique was offered. Untener believed that his ministry demanded that he instill in his presbyterate the habit of seeking and offering critique. His insights endure (Untener 1999).

Group Preparation

FIYH wisely recommends that preaching is best prepared in a community of faith. This group may be other preachers who are listening to the texts and sharing the fruits of their own prayer and study of the texts. They can and should also share how they understand the scriptural texts and liturgy as it addresses and challenges the current context and specific lives of the people they serve. The group may also consist of the future listeners of the preaching who gather to attend to the scriptural and liturgical texts and share what they say to them in terms of good news, challenges, motivation for action, and celebrating the Sunday liturgy. Sometimes the gathering is a parish staff that regularly takes time to reflect on community life in view of the scriptural and liturgical texts. They, too, can assist a preacher with images and insights that can be incorporated into the incubation process as the preaching event evolves. Group preparation is a virtually fail-safe way of guaranteeing a freshness in this ministry that relentlessly asks the preacher for winged words for life.

Conclusion

Under the influence of the Roman orator Cicero (*De Oratore*, 2.1.15), Augustine outlined three ways one becomes an effective speaker: (1) learning from a book of rules and principles, (2) watching persuasive speakers who do it well and imitating them, and (3) doing it yourself and discovering from experience what works and what doesn't (*De Doctrina Christiana*, 4.4). We would add to these the cultivation of three others: (1) a biblically, theologically, and liturgically sound vision of preaching, (2) pastoral attitudes that serve the people, and (3) homiletic habits that will carry a preacher into a lifelong commitment to preaching and a joyful ministry of the Word. It is particularly to this last end that teachers of preaching gratefully ply their craft.

Bibliography

Hoefler, Richard Carl. *Creative Preaching & Oral Writing*. Lima, OH: CSS Publishing, 1978.

Lonergan, Bernard J. F. *Method in Theology*. Minneapolis: Seabury Press, 1972.

Rilke, Ranier Maria. *Duinesian Elegies*. Translated by Elaine E. Boney. Chapel Hill: University of North Carolina Press, 1975.

Ritter, Simone M., and Ap Dijksterhuis. "Creativity—the Unconscious Foundations of the Incubation Period." *Frontiers in Human Neuroscience* 8 (2014). http://doi.org/10.3389/fnhum.2014.00215.

Untener, Kenneth. *Preaching Better: Practical Suggestions for Homilists*. Mahwah, NJ: Paulist Press, 1999.

Roman Catholic Teaching on Preaching
A Postconciliar Survey
Con Foley and Richard N. Fragomeni

Introduction

Preaching has been an essential part of the Christian tradition since its beginning. When this speech-proclamation-event is examined over the centuries—as our colleagues have done in the six essays that comprise the next part of this volume—the varieties of forms and contexts that emerge are notable. Ordinarily these evolve out of the needs and contexts (see 233ff. below) of communities receiving the preached message. Sometimes preaching has been regulated by various manifestations of church leadership (Stewart-Sykes 2001).

The Roman Catholic Church launched an extensive renewal of its understanding of self and mission at Vatican II (1962–1965). Part of this renewal was reimagining the role of liturgy and preaching for revitalized communities of the baptized. In various documents, promulgated during or after Vatican II, definition and direction were provided about the liturgy and its preaching.

While there are many kinds of preaching within the tradition of the Roman church—many referenced and illustrated in this volume—official documents concern themselves mostly with the homily (see 156ff. below). With this emphasis on the homily, there was a seismic shift concerning what the preacher was to preach at Sunday Eucharist.

Previously preachers would offer a "sermon," usually apologetic or moralistic preaching, intended to persuade or educate Roman Catholics about doctrine and moral understanding or behaviors expected of them. Preachers often used preaching manuals to create a series of sermons delivered on consecutive Sundays around a common theme, e.g., the Ten Commandments or the seven sacraments. While the sermon was considered a necessary part of Sunday worship, it was not an essential part. The *Baltimore Catechism*, for example, does not include the Scriptures or preaching as a principal part of the Mass but instead lists the principal parts as consecration, offertory, and priest's communion (*Baltimore Catechism* 1891, question

932). You could miss the entire "Mass of the Catechumens," including the sermon, and still fulfill your Sunday obligation. That changed with Vatican II, which instructed that the homily was the premier form of preaching and an integral part of the Eucharistic Liturgy.

The remainder of this essay will first offer a chronological survey of official Roman Catholic understandings of preaching as developed in conciliar and postconciliar documents that pertain to the universal Roman Catholic Church. Thus we will not consider any documents from groups of bishops for some particular country or region (e.g., *Fulfilled in your Hearing* [FIYH]), so frequently referenced in this volume. Next we will offer a series of observations concerning understandings of preaching—especially liturgical preaching—from these documents.

A Chronological Survey (1963–2015)

1962: Sacrosanctum Concilium (SC)

Sacrosanctum Concilium was the first promulgated document of Vatican II. Like virtually all the documents of this council, it emphasized the importance of Scripture. *SC* makes clear that "the primary source of the sermon . . . should be scripture and liturgy, for in them is found the proclamation of God's wonderful works in the history of salvation, the mystery of Christ ever made present and active in us, especially in the celebration of the liturgy" (*SC*, no. 35.2). Through the homily, "the mysteries of the faith and the guiding principles of the christian life are expounded from the sacred text" (*SC*, no. 52). "Sacred text" not only refers to the Scriptures but also includes other texts from the ordinary or proper of the day's Mass (*Inter Oecumenici* [*IO*] no. 54).

SC confirms the importance of preaching, asserting that "the ministry of preaching should be carried out properly and with the greatest care" (*SC*, no. 35.2) for the homily "forms part of the liturgy itself" (*SC*, no. 52). The principle that the homily is an essential part of the liturgy and that there is an extricable link between Word and Eucharist is referenced multiple times in this document (*SC*, nos. 35, 48, 56, 106). *SC* concludes that the homily should be omitted only for serious reasons (*SC*, no. 52).

1965: Dei Verbum (DV)

Dei Verbum, another principal document of Vatican II, focused primarily on the role of Scripture study and methods of biblical interpretation. With regard to the homily, *DV* explicitly states that "all the preaching of the church . . . should be nourished and ruled by sacred scripture" (*DV*, no. 21). Preachers are urged to engage in diligent sacred reading and careful study of Scripture so that, in the words of Jerome (d. 420), none of them will become "empty preachers of the word of God to others, not being hearers of the word in their own hearts" (*DV*, no. 25). According to *DV*, reading and knowledge of the Scriptures should be nourished by private prayer (*DV*, no. 25) so that through the homily the preacher may enlighten the minds, strengthen the wills, and set the hearts of the faithful on fire with the love of God (*DV*, no. 23).

1965: Presbyterorum Ordinis (PO)

Promulgated just three weeks after *DV*, *Presbyterorum Ordinis* stresses that "it is the first task of priests as co-workers of the bishops to preach the Gospel of God to all" (*PO*, no. 4). This document acknowledges that the circumstances of the world make preaching very difficult. In order for preaching to be most effective, the Word of God ought not to be explained in an abstract and general way but "by an application of the eternal truth of the Gospel circumstances of life" (*PO*, no. 4). This document, however, does not give any practical guidance or direction as to how this can be achieved.

1975: Evangelii Nuntiandi (EN)

An apostolic exhortation issued by Paul VI (d. 1978), *Evangelii Nuntiandi* focuses on the topic of evangelization. Evangelization is "the essential mission of the Church" (*EN*, no. 14) and preaching is central to that mission (*EN*, no. 17). Highlighting the importance of preaching as proclaimed by Paul (Rom 10:14, 17), *EN* sets forth three general elements that must be present for authentic evangelization: preaching (1) "hope in the promises made by God in the new Covenant in Jesus Christ, (2) "God's love for us and of our love for God," and (3) "brotherly love for all . . . the capacity of giving and forgiving, of self-denial, of helping one's brother and sister" (*EN*, no. 28).

While there are many ways preaching may be used in evangelization, *EN* identifies the homily as "an important and very adaptable instrument in evangelization" (*EN*, no. 43). The preacher must have "true spiritual sensitivity for reading God's message" (*EN*, no. 43) in human events and situations. The faithful expect much from the homily and they can benefit greatly if it is "simple, clear, direct, well-adapted, profoundly dependent on Gospel teaching and faithful to the Magisterium, animated by an apostolic ardor coming from its own characteristic nature, full of hope, fostering belief, and productive of peace and unity" (*EN*, no. 43).

Paul VI stresses that homilists must take their preparation seriously so that the homily is enriching and possesses depth. Special attention should be paid to "the dignity, precision and adaptation" (*EN*, no. 73) of language as well as ongoing development of rhetorical and communication skills. It is the role of bishops to ensure that preachers receive adequate training that can give them the confidence and enthusiasm to proclaim Jesus Christ (*EN*, no. 73). According to *EN*, another essential condition for effective preaching is "witness of life" (*EN*, no. 76). This means that the preacher must have "a reverence for truth . . . even at the price of personal renunciation and suffering" (*EN*, no. 78). God is the first truth and it is the role of the homilist to search for this truth, to study it, and to communicate it. The preacher must be a person who "never betrays or hides truth out of a desire to please people, in order to astonish or shock, nor for the sake of originality or the desire to make an impression" (*EN*, no. 78).

1981: Introduction (Proemium) of the Ordo Lectionum Missae, editio typica altera (OLM1981-Pr)

This introduction to the Lectionary, like *SC*, emphasizes the homily as an essential part of the liturgy and confirms that its main function is to "lead the community of the faithful to celebrate the Eucharist actively" (*OLM1981-Pr*, no. 24). It sketches out a few rules of thumb but goes into no real depth, noting only that the homily must be "truly the fruit of meditation, carefully prepared, neither too long nor too short, and suited to all those present, even children and the uneducated" (*OLM1981-Pr*, no. 24).

1993: The Interpretation of the Bible in the Church (Pontifical Biblical Commission [PBC], 1993)

This document was presented by the PBC to John Paul II in 1993. It addresses preaching in the final part of the document regarding the "Interpretation of the Bible in the Life of the Church." Specifically it states that the ministry of preaching, especially the homily, should draw "spiritual sustenance" from the Scriptures and be "adapted to the present needs of the Christian community" (PBC, no. 4.C.3). Although he need not explain the biblical texts in detail, the preacher should be able to convey "the central contribution of the texts" in his homily (PBC, no. 4.C.3). This means that the features of the text that are "most enlightening for faith and most stimulating for the progress of the Christian life" should be presented in a manner that is sensitive to the "actualization and inculturation" of the message (PBC, no. 4.C.3). To achieve this, the preacher should employ "good hermeneutical principles" and quality exegetical publications.

The PBC notes that the tone of the homily is also important. The obligations incumbent on believers should never overshadow the "principal characteristic" of the biblical message which is "the good news of salvation freely offered by God." So it is crucial that the preacher explains the Scriptures in such a way that is challenging but positive (PBC, no. 4.C.3).

1999: The Priest and the Third Christian Millennium: Teacher of the Word, Minister of the Sacraments and Leader of the Community (PTCM)

This document from the Congregation for the Clergy highlights the relationship between the quality of preaching and the spiritual life of the priest. An active personal prayer life makes the preached word more convincing because the message "comes from a prayerful, sincere heart which is aware that sacred ministers are bound not to impart their own wisdom but the Word of God and ceaselessly to invite all to holiness." If the task of preachers is to "enthuse and purify the conscience" of the faithful, this cannot be achieved through "irresponsible and indolent improvisation" (PTCM, no. 2.2). In addition to using Sacred Scripture as a primary resource, the preacher may also wish to refer to the lives of the saints that carry "renewed significance in contemporary circumstances" and can provide vital homiletic material (PTCM, no. 2.2).

This document urges the priest to "cultivate the formal aspects of preaching," including more specialized rhetorical skills, utilizing "elegant, accurate, and accessible language," and cultivating a pleasant speaking voice (PTCM, no. 2.2). Perhaps one of the more significant insights here is that the priest should have the humility to be receptive to advice from fellow clergy and the faithful. It is recommended that the preacher seek comments on the content, theological and linguistic quality, style, and duration of the homily in an ongoing effort to improve his preaching skills (PTCM, no. 2.2).

2002: Institutio Generalis Missalis Romani (IGMR2002)

This general instruction is associated with the 2002 Roman Missal. It was originally translated into English in 2003 and retranslated in 2010, although the Latin text remained unchanged. It reminds readers that because the aim of the homily is "the nurturing of the Christian life," the preacher must "take into account both the mystery being celebrated and the particular needs of the listeners" (*IGMR2002*, no. 65). Resonant with *IO* (no. 54, noted above), this instruction confirms that the homily addresses "some aspect of the readings from Sacred Scripture or of another text from the Ordinary or the Proper of the Mass of the day" (*IGMR2002*, no. 65). The physical positioning of the preacher when delivering the homily is extended beyond the two places (ambo and chair) mentioned in the *OLM1981-Pr* (no. 26). It further notes that the priest may stand in "another worthy place" (*IGMR2002*, no. 136) when appropriate.

2004: Redemptionis Sacramentum (RS)

This instruction from the Congregation for Divine Worship and the Discipline of the Sacraments confirms the position of *IGMR2002* that the homily should expound "the mysteries of the Faith and the norms of Christian life from the biblical readings and liturgical texts . . . and provide commentary on the texts of the Ordinary or the Proper of the Mass." To this last phrase it adds something not contained in the Missal: "or of some other rite of the Church" (*RS*, no. 67). This addition appears to give homilists license to preach not only on "sacred texts" other than the biblical readings and texts of the Mass but also ritual actions that are central to such rituals, such as the reception of Communion or the anointing with oil. The US bishops anticipated this move in their 2003 *Introduction to the Order of Mass* when they noted that in the homily "the mysteries of faith and the guiding principles of Christian living are expounded most often from the Scriptures proclaimed," then adding "but also from other texts and *rites* of the liturgy" (USCCB 2003, 92).

RS also confirms that the diocesan bishop must be diligent in ensuring that priests are in compliance with the magisterial instructions on the homily and places the ultimate responsibility for oversight on the bishop (*RS*, no. 68).

2007: Sacramentum Caritatis (SaCar)

Following the 2005 Roman Synod on the Eucharist, Benedict XVI (b. 1927) issued this apostolic exhortation that emphasizes the "intrinsic bond" between the Liturgy of the Word and the Liturgy of the Eucharist (*SaCar*, no. 44). The homily must reflect this reality, and ministers should "preach in such a way that the homily closely relates the proclamation of the Word to the sacramental celebration and the life of the community" (*SaCar*, no. 46). Benedict XVI bluntly notes, "[T]he quality of homilies needs to be improved" (*SaCar*, no. 46). The purpose of the homily is "to foster a deeper understanding of the word of God, so that it can bear fruit in the lives of the faithful" (*SaCar*, no. 46). He notes the importance of keeping the "catechetical and paraenetic aim of the homily" in mind and also allows for homilies to be oriented around certain themes (*SaCar*, no. 46). The preacher, however, should judge the occasion and frequency of thematic homilies carefully. These homilies should address "the great themes of the Christian faith," particularly the "four 'pillars' of the *Catechism of the Catholic Church* . . . namely: the profession of faith, the celebration of the Christian mystery, life in Christ and Christian prayer" (*SaCar*, no. 46).

This exhortation strongly recommends mystagogical catechesis as an approach that could be used to "lead the faithful to understand more deeply the mysteries being celebrated" (*SaCar*, no. 64). Although liturgical preaching is not expressly mentioned as a form of mystagogical catechesis here, a preacher might usefully employ a mystagogical approach (see 134ff. below) to help hearers gain a "vital and convincing encounter with Christ" (*SaCar*, no. 64), leading to deeper faith and understanding.

2010: Verbum Domini (VD)

This apostolic exhortation follows the 2008 Roman Synod on the Word of God in the life and mission of the church. In it Benedict XVI stresses that in listening to the homily "the faithful should be able to perceive clearly that the preacher has a compelling desire to present Christ, who must stand at the centre of every homily" (*VD*, no. 59) To achieve this, the homilist must not only study the sacred text but also spend time in meditation and prayer with it. Benedict XVI recommends *lectio divina* as a practice that can help the homilist preach with conviction and sets out the basic steps of *lectio divina* in this document (*VD*, nos. 86–77). Benedict also recommends that "competent authorities" should prepare practical publications to assist homilists in exercising the ministry of preaching (*VD*, no. 60).

2013: Evangelii Gaudium (EG)

Pope Francis's (b. 1936) first apostolic exhortation gives considerable attention to the homily at the very heart of the document (*EG*, nos. 135–59). He identifies the homily as "the touchstone for judging a pastor's closeness and ability to communicate to his people" (*EG*, no. 135). Francis characterizes the homily as an opportunity to facilitate "dialogue between God and his people" (*EG*, no. 137) and for this reason the homily should not take on "the semblance of a speech or lecture" (*EG*, no. 138). In his view, the essential task of the preacher is not catechesis but to join "loving hearts, the hearts of the Lord and his people" (*EG*, no. 143). In this way, the homilist becomes an intermediary whose heart must be "on fire" if he is to reach the hearts of the people (*EG*, no. 144).

Unlike most church documents, Francis includes practical suggestions for homily preparation. First, he stresses that sufficient preparation time is required: preachers who don't carve out the necessary time to prepare are "dishonest and irresponsible" with the gifts that they have received (*EG*, no. 146). When preparing his homily, the preacher needs to keep in mind the needs of his congregation and "to contemplate his people" in addition to contemplating the Word (*EG*, no. 154). This means developing "a broad and profound sensitivity to what really affects other people's lives" (*EG*, no. 155).

How a homily is delivered is as important for Francis as its content. He recommends that preachers cultivate the art of using images (*EG*, no. 157) and to speak warmly and from the heart. Simple language, a clear order, and a positive message that "does not leave us trapped in negativity" (*EG*, no. 159) are necessary elements of good preaching.

While only a section of *EG* directly addresses homiletics, themes throughout the exhortation also inform good preaching (Foley 2014). Francis's emphasis on joy, mercy, and evangelization are prominent throughout the text, as is his consistent use of "heart" language and his positive view of the human person (*EG*, no. 274). Also enriching for the preacher are his treatment of the "challenges of today's world" (*EG*, nos. 52–75), the inclusion of the poor in society (*EG*, nos. 186–216), and the common good and peace in society (*EG*, nos. 217–37).

2014: The Homiletic Directory (HD)

Issued by the Congregation for Divine Worship and the Discipline of the Sacraments, HD is a response to Benedict XVI's request (*VD*, no. 60) that a directory be prepared to assist preachers in their ministry. While the introduction states that it "seeks to assimilate the insights of the past fifty years" (HD, no. 3), it offers additional resources, e.g., principles to help preachers interpret the Scriptures and practical suggestions for incorporating dogma into the Sunday homily.

The homily is redefined as "an act of worship" whose purpose is "not only to sanctify people, but to glorify God" (HD, no. 4); this resonates with the purposes of liturgy defined by *SC* (no. 7). HD emphasizes the *Catechism of the Catholic Church* (CCC; HD, no. 23). Preachers are encouraged to consult CCC as "an invaluable resource" to help "provide doctrinal and moral catechesis during the homily." The three primary criteria set out in CCC for interpreting Scripture are recommended (HD, no. 17) as guides to homilists to enable preaching "about the deepest meaning of Scripture" (HD, no. 21).

A second section—*Ars Praedicandi* (Lat. for "the art of preaching")—illustrates how the preacher can more deeply reflect "the biblical readings provided in the liturgy through the lens of the Paschal Mystery of the crucified and risen Christ" (HD, no. 37). HD contains an extended appendix, detailing how sections of CCC and church doctrine can be linked to each Sunday in the three-year Lectionary cycle.

Five Trajectories about Preaching

Having offered this survey of universal Roman Catholic documents concerned with preaching since Vatican II, it is now helpful to highlight some of the convergences or trajectories in these documents that illuminate shifts in the understanding and practice of preaching since 1963.

There Is Preaching and There Is Liturgical Preaching

The official Roman Catholic texts speak of preaching in a generic way but more specifically and frequently address liturgical preaching, i.e., the homily. In general, the importance of preaching as a singularly necessary speech-event for the proclamation of the Gospel is acknowledged throughout these documents. On the other hand, the central significance of the liturgical dimension of preaching is consistently underlined. No doubt, this is because of the regularity of this kind of preaching in the Christian communities around the world. Preaching as part of the Sunday eucharistic gathering is without doubt the most frequent kind of preaching that occurs in Roman Catholic communities as, for example, compared to parish mission preaching that may happen only once a year.

One of the more significant contributions of this emphasis on the homily is the theological transformation of "hearers" from objects of the preaching to subjects in the preaching event (see 162 below). Francis underscores this perspective when he speaks of homilists as intermediaries in the dialogue between God and God's people (*EG*, no. 143). As a centrifugal force in Roman Catholic preaching, the homily should inspire every other type of preaching to be equally respectful of all hearers as partners in these revelatory events.

The Centrality of Scripture

An unmistakable and dominant flow throughout these documents is the relentless emphasis on the centrality and necessity of Scripture for the preaching event. This emphasis is grounded in and resonant with the stress on the Word of God for the life of the church that echoes through virtually every document of Vatican II. It is true that these documents have provided a wide homiletic vision, allowing for discourse on other "sacred texts" besides the Scriptures, the mysteries being celebrated, and even other rites of the church (*RS*, no. 67). These expansions could be interpreted as an implicit recognition not only of the dual sources of revelation held by the Roman Catholic Church—i.e., Scripture and tradition—but also how some theologians have recognized that the "catholic" imagination is ultimately a "sacramental" imagination (Hilkert 1997). Despite this widening to more liturgical and sacramental preaching, these documents make clear that the Scriptures—especially as reconfigured in the Lectionary—are pivotal for preaching that calls itself catholic.

For liturgical preaching, this trajectory has been given a new embodiment in the three-year Sunday Lectionary: one of the great gifts of Vatican II–inspired reforms. Although not addressed in official documents, the distinction between Bible as Scripture and Lectionary as Scripture is essential. This distinction is considered by scholars (see 119 below), and Lectionary commentaries have been written to assist preachers in wrestling with this difference (Bergant 1999, 2000, 2001).

The Ministry of the Preacher

The documents accent many points about the preacher. Three are especially notable. First, there is an insistence that the preacher be a person deeply engaged in a life of Scripture study and contemplation. The preacher is to not only know the scriptural texts but also be inspired by them. To this end, *lectio divina* is a highly recommended practice.

Lest the preacher think only abstractly and theoretically about the Scripture, there is a second clear injunction that the preacher must know the life situations of people who are the hearers and participants in such preaching. Having a lived knowledge of the assembly allows for an unmistakable vibrancy of the Word with distinctive accents of the local communities. There is no hearing of the Word if it is not contextual (see 233ff. below).

Finally, the preacher—especially the homilist—is called to be a mystagogue. Mystagogues probe the depths of the mysteries being celebrated in prayer, action, and song. They can poetically feed and stimulate the religious imagination of the assembly. Key for becoming a mystagogue is an immersion into the vast richness of the liturgical tradition of the feasts, seasons, saints, prayer texts, tunes, and lyrics that comprise our shared prayer. Part of honing this skill comes from simultaneously immersing oneself in the poetry, music, art, and artistry of the local context. The mystagogical preacher speaks from the overwhelming beauty of this vast treasury.

The Liturgical Bible

The liturgical facet of this treasury has a name: the liturgical Bible. As noted above, these documents assert the undeniable significance of the Scriptures; for the homily, this is the reimagined Bible in the form of a lectionary. At the same time, the documents announce a startling new permission for preachers. While the Lectionary is central to the homily, the official documents set up another source for liturgical preaching. The preacher is now allowed—without ignoring the significance of the Scriptures or biblical-lectionary to Roman Catholic preaching—to engage the vast array of texts, tunes, symbols, and rites that are part of the liturgical action. For instance, one could imagine a preacher using as the centerpiece of a homily in times of distress, terrorist activity, or the all too often mass shootings that are a part of the global reality today a section from one of the eucharistic prayers for reconciliation.

These expansions in preaching parameters for Roman Catholics—distinctive from some Christian traditions that emphasize that the Bible alone is the preaching source—have been bolstered by contemporary scholarship that asserts that the Bible is actually "born of the liturgy." Thus, for example, Chauvet will assert from an "empirical" perspective that Christian assemblies—especially gathered for Eucharist and baptism—were "the decisive crucible where the Christian Bible was formed" (Chauvet 1995, 197).

The Need for Preparation

These official texts not only suggest but also seem to make it a moral obligation on the part of the preacher to prepare well for this ministry. This clarion call is particularly relevant to the homily. Furthermore, preparation requires a method. Admittedly, while the bulk of the documents under consideration are stronger on theory than practice, on concepts rather than procedures, recent Vatican texts have been more explicit, especially in outlining homiletic methods. *EG* is particularly notable here.

One interesting addition to the official discourse on homiletic preparation is found in the Homiletic Directory. In the appendix to this document, the Vatican has gone to great lengths to harmonize the Sunday Lectionary cycle of texts with certain quotations from the CCC. The caveat for preachers is not to think that such suggestions mean that the homily should once again become essentially a tool for catechesis. Rather, it could be seen as a prompt toward a richer understanding of the mysteries, best celebrated in symbol and symbolic language.

Conclusion

As colleagues from other Christian denominations sometimes note, the Roman Catholic Church is rich in law. In particular, we have much universal law and local directives about worship, sacraments, and even preaching. While this plethora of prescriptions can be experienced as an unwelcomed weight, the universal teachings about preaching in the Roman Catholic Church that we have rehearsed here, on balance, seem much more liberating than constricting. Overall, these instructions are theologically cogent, pastorally cued, well-grounded in Scripture and tradition, and focused on effective ministerial practice rather than some hermetically sealed orthodoxy. Never before, in the history of the Roman Catholic Church, has there been so much rich teaching about preaching and homiletics in such a short period of time. It is a treasure that needs to be engaged, honored—critiqued where necessary—but largely and energetically embraced.

Bibliography

Baltimore Catechism. http://www.sacred-texts.com/chr/balt/.

Bergant, Dianne, with Richard Fragomeni. *Preaching the New Lectionary.* Collegeville, MN: Liturgical Press, 1999, 2000, 2001.

Chauvet, Louis-Marie. *Symbol and Sacrament: A Sacramental Reinterpretation of Christian Existence.* Translated by Patrick Madigan. Collegeville, MN: Liturgical Press, 1995.

Foley, Edward. "The Homily in the Context of *Evangelii Gaudium*." *Pray Tell* (blog). August 13, 2014. http://www.praytellblog.com/index.php/2014/08/13/the-homily-in-the-context-of-evangelii-gaudium.

Hilkert, Mary Catherine. *Naming Grace: Preaching and the Sacramental Imagination.* New York: Continuum, 1997.

Pontifical Biblical Commission. *The Interpretation of the Bible in the Church.*
  http://catholic-resources.org/ChurchDocs/PBC_Interp-FullText.htm.
Stewart-Sykes, Alistair. *From Prophecy to Preaching: A Search for the Origins
  of the Christian Homily.* Leiden: Brill, 2001.
USCCB. *Introduction to the Order of Mass.* Washington, DC: USCCB, 2003.

Historical Perspectives

Preaching in the New Testament

vanThanh Nguyen

Introduction

Although preaching is one of the most demanding tasks of ministry, it is an essential component of bearing witness to Christ. Paul states, "Woe to me if I do not preach the gospel" (1 Cor 9:16), and again, "But how can they call on him in whom they have not believed? And how can they believe in him of whom they have not heard? And how can they hear without someone to preach?" (Rom 10:14). Indeed, preaching is an act of bearing witness that every Christian minister must frequently and enthusiastically perform. Since preaching is an art, effective preaching takes time, energy, and tremendous skills in order to establish an encounter with the Word. To preach well also requires creativity and personal conviction. Furthermore, in this day and age, when our churches are becoming more ethnically diverse, contextualizing and establishing cultural rapport with one's assembly is crucial in the proclamation of the Christian message (see 233ff. below).

The aim of this essay is to show that even in our digital world, preaching remains an essential aspect of Christian witness and mission. The essay begins by showing that as a prophet, Jesus taught with authority and power, revealing the mystery of God's reign through storytelling. More than just telling stories, however, Jesus spoke often in parables that were subversive and counterintuitive, grabbing the attention of those who heard them. Jesus' parables have the potential to transcend space and time as well as their original context to speak to us today in messages that are still pertinent and images that are still powerful. Not surprisingly, therefore, the apostles and disciples were commissioned to preach the Good News of Jesus Christ to the ends of the earth. The book of Acts gives numerous instances of effective preaching. One of the finest examples is Paul's sermon at the Areopagus in Acts 17:22-31, an outstanding illustration of cross-cultural missionary preaching in the New Testament.

Jesus the Parabolic Preacher

Prophet of the Reign of God

Jesus asked his disciples: "Who do people say that I am?" They answered, "John the Baptist; and others, Elijah; and still others, one of the prophets" (Mark 8:27-28; also Matt 16:14; Luke 9:19). People saw Jesus as a prophet. When Jesus entered Jerusalem, for example, the crowds rejoiced, singing hymns and chanting, "This is the prophet Jesus from Nazareth in Galilee" (Matt 21:11). Matthew recounts that the chief priests and the Pharisees were greatly offended by what Jesus said and therefore wanted to arrest him, but they feared the crowds "because they regarded him as a prophet" (Matt 21:46). The crowd's recognition of Jesus' prophetic character actually prevented him from being arrested. Even Jesus' opponents saw him as a prophet. Herod Antipas believed that Jesus was the prophet John, whom he had beheaded and had been raised from the dead (Mark 6:16). In the story of the repentant woman who anointed his feet, Simon the Pharisee must have considered Jesus a prophet when he asked himself, "If this man were a prophet, he would have known who and what kind of woman this is who is touching him—that she is a sinner" (Luke 7:39).

Jesus' own disciples also identified him as a prophet. As two distraught disciples traveled to Emmaus, a stranger appeared and inquired of them about the things that they were discussing. They replied, "The things about Jesus of Nazareth, who was a prophet mighty in deed and word before God and all the people" (Luke 24:19). Likewise, the Gospel of John bears witness to the identification of Jesus as a prophet. Already in the prologue, the fourth evangelist introduces Jesus as a prophet (John 1:14-18) and more explicitly as *the* prophet "about whom Moses in the law and also the prophets wrote" (John 1:45). In the story of the Samaritan woman, after Jesus recounted her past history, she became amazed and said to him, "Sir, I see that you are a prophet" (John 4:19). Having been healed by Jesus, the man born blind confidently declared to his interrogators, the Pharisees, that Jesus was a "prophet" (John 9:17). Jesus also seemed to refer to himself as a prophet when he testified, "[A] prophet has no honor in the prophet's own country" (John 4:44; Atkins 2013, 281–82).

Prophet is a reliable description of Jesus, since this is well attested in all four gospels and throughout the New Testament (Kaylor 1994). More important, Jesus saw himself as a Spirit-filled prophet whose mission was to bring about the reign of God here and now. If we read the gospels carefully, especially the Synoptics, we will see that Jesus was driven by a burning vision (Fuellenbach 1997, 3). Jesus expressed it this way, "I came to bring fire to the earth, and how I wish it were already kindled" (Luke 12:49).

What is this fire that was apparently burning within him and that he wanted to cast into this world? The answer to that question is succinctly expressed in his inaugural address in Mark 1:15, "The time is fulfilled, and the kingdom of God has come near; repent, and believe in the good news." His vision is nothing else than the arrival of the reign of God. It is a vision that will radically transform the world and will turn everything upside down. It is a vision in which the poor and the rich will joyfully dine at the same table, where enemies begin peacefully to embrace each other, where sinners are reconciled, where the outcasts of society are sheltered, and where the poor, the lame, and the blind are treated justly (Luke 7:22). Indeed, the reign of God is the key. It is everything for which he stands. It is the meaning of his life and the focus of his ministry. To live is to live for the reign of God. To labor is to labor for it. It is this fiery vision of the reign of God that Jesus preaches and for which he suffers and dies.

What does Jesus mean by the "kingdom of God"? Unfortunately, Jesus never defined it in concrete terms. He simply gave examples, illustrations, or similes using common and ordinary images, such as fig trees and mustard seed, fish and sheep, or wheat and weeds to describe not an imaginary realm from another world but an activity of God that is justice, peace, life, and joy permeating the lives of ordinary people and events. To captivate his audience and help them grasp its hidden meaning, Jesus frequently used parables as the favorite storytelling method to teach as well as to proclaim his vision (Reid 2014, 208). *Parabole* in Greek literally means "to set beside" or "to throw beside." This is why the parables of Jesus normally involve a comparison between the everyday and the transcendent, the earthly and the heavenly; so much so that John Fuellenbach defines parable as "an earthly story with a heavenly meaning" (Fuellenbach 1997, 71).

The Message of the Reign of God

What Jesus preached was first and foremost justice. Although the term "justice" (Gr., *dike*) is seldom used in the gospels, if one reads the gospels carefully, justice is one of the central themes that Jesus stressed repeatedly (Herzog 2000). We hear it in the parable of the "Unjust Steward" (Luke 16:1-8) who squanders his master's property and is called to make an account of his stewardship. Jesus also told the man in "Parable of the Rich Fool" (Luke 12:16-21), whose only concern is to acquire riches of this world, to begin to share or otherwise to be condemned. In the kingdom of God where justice truly reigns, one's salary does not depend on one's strength or on the hours of one's labor, but everyone gets paid equally and generously, as is depicted in the "Parable of the Workers in the Vineyard" (Matt 20:1-16).

For Jesus, justice was primarily "a matter of relationship" (Fuellenbach 1997, 157). To be just is to be in right relationship with God, with oneself, with one's neighbor, and with creation as a whole. Thus, justice is not some abstract concept but has to be defined in concrete and specific terms. Jesus' parable of the "Persistent Widow" (Luke 18:1-8) is a good example. For Jesus, defending the poor and the marginalized of society—in this case the widow—was what the reign of God was all about. The "Good Samaritan" (Luke 10:29-37) is another example of what it means to act justly and righteously in the eyes of God. The parable of the "Rich Man and Lazarus" (Luke 16:19-31) teaches that injustice done to another person is intolerable, and whoever does this will be excluded from the reign of God. If we examine the gospels closely, therefore, we will see that doing justice was the primary focus of Jesus' proclamation of the reign of God. His vision was to establish a kingdom of justice. His mission was fundamentally about inviting people to commit themselves to live in a new society where justice reigns for all—and not in the future but here and now.

Jesus did not only preach about doing justice; he invited people to live in peace. The word "peace" (Gr., *eirene*; Heb., *shalom*)—which means "wholeness," "perfect welfare," or "complete harmony"—appears very frequently in the gospels. When Jesus used the word "peace," he implied more than just the absence of war. It is rather a state of wholeness or reconciliation with God and people. When the woman afflicted with a hemorrhage was cured of her illness, Jesus not only healed her physical infirmity but also reintegrated her back into society as a full member of the community with the words "Go in peace" (Mark 5:34). On another occasion, when Jesus was dining with the Pharisees and with his disciples, a sinful woman courageously came, washed his feet with her tears, and anointed them with perfume (Luke 7:36-50). On that occasion, Jesus not only forgave her sins but also restored her back to wholeness as a member of the community, again with the words "Go in peace" (v. 50).

What is peace for Jesus? It is, primarily, restoring people to a "right relationship" with God and with people. It is making people and society completely whole, a state "wherein greed will end, exploitation will cease, and an entirely new social order will take over" (Fuellenbach 1997, 168). In the "Parable of the Tenants" (Mark 12:1-9), for example, Jesus envisioned a new society where complete harmony exists between landowners and tenant farmers. The promotion of such peace is so vital that Jesus commissioned the seventy disciples to go to every town and village and share it freely (Matt 10:10-12). Furthermore, in the "Beatitudes," Jesus blessed those who are bearers of peace, for they are called "children of God" (Matt 5:9). Jesus' vision was to establish a kingdom of peace here on earth.

The reign of God is also a kingdom of life. The evangelist John tells us that Jesus came so that people may have life and have it more abundantly (John 10:10). Jesus is also the way, the truth, and the life (John 14:6); whoever abides in him will have life and bear much fruit (John 15:1-10). In the Synoptic Gospels, Jesus did not frequently preach about life, he begot life. Wherever he went, he generated life; whomever he touched or whoever touched him was invigorated with new life. Jesus came to bring life into this world. He gave new life to those who were possessed by demons; he cured people of their illnesses and forgave their sins so that they might begin to live life more fully. He gave sight to the blind, cured the lame, cleansed the lepers, opened the ears of the deaf, and raised the dead to new life (Luke 7:22). And when people were hungry, he gave them bread to eat to sustain them (Mark 6:34-44; 8:1-9).

Jesus' vision of the reign of God was a kingdom of abundant life. It might start with something as small as a mustard seed, "but when it has grown it is the greatest of shrubs and becomes a tree, so that the birds of the air come and make nests in its branches" (Matt 13:32). It is also "like yeast that a woman took and mixed in with three measures of flour until all of it was leavened" (Matt 13:33). In other words, life in the reign of God has tremendous effects, although it seems insignificant and ordinary in the beginning. It is contagious; it spreads like wild flowers. It is like the "sower" who simply takes a handful of seeds and scatters them without worrying where they might fall; yet at harvest time, he collects an extraordinary yield (Mark 4:3-8). The reign of God as envisioned by Jesus was full of vitality and life.

Finally, the reign of God is also a kingdom of joy and delight. It is good news because the Messiah has come to deliver his people. It is time, therefore, to be glad and rejoice, to laugh and dance, to sing and shout for joy because the Savior is born (Luke 1:14, 44, 47, 58; 2:10-11). Indeed, with the arrival of Jesus a new era dawns. The Gospel of Luke particularly accentuates this mood of joy not only in the infancy narratives but also throughout his gospel. Joy is a major theme in Jesus' parables. In the "Parable of the Lost Sheep" (Luke 15:1-7), we are told that the shepherd goes through extraordinary measures to find the one lost sheep, and when he finds it, he places that sheep on his shoulders, rejoicing. Likewise, the woman who had lost the coin carefully sweeps the whole house and searches for it, and when she finds the coin, she too is filled with joy and calls her friends and neighbors to rejoice with her (Luke 15:8-10). We are told that even the angels in heaven rejoice. Similarly, in the "Parable of the Lost Son" (Luke 15:11-32), the loving father waits and longs for his son's return, and when he finally does return, the father embraces and kisses him tenderly. Furthermore, he restores the honor of the lost son by killing the fatted calf, so that the whole village could come to celebrate and rejoice. No one is excluded. It is like dining at the "Great Banquet" (Luke 14:15-24) where the rich and the poor, the lame and the blind, servants and masters, all sit at the same table delighting in the presence of God and one another.

The Preaching of the Apostles

Speeches in the Acts of the Apostles

The risen Lord commissioned his disciples to bear testimony about him "in Jerusalem, throughout Judea and Samaria, and to the ends of the earth" (Acts 1:8), which the early apostles and disciples frequently and enthusiastically performed. The book of Acts gives us numerous examples of powerful preaching. Peter, for example, delivered eight significant speeches scattered throughout the first part of Acts (1:16-25; 2:14-40; 3:12-26; 4:8-20; 5:29-32; 10:28-43; 11:5-17; 15:7-11). Peter's two most notable proclamations led to the outpouring of the Holy Spirit, namely, the Jewish (2:14-40) and the Gentile Pentecost (10:28-43). Although Stephen gave only one speech (7:1-53), his is the longest in Acts. James, the brother of Jesus and the leader of the Jerusalem church, gave two short but important speeches that changed the course of the church's mission (15:13-21; 21:20-25). Paul, who dominates the second part of the book of Acts, delivered three mission speeches (13:16-41; 14:15-17; 17:22-31), five defense speeches (22:1-21; 24:10-21; 26:2-27; 27:21-26; 28:17-28), and one farewell speech (20:18-35).

There are approximately twenty-eight speeches in Acts (Soards 1994). The form and rhetoric (see 200ff. below) of these speeches are related to Greco-Roman historiography, which aims to produce a dramatic effect and to aid the author's purpose in communicating his message. The genres or types of speeches found in Acts are diverse, consisting of missionary, evangelizing, indictment, defense, farewell, constitutive, and political speeches. While it is not easy to assess the historical accuracy of these speeches, it is appropriate to assume that they are accurate summaries that were composed by Luke, the author of Acts. What is most fascinating about these speeches is that each one is composed appropriately for the occasion. One of the finest examples is Paul's sermon at the Areopagus in Acts 17:22-31 (Nguyen 2014).

Paul the Missionary

Paul probably arrived in Athens sometime in early spring of 50 CE. He had come from the north, leaving Timothy and Silas behind to care for newly founded communities (Acts 17:14-15). Paul had caused an uproar in many of the towns and cities he had previously visited; in Thessalonica his friends had to slip him away to safety in the night. His opponents kept pursuing him wherever he went. Paul had hoped that in a bigger city like Athens, he might be able to elude his opponents a little more easily.

Curious about the disturbing new message and "foreign deities" that were being promoted around the city, the Council of Areopagus summoned Paul to present his case. The Areopagus, or "Rock of Ares," is located on the northwestern side of the Acropolis, which in ancient Athens functioned as the high court of appeal for civil (also possibly criminal) cases. During Paul's time, however, the Romans called it "Mars Hill," a platform for discussing the religious life of the city. Perhaps Paul's preaching about Jesus and the resurrection (Gr., *anastasis*) had led some to assume that Paul wanted to introduce new deities, named "Jesus and *Anastasis*" (Acts 17:18). The notion of the dead rising to life was a novelty to the Athenians.

Athens was the center of Greek culture and philosophy, widely considered the cradle of Western civilization and the birthplace of democracy. Although Athens was well past its golden age by the time Paul arrived, it was still considered the greatest university city of its time, and intellectuals from all over the Roman Empire were drawn to it. One customary activity of the Athenian intellectuals was to gather in public squares and marketplaces to argue and debate new theories and ideas. Athens was not just an intellectual hub, it was also a religious center. Temples and shrines dedicated to all sorts of gods and goddesses were found everywhere in the city. At every turn there were statues of idols, gods, and goddesses. There was even a shrine dedicated to an "unknown god."

Paul seemed to have done his homework well. He must have spent considerable time watching, listening, and learning the Athenians' culture and customs (17:23). His speech indicates that he understood the local philosophies and was quite knowledgeable about the Greek and Roman gods. The words he spoke were very familiar to the Athenians. "The God who made the world and everything in it" (17:24) comes straight out of Stoic philosophy. "In him we live and move and have our being" (17:28) is from the Greek philosopher Epimenides of Knossos (sixth or seventh century BCE). "For we too are his offspring" (17:28) comes from the well-known poet Aratus of Soli (d. 240 BCE). Paul engaged the Athenians by using their own philosophies and practices, demonstrating that he was familiar with their cultural milieu and spoke a language they could understand.

Even though greatly distressed by the many idols, Paul did not chastise them for their beliefs. Instead, Paul sought to meet the Athenians on their own ground, saying, "I see that in every respect you are very religious" (17:22). He was careful and respectful throughout the whole speech, neither mocking their idols nor being judgmental or self-righteous. Paul gently corrects, using "we" instead of the more accusatory "you" (17:28-29). Paul had respectfully contextualized the Gospel message for his audience.

Paul the Skillful Orator

While Paul demonstrated a conciliatory attitude toward the Athenians, he refused to water down the Gospel message. Paul stood firm regarding the message of the Gospel, criticizing pervasive idolatry and religious pluralism. He challenged his listeners to abandon their old ways of honoring idols and worship the one true God. Paul sought to convince the Athenians by means of a rhetorical argument. Paul stood in their midst, the position of a Greek orator, and addressed his audience according to the conventional pattern of Greco-Roman rhetoric (see 201–2 below). The sermon itself (17:22-31) is the centerpiece of the whole episode of Paul's time in Athens, sandwiched between the opening scene that sets the stage for the sermon (17:16-21) and the closing scene that ends with a report of mixed reviews (17:32-34).

Paul begins the sermon with a rhetorical technique called *exordium* or introduction (vv. 22-23a), designed to establish rapport and credibility with his listeners. He complimented them for being "extremely religious in every way." After this opening commendation, however, Paul immediately declared his intended goal of the speech: "What therefore you unknowingly worship, I proclaim to you" (v. 23b); he wishes to make the Unknown God known. This rhetorical technique is called the proposition (Lat., *propositio*). The next portion of the speech is the proof (Lat., *probatio*; vv. 24-29), which displays the basic argument of the case. Paul quoted several previously noted poets and philosophers as "testimonies" to strengthen the argument that this Unknown God is none other than the Creator who "made the world and all that is in it" and who "is not far from anyone of us." Paul tried to convince the Athenians that those images "fashioned from gold, silver, or stone by human art and imagination" (v. 29) are mere distortions of the image (Gr., *eikon*) of the one, true God. Paul pointed out to the Athenians that their time of "groping search" or fumbling in the darkness is over. Paul then concluded the sermon with an exhortation (Lat., *peroratio*; vv. 30-31), which attempts to persuade his listeners to take the right course of action by declaring that God has "overlooked the times of ignorance" and is now demanding people everywhere "to repent." Paul does not seek to add a new god to the Athenian Pantheon; rather, he calls them to repentance. Paul also deferred the controversial issue of "the resurrection" (17:18, 30) until now. Paul used this rhetorical strategy of deferral or the "subtle approach" (Lat., *insinuatio*) very deftly.

While the sermon has elements of judicial rhetoric, Paul's purpose was ultimately deliberative, seeking to change his audience's beliefs and behavior. He did so with great sensitivity and rhetorical skill, drawing on the ideas and language of his listeners to establish points of contact with them. He used whatever persuasive tools he had acquired to engage the Athenians' worldview and philosophy. At the mention of the resurrection of the dead, however, some sneered while others walked away in disbelief. In general, the Greeks regarded the resurrection of the body as an absurdity and thus were not interested in it. Nevertheless, Paul's speech was not completely unsuccessful. The Athenians did not violently oppose Paul's argument and belief, and they considered hearing him "some other time" (v. 32). Also, there were a few who actually believed, such as Dionysius and a woman named Damaris.

Conclusion

Jesus—the parabolic preacher—was a Spirit-filled prophet whose mission was to bring about the reign of God that was already being realized. He envisioned a society in which justice, peace, abundance of life, and joy completely reign, not in some imaginary realm, but here and now. This vision of the reign of God inspired Jesus to say what he said and compelled him to do what he did; it gave meaning to his life and became the focus of his ministry. The reign of God summarizes the life and ministry of Jesus.

Paul's sermon at the Areopagus is an outstanding example of cross-contextual missionary preaching found in the New Testament. While showing cultural sensitivity to the Greeks, Paul proclaimed the Christian message with integrity and boldness. The sermon conveys many insightful lessons and implications for preachers today, for example, the need to contextualize and transpose the Gospel with care and creativity so as to engage with all sorts of listeners, even nonbelievers. Effective preachers must display rhetorical skill as well as flexibility and firmness. While establishing rapport with the assembly, preachers must also remain faithful to the Christian message, avoiding hasty accommodation to the dominant culture and inviting authentic transformation.

Bibliography

Atkins, J. D. "The Trial of the People and the Prophet: John 5:30-47 and the True and False Prophet Traditions." *Catholic Biblical Quarterly* 75, no. 2 (2013): 279–96.

Fuellenbach, John. *The Kingdom of God*. Maryknoll, NY: Orbis Books, 1997.

Herzog II, William R. *Jesus, Justice, and the Reign of God: A Ministry of Liberation*. Louisville, KY: Westminster-John Knox, 2000.

Johnson, Luke Timothy. *Prophetic Jesus, Prophetic Church: The Challenge of Luke-Acts to Contemporary Christians*. Grand Rapids, MI: William B. Eerdmans, 2011.

Kaylor, R. David. *Jesus the Prophet: His Vision of the Kingdom on Earth*. Louisville, KY: Westminster/John Knox, 1994.

Nguyen, vanThanh. "Paul's Sermon at the Areopagus." *The Bible Today* 52, no. 4 (2014): 213–18.

———. *Stories of Early Christianity: Creative Retelling of Faith and History*. Liguori, MO: Liguori Publications, 2013.

Reid, Barbara. "Jesus: Parabolic Preacher." *The Bible Today* 52, no. 4 (2014): 207–11.

Soards, Marion L. *The Speeches in Acts: Their Content, Context, and Concerns*. Louisville, KY: Westminster-John Knox Press, 1994.

Preaching in the Early Christian Church

Alden Bass

Introduction

Since the liturgical reforms of the mid-twentieth century, homilists have returned to the preachers of the patristic era for inspiration and guidance. Early Christian preaching has become a model for contemporary preachers because of its dynamic style and creative hermeneutical methods. Patristic sermons present a trove of exegetical, rhetorical, and theological resources for contemporary preachers.

Although preaching has always been central to Christian worship, the homily took centuries to emerge into something resembling its current form. As followers of Jesus moved from synagogue to households to meeting halls and basilicas, the mode of communication shifted to fit their new surroundings and the changing needs of the community. As an oral event, preaching did not leave a significant written trace for several generations; not until the third century were homilies preserved in any number, when the students of the brilliant teacher Origen (d. 253–54) collected and passed down nearly three hundred of his sermons as exemplars of the exegetical art. With the legalization of Christianity in the fourth century, preaching became a fully public affair, and preaching proliferated; people flocked to hear the great orators of the age such as John Chrysostom (d. 407), Gregory Nazianzus (d. 390), Basil (d. 379), Ambrose (d. 397), Ephrem (d. 373), and Augustine (d. 430). This period witnessed rapid growth both in the quantity and quality of Christian preaching and established a benchmark for all future preachers. The sermons of these homiletic masters were transcribed for posterity and were used as models for lesser preachers throughout the Middle Ages. The quality of preaching declined in the fifth and sixth centuries, although lights such as Leo the Great (d. 461), Jacob of Serug (d. 521), Caesarius of Arles (d. 542), and Gregory the Great (d. 604) continued to shine from pulpits across the Mediterranean.

From Prophecy to Preaching: Second and Third Centuries

Alistair Stewart-Sykes has defined the homily as "oral communication of the word of God in the Christian assembly" (Stewart-Sykes 2001, 6). The New Testament provides many examples of kerygmatic, or missionary preaching, but few references to the type of communication that occurred within a congregation. The references that do remain indicate that the "Word of God" was a fluid concept that could be discovered through Spirit-led conversation. For instance, in the Emmaus narrative (Luke 24:13-35), the Word is revealed in "speaking" together rather than in Scripture itself. The Greek term *homilia* originally meant conversation; it did not receive its present meaning until the third century. Likewise in the Johannine community, it was the Paraclete, or "spirit of truth," who would guide the disciples into truth (John 16:13). This Spirit was gifted to different individuals, sometimes called prophets, and the Word was communicated to the assembly (Gr., *ekklēsia*) during weekly meetings. Since apostolic times, this process was connected to the eucharistic meal (Acts 20:11; Justin, 1 *Apologia* 65.2-5; 67.5). Thus, the origins of Christian preaching lie in the prophetic table-talk of the first few centuries.

These Spirit-led conversations were dialogical, consisting of two elements. The first was prophetic exhortation, which was the functional equivalent to modern preaching. Paul instructed the Corinthian church: "When you come together . . . let two or three prophets speak, and let the others weigh what is said" (1 Cor 14:26-29). Prophecy could refer not only to oracular revelations from God but also charismatic exegesis of Torah or simply extemporaneous moral exhortations. The "homilies" (Gr., *homilia*) of the *Acta Pauli* from the mid-second century are conducted entirely as prophetic speeches. Prophets could be located within a given congregation (1 Cor 14; Ignatius, *Ad Philadelphienses* 7.1-2) or they might be itinerants (*Didache* 11–13). Traveling apostles, prophets, and teachers were normal in the apostolic period (cf. 3 John 5–8); John the Revelator probably belonged to an itinerant prophetic circle in the Roman provinces of Asia (Rev 22:9). Charismatic gifts were in no way restricted and could be received by persons of any social standing, ethnic background, or gender (cf. Philip's daughters in Acts 21:9).

The second aspect of early Christian homilies was *diakrisis* (Lat. for, lit., "judgment"), the debate and critical discussions of prophecy and Scripture held around the table in the assembly. This is what Paul meant when he counseled the Corinthian church to "weigh what is said" (cf. 1 Thess 5:21). Judgment was necessary because some "false" prophets used their gift as a cloak for vice (cf. Rev 2:20; Hermas, *Mandates* 11.12; *Didache* 11.6). Scripture was used as the standard for judgment, as was the creed (Lat., *symbolum fidei*), although the creed itself was subject to the same process of communal discernment (cf. *2 Clement*). By the early third century, this process could still be observed in the church at Carthage, although it took place outside of the assembly (Tertullian, *De Anima* 9.4). Over time, as the authority of Scripture increased and new revelations ceased to be accepted, the role of arbiter transferred to an individual teacher or church leader.

Though the development of the homily occurred unevenly in different regions, the entire trajectory can be traced through the church of Smyrna. In the first century, the church was subject to one of the original prophetic oracles in the book of Revelation (1:11), of which the perceived apostolic origins may have curtailed criticism. By the time of Polycarp (d. 167), however, the church discerns together concerning the Word of God. Ignatius (d. 117) wrote to Polycarp to encourage him to "make a conversation" (Gr., *homilia poiein*) in order to reveal the evil arts, or false prophecy (Ignatius, *Ad Polycarpum* 5.1). A century later, when the city had become a center of rhetorical education, the Greek term *homilia* had assumed its set meaning; the *Vita Polycarpi* refers to the homilies of Polycarp in the modern sense of sermons. Even at this late date, however, it is noteworthy that this was not a single speech but rather a series of short talks given by presbyters followed by the bishop's teaching (*Vita Polycarpi* 22). This practice reflects the earlier situation wherein glosses on the Word were given in turn and continued at least through the time of Chrysostom in the fourth century (*De Beato Philogon* 3; cf. *Apostolic Constitutions* 2.57).

That early Christian homilies focused on charismatic prophecy rather than Scripture was in part a practical issue; early house churches would not have been able to afford copies of the Scriptures and probably would have continued to audit Scripture in the synagogue for several generations. Gradually, however, copies of Scripture were obtained by house churches and—alongside the new revelations of the apostles—read aloud in the assembly. Writing from Rome around 150, Justin (d. 165) provides a clear description of early Christian preaching: a lector reads aloud a lengthy section of the Old or New Testament "as long as time permits." He continues: "[T]hen, when the reader has finished, the one presiding gives an address, urgently admonishing his hearers to practice these beautiful teachings in their lives. Then all stand together and recite prayers" (1 *Apologia* 67.3-5; trans. Jungmann 1960, 42). The reading of Scripture was followed by an extemporaneous speech (Gr., *logos*) delivered by the one who presided over the assembly. The speech was not a formal discourse, which would have been out of place in the intimate setting of a household, but rather an explanation of the text just read (Gr., *nouthesia*) and an exhortation (Gr., *proklesis*). Tertullian (d. before 240) provides a second witness to liturgical preaching, writing from Carthage about forty years after Justin (*Apologeticum* 39.3-4; *De Anima* 9.4). By the mid-third century, some form of lectionary had developed, and preaching became increasingly exegetical as it followed a continuous reading of the Scriptures (Lat., *lectio continua*) as the sermons of Origen in Egypt and Hippolytus (d. 235) in Italy demonstrate. Moreover, the custom of allowing lay people to preach disappeared around this time, as bishops took exclusive control of the pulpit, with few exceptions.

Thus, preaching retained a spontaneous, oracular quality through the third century. This was the case especially in communities where Greek was not the first language, such as Gaul, North Africa, and East Syria. Scripture would have been read aloud in Greek, and then immediately translated into Latin or Syriac, likely with explanatory comments in the manner of a Jewish targum. By the early fourth century, however, biblical translations were widely available, and preaching was being done not only in the imperial languages but also in local dialects such as Punic, Syriac, Gothic, and later Armenian and Coptic, either by native speakers or through translation.

As household assemblies gave way to what Stewart-Sykes characterizes as "scholastic social organizations" (Stewart-Sykes 2001, 88–91) with independent meeting places, the Word of God was communicated in increasingly sophisticated ways. Justin and Tertullian refer to preaching in the Sunday assembly, but by the mid-third century, preaching was not confined to eucharistic celebrations (which frequently occurred on Fridays as well as Sundays) but often took place on a daily basis. The "precepts and the gospel of the Lord" were read in Carthage daily (Cyprian, *Epistula* 39.4.1) and Cyprian preached "often" (Pontius, *Vita Cypriani* 3.5). While a presbyter in Caesarea Palestine in the 240s, Origen preached "almost every day," probably in the early morning before work began (Pamphilius, *Apologia pro Origene* 9.6-7). Soon, the preacher's voice was the voice most heard in the public arena, far more than any other orators in the city. Such consistent and continuous preaching led to the formation of a distinct and cohesive Christian culture.

The Golden Age of Preaching: Fourth Century

Preaching slowly transformed from private exhortation to public proclamation. By the beginning of the fourth century, many Christian communities had acquired enough wealth and social standing to buy or build monumental meeting halls situated prominently in urban centers (see Porphyry's complaint, *Adversus christianos* fragment 76). Western Christians adopted for their meeting places law courts (Lat., *basilica*) where trained orators deliberated rather than Greek temples where priests celebrated the mysteries; this decision reflects the centrality of oratory in the liturgy as well as the forensic bent of their preaching. The transition to public cult was complete with the Constantinian settlement of 313, which granted Christianity the status of an approved religion (Lat., *religio licita*). The new religion spread rapidly both geographically and socially. Membership increased steadily from the third century, in part because of persuasive preaching (see Origen, *Homiliae in Numeros* 13.7; *Homiliae in Jeremiam* 4.3). Not only were there more churches but there were also more worship spaces where sermons could be given, such as sanctuaries of the martyrs (Lat., *martyria*); catechumens were often taught in the vestibule of the baptistery, which was a separate building. Preachers spoke from an episcopal seat (Lat., *cathedra, thronus*) on a raised platform in the apse (Lat., *exedra*) surrounded by seated presbyters and separated from the people by a series of steps. In the ancient world, sitting was a posture of authority, most notably the posture of the schoolmaster. The assembly, which was divided by gender in many churches, stood during the sermon, sometimes for several hours.

The Preacher

The architectural shift from houses to halls corresponded to a social shift from the congregation to what we might call an "audience," and a parallel rhetorical shift from *paraenesis* (Gr. for "exhortation") to persuasion. Christian preaching drew crowds from across the social ranks of the empire, and as more educated people joined the "audience," expectations for the rhetorical quality of the sermon heightened; in the words of Gregory Nazianzus, the public "did not look for priests, but for orators" (*Oratio* 42.24-25). Preachers often understood themselves to be one more form of entertainment in the city alongside the hippodrome, the circus, civic festivals, and the theater (Augustine, *Enarrationes in Psalmos* 80.23). Sermons were calculated to give pleasure to the crowd and often concluded with applause; at times claques were even hired to congratulate the preacher. According to Eusebius (d. ca. 339), the sermons of the bishop of Antioch, Paul of Samosata (d. 275), resulted in fans jumping up and down "as occurred in the theater" (*Historia Ecclesiastica* 7.30.9). Gregory of Nazianzus actively sought applause (*Oratio* 36.4), as did his rival Eunomius (d. ca. 393; Gregory of Nazianzus, *Oratio* 27.1). Basil was also taken with acclaim (*Homilia*

11.5) as was Augustine (*Enarrarationes in Psalmos* 141.8) and Fulgentius of Ruspe (d. 533; Ferrandus, *Vita Fulgentii* 27). John Chrysostom expressed some reservations about the cheering, but his criticism was offered so eloquently that it earned him a standing ovation (*Homiliae in Acta Apostolorum* 30.3-4). Oratorical prowess sometimes overshadowed the pastoral purpose of preaching, so that some preachers rushed into the church "to flatter the audience, thinking not about the cure of the soul, but only the beauty of words" (Ps.-Athanasius, *Homilia de Semente* 4).

A more educated and elite group was drawn not only into the assembly but also into the pulpit. A leading lawyer in the courts of Carthage, Cyprian was rushed up the episcopal ladder to become the "primate of Africa" within a year of his baptism; his rhetorical training guaranteed him that eloquence for which he was forever famous (Pontius, *Vita Cypriani* 1.1; 2.2). Similarly, Ambrose, a governor of north Italy trained in law and rhetoric, was famously drafted as bishop before he was even baptized. It was the charm (Lat., *suavitas*) of Ambrose's panegyric on New Year's Day 385 that won over the young African orator Augustine (*Confessiones* 5.13.23), who would become one of the most influential homileticians in the West. Besides being drawn from the legal professions, bishops such as Gregory of Nazianzus and Augustine also came from the ranks of the academy. Bishops who did not already have a rhetorical education attended the prestigious schools of the Mediterranean world such as Athens, Alexandria, Beirut, Rome, and Bordeaux. After Constantine, ecclesiastical careers became more powerful, and thus more coveted positions; clerical positions in turn became increasingly competitive. Thus Libanius (d. ca. 393)—the famous teacher of rhetoric—rued that his best student, John "Chrysostom" (Gr. for "golden-mouthed"), was stolen by the Christians (Sozomen, *Historia Ecclesiastica* 8.2.2.5).

As public figures, Christian bishops spoke not only for the community but also for the city and the empire. During the fourth century, preaching moved from its persistent focus on the Word of God to include social and political issues. Sermons addressed common civic challenges such as the accumulation of wealth or responded to natural disasters such as earthquakes, famines, and epidemics (e.g., Severus of Antioch, *Homilia* 19). Current events were also treated in sermons, as in John Chrysostom's Lenten series *Homilies on the Statues*, delivered in Antioch after the famous riots of 387. There are more thematic sermons in this period, and even the traditional exegetical sermon changes in significance. Doctrinal questions that once prompted internal debate now carried political import. For example, the preaching of the dissident presbyter Arius in Egypt (d. 336) that sparked a century of political and theological controversy demonstrates that preaching was no longer merely speculative.

Rhetoric and Style

Although the socially elite and refined urban classes now present in the assemblies demanded well-spoken sermons, Christianity at its core was a religion of the masses. As early as the second century, there was a tension between high- and low-style preaching, and some of the earliest surviving homilies, such as Melito of Sardis's *Paschal Homily* and Pseudo-Cyprian's *Against the Judeans*, display an exceedingly polished delivery derived from Hellenistic models. Christians eventually developed their own distinct rhetorical discipline rooted in the humble and unornamented style of Scripture. Cyprian termed this style *mediocritas* (*Epistola* 53.1), an expression that referred both to the personal modesty of the speaker and to the rhetorical style adapted from Cicero's *simplicitas* (*De oratore* 1.117; cf. 201f. below). Following Cyprian, Augustine claimed to speak in a colloquial style called *sermo humilis* or "common speech." John Chrysostom advised that "a [preacher's] diction be poor and his style simple and plain; but let him not be unskilled in the knowledge and accurate explanation of doctrine" (*De sacerdotio libri* 4.6). Despite these caveats, such highly educated preachers could not help but preach rhetorically sophisticated sermons. Augustine assured his people that preaching simply did not exclude preaching "with great eloquence" (Lat., *ex multa eloquentia*; *Contra Cresconium* 1.1.2), and when Caesarius of Arles used "common language" (Lat., *pedestri sermone*) he felt the need to apologize to the "erudite ears" in his audience (*Sermo* 86.1).

Whereas Greek and Latin preaching drew on Hellenistic modes of persuasive speech, Syriac preaching took an entirely different course. Marrying theology and poetry, sermons were less argumentative and more poetic; sometimes verse homilies were sung to the accompaniment of instruments such as the harp. One of the greatest early Christian preachers was Ephrem of Nisibis (d. 373), the father of the hymnic homily. These sermons, called *madrashe*, consisted of stanzas sung by the preacher and a refrain given by the congregation. Ephrem also adapted the ancient genre of the dialogue poem (Syr., *memre*), which takes the form of an imagined argument between two biblical characters in order to highlight the dramatic tension within the biblical narrative. These verse homilies effectively explore the psychological dimension of the stories while simultaneously revealing the theological teaching of the passage. Ephrem became the model for fifth-century preachers such as Narsai (d. 503) and Philoxenus of Mabbug

(d. 523). Jacob of Serug, known as the "flute of the Holy Spirit and the harp of the orthodox church," was famous for his nearly eight hundred homiletical poems. By incorporating music and metrical verse into their homilies, the Syriac poet-preachers opened a new path in preaching, which has yet to be explored in the Western church.

Types of Sermons

Liturgical sermons took multiple forms and can be classified on the basis of circumstance or content. With regard to circumstances, there exists Sunday, weekly, festal, and panegyric sermons. Sunday and weekly sermons were given during the liturgy and were generally based on the scriptural passages read during the service. Festal sermons were delivered on major feasts of the liturgical calendar. Easter quickly emerged as the central feast of the Christian year, and the most ancient homilies are paschal, e.g., *On the Pascha* (Gr., *Peri Pascha*) of Melito of Sardis (d. ca. 180) and *On the Holy Pascha* (Lat., *In Sanctum Pascha*) of Pseudo-Hippolytus (fourth century). Feasts commemorating martyrs, saints, and other important individuals were celebrated with panegyric sermons, which often assumed the rhetorical traits of the Hellenistic panegyric tradition.

Preaching can also be categorized by content, which includes kerygmatic, catechetical, mystagogical, exegetical, and thematic sermons. Kerygmatic, or missionary, preaching was aimed at winning nonbelievers to the faith. Though few examples of this type of preaching remain, it was undoubtedly practiced by great missionaries such as Ulfilas (d. ca. 382) in the region of the Danube and Patrick (d. ca. 460) in Ireland. Those who were persuaded were subject to a period of catechesis, lasting from a week to several months, intended to initiate them into the world of Christian beliefs and practices, culminating in baptism. A collection of nineteen *Catechetical Lectures* preached by Cyril of Jerusalem (d. 386) in 348 survives, as do many of Augustine's catechetical Lenten homilies from the early fifth century. Following baptism, the newly baptized received a week or so of special daily instruction called mystagogy (see 134ff. below) that explained the sacred liturgical rites and the doctrine of the creed. Eight *Mystagogical Homilies* of Cyril (or John) of Jerusalem remain, as well as important collections by Ambrose, John Chrysostom, Gaudentius of Brescia (d. 410), Theodore of Mopsuestia (d. 428), Augustine, and Quodvultdeus (d. ca. 450).

Taxonomy notwithstanding, nearly all preaching was exegetical at some level. One exception is the thematic sermon, given in the event of natural disasters such as earthquakes (Chrysostom, *De terrae motu*) or political crises, such as the sack of Rome (Leo I, *Sermo* 84); yet even here exegesis was a dominant mode. Numerous passages—often dozens—were cited in a single sermon. Preachers generally explained a passage phrase-by-phrase, and the exposition was usually followed by practical application for the hearers. This pattern could constitute the entire sermon or be repeated throughout in cycles. Sometimes preachers would simply dramatize biblical stories, inventing dialogue to make a passage more exciting. These narratives provided a rich source of moral examples. At other times, texts were interpreted typologically or allegorically, drawing both on rabbinic and Hellenistic reading strategies. The use of illustrations varied from preacher to preacher; some used hardly any, except those drawn from Scripture (like Cyril of Jerusalem). Others advanced scenes from daily life, such as John Chrysostom. Gregory of Nazianzus used illustrations drawn from pagan authors; Basil is famous for his illustrations drawn from nature. Anecdotes from the lives of the saints were employed from the fourth century onward. Many sermons close with a trinitarian doxology.

The Homiletic Tradition: Fifth and Sixth Centuries

The end of late antiquity saw the continued refinement of the preaching art in people such as Peter Chrysologus (d. ca. 450), Sidonius Apollinaris (d. 489), and Avitus of Vienne (d. ca. 518). The main feature of this period, however, is the emergence of a canon of master homilists who would provide models for imitation throughout the Middle Ages. Abraham of Ephesus (mid-sixth century) in his *Homily on the Annunciation* admitted to employing material from earlier preachers who had already treated his themes: Athanasius (d. 379), Basil, John Chrysostom, Cyril of Alexandria (d. 444), Proclus of Constantinople (d. ca. 447), and Gregory. Sometimes preachers did not simply borrow outlines or passages, but whole sermons were read verbatim. Augustine commended those unable to craft their own sermons "to learn by heart and preach those of acknowledged masters" (*De Doctrina Christiana* 4.29.62). By the time of Gregory the Great at the end of the sixth century, it had become common practice for bishops to recite the text of an acknowledged teacher of the church.

To facilitate such imitation, collections of sermons called homiliaries were assembled and published, the earliest of which (a Latin translation of Chrysostom's sermons) dates back to the early fifth century. These collections were organized variously to address liturgical seasons, feasts of the saints, or a series of biblical themes. Collections of Augustine and Chrysostom were the most popular, but homiliaries such as the Eusebian

Gallicanus could also contain a bouquet of lesser-known preachers such as Genesius of Arles (d. ca. 303), Honoratus of Arles (d. 429), and Maximus of Riez (d. 460). These collections were particularly useful in rural areas (Lat., *parrochiae*) where bishops often lacked education. Caesarius of Arles distributed such collections to clergy in France, Gaul, Italy, and Spain (*Vita Caesarii* 1:55).

This period also witnesses the first theological reflections on the act of preaching itself, most notably Augustine's homiletic handbook, *On the Form of Teaching Suitable for Christians* (Lat., *De Doctrina Christiana*). Augustine synthesized Latin Christian preaching into a distinct, rhetorical discipline, utilizing the tripartite division of classical rhetoric: *logos*, *ethos*, and *pathos* (see 201 below). He adapted the three goals of Ciceronian rhetoric—to teach, to please, and to move—for Christian preaching. The preacher was "not only to teach that he may instruct and to please that he may hold attention, but also to persuade that he may be victorious" (*De Doctrina Christiana* 4.13.29). Still, centuries would pass before the relationship between preaching and sacramental worship was satisfactorily elaborated. Origen hinted at a productive path in his oft-repeated phrase "bread of the Word, bread of the Eucharist," a concept Hilary of Poitiers (d. ca. 368) also utilized (*Tractates in Psalmos* 127.10). This idea was echoed by the Second Vatican Council, which speaks of "two tables" in relation to the dignity of God's Word, the ministry of the ordained and the relationship of the Word and sacrament in the Eucharist (*DV*, no. 21; *PO*, no. 18; *SC*, nos. 48 and 51).

By the close of the patristic era, the majority of preaching was derivative, concerned with either catechetical or doctrinal explication, often with a polemical thrust or tedious moralizing; the most creative and dynamic preaching was increasingly relegated to monasteries. For the average layperson, the practice of reading the sermons of past masters indicated, in the words of Brilioth, that "the liturgy had smothered the sermon, making it a mere section of the liturgy, which could only happen in an era when exposition of Scripture had dried up and when the spirit of prophecy had departed from the church" (Brilioth 1961, 68). It would be several centuries before the church recovered the prophetic fire, with its exegetical brilliance and rhetorical heat of the early preachers.

Bibliography

Brilioth, Yngve. *A Brief History of Preaching*. Translated by K. E. Mattson. Philadelphia: Fortress Press, 1965.

Dunn-Wilson, David. *A Mirror for the Church: Preaching in the First Five Centuries*. Grand Rapids, MI: Eerdmans, 2005.

Fatti, Federico. "Preaching." *Encyclopedia of Ancient Christianity*. Downers Grove, IL: InterVarsity Academic, 2014.

Harrison, Carol. *The Art of Listening in the Early Church*. Oxford: Oxford University Press, 2013.

Hunter, David, ed. *Preaching in the Patristic Age*. New York: Paulist Press, 1989.

Jungmann, Josef. *The Early Liturgy*. Translated by Francis Brunner. London: Darton, Longman & Todd, 1960.

Old, Hughes Oliphant. *The Reading and Preaching of the Scriptures in the Worship of the Christian Church*. Vol. 2: *The Patristic Age*. Grand Rapids, MI: Eerdmans, 1998.

Olivar, Alexandre. *La Predicación Cristiana Antigua*. Barcelona: Herder, 1991.

Osborn, Ronald. *Folly of God: The Rise of Christian Preaching*. St. Louis: Chalice Press, 1997.

Stewart-Sykes, Alistair. *From Prophecy to Preaching: A Search for the Origins of the Christian Homily*. Leiden: Brill, 2001.

Medieval Preaching

Carolyn Muessig

Defining Medieval Preaching

Medieval preaching was variegated. The theologian Alan of Lille (d. 1203) described it as "a manifest and public instruction of morals and faith, serving the formation of humanity and coming forth from the path of reason and the fount of authorities" (*Summa de arte praedicatoria, caput primum*). This definition covers a great deal of what constituted medieval preaching but, as we will see, it also sets limits on its expansiveness. Indeed, the Latin term *sermo* ("sermon") had a multifaceted meaning. From early in the Christian tradition, particularly with Augustine (d. 430), *sermo* had different meanings that were in some respects interchangeable with the words *tractatus* (Lat. for, lit., "a treatment") and *omelia* (Lat. for "homily"). The word *sermo* could mean, among other things, discourse, conversation, language, or word. *Tractatus* could pertain to any learned commentary, whether it was religious or nonreligious, oral or written. The term *omelia* could mean a colloquy, exposition, discourse, or sermon (Hall 2000, 203–55).

"Homily" and "sermon" were the terms used most often during the medieval period. Although these two words were often interchangeable, there was sometimes a distinction made between them. A concise and helpful definition of the terms sermon and homily that demonstrates these differences has been put forward by Tom Hall:

> The most important such distinction in use today holds that a sermon is fundamentally a catechetical or admonitory discourse built upon a theme or topic not necessarily grounded in Scripture, whereas a homily is a systematic exposition of a pericope (a liturgically designated passage of Scripture, usually from a Gospel or Epistle) that proceeds according to a pattern of *lectio continua*, commenting on a given passage verse by verse or phrase by phrase. (Hall 2000, 205)

Keeping these specific definitions in mind, preaching could also be delivered in a variety of ways that move beyond neat classifications. For example, George Ferzoco has pointed out that hermit saints and wandering preachers often were renowned not so much for what they preached but for how they lived their lives. Their actions were viewed as sermons rather than any public speech. The transmission of a sermon, therefore, was not necessarily an aural event. Regina Schiewer (1998) has shown how the reception of a sermon could happen without the presence of a preacher, as in the case of German Observant Dominican nuns who sometimes read vernacular sermon collections. This was a fairly widespread practice in monastic houses. Michel Zink has notably termed the reading of sermons as "preaching in an armchair" (Zink 1976, 478).

This chapter will consider the diverse modes of medieval preaching that embrace a large chronological and geographical sweep from sixth-century Merovingian Gaul to early sixteenth-century Italy.

Who Could Preach?

In the church of the patristic era (see 51ff. above), preaching was mainly an episcopal function. Although the bishop never relinquished this role, it was increasingly appropriated by different sorts of religious figures. During the sixth and seventh centuries, monks such as Columbanus (d. 615) were energetic missionaries who evangelized large areas of Western Europe. During the Carolingian Reform, priests were called on to become more involved in the ministry of the Word. The *Admonitio Generalis* of 789 stated that priests were to preach in all parishes to the people. By the late eleventh and early twelfth century, a debate arose concerning monastic preaching. Benedictine monk-priests like Rupert of Deutz (d. 1129) argued that monks, as long as they were priests, could preach. Priests, and in particular the canons regular in the twelfth century, argued that preaching was strictly a sacerdotal function. This debate continued throughout the Middle Ages.

The debate between priests and monks concerning the right to preach was just the beginning of an eruption of conflicts regarding preaching authority. Rolf Zerfaß has shown that one area of major contention in the twelfth century was the issue of lay preaching. Some clerics debated whether the laity should have the right to preach, or at least have the right to give moral exhortation. These disputes show that lay preaching was a point of anxiety for the medieval church.

Lay preaching came in different forms. In the twelfth century some lay preachers embraced voluntary poverty and itinerancy. In Italy in the thirteenth century, the best examples of this were the Humiliati and the early Franciscans—most notably Francis of Assisi (d. 1226) himself. On the other hand, lawyers and kings were known to deliver sermons. Although preaching by secular leaders was an infrequent practice, it was not unique. In the tenth century in Constantinople, Emperor Leo VI (d. 912) preached on liturgical and theological topics. In the fourteenth century, King Robert of Naples (d. 1343) preached about Angevin saints such as Louis IX; undoubtedly this helped enhance the authority of Robert's Angevin lineage. Preaching by secular leaders occurred in the kingdom of Aragon; King Charles IV of Bohemia (d. 1378) preached in 1328 and in 1347.

In the fourteenth century, Robert de Basevorn again raised the issue about lay preaching and also debated if women had the right to preach. He concluded that laymen should not preach without authorization, and that women should never preach. On occasion, however, women were given the opportunity to preach. The most notable example is the Benedictine nun Hildegard of Bingen (d. 1179), who carried out four separate preaching missions with papal permission. Other women preached with ecclesiastical approval during the medieval period, such as Rose of Viterbo (d. 1252) and Humility of Faenza (d. 1310). It is interesting to note that women who were granted the right to preach often were involved in reform or preaching against heresy: Hildegard preached against the threat of the heresy of the Cathars and for ecclesiastical reform, while Rose of Viterbo preached against the "heresy" of the papal enemy Frederick II (d. 1250).

Regardless of the opportunities for different sorts of people to preach, the most likely individuals to deliver a sermon in the Middle Ages were priests. By the thirteenth century, mendicant friars, in particular Franciscans and Dominicans, became the leading figures in the burgeoning field of preaching. Although there is little surviving evidence of the sermons of the founders of these orders—respectively, Francis of Assisi and Dominic de Guzmán (d. 1221)—their legacy is well documented. David d'Avray has sketched how the evolution of the mendicant orders was greatly influenced by those friars who received their formation at the University of Paris where they acquired and developed a sense of identity as learned preachers. Hervé Martin—relying on chronicles, municipal and parish accounts, university archives, and friary archives as well as sermons—delivers a compelling and detailed account of the preacher's profession. Martin can account for 2,800 men who preached over the period from 1350 to 1520 in northern France; the majority of them were mendicants (Martin 1988, 615). Their profession was shaped by the acquisition of knowledge, the use of preaching tools, and the application of oratorical techniques to preaching (Martin 1988, 617).

Among Latinate clerics and monks, sermons were able to be diffused widely around western Europe because they were recorded in Latin, the *lingua franca* of learned medieval clerics. From the early thirteenth century, model sermon collections produced at Paris—the center of learning and training for preaching and theology in the later Middle Ages—had a great impact on the diffusion of sermons. The collections of famous preachers such as the Cistercian Bernard of Clairvaux (d. 1153), the Augustinian canon Jacques de Vitry (d. 1240), the Franciscan Bonaventure (d. 1274), and the Dominican James of Voragine (d. 1298), as well as the collections of Augustine and Gregory the Great (d. 604), were copied and circulated and became the main staple that educated preachers used in the construction of their sermons. In many ways, these collections were the descendants of the homiliaries that were produced during the Carolingian reform. The homiliary of Paul the Deacon (d. 799), in particular, was one of the most enduring pastoral legacies of the Carolingians. At the bidding of Charlemagne (d. 814), Paul produced a compendium of patristic homilies and sermons that were organized according to the liturgical calendar.

How Medievals Preached

Evidence for preaching in the vernacular and its association with multilingualism can be found as early as the ninth century in canon 17 of the Third Council of Tours (813). This canon required that preachers not only teach their flocks the basic tenets of the Catholic faith but also deliver them in a Romance or Germanic language so that all people could understand them easily. Sermons preached to the laity would normally have been delivered in the vernacular, and those preached to the clergy and monks would have been delivered in Latin. Therefore, even if sermons were written and preserved in Latin, the onus was on the preacher to translate them into a language that could be grasped by his congregation. This was a common task for many medieval preachers as most model sermons, until the fourteenth century, were normally preserved in Latin whether or not they were uttered in the vernacular.

In addition to the literary bilingualism of the preacher and scribe, there is evidence that some sermons contained words actually spoken in a mixture of Latin and vernacular phrases. Raoul of Châteauroux once attended a sermon at the Paris beguinage given by the Dominican preacher William of Auxerre (d. 1294). He describes William of Auxerre quoting Apocalypse 14:7 in Latin: *Adorate Dominum qui fecit celum et terram, mare et omnia que in eis sunt*; then Raoul reports that the preacher provided a French gloss on this New Testament text (Bériou 1998, 1:234, n64). This is significant because it indicates that preachers did use Latin quotations from the Bible and then provided biblical exegesis of the Latin using the vernacular. Preachers entwined sacred and secular languages to create an accessible form of biblical exegesis for their listeners—in this case, the beguines of Paris.

Preachers endeavored to preach in a language that their hearers would entirely understand. We see this with Bonaventure who, while giving a sermon before the people of Montpellier on Christmas, spoke in French, although his native language was Italian (*Sermo de tempore* 18). When preaching before the nuns of Saint-Antoine-des-Champs in Paris, he apologized most eloquently for his alleged poor French but stated that any language deficiency would not devalue the Word of God (*Sermo 1, de sancto Marco Evangelista*). When he preached to his learned Franciscan brothers in Paris, he did so in Latin. Indeed, we have evidence from chronicles and saints' lives indicating that preachers were bilingual and sometimes trilingual. The French preacher Yves de Tréguier (d. 1303) was reported to have preached in three different languages—French, Breton, and Latin—using the language that best fit the needs of what his hearers required (Martin 1988, 26).

Although preaching manuals (Lat., *artes praedicandi*) called for preachers to deliver their sermons in a thoughtful tone and to avoid buffoonery, preachers were known to use, among other flourishes, songs and mimicry in their preaching. In the late Middle Ages, some preaching was more like theater than liturgy. In 1515, a Franciscan Observant friar, identified in some sources simply as Oliver, preached a sermon on Good Friday in Metz, France. A contemporary, Philippe de Vigneulles (d. 1527/8), described it in his *Chronicle*. In the Church of St. Peter, Oliver had a tabernacle constructed so it looked like a chapel in which he hid two people and a wooden cross. When it came to the part of the sermon when the preacher cried to the congregation, "Have mercy," and he began to describe the crucifixion of Jesus, one of the people hidden in the chapel hit hard on an anvil with a large hammer three times for every nail that went into the hands and feet of Jesus. At that moment when many members of the congregation were welling up with tears, Oliver raised the hidden cross from the tabernacle and elevated the host while a flaming torch lit this spectacle. Then, when the sentence of Pilate had been given, Oliver had one of the people from inside the chapel blow a trumpet three times. The chronicler observed that these dramatic flourishes filled the congregation with compassion: "Because of this, the people were amazed and very sorrowful" (Bruneau 1933, 4:190). The account of the Passion message, fortified with images, props, and words, was understood as having a powerful influence on the worshipers.

Where Medievals Preached

The places in which preachers could deliver a sermon mirror developments in medieval pastoral care. Early medieval sermons were closely tied to the church as they were often delivered during Mass when the priest gave an exposition on the gospel reading. With the spread and development of monasticism throughout western Europe in the central Middle Ages, the monastery became a site where preaching often occurred. Here, the abbot would deliver sermons in chapter to his brethren. Bernard of Clairvaux wrote a series of sermons on the Song of Songs. This collection circulated widely among the various Cistercians and beyond, becoming one of the most evocative and enduring homiletic collections produced in the Middle Ages in its encouragement of the listener to cultivate an interior and intimate relationship with God.

Nuns also preached in their convents. As early as the sixth century, the queen and nun Radegund of Poitiers (d. 587) was reported to have frequently preached in her convent of the Holy Cross. As mentioned earlier, the Benedictine polymath Hildegard of Bingen preached to her sisters at Ruperstberg. In the late Middle Ages, Observant convents became places for female preaching. The Franciscan nun Caterina Vigri (d. 1463) delivered numerous sermons to her sisters that reflected trends in humanistic learning. The Observant Dominican nun and sacristan Tommasina Fieschi (d. 1534) preached collations or "evening sermons" to her sisters during key liturgical points of the year: Maundy Thursday, the Annunciation, and the Nativity. Her preaching portrays an intimate and intense relationship with the Virgin Mary and Christ.

The monastery, however, was not the only place where preaching thrived and it increasingly became an outdoor activity in the preacher's bid to deliver an impromptu and heartfelt message. In the late eleventh and early twelfth centuries in France, charismatic preachers expounding church renewal and apostolic simplicity—themes associated with the Gregorian Reform—appeared on the scene. Among the most outstanding were Henry of Lausanne (d. ca. 1148) and Robert of Arbrissel (d. 1116). Their peripatetic lives and practices of voluntary poverty captured the imagination of many. These preachers were, at least initially, supported by church officials to enliven the faithful to recognize the need for ecclesiastical and personal reform. As with the case of Henry of Lausanne, however, such preaching sometimes incited some listeners to turn against the church. This led to Henry's eventual imprisonment as a heretic in 1148.

Itinerant, outdoor preaching came to be associated with the mendicant orders who served in the front line of the church in its endeavor to win back the disaffected. At the Fourth Lateran Council, Pope Innocent III (d. 1216) made it one of his main objectives to establish a group of men to assist bishops in their preaching. Innocent III ordered,

> We therefore decreed by this general constitution that bishops are to ap-point suitable men to carry out with profit this duty of sacred preaching, men who are powerful in word and deed and who will visit with care the peoples entrusted to them in place of the bishops, since these by themselves are unable to do it, and will build them up, by word and example. The bishops shall suitably furnish them with what is necessary, when they are in need of it, lest for want of necessities they are forced to abandon what they have begun. (Tanner 1990, 1:239)

This role was assumed by the mendicant orders, particularly the Franciscans and Dominicans, which were both founded in the first quarter of the thirteenth century.

Several superstar mendicants emerged in the fifteenth century, whose reputation attracted hundreds of listeners, making the public square the only space that could accommodate their enraptured audiences. Observant preachers, such as the Franciscans Bernardino of Siena (d. 1444) and John of Capistrano (d. 1456) and the Dominicans Vincent Ferrer (d. 1419) and Girolamo Savonarola (d. 1498), drew large crowds eager to hear and to see their remarkable preaching. The success of their preaching coincided with the development of outdoor portable pulpits. These could be placed in the middle of town squares as well as graveyards or next to outdoor preaching crosses or in front of churches. Many images of Bernardino of Siena show him on a portable pulpit preaching to large audiences in the middle of a piazza. In one of his sermons, Bernardino went so far as to argue that if the listeners had to make a choice between attending a sermon or attend-ing church, they should choose the sermon. This was because listening to sermons could strengthen one's belief, while hearing Mass did not expli-cate Christian doctrine. In the eyes of this influential preacher, the sermon became a self-contained act that was superior to the Mass. The hearing of a sermon, like the reception of a sacrament, could bring grace.

What Was Preached

Within monasteries and convents a pervasive use of biblical verses and phrases was the core of sermon construction. Bernard of Clairvaux described Scripture as food to be digested and regurgitated, that is, to be thought upon on and recalled effectively. Listening to sermons assisted in this process because Bernard's preaching—like many monastic sermons—was infused with scriptural texts. Outside of the cloister, generally speaking, preaching was concerned with relaying the basics of Christian faith. The parish priest focused on teaching the creed, the Ten Commandments, the works of mercy, and saying the *Pater Noster* and the *Ave Maria*.

In the later Middle Ages, however, there is evidence that more sophisticated sermon content was delivered to the laity. Martin argues that late medieval preachers taught their congregations not only the articles of the creed but also difficult theological issues like the Trinity (Martin 1988, 619). Preachers used liturgical occasions to teach and instill faith and ritualistic practices. For example, sermons preached on the feasts of the Exaltation of the Cross (September 14), the Invention of the Cross (May 3), and Good Friday often invited the laity to venerate the cross through developing an intimate relationship with the suffering Christ. Sermons preached on saints' days were opportunities for preachers to offer up models of holiness for their listeners to imitate. The feast days of virgin martyrs such as Cecilia provided the renowned thirteenth-century preacher Jacques de Vitry (d. 1240) the opportunity to discuss paragons of female piety, especially in his preaching to beguines. When giving a sermon on the feast day of Augustine of Hippo, preachers sometimes included the moment when the saint threw himself under a tree and wept during his anxious conversion to Christianity. This scene was frequently used by preachers as an opportunity to speak about conversion and penitence.

Preachers, however, also used sermons to convey prejudices, hatred, and violence. Bernardino of Siena encouraged belief in witches and insisted that they be violently punished. In his tireless attempts to replace Jewish bankers with Christian ones, another Franciscan Observant, Bernardino of Feltre (1439–1494), preached against the Jews and their practice of usury. Part of his anti-Semitism included preaching the blood libel of the child Simon of Trent (d. 1475), whom many Christians believed had been killed by Jews.

When and Why They Preached

Medieval sermons were often tied to the liturgical calendar. The expectation was that the parish priest would address his congregation on Sundays and feast days during the Mass at some point after the gospel reading. The Carolingian Reform Synods of 813 required that preaching take place not only in cities but also in all parish churches. In monastic settings, preaching was sometimes tied to meditative processes that invited the community to contemplate union with God. With the broadening of clerical education and the rise of the mendicant orders in the thirteenth century, preaching became more widespread and frequent. It could occur on a number of occasions: the dedication of a church, crusading missions, councils, and ordinations. Preachers were known to deliver sermons and to organize processions in order to ward off drought, disease, and earthquakes. The repetition of sermon themes taken from the liturgical calendar over decades and centuries of preaching helped instill Christian learning across medieval western Europe. In this regard, the gradual conversion of Europe was assisted through preaching.

By the later Middle Ages, high hopes were attached to preaching. Sermons were viewed in some circles as a method to cure societal evils. Preachers like Bernardino of Siena were frequently invited by civic authorities to preach in an attempt to instill calmness and harmony during tense political times. It was for this reason that he was invited to Siena in 1427. Preaching over a period of seven weeks, from August 15 to October 5 in the Piazza del Campo, Bernardino did not use the traditional liturgical *thema* that normally would have been used for sermons preached during this time. Instead, he substituted them with what he saw as more appropriate thematic choices from Scripture to preach peace to his audience. Therefore, the themes of these sermons were not so much tied to the daily liturgy as to the daily lives of men and women; they were tailor-made to the measure of Sienese civic and personal struggles.

This motivation in Observant preaching at the end of the Middle Ages demonstrates an optimism that some preachers had in regard to their vocation. The highest aspirations preachers held would be to assist their listeners on the path to perfection. Whether or not medieval preachers did successfully direct their audiences to this end is next to impossible to know, as we cannot ask their listeners what happened. Sometimes, however, we do come across evidence that gives insight to listeners' responses and to an indication of an inner transformation. In Florence, the great Observant preacher of the Dominicans, Giovanni Dominici (d. 1419) wrote vernacular sermons and preached to wide-ranging audiences. Describing Dominici's preaching, the Florentine notary Ser Lapo wrote to a friend,

> I tell you that I have never heard such a sermon, nor such preaching. It really looks as though the friends of God are on the rise again, to reform the clerics and laity. And he's supposed to preach here at Lent; he's coming from Venice, where everyone follows him about. You'll think you're hearing a disciple of St. Francis and be revived. All of us either wept or stood stupefied at the clear truth he showed to the people. (Mazzei 1880, 1:228)

Conclusion

Preaching in the Middle Ages provided a solid foundation in the development of belief, ritual, and devotional fervor. Successful preachers adapted their sermons to teach the hearers the intricacies of faith and sometimes to move them to emotion so as to heighten their belief. Many late medieval preachers held a conviction that the power of preaching could change lives, and the appeal to emotion was one way to initiate this change. In a world where hearing a sermon, in some instances, was more important than the Mass, we see that preaching became increasingly vital as a means of Christian formation as the Middle Ages wore on. By the eve of the Reformation, listening to sermons had taken on a quasi-sacramental quality.

Bibliography

Alan of Lille. *Summa de arte praedicationum. Patrologia Latina* 210, coll. 111C-196A. Paris: Migne, 1855.

Antonopoulou, Theodora. *The Homilies of Leo VI*. Leiden: Brill, 1997.

d'Avray, David. *The Preaching of the Friars: Sermons Diffused from Paris before 1300*. Oxford: Clarendon Press, 1985.

Bériou, Nicole. *L'Avènement des maîtres de la parole. La prédication à Paris au XIIIᵉ siècle*. Série moyen âge et temps modernes 31. 2 Vols. Paris: Institut d'études augustiniennes, 1998.

Blamires, Alcuin. "Women and Preaching in Medieval Orthodoxy, Heresy and Saints' Lives." *Viator* 26 (1995): 135–53.

Bonaventure. *Sermones de tempore, de Sanctis, de B. Virgine Maria, et de diversis*. In *Opera omnia*. Ed. PP. Collegii a S. Bonaventura, vol. 9. Quaracchi: Ex Typographia Collegii S. Bonaventurae, 1901.

Bruneau, Charles, ed. *La Chronique de Philippe de Vigneulles*, Tome 4 [de l'an 1500 à l'an 1525]. Metz: Societe d'histoire et d'archeologie de la Lorraine, 1933.

Bruzelius, Caroline. "The Architecture of the Mendicant Orders in the Middle Ages: An Overview of Recent Literature." *Perspective* 2 (2012): 365–86.

Dalarun, Jacques. *L'impossible sainteté. La vie retrouvée de Robert d'Arbrissel, fondateur de Fontevraud*. Paris: Cerf, 1985.

Ferzoco, George. "Preaching by Thirteenth-Century Italian Hermits." In *Medieval Monastic Preaching*. Studies in Intellectual History 90. Edited by Carolyn Muessig, 145–58. Leiden: Brill, 1998.

Hall, Tom. "The Early Medieval Sermon." In *The Sermon*. Typologie des sources des moyen âge occidental, fascicules, 81–83. Edited by Beverly M. Kienzle, 203–69. Turnhout: Brepols 2000.

Kienzle, Beverly M., and Pamela J. Walker, eds. *Women, Preachers, and Prophets through Two Millennia of Christianity*. Berkeley: University of California Press, 1998.

Kienzle, Beverly M., ed. *The Sermon*. Typologie des sources des moyen âge occidental, fascicules, 81–83. Turnhout: Brepols, 2000.

Martin, Hervé. *Le métier de prédicateur à la fin du moyen âge 1350–1520*. Paris: Cerf, 1988.

Mazzei, Lapo. *Lettere d'un notaro a un mercante del secolo XIV*. Edited by Cesare Guasti. 2 vols. Florence: Successori Le Monnier, 1880.

McKitterick, Rosamond. *The Frankish Church and the Carolingian Reforms 789–895*. London: Royal Historical Society, 1977.

Mooney, Catherine M. "Authority and Inspiration in the *Vitae* and Sermons of Humility of Faenza." In *Medieval Monastic Preaching*. Studies in Intellectual History 90. Edited by Carolyn Muessig, 123–44. Leiden: Brill, 1998.

Mostaccio, Silvia. *Osservanza vissuta osservanza insegnata: La domenicana genovese Tommasina Fieschi e i suoi scritti 1448 ca. – 1534*. Florence: Olschki, 1999.

Muessig, Carolyn. "Sermon, Preacher and Society in the Middle Ages." *Journal of Medieval History* 28 (2002): 73–91.

———. "Bernardino da Siena and Observant Preaching as a Vehicle for Religious Transformation." In *Observant Reform in the Later Middle Ages and Beyond*. Brill's Companions to the Christian Tradition 59. Edited by James Mixson and Bert Roest, 183–203. Leiden: Brill, 2015.

Pryds, Darlene. "Monarchs, Lawyers, and Saints: Juridical Preaching on Holiness." In *Models of Holiness in Medieval Sermons*. Textes et études du moyen âge 5. Edited by Beverly M. Kienzle et al., 141–56. Louvain-la-Neuve: FIDEM, 1996.

———. "Proclaiming Sanctity through Proscribed Acts: The Case of Rose of Viterbo." In *Women, Preachers, and Prophets through Two Millennia of Christianity*. Edited by Beverly M. Kienzle and Pamela J. Walker, 159–72. Berkeley: University of California Press, 1998.

Roberts, Phyllis. "Preaching and Sermon Literature, Western European." In *Dictionary of the Middle Ages*. Edited by Joseph Strayer, 10:75–82. New York: Charles Scribner's Sons, 1988.

Schiewer, Regina. "Sermons for Nuns of the Dominican Observance Movement." In *Medieval Monastic Preaching*. Studies in Intellectual History 90. Edited by Carolyn Muessig, 75–92. Leiden: Brill, 1998.

Vigri, Caterina. *Le sette armi spirituali.* Edited by Antonella Degl'Innocenti. Florence: SISMEL, 2000.

Werminghoff, Albert, ed. "Concilium Turonense." In *Monumenta Germaniae Historica.* Leges Sectio 3, Concilia, 2:1. Hannover-Leipzig: Hahn, 1906.

Zerfaß, Rolf. *Der Streit um die Laienpredigt. Eine pastoralgeschichtliche Untersuchung zum Verständnis des Predigtamtes und zu seiner Entwicklung im 12 und 13 Jahrhundert.* Freiburg: Herder, 1974.

Zink, Michel. *La prédication en langue romane avant 1300.* Paris: H. Champion, 1976.

Preaching from Trent to the Enlightenment

Robert Bireley

Scholars are coming to realize that in the sixteenth and seventeenth centuries the pulpit served as the principal medium of mass communication. Preaching during the period from the Council of Trent into the Enlightenment, from roughly 1563 to 1780, exhibited considerable diversity in both content and style. The late Middle Ages had suffered no lack of preaching, especially by the Dominican and Franciscan friars (see 64 above). The problem was with the content not the extent of preaching. The Fifth Lateran Council in 1516 bemoaned the twisting of the sense of Scripture by apocalyptic preachers who threaten "various terrors, menaces, and many other evils, which they say are about to arrive and are already growing" (Tanner, 1:635). They have "invented miracles, new and false prophecies and other frivolities hardly distinguishable from old wives' tales." So congregations "are withdrawn by their sermons from the teaching and commands of the universal church" (Tanner, 1:636). Superiors were to examine all preachers, whether regular or secular, and guarantee to the local bishop or other authority their life, competence, and doctrine

The Fifth Lateran Council prepared the way for the Council of Trent (1545–1563). In 1547 this council declared preaching to be "the principal duty of bishops" (*praecipuum episcoporum munus*): the bishop was personally bound to this and required to find a substitute if he were legitimately impeded. Pastors bore the same responsibility for their parishes; they or competent substitutes were expected to preach "at least on Sundays and solemn feasts, according to their own and their hearers' capacity what it is necessary for all to know with a view to salvation by proclaiming briefly . . . the vices they must avoid and the virtues they must cultivate so as to escape eternal punishment and gain the glory of heaven" (Tanner, 2:669), words adapted from the second Rule of Francis of Assisi (d. 1226) and pointing to moralistic preaching. This was repeated in a decree at the end of the council in 1563. Here, pastors or their substitutes were also expected to preach daily or at least three times a week during Lent and Advent

(Tanner, 2:763). In fact, most of the series of Lent and Advent sermons were delivered by religious priests. The decree on seminaries called for instruction in homiletics.

Many treatises on preaching, the *Ars Praedicandi*, appeared in the late Middle Ages, and they usually dealt with the "thematic sermon," a style associated with scholasticism and usually intended for an educated congregation. The Christian humanist Erasmus published a treatise on preaching—the *Ecclesiastes* in 1535, so before the Council of Trent—that was to have significant influence even though it lacked clarity. He called the sermon a *concio* or exhortation addressed to a popular audience, a word taken over from Jerome (d. 420), and he related it to the *genus deliberativum* or persuasive speech, a form used in ancient Rome to persuade a deliberative body. So he endorsed the use of classical literary forms and rhetorical devices for use in Christian preaching (see 200ff. below). He also advocated a return to the Scriptures and to the "Fathers of the Church" as sources for preaching and recommended especially the sermon based on a particular text of Scripture. Following Trent, Charles Borromeo (d. 1584) issued his *Instructions for Preaching the Word of God* (Lat., *Instructiones praedicationis verbi Dei*, 1576), which were widely disseminated along with those of other reforming bishops. His focus, broadly similar to that of Trent, was on sin, occasions of sin, virtues, and then on the sacraments and church customs. A moralism pervaded his *Instructions*.

Two other important authors were Agostino Valerio (d. 1606), bishop of Verona and a protégé of Borromeo, who published his *Three Books on Ecclesiastical Rhetoric or the Manner of Preaching* (Lat., *De rhetorica ecclesiastica sive modo praedicandi libri tres*, 1574), and the Spaniard Louis of Granada (d. 1588) who published his work of a similar title in 1576. Both of them drew heavily on classical rhetoric: Valerio on Aristotle (d. 322 BCE) and Louis of Granada on Cicero (d. 43 BCE) and Quintilian (d. ca. 100 CE). This classical rhetoric outlined five steps in the development of a sermon: (1) invention with the help of commonplaces; (2) the order in a sermon of exordium, narration, division, confutation, and peroration; (3) figures of speech and of words; (4) organization and reflection to help memory; and (5) instruction on voice and action. This classical rhetoric was taught at the Jesuits' Roman College, the Sapienza, and other Roman institutions; it was then enshrined in the Jesuits' Plan of Studies (Lat., *Ratio Studiorum*) and transmitted to the Jesuit colleges and the new seminaries called for by the Council of Trent.

The renewal of preaching, first in Rome and then beyond, maintained ideals of the humanism of the Renaissance. It aimed at persuasion, to abhor vice and embrace virtue; it summoned to conversion and to the sacrament of confession. Preaching also contributed greatly to the transformation of Catholic Christians into Roman Catholics, with their center in the Eternal City, Rome. Criticism of the church, which had been widespread in the years leading up to Trent, disappeared from sermons. Sermons proclaimed Roman Catholic doctrinal positions on the basis of Scripture and tradition; disputes with Protestants were rare. Preaching in Rome also revived on a more popular level with the homily or *sermo evangelicus*.

Preaching was central to Italian culture during the early modern period. Its often theatrical nature drew crowds and moved them. Sermons appealed to the imagination and elicited active participation. The two most prominent preachers in Italy in the sixteenth century were the Franciscans Cornelio Musso (d. 1574) and his protégé Francesco Panigarola (d. 1594). Called "the Italian Demosthenes," Musso was the first, contemporaries thought, to preach eloquently in Italian in both an embellished and a simple style. He preached the inaugural sermon at Trent in 1545 and played a significant role in the council. He effectively combined humanist rhetoric with Franciscan values. One observer contended that his verbal descriptions rivaled the paintings of the great artists. Sometimes he addressed the first half of a sermon to the elite and the second half to the ordinary people. Panigarola, who preached frequently in Rome in St. Peter's and in Santa Maria in Aracoeli, was known for crafting rich word images. Both Musso and Panigarola published their sermons that were then employed as models for preachers as well as devotional reading for the laity. Lent and Advent sermons predominated in their printed sermons, which might be considered literature. Robert Bellarmine, on the other hand, was hostile to classical forms and favored the homily. In Rome itself, preaching now glorified the city as the center of a restored Roman Catholicism, and criticism of the church was off limits.

Preaching stood out as an event in early modern Italy that required active participation; it was a ritual. The preacher himself had the principal role. Often his clothing, his gestures, and his voice called to mind a prophet of the Hebrew Scriptures. One well-known preacher usually bowed before the Blessed Sacrament or the crucifix if the sermon was held outside, as it often was, acknowledged the congregation, and then prayed with outstretched hands. Next he venerated the crucifix once again and recited the Hail Mary in a voice that the congregation could hear. He then gave his cloak to an assistant before climbing into the pulpit and uncovering his head. Then he announced his chosen theme and began the sermon, during which he often directly addressed his audience. Preaching was frequently associated with eucharistic devotion, especially in the *quarant'ore* or Forty

Hours devotion where the consecrated Host was adored for a continual forty hours while preachers took turns exhorting the congregation.

In Germany, the *postils* played an important role for preaching, more so than in other countries. These were collections of sermons or sermon outlines that circulated widely, the early modern equivalent of "homily helps." They were meant to help priests prepare their sermons or even to be read as sermons themselves. The acronym *postil* comes from the Latin *post illa verba textus*, that is, "after the words [of the gospel preach the following] text."

The use of *postils* had become a practice during the later Middle Ages, and it greatly increased with the advent of printing. Normally there were two sets of *postils*, one for the Sundays of the year and the other for feast days, of which there were many more than there are now. The epistle and gospel readings selected for Sundays dated back to the early Middle Ages, and it was thought that they covered all the basic doctrines and teachings of the church. For example, the gospel reading for the Second Sunday after Epiphany, which told the story of the marriage feast at Cana, provided an opportunity to preach on marriage. Some of the folio volumes of *postils* contain eight to ten sermons for a Sunday. In many German towns and cities, there frequently existed endowed preaching positions, and sermons were delivered in a separate service in the afternoon following a homily during the morning Mass. *Postils* were published in Latin and German; many priests could develop a German sermon from a Latin outline.

John Eck (d. 1543), a professor at the University of Ingolstadt and Luther's (d. 1546) first major opponent, published three volumes of sermons by 1530, three years after Luther's first *postils* appeared. They included traditional material along with challenges to Luther's interpretations of Scripture. By 1532, four series of one hundred sermons came from the pen of Friedrich Nausea (d. 1552), preacher at the cathedral in Mainz; they too were often directed in large part against Luther. One estimate claims that from 1530 to 1555 approximately 132,000 complete sets of Roman Catholic *postils* had been printed in which a principal theme was the refutation of Protestant understandings of Scripture. *Postils* were handed down from pastor to pastor in the parishes. Thus, Trent did not initiate a new period of preaching. It did aid preaching indirectly by clarifying doctrine and by calling for a better seminary education; the new Jesuit colleges were more effective for the education of priests. Synods held in 1547 at the time of the Augsburg Interim, when Roman Catholics briefly secured the upper hand in Germany, emphasized preaching anew. German Roman Catholic *postils* took up many themes that were meant to be conciliatory toward Protestants and represented a *via media*: i.e., a piety that was Christocentric; gave less attention to the veneration of saints and the unearned character of God's mercy; that recognized that good works were the fruits of faith and that the Spirit stirred up faith through the preaching of the Word; and admitted that the immorality of the popes and the German clergy bore the brunt of the responsibility for the spread of heresy.

Starting in 1570 the tone of Catholic *postils* changed again, and they revealed the growing tension between Roman Catholics and Protestants. They became more aggressive and took on Counter-Reformation features. That year Michael Buchinger (d. 1571?), a priest of Colmar in Alsace, published the first of his *postils* that demonized Protestants; they were to go through forty-eight printings.

From the pen of Martin Eisengrein (d. 1578), a convert who moved from Vienna to Ingolstadt, came *postils* on the Sunday pericopes intended for parish priests that asserted the Roman Catholic position on papal primacy, indulgences, the cult of the saints, and communion under one species. The Jesuit Peter Canisius (d. 1597) released his first collection of *postils* in 1591 that vigorously defended tradition and the decrees of Trent. Such *postils* were becoming an instrument to consolidate the Roman Catholic party in the empire. From 1600 to 1620, more *postils* appeared than in any other twenty-year period since Luther came on the scene, and foreign authors like Cardinals Bellarmine and Baronius (d. 1607) were contributing them from Rome. The Thirty Years War broke out in 1618.

By the late Middle Ages, preaching had reached most of France except for the most isolated rural or mountainous regions. Yet there was nowhere near the number of published sermons in the sixteenth century in France as in Germany or Italy. After 1560, with the outbreak of the Religious Wars, sermons became more militant and political. The mendicant orders did much of the preaching. The sermon required by Trent was usually a brief instruction delivered at Mass and rarely reprinted. A full-dress sermon was normally given at a different time, often in the afternoon on Sundays, feast days, and especially in Lent and Advent. It normally went on for one hour. Borromeo's *Instructions on Preaching* and Valerio's *Three Books on Ecclesiastical Rhetoric* exercised considerable influence on preachers in France. It was in France also that the new style of the popular rural mission first took hold. Vincent de Paul (d. 1660), with his little band of four that would become the Congregation of the Mission, undertook its first mission in February 1617 in the parish of Villepreux on the lands of his patroness, Madame de Gondi. They took up residence in an abandoned house and then began to reach out to the reserved peasants. The missionaries began by instructing the children in catechism and teaching them the hymns to be sung at the services. Catechism would become a feature of a mission, which lasted three weeks. Gradually the adults began to overcome their reservations and soon they filled the church for the sermon given according to the "Little Method" of Vincent, which contrasted with the revived classicism. At the end, most of the parishioners went to confession and approached the altar for Holy Communion. Before they left the parish, Vincent and his companions organized a *charité*, a group of women who were to minister to the needs of the poor. The *charité* would become a standard feature of the missions of Vincent and his companions and eventually would result in the foundation of the Sisters of Charity.

The Society of Jesus and Mary, or the Eudists, founded in 1643 by John Eudes (d. 1680), and especially the Jesuits took up the work of the rural parish missions. Prominent among the Jesuits was Julian Maunoir (d. 1683), the "Apostle of Brittany," who led four hundred missions from 1640 to 1683, usually ten a year from four to five weeks each. Upwards of thirty thousand people attended some missions, where Maunoir was assisted by a large team of local diocesan priests and where the main sermons were held outside in a field or in the village or town square. The pastor of the parish, the bishop, or a local landowner invited him. Maunoir normally opened the mission on a Saturday afternoon with a solemn procession after Vespers, followed by a sermon outlining the schedule of the mission and urging participation. An early silent Mass on Sunday morning was followed by a dialogue in which Maunoir put questions to the congregation and took questions from them, thus acquiring some idea of their mentality. Then came the first-morning sermon. Afterward followed "break-out" sessions for catechesis—which constituted a major feature of a mission as it had for Vincent—and the learning of the peculiar Breton *cantiques* or didactic religious poems to be sung throughout the mission, along with opportunity for confession. Two further sermons followed in the course of the day, one at 10:00 a.m. and another at 4:00 p.m. in winter or 5:00 p.m. in summer. The rest of the day was filled with catechesis, *cantiques*, and confessions. The day ended with Benediction of the Blessed Sacrament and night prayers. The subjects of the initial sermons were taken for the most part from the first week of the *Spiritual Exercises* of Ignatius of Loyola (d. 1556): the purpose of our existence, the four last things (death, judgment, heaven, and hell), sin and forgiveness, the sacraments (especially confession and Holy Communion), and the rewards of heaven. A highlight of the mission was the General Communion for the Dead through which the participants could obtain a plenary indulgence for the souls in purgatory. The mission concluded with a grand procession that featured tableaux of scenes from the life of Jesus or of the sacraments that were staged by parishes from the area. Benediction of the Blessed Sacrament and a final sermon by Maunoir on the Passion of Christ brought the mission to a conclusion. Afterward a cross was frequently erected in the church or outside it to remind the parishioners of the graces of the mission.

In 1660, Vincent Huby (d. 1693) founded the first Jesuit retreat house, also in Brittany, at Vannes. The retreats ran from Tuesday evening until the following Wednesday morning, with two retreats a month. The retreat house could accommodate up to three hundred men; clergy and laity, nobility and commoners made the retreat together. Here too the talks followed more or less the *Spiritual Exercises*, building up to a general confession and then prayer on the life of Christ leading to an election. Retreat houses then eventually spread to other French cities and to Prague, Munich, and Rome. Not to be outdone, a French noblewoman in Vannes of considerable means, Catherine de Francheville (d. 1689), seeing the men crowding to the men's retreat house, undertook to establish a retreat house nearby for women and, after overcoming formidable obstacles, finally succeeded in 1674.

French pulpit oratory rose to the level of literature in the second half of the seventeenth century. Most prominent were the court preachers Bishop Jacques Bénigne Bossuet (d. 1704) and the Jesuit Louis Bourdaloue (d. 1704). A native of Dijon, Bossuet spent much of his time in Paris from 1659 to 1681 at the court of Louis XIV (d. 1704), serving from 1670 as tutor to the dauphin. It was during this time that he preached his most celebrated sermons, panegyrics of saints, and funeral orations, as well as Advent and Lent sermons. He embodied French classical elegance with his periodic sentences and sonorous voice, combining reason, balance, and order and drawing extensively on the Bible and Augustine (d. 430). He spoke out clearly against the king's adulteries, threatening him with damnation, while at the same time recognizing Louis's role in unifying France. After 1682, he returned to Meaux where he had been named bishop but remained active in the controversies of the time, especially Jansenism and Gallicanism. Bourdaloue made a brilliant debut with his Advent sermons at St. Louis in Paris in 1669. In 1679, he became the ordinary preacher of the king and the court, and he also preached in other churches in Paris. He combined a healthy reason and a vivid imagination with a profound knowledge of the human heart. Basically a moralist, he did not mince words as he pilloried the vices and disorders of the court and city, but he opposed Jansenist rigorism, its view on predestination, and its severe limitation on the reception of Holy Communion.

When we move east to Catholic Germany, and especially to the baroque preaching of the Habsburg monarchy and Bavaria, we find a generally more optimistic tone and a wide variety of types of sermons. Sermons were given in light-filled churches where magnificently carved pulpits seemed to be suspended in space from which the preacher delivered the Word of God. There was a wide variety of sermon types. Sermons on Sundays—sometimes three a day, at Mass in the morning, in the afternoon, and again at night— on Marian and saints' feast days, at marriages and funerals made up the chief genres. Preaching also accompanied important events of city and state, jubilees of the dynasty, the start of war, the conclusion of peace as well as rituals seeking deliverance from plagues, fires, and floods. There were also moral sermons denouncing drinking, dancing, female fashions, luxury, and frivolity. Preachers drew on a wide variety of sources: Scripture, commentaries on Scripture, *postils*, the Missal, and the Breviary and often encyclopedias and histories that provided examples from nature and from history. God governed the world. Whoever sought to evoke God's glory and greatness, love and mercy, needed to vary, pile up, and surpass the standard images and metaphors of the day. The preacher had to adapt to his congregations. Underneath all the examples, word pictures, and tales there yet remained the structure and the ordinary progression of a human-ist oration. Jeremias Drexel (d. 1638), a prominent preacher at the court of Bavaria during the early baroque period, advised that a sermon should not exceed one hour. Preachers often took an hourglass or a pocket watch with them into the pulpit.

Perhaps the most prominent baroque preacher was the Discalced Augustinian friar Johann Ulrich Megerle (d. 1709), better known as Abraham a Santa Clara, who was born in Baden but spent most of his active life in Vienna where he died. In addition to preaching, Abraham also authored a wide variety of books and pamphlets, and he warned vigorously against the advance of the Turks in the 1680s. He too preached at court, for Emperor Leopold (d. 1705), but he frequently addressed the common people, and his style was much more popular than the elite French preachers. His vocabulary left a permanent mark on the German that people spoke in Austria and especially in Vienna. The poet Friedrich Schiller (d. 1805) characterized him as a preacher of great originality, wit, and cleverness. He was a powerful, colorful preacher who could mimic with great effectiveness and tell stories entertainingly. His insight into human nature and into the popular mind stood out, and he preached on every considerable topic. He did not fear criticizing the morals of the court, and when reprimanded for denouncing female fashions at court too vigorously, he announced the following Sunday that in the future he would no longer preach vigorously against shameful female dress.

Another prolific preacher of the baroque period was the Capuchin Prokop of Templin (d. 1680). A convert from Lutheranism, he left behind more than 2,600 sermons that he delivered in Bohemia and Austria.

The baroque and the Enlightenment periods overlapped somewhat in the late seventeenth and early eighteenth centuries. There continued to be a great deal of preaching during the Enlightenment, but its tone and content changed to a degree. Interestingly, no individual Roman Catholic preachers stand out in the Enlightenment as did in the previous periods. Generally, the Enlightenment tended to reduce religion to God, virtue, and the afterlife, and this influenced Catholic preaching. Enlightenment figures downplayed many devotions and feasts emphasizing the simple service of God. Sermons became more didactic, drawing on Scripture and reason as well as the Catechism of the Council of Trent and the Catechisms of Peter Canisius. Narratives, legends, anecdotes, and examples were banished. Sermons became shorter. A natural, utilitarian morality came to the fore, still based on the Ten Commandments and often supportive of obedience to the growing state. Preachers also addressed the rights and responsibilities of each estate and stages of life.

Popular missions continued in the rural areas, especially of western and southern Europe. Indeed, the period from 1680 to 1750 has been called "the golden age" of the missions in Europe, which saw a transformation of the countryside. In Italy, the Jesuit Paolo Segneri the younger (d. 1713) continued missions throughout Italy in the theatrical style of his uncle, Paulo Segneri (d. 1694). Alphonsus Liguori (d. 1787) began his work of evangelization that would result in the foundation of the Redemptorists. Yet many churchmen were suspicious of the genuine results of the missions; "conversions" based on an emotional experience were often short-lived. Such was the view of Italian bishops gathered at Pistoia in 1786, shortly before the events of 1789 would start to convulse Europe.

Because of the vastness of the topic of preaching, Spain and the Americas have not been discussed in this contribution. Spain did not produce preachers at court of the caliber of Bossuet, Bourdaloue, or Abraham a Santa Clara. Yet, preaching did flourish in Spain. The treatise of Louis of Granada has been noted. A great many published sermons circulated, both for reading and as helps for other preachers, such as the volume of more than six hundred pages of Andreu Capella (d. 1609), bishop of Urgell in Catalonia, for Sundays of the year and for Lent published in 1596. The Jesuit Eusebio Nieremberg (d. 1658) published a compendium of homilies, *La Practica del Catecismo Romano y Doctrina Christiana*, which combined catechetical instruction with sermons and long remained popular in Spain as the "Eusebio." Homilies of from five to ten minutes were often given at Mass with the sermons delivered later in the afternoon and especially in Lent and Advent when there were sermons several times a week, usually delivered by members of religious orders. In 1574, the parish of the village of Salmeron near Cuenca in Spain sued its pastor because he did not preach and so compelled him to hire a Franciscan from a nearby convent to do so. Rural missions were also conducted in Spain. The well-known Jesuit preacher Pedro de Calatayud (d. 1773) was conducting missions in Catalonia at the time of the suppression of the Jesuits in Spain in 1763.

With regard to the Spanish Empire in the New World, there were fundamentally two types of preaching, one for the European population and one for the Amerindians. The former aimed at the exhortation of the people to live a better Christian life, and it did not differ greatly from what was employed in Europe. The latter envisioned the evangelization of the Amerindians. This made use of a much simpler style, and it required a great deal of linguistic ability in order to reach the many different Amerindian populations. Its more specific goal was to uproot the remnants of paganism and idolatry among the Amerindians. The two types are illustrated by two works of the Jesuit teacher of rhetoric in Peru, José de Arriaga (d. 1622), *Of the Christian Preacher* (Lat., *Rhetoris Christiani*) of 1619 and *Extirpation of Idolatry in Peru* (Lat., *Extirpacion de la idolatria en el Peru*).

Bibliography

Abbott, Don Paul. *Rhetoric in the New World: Rhetorical Theory and Practice in Colonial Spanish America*. Columbia: University of South Carolina Press, 1996.

Bayley, Peter. *French Pulpit Oratory, 1598–1650: A Study in Themes and Styles; With a Descriptive Catalogue of Printed Texts*. Cambridge, UK: Cambridge University Press, 1980.

Chatellier, Louis. *The Religion of the Poor*. Translated from the French. Cambridge, UK: Cambridge University Press, 1997.

Frymire, John. *The Primacy of the Postils: Catholics, Protestants, and the Dissemination of Ideas in Early Modern Germany*. Leiden: Brill, 2010.

Herzog, Urs. *Geistlich Wohlredenheit. Die katholische Barockpredigt*. Munich: Beck, 1991.

Michelson, Emily. *The Pulpit and the Press in Reformation Italy*. Cambridge, MA: Harvard University Press, 2013.

Schneyer, Johann Baptist. *Geschichte der katholischen Predigt*. Freiburg: Seelsorge Verlag, 1969.

Preaching before Vatican II

Guerric DeBona

When *Sacrosanctum Concilium* (*SC*) restored the homily in 1963, it appeared to some that Roman Catholic evangelism was finally moving into the twentieth century. Long shaped by the guidelines established at the Council of Trent (1546–1563), the first synod (1791), and provincial councils of Baltimore (1829–1849), Pope Pius X's *Acerbo Nimis* (1905), the 1917 *Code of Canon Law* (*CIC*1917), together with other ecclesial documents on evangelism, Roman Catholic preaching in the United States seemed to have very little new to recommend itself before the promulgation of *SC* (McNamara 1975). Since the time of John Carroll (d. 1815) there was more than a tendency to use the Sunday sermon as a time for announcements, catechetics, and sometimes politics, with little relationship to the Sunday liturgy or its readings (McNamara 1975, 41). Then there were the challenges of preaching in a country suffused with nativist, anti-Catholic sentiment, the complicated cultural politics of immigration, and a church more or less dominated by ritual rather than the Word. The resulting narrative is often that from the colonial period to the modern age, the weight of Roman Catholic preaching fell on priests with little or no formation in homiletics and who thrived in a parochial environment less prophetic than it was educative and functional.

There are problems with such a simplified scenario. Preaching by Roman Catholics in the United States has been underresearched and underreported and requires some demythologizing. The decades before the restoration of the homily in 1963 were surprisingly vital times for Roman Catholic preaching in the United States. Because of the concise nature of the essays in this volume, this essay will attempt to demystify three "myths" about early twentieth-century Roman Catholic preaching in the United States. The following narrative is meant to be more suggestive than exhaustive but hopefully both provocative and contributory.

Myth Number 1: *Roman Catholicism's authoritarian and clerical structures made any renewal of preaching—including preaching by the laity—impossible until Vatican II.*

Few would argue with the view that *CIC*1917 defined preaching as largely the function of the magisterium (i.e., the teaching faculty of the church), with the pastor serving as delegate (Provost 1983, 134–58). From this perspective, the laity was simply a passive recipient of the teaching church through its hierarchical and bureaucratic structure. Yet decades before *Lumen Gentium* would redefine the church as the People of God (e.g., *LG*, no. 9), preaching was being revitalized at the grassroots level in the twentieth-century Roman Catholic United States and beyond through liturgical renewal, a rise in diverse forms of evangelization, and Catholic Action groups. The reforms began in Europe as early as 1830 with the "liturgical movement" and its influential pioneers, such as Lambert Beauduin, OSB (d. 1960). Their attention to the Christian assembly as the core of worship set in motion a push for the full participation of the faithful in what Beauduin in his 1909 address called "The Full Prayer of the Church" (Funk 1990, 700). This would affirm the active role of the hearers of the Word. By 1903, Pius X (d. 1914) promulgated a *motu proprio* (Lat. for, lit., "on his own impulse") on church music (It., *Tra le Sollecitudini*, "Among the Concerns"), advising active participation by the laity in the sacred mysteries; in 1905 he issued the decree *Sacra Tridentina* (Lat. for "The Holy [Council] of Trent"), urging congregants—including children—to engage in more frequent communion. In the United States, pioneering liturgists such as Virgil Michael, OSB (d. 1938), and others set a new agenda for participative worship. In a sense, the renewal of the Sunday homily in *SC* reached its desired and natural outcome only after decades of liturgical reform that sought to transform the faithful listeners as active and fully participative members of the assembly. This would also include some strong inroads in the early twentieth century in the revitalization of preaching committed to engaging active hearers of the Word.

Jay Dolan has demonstrated that there was a "Catholic revivalism" in the early nineteenth-century United States, which began to reconfigure preaching in new and transformative ways. In Dolan's reading, a window suddenly opened, highlighting the strong connection between listening to preaching, religious experience, and popular piety. The emergence of a Roman Catholic evangelical subculture was "a new variety of religious experience as far as Catholic America was concerned and its widespread and prolonged popularity indicated that the spirit of evangelism was becoming a major current in the mainstream of Catholic piety" (Dolan 1978, 187). Grounded in a vision of Roman Catholic evangelism and conversion, preaching became a channel for revitalizing piety that could invigorate the institution. This preaching could take a variety of forms, from "mission sermons" preached in urban parishes to more informal events in rural environments (see 78–80 above). The overall effect of such evangelism was to prioritize the experience of the hearer, deepen the faith of the baptized, and lead them to more devotion. Some rural evangelism was characterized by somewhat quirky, itinerant preaching such as the "Gospel Wagon" of Father Boniface Spanke (d. 1942) in Arkansas, whose apologetic preaching in 1913 was intended to counter the vehement anti-Catholicism in magazines such as *The Menace* (Kodell 2010, 257–85).

Laymen and laywomen in Catholic Action groups in the United States played a particularly important role in shaping and revitalizing preaching in the early part of the twentieth century, especially when it came to apologetics. With the rise of anti-Catholic and anti-immigrant sentiment aimed at protecting the rights of native-born citizens in this country in the 1920s—a problem that culminated in the landslide defeat of Governor Al Smith in the 1928 presidential election—the National Catholic Welfare Conference (NCWC) charged members of the National Council of Catholic Men and the National Council of Catholic Women to organize street preaching or "Evidence Guilds" to correct popular, often diabolical notions of Roman Catholicism. These guilds reached something of an apogee in the first half of the 1930s, and there is notably an interesting involvement of college women from Rosary College in River Forest, Illinois, who engaged in street preaching on such topics as "Why Priests Don't Marry" and "Why Honor the Blessed Virgin" (Campbell 1986, 380–83). Started by the English layman Vernon Redwood (d. 1954) in 1918 and then extended throughout the 1920s by husband and wife Frank Sheed (d. 1982) and Maisie Ward (d. 1975), Catholic Evidence Guilds trained licensed speakers to preach. They emerged in the United States throughout the early 1930s in strategic urban locations such as Baltimore (1931), Washington (1931), Oklahoma City (1932), Detroit (1934), Philadelphia (1934), and Buffalo (1935) (Campbell 1986, 374; Russell 1948, 301–17). The guilds were more widespread, however, than just cities and included an eclectic group of preachers. Priests, seminarians, and laity alike spoke in a wide variety of venues from prisons to streets to rural country farms. According to *Catholic Action*, the journal for the NCWC, street preaching sessions of the Catholic Evidence Guild attracted twelve thousand people in 1942 (*Catholic Action* 1942, 27). By 1946, the Confraternity of Christian Doctrine was sponsoring a "Street Preaching Institute" and published *The Apostolate of Good Will: A Manual of Street Preaching*.

The laity in the first half of the twentieth century was far from apathetic when it came to effective preaching and often campaigned for its revitalization. Under the supervision of Archbishop John Noll (d. 1956)—the episcopal chair for the organization of the laity of the NCWC—the "Crusade for

Fruitful Preaching" emerged as a corrective to what appears to have been a growing trend in the late 1930s, i.e., the "omission of the sermon at the Sunday Mass" (NCWC 1937, folder 20). In 1937, the pioneering laywoman at the center of the movement—Swiss-born Helene Froelicher—wrote to Noll informing him that "400 crusaders signed a petition for a more vital preaching and hearing of the word of God" (Froelicher 1937), after which the archbishop granted her an interview. Froelicher even traveled to Rome to petition Archbishop Amleto Giovanni Cicognani, apostolic delegate to the United States, to have the Holy See grant a solemn proclamation for a feast of "Christ the Divine Preacher" (Froelicher 1938).

Moreover, the Catholic Evidence Guild brought its considerable experience to bear on helping to make the Sunday sermon more intelligent and succinct. Remarkably, in 1942, O'Brien Atkinson published a guide to the Sunday sermon from the point of view of the assembly, titled *How to Make Us Want Your Sermon*. In the preface Atkinson states that "this text is a plea for better understanding. It tries to bring to you the story of what happens to the words of your sermon after they leave your lips; a story that no one else is so well fitted to tell as the layman" (Atkinson 1942, v). Atkinson's text would anticipate by four decades the well-deserved attention the listening assembly would receive in *Fulfilled in Your Hearing* (FIYH 1982).

Myth Number 2: *Since Roman Catholicism failed to secure much in the way of an intellectual tradition in the United States, preaching and the study of preaching was neglected.*

John Tracy Ellis (d. 1992) famously lamented the dearth of intellectual life at US Roman Catholic colleges and universities in 1955, a strange condition for arguably one of the most powerful and influential subcultures in modern history (Ellis 1955, 351–88). It is true that Roman Catholic intellectual life did not produce many scholars and most sermons were probably far from theologically or biblically informed. At the same time, however, there was a considerable amount of practical Roman Catholic education that was catechetical and missiological; similarly, preaching was less heuristic and more pragmatic. Consequently, there was a good deal of homiletic literature being produced by both Protestants and Roman Catholics that included preaching plans for parish missions, catechetics, and the Sunday sermon.

Preaching missions have a long history in Catholic homiletics and found a resurgence in the United States in the nineteenth century. According to James P. McCartin, the function of these missions was to draw the faithful into a deeper and more pious union with God (McCartin 2010, 46ff). Religious orders such as the Jesuits, the Redemptorists, the Passionists, and others developed a specific ministry devoted to planning weeklong parish missions and many such preachers traveled extensively. One of the most prolific of these mission priests was Paulist Walter Elliott (d. 1928), who wrote and spoke profusely about preparing parish missions for those conducting these appeals. In his *Manual of Missions* (1922), for example, Elliott advised "a direct appeal to sincerity—a gentle but serious arraignment in the court of conscience. Endeavor to arouse heroic courage, the martyr spirit. Bring the soul face to face with Jesus Christ" (Jonas 1988, 214). The mission would often culminate in sacramental confession, Mass, and the devout reception of communion. More often than not, the rhetorical tactics of mission preaching were quite dramatic and obviously geared to increase the devotional life of the congregation, a kind of recapitulation of the Roman Catholic Revivalism of the previous century.

In the decades before Vatican II, there was a surprising interest in homiletic pedagogy, first at the seminary level but later more generally. As if to underline the importance of the study and preparation of preaching, in 1898 a monograph on clerical studies at St. John's Seminary in Brighton, Massachusetts, outlined the substantial work of the preacher as threefold: "to be sufficiently acquainted with his subject; next, he has to accommodate it to his hearers; thirdly, he has to speak the discourse thus prepared in a way to awaken their attention and sustain their interest" (Hogan 1898, 344). Between 1911 and 1918, the homiletic curriculum at St. John's was substantially augmented (Sexton and Riley 1945). In 1910, John P. Chidwick (d. 1935)—president of St. Joseph's Seminary in Dunwoodie, New York—published a pamphlet on *The Teaching of Homiletics in our Seminaries* for the Catholic Educational Association. It is clear that seminary education took sermon preparation very seriously: "There is an art, not only in delivery, but also in the preparation and presentation for our sermon matter, in the construction and development of our discourse, in the building of a paragraph and a climax in the selection of our thoughts and arguments and in their application" (Chidwick 1910, 10). As further advice, Chidwick suggests that "the Holy Bible must be our principal armory and the chief source whence shall flow the living waters from our lips" (Chidwick 1910, 11).

There appears to have been a great deal of interest and writing around the topic of sacred oratory in both books and journals. In 1903, Thomas J. Potter published one of the most important books in English on preaching, *Sacred Eloquence or The Theory and Practice of Preaching*. Potter included methodological outlines with a "leading idea" and "three points," an organizational feature that would become a standard for generations. As Joseph Connors has demonstrated, there were no less than nine Roman Catholic

authors of homiletic treatises in English published from 1900 to 1935. These
were followed by a "second generation" of homiletic guides that extended
to 1961 (Connors 1962, 340ff.). Perhaps the most influential and substantial
of these were works by Msgr. Hugh T. Henry (d. 1946): *Hints to Preachers*
(1924), *Papers on Preaching* (1925), and *Preaching* (1941). The latter volume
constitutes something of a comprehensive guide to sacred eloquence and
rhetoric, with methodological advice, together with extensive quotations
from past orators for everything from writing the sermon to the organization of a secular panegyric. Henry and others had a tremendous impact on
the continuing homiletic education of clergy through journals that offered
more theoretical explorations of the sermon, especially *American Ecclesiastical Review* and *Homiletic and Pastoral Review*. Henry was hired as associate
professor of homiletics at Catholic University (CUA) in 1919 and subsequently Fulton Sheen (d. 1979) became an instructor in apologetics there
in 1927. According to the "Courses of Study Catalogue" for 1926–1927, the
homiletics department at CUA offered remote and proximate preparation
for the sermon, providing coaching to groups and individuals. In 1933, CUA
established a "Preaching Institute," offering a six-week course of intensive
training in sermon composition, voice training, and delivery skills. The institute also boasted of using electrical voice reproduction, "thus familiarizing
the preacher with his own voice and his own peculiarities" (CUA 1933, 55).

Myth Number 3: *Since Roman Catholic preaching before Vatican II was parochial,
urban, and oriented toward immigrants, the evangelism during that period was
defined by local neighborhood demographics.*

By 1900, Roman Catholicism had amassed what some considered to be
an empire of immigrants in the United States, with twelve thousand priests
and fifty thousand women religious staffing more than twelve thousand
parishes and missions and thirty-three hundred schools, this population
having quadrupled between 1860 and 1900. By 1920, this population was
close to 20 million, and by 1930, Roman Catholics would account for 20
percent of the general public of the United States (Morris 1997, 113–14).
The "Catholic culture" fostered a network of catechesis unlike anything
anyone had ever before seen, with religious women teaching tirelessly
from the Baltimore Catechism in parochial schools and to children from
public schools in special religious education classes across the United States.
Similarly, the Sunday sermon often brought practical catechetical questions
to the fore in a worshipful setting, comfortable for the immigrant Roman
Catholic Church. Such an enclosed infrastructure seemed to leave little
room for evangelical outreach.

There is, however, another story to be told concerning Roman Catholic preaching during the middle of the twentieth century that renders preaching more global, eclectic, and cosmopolitan; it would also help to bring US Roman Catholicism out of the margins and into the mainstream culture by the end of the Second World War. A rather fortuitous moment in the history of preaching—and US Roman Catholicism—occurred in 1926, when the National Broadcasting Company (NBC) was formed. By the beginning of the 1930s, radio was the most important instrument of instant communication in the nation, with 12 million listeners in 1930, a number that would almost triple by the end of the decade. One of NBC's mandates was to offer a variety of religious programming, donating free blocks of time to Roman Catholics, Protestants, and Jews. The most significant result of this policy for Roman Catholics was the appearance of the "Catholic Hour" in March 1930, with Fulton J. Sheen as its first guest speaker (NCWC 1930, folder 5). After consultation with the Federal Council of Churches, NBC stipulated that only nationally recognized figures, such as Sheen and Baptist Pastor Harry Emerson Fosdick (d. 1969), would be broadcast on these shows (Hangen 2002, 21ff.). This lineup of prominent speakers drew a wide variety of listeners and changed the history of preaching in the United States. The audience for Roman Catholic religious radio was invariably a mix of believers and nonbelievers who were being gathered together not in an ecclesial space, or even a revival tent, but in living rooms across the nation.

The purpose of the Catholic Hour was not so much apologetic as it was to be descriptive of Roman Catholic dogma, morals, and the perceived history of the Roman Catholic Church; it was not intended to be defensive. Although the purpose of the Catholic Hour was in line with the Evidence Guild's goal to explain Catholic teachings in the context of anti-Catholic sentiment, the program was also clearly aligned with Catholic Action in relying on extensive lay involvement and even the circumstances of everyday life with which to evangelize. The faithful engine behind the success of Roman Catholic preaching on the airwaves was the Roman Catholic laity, advised by the various bishops from the NCWC. If the speakers on the Catholic Hour were clerics with some significant reputation, then it was the National Council of Catholic Men who negotiated the programming and the broadcast opportunities to various national networks. The speakers would be subject to a variety of conditions, including vetting them for ecclesiastical approval. The programming was often topical but intended to have wide appeal, especially to a general Christian audience. Some of Sheen's early preaching topics from the Catholic Hour were on

Palm Sunday ("The Pulpit of the Cross") and Easter ("Dying and Behold we Live"). Perhaps the most popular feature of the show was a "Question Box," in which Sheen would regularly save a portion of the program to answer questions submitted ahead of time by listeners, Roman Catholic and non–Roman Catholic alike. Since NBC did not censor the programs, it was up to the National Council of Catholic Men to supervise the script before the Catholic Hour was broadcast on NBC and its affiliates. Needless to say, there was a good deal riding on the specifics of each script. The preachers for these broadcasts were carefully vetted.

Besides Fulton Sheen, other famous guest speakers included the Jesuit Daniel A. Lord (d. 1955), who helped to draft the Production Code for Hollywood in 1930, and Paulist James Gillis (d. 1957) of *The Catholic World*. Both NBC and the National Council of Catholic Men were very interested in keeping the programming directed toward a general US audience and not simply a Roman Catholic one. In this regard, certain aspects of Catholic social teaching could be helpful in understanding contemporary cultural issues. For example, in December 1954 John La Farge, SJ (d. 1963), offered a program on desegregation.

NBC's interest in featuring nationally known figures for its religious broadcasting was visionary. The "golden-voiced" Sheen (as *Time* magazine called him in 1946), for example, made his reputation as a celebrity preacher first on the radio and then (as bishop) on television in 1951 with the *Life Is Worth Living* series. At the same time as the Catholic Hour debuted on NBC, Columbia Broadcasting System (CBS) hired a quite controversial Catholic personality who made a unique contribution to radio preaching. A self-styled "radio priest," Charles Coughlin (d. 1979) introduced what one media group characterized as a "dramatic harangue." Eventually, Coughlin acquired as many as 10 million listeners, even as he became anti-New Deal, anti-Roosevelt, and anti-Semitic (Hangen 2002, 30ff.). Eventually, he was forced off the air by the National Association of Broadcasters in 1940. He continued airing his view in editorials in his newspaper, *Social Justice*. Under threat of indictment by the attorney general, however, his bishop put an end to his political activities and his newspaper, although he remained a parish pastor until he retired in 1966.

In retrospect, it is difficult to overestimate the unique form of preaching that emerged through the convergence of technology (see 254ff. below), celebrated clerics, and a culture profoundly influenced by the Great Depression and World War II. Keenly sensitive to a variety of listeners, radio preaching allowed for a ballooning of interest in Roman Catholicism and in religion more generally at a time of high economic and domestic anxiety. President

Franklin D. Roosevelt's famous "fireside chats" reassured the nation, even as religious celebrities helped even further to calm cultural tensions. Oratory has always participated in what Aristotle called the power of "ethos" or the aura of the speaker (see 201 below), and celebrity priests like Sheen and Coughlin certainly gave credibility to preaching like never before by creating an intimate bond with their listeners. Sheen reportedly received as many as six thousand letters a week, an enviable load of fan mail that rivaled many a Hollywood movie star. More important, perhaps, is that twentieth-century preaching was part of a mass cultural movement in which the listener helped to shape the message. In response to a growing sense of devotions among Roman Catholics, Holy Cross priest Patrick Peyton (d. 1992) began a Family Rosary Crusade in 1942 and, like his contemporaries, helped to galvanize religious sensibilities and piety first through radio and then television.

As a final aside, it is interesting to note that after almost fifteen years of Catholic Hour broadcasts, the two top box office films for 1944 and 1945 (*Going My Way* and *The Bells of St. Mary's,* respectively) dealt with priests, nuns, and the drama of parochial education. Would such popularity ever have been possible without this new, mass preaching effort by Roman Catholics? Read one way, this combination of lay involvement, strategic homiletic planning by some clergy, mass communication, and the appeal of priest celebrities helped move the anti-Catholic United States of the 1920s to a celebration of Roman Catholic parochial life with an Oscar for best picture in 1944. In the end, US Roman Catholic preaching in the first half of the twentieth century may not have directly anticipated the formal demands of what would become the restored homily of Vatican II, but such discourse almost certainly helped to shape and mainstream the Roman Catholic Church in the United States and to claim a new generation as hearers of the Word in a post–World War II world.

Bibliography

Atkinson, O'Brien. *How to Make Us Want Your Sermon*. New York: Joseph Wagner, 1942 [repr. 2012].

Campbell, Debra. "Part-Time Female Evangelists of the Thirties and Forties: The Rosary College Catholic Evidence Guild." *U.S. Catholic Historian* 5, no. 3 (1986).

Catholic Action. "Street Preaching Sessions Attract 12,000 Persons." October edition (1942).

Catholic University of America. *Announcements*. Summer: June 23 to August 3 (1933).

Chidwick, John P. *The Teaching of Homiletics in Our Seminaries*. Columbus, OH: Catholic Educational Association, 1910.

Connors, Joseph M. "Catholic Homiletic Theory in Historical Perspective." PhD Diss., Northwestern University, 1962.

Dolan, Jay P. *Catholic Revivalism: The American Experience, 1930–1900*. Notre Dame, IN: University of Notre Dame Press, 1978.

Ellis, John Tracy. "American Catholics and the Intellectual Life." *Thought* 30, no. 3 (1955).

Froelicher, Helene. Letter to the Most Reverend John F. Noll, September 28. General Secretary-Executive Department Records. General Administration Files. Organizations: Lay: Crusade for a More Fruitful Preaching. Catholic University of America: Archives, Box 75, Folder 20, 1937.

———. Letter to the Most Reverend Amleto Giovanni Cicognani, October 31. General Secretary-Executive Department Records. General Administration Files. Organizations: Lay: Crusade for a More Fruitful Preaching. Washington, DC: Catholic University of America: Archives, Box 75, Folder 21, 1938.

Funk, Virgil C. "The Liturgical Movement." In *The New Dictionary of Sacramental Worship*. Edited by Peter E. Fink. Collegeville, MN: Liturgical Press, 1990.

Hangen, Tona J. *Redeeming the Dial: Radio, Religion and Popular Culture in America*. Chapel Hill: University of North Carolina Press, 2002.

Hogan, J. B. *Clerical Studies*. Boston: Marlier, Callanan and Co., 1898.

Jonas, Thomas J. *The Divided Mind: American Catholic Evangelists in the 1890s*. New York: Garland, 1988.

Kodell, Jerome. "The Gospel Wagon of Father Boniface Spanke, OSB." *American Benedictine Review* 61, no. 3 (2010).

McCartin, James P. *Prayers of the Faithful: The Shifting Spiritual Life of American Catholics*. Cambridge, MA: Harvard University Press, 2010.

McNamara, Robert F. *Catholic Sunday Preaching: The American Guidelines: 1791–1975*. Washington, DC: Word of God Institute, 1975.

Morris, Charles R. *American Catholic: The Saints and Sinners Who Built America's Most Powerful Church*. New York: Random House, 1997.

National Catholic Welfare Conference. General Secretary-Executive Department Records. Information Media. Radio Broadcasts: Catholic Hour. Washington, DC: Catholic University of America. Archives, Box 35, Folder 5, 1930.

————. General Secretary-Executive Department Records. General Administration Files. Organizations: Lay: Crusade for a More Fruitful Preaching. Washington, DC: Catholic University of America: Archives, Box 75, folders 20–21, 1937.

Provost, James H. "Lay Preaching and Canon Law in a Time of Transition." In *Preaching and the Non-Ordained: An Interdisciplinary Study*. Edited by Nadine Foley. Collegeville, MN: Liturgical Press, 1983.

Russell, W. H. "The Catholic Evidence Guild in the United States." *Lumen Vitae* 3 (1948).

Sexton, John E., and Arthur J. Riley. *History of St. John's Seminary, Brighton.* Boston: Roman Catholic Archdiocese of Boston, 1945.

Preaching after Vatican II

Guerric DeBona

A pivotal and defining moment in our understanding of Roman Catholic preaching emerged from a renewed ecclesiology. Vatican II's *Lumen Gentium* (*LG*) acknowledged the crucial importance of the "people of God" as the foundation of the church where the Spirit dwells when it noted that "the Spirit dwells in the church and in the hearts of the faithful as in a temple" (*LG*, no. 4). Reminding us that the baptized whom Christ has claimed as his own cry out until he comes again, this document teaches that "[the Spirit] prays and bears witness to them that they are his adopted children" (*LG*, no. 4). *Gaudium et Spes* (*GS*) further clarified the evangelical role of a church in dialogue noting that "in every age the church has the duty of reading the signs of the times and of interpreting them in light of the Gospel" for the world (*GS*, no. 4). The church defines its mission to carry out Christ's own incarnate ministry, enfleshing the Word in the world in the context of the "universal call to holiness." To this end, *Sacrosanctum Concilium's* (*SC*) restoration of the ancient homily (*SC*, no. 52) signaled a new impetus for preaching more broadly for both the preacher and the hearer of the Word: called to abide in a pastoral, contextualized space, in dialogue with the liturgy, the Scriptures, and the world. This renewed, more expansive vision of the ministry of the Word for ordained and laity alike has influenced the way that the Roman Catholic Church has come to understand the crucial role of the assembly, the homiletic text, and the mission to evangelize.

The Turn toward the Assembly

Attending to the needs of the listener during an oration is at least as old as the art of rhetoric itself. Augustine's (d. 430) *De Doctrina Christiana* (4.12.27-28) as well as the Council of Trent (1545–1563) acknowledged the importance of the hearer in the speech act. The latter states that preachers ought to be sensitive to the hearer, teaching "according to their own and their hearers' capacity, what is necessary for all to know with a view to salvation, by proclaiming briefly and with ease of expression" (Tanner,

95

2:669). *SC*, however, envisions the assembly not only as those to whom the homily is addressed but also a constitutive dynamic of preaching itself. Recognizing the dialogical character of liturgy as the action of Christ's head and members (*SC*, no. 7), *SC* characterizes the assembly's hearing of the Word as a participation in the proclamation of the Lord's saving works, which "in a spirit of thanksgiving will be led on to a fruitful participation in the mysteries of salvation" (*SC*, no. 10). Further, in order to strengthen the assembly's participation in the saving works of God throughout salvation history, *Dei Verbum* and *SC* famously opened up the "Table of the Word," calling for a revision of the Lectionary, "so that a richer fare may be provided for the faithful at the Table of God's word" (*SC*, no. 51).

In some sense, the liturgical reforms of *SC* powerfully lay claim to a new evangelization, to preach the Gospel to all nations. *LG* spells out this new vision by teaching: "The Lord desires that his kingdom be spread by the lay faithful also: the kingdom of truth and life, the kingdom of holiness and grace, the kingdom of justice, love and peace" (*LG*, no. 36). Therefore when the 1983 Code of Canon Law was promulgated, special attention was given to a revitalized evangelization in canon 211. To this end, the assembly becomes a visible sign of Christ's presence in the Eucharist (*SC*, no. 7), sanctified by "the sacramentality of the Word in the Liturgical assembly" (Janowiak 2000, 167ff.). So nourished by the Word, the baptized can harvest these riches and share them through their apostolic work of teaching and preaching (*Catechism of the Catholic Church* [CCC], nos. 864, 910, 1102). Such a reaffirmation of the role of the baptized, whose faith is to be deepened by the homily (*Fulfilled in Your Hearing* [FIYH], no. 43), contributed to the flourishing of preaching by the laity, e.g., their preaching alongside the ordained during retreats and in parish missions.

There were at least three cultural-contextual factors surfacing during the 1960s in the United States that helped to underline the vital role of the assembly in preaching. A propositional, deductive style of preaching had dominated the landscape as epitomized in John A. Broadus's very influential *A Treatise on the Preparation and Delivery of Sermons* (1870). Narrative preaching—informed by a kind of experiential methodology as embedded in the parables of Jesus—began to turn away from this style. Narrative preaching methodologies—both innovative and experiential—were essentially inductive and focused on the ability of the congregation to act as a community of interpreters (see 117 below). These methodologies were indebted, at least in part, to the legacy of Friedrich Schleiermacher's (d. 1834) hermeneutics and its emphasis on how people understand or receive texts. Supporting this shift in emphasis were advances in biblical studies by scholars such as C. H. Dodd (d. 1973) who, along with others, sought to recover the dynamic or "kerygmatic" nature of New Testament preaching (see 41ff. above). This approach underscored preaching that was not turned in on itself as simply moral instruction but was intended to engage the hearer at a profound level by announcing the resurrection of Christ to all believers.

A second factor that helped underscore the centrality of the assembly in the preaching act was the emergence of new educational and communication theories. John Dewey (d. 1952) and A. F. Bentley's (d. 1957) *Knowing and the Known* (1949), for example, championed ideas about the retention of knowledge based on an *interactional* model, in which the listener is invited into the act of communication. This new thinking challenged the prevailing *actional* model, in which the listener was wrongly imagined to remain utterly passive. The shift from speaker-dominated communication to a focus on the receiver not only suggests a more accurate representation of a communal interaction but also would have lasting and wide-ranging effects in preaching, in the workplace, and in the classroom.

A third factor affecting the reimagining of preaching in the 1960s was mass communication in the forms of radio, television, and film that already had shaped society during the twentieth century. For decades Hollywood had adapted and created narratives that accompanied us through the Great Depression, two world wars, and the threat of a nuclear armageddon. By the 1920s, radio was the nation's companion through sports triumphs and national tragedies, presidential addresses and religious revival. In the 1960s living rooms became centers for debating our involvement in Southeast Asia as families watched the war unfold before them in living color.

The postconciliar documents of the Roman Catholic Church (see 26ff. above) clearly recognize the participative role the listener plays in collaborating in the speech act as well. Although it concerns itself exclusively with the Sunday homily, FIYH considers the assembly first and concerns itself with how preaching empowers those gathered to act in mission because "the primary reality is Christ in the assembly, the People of God" (FIYH, no. 4). Indeed, preaching exists neither for the sake of the preacher nor the text but for the faithful. "The community that gathers Sunday after Sunday comes together to offer God praise and thanksgiving, or at least to await a word that will give a meaning to their lives and enable them to celebrate Eucharist" (FIYH, no. 14).

In 2008 Benedict XVI (b. 1927) convened a synod in Rome on God's Word. In his post-synodal exhortation *Verbum Domini*, Benedict says that the homily "is a means of bringing the scriptural message to life in a way that helps the faithful to realize that God's Word is present and at work in their everyday lives" (*VD*, no. 59). The US Catholic bishops, in *Preaching the Mystery of Faith* (PTMOF), underline this teaching by recognizing that the homily should establish a " 'dialogue' between the sacred biblical text and the Christian life of the hearer" (PTMOF, 29). The conversation between God's Word and God's people is diverse. The bishops acknowledge the diversity of those gathered to hear the word in the United States today and the challenges of such complexity. "We know, for example, that through immigration the Catholic population is increasingly diverse in its cultural and ethnic makeup, and this diversity is a great blessing for our Church and our country, but it also raises new challenges for those who preach in such settings" (PTMOF, 4; see 233ff. below).

While priests and deacons have been called to see the proclamation of the Gospel as their primary ministerial task, increasingly laywomen and laymen have also been called to preach the Gospel in ways that respect the gifts of their own culture and context. The growing diversity of our assemblies has changed the way churches think about preaching. Since Vatican II, our assemblies have grown more ethnically diverse in North America—especially with the growing number of immigrants from Mexico, Central and South America, as well as those from Asia and Africa. Keenly aware of these challenges, Pope Francis (b. 1936) reminds us that "what is called for is an evangelization capable of shedding light on these new ways of relating to God, to others and to the world around us, and inspiring essential values. It must reach the places where new narratives and paradigms are being formed, bringing the word of Jesus to the inmost soul of our cities" (*Evangelii Gaudium* [*EG*], no. 74). Francis reckons the cities of the world as privileged sites of the new evangelization. "New cultures are constantly being born in these vast new expanses where Christians are no longer the customary interpreters or generators of meaning" (*EG*, no. 73). In the spirit of Vatican II, *EG* encourages a homiletic that is both diverse and dialogical, breaking through established personal and social boundaries. "Each Christian and every community must discern the path that the Lord points out, but all of us are asked to obey his call to go forth from our own comfort zone in order to reach all the 'peripheries' in need of the light of the Gospel" (*EG*, no. 20). Aware that the baptized are "missionary disciples," Francis extends the call of the listener beyond the assembly into a respectful "personal dialogue" (*EG*, no. 128), proclaiming the Gospel message to different cultures (*EG*, no. 132). The faithful listener becomes the agent of the new evangelization.

The Expansion of the Preaching Text

The turn toward the assembly has had a direct influence on how we understand the preaching text as well. Of significance in this regard was a shift from what could be called an essentialist model focused on what a text *means* in and of itself, to one that is more phenomenological, i.e., concerned with what a text is actually *doing* in a given context. For centuries sacred oratory followed the paradigm Aristotle (d. 322 BCE) outlined in his *Rhetoric*, including principles of deduction he established as normative for the speech act (see 201 below). Deductive preaching poses a proposition at the beginning and then tries to prove the case, much like a prosecutor would state a case against a defendant. Analogously, preachers often stated a proposition and then demonstrated—typically in three ways—how and to what extent the statement was true or false.

The preaching reforms of the 1960s, however, inverted this propositional, deductive method. This so-called New Homiletic (see 221ff. below) was a more inductive approach that presumed a dialogue among the preacher, the text and the assembly. The inductive approach invites the hearer to participate in the "text" by beginning with the particularities of everyday life that eventually allow the preacher to move to a conclusion. Induction is, by its very nature, a *process* that begins with the historical-contextual horizon of a particular assembly and engages these hearers in a conversation. *GS* stresses the need to engage with one's context and even to adapt preaching to the languages and concepts of people, thereby providing a kind of meta-principle for evangelization:

> [The church] profits from the experience of past ages, from the progress of the sciences, and from the riches hidden in various cultures. . . . The church learned early in its history to express the Christian message in the concepts and languages of different peoples. . . . Indeed, this kind of adaptation and preaching of the revealed word must ever be the law of all evangelization. In this way it is possible to create in every country the possibility of expressing the message of Christ in suitable terms and to foster vital contact and exchange between the church and different cultures. (*GS*, no. 44)

Similarly, FIYH recommends that the homily is developed precisely by an induction method. Specifically, it suggests beginning "with a description of a contemporary human situation which is evoked by the Scripture texts. . . . [Then] turn to the Scriptures to interpret this situation, showing how the God described therein is also present and active in our lives today" (FIYH, no. 65). Preaching by induction, therefore, takes into account the diversity of the assembly while moving the hearer to a faith experience as part of a contextualized event, enabling people "to lift up their hearts, to praise and thank the Lord for his presence in their lives" (FIYH, no. 67). Such an expansion of the preaching event parallels the emphasis of various models of contextual theology that take seriously people's social location.

In this digital age (see 254ff. below), the preaching text faces significant cultural challenges, with the advent of new technologies that can render the written text—and the theological and biblical associations of that text— increasingly irrelevant. With the deluge of words and images that bombard us on a daily basis from innumerable personal and digital sources, it is possible that our preaching becomes just one more text among many. Some contemporary philosophers have expressed serious mistrust for the grand or "meta-narratives" that dominated the previous centuries, including the Christian narration of salvation history; in their place, a pastiche of smaller, "micro-narratives" are emerging.

This digital barrage of words and images, launched in an era whose mistrust of the sweeping story questions the very validity of salvation history, raises serious challenges for the preacher today. For example, what would be the preacher's theological anchor without a belief that God has intervened throughout all of human history? What are the common reference points and shared symbols in an age marked by fragmentation that the preached text might deploy to engage a congregation? Without a shared salvation history, how does a preacher hope to connect with a local community whose members experience much fragmentation in their lives, yet yearn for some coherence, even clarity? Finally, what is the power or even effectiveness of preaching—whether eight minutes in a liturgical assembly or some interfaith gathering, or even fifty minutes during some parish mission or retreat—when Facebook messages, tweets, instant messages, and so many other media flood the lives of believers and seekers?

Preaching in the contemporary age is challenging but can be energized and invigorated by the mission to evangelize with joy. *Ad Gentes Divinitus* called the church into a renewed relationship with all people "to be the 'universal sacrament of salvation' . . . and in obedience to the command of her founder . . . strives to proclaim the gospel to all" (*AGD*, no. 1). That commission takes us beyond language and into the power of witnessing to God's love and mercy in the world. As Francis notes,

> Being Church means being God's people, in accordance with the great plan of his fatherly love. This means that we are to be God's leaven in the midst of humanity. It means proclaiming and bringing God's salvation into our

world, which often goes astray and needs to be encouraged, given hope and strengthened on the way. The Church must be a place of mercy freely given, where everyone can feel welcomed, loved, forgiven and encouraged to live the good life of the Gospel. (*EG*, no. 114)

It is when we are authentically ecclesial that we become the graced bearers of God's Word to the world.

By Whose Authority?

Many Christian preachers today face what could be considered a crisis of authority. In a seminal work, Fred Craddock characterized the preacher "as one without authority" (Craddock 2001). While the homily was experiencing a resurgence in the 1970s, traditional secular and religious leadership faced its own dismantling of authorities in the wake of scandals such as Watergate and the church's sexual abuse crisis. Like the homiletic text itself, all authority might be read as diminished and altogether relative. Additionally, in a society that is increasingly secular, individualistic, and hybrid, the preacher is challenged to craft a proclamation that is cohesive and feels in some way organic. In the face of such challenges, some communities have negotiated an utterly democratic form of preaching in which several share the role of preacher at the same proclamation. Lucy Atkinson Rose (Rose, 1997), for example, suggests giving equal voice to all in the congregation to articulate the sermon.

The Roman Catholic tradition has defined who will preach and under what circumstances (see 267ff. below) and will continue to shape its own vision of preaching; it also must come to grips with the contemporary challenges to preaching authority. Furthermore, proclamation cannot be separate from the pastoral care of God's people or what Francis calls "the art of accompaniment, which teaches us to remove our sandals before the sacred ground of the other (cf. Ex 3:5). The pace of this accompaniment must be steady and reassuring, reflecting our closeness and our compassionate gaze which also heals, liberates and encourages growth in the Christian life" (*EG*, no. 125). Thus the preacher needs to be mercifully present and willing to listen. Preaching so tuned to this new evangelization will continue to evolve, even while preachers interpret the signs of the times through the Good News of Jesus Christ for the sake of all of God's holy people.

Bibliography

Craddock, Fred B. *As One without Authority*. 4th ed. St. Louis: Chalice Press, 2001 [1971].

Janowiak, Paul. *The Holy Preaching: The Sacramentality of the Word in the Liturgical Assembly*. Collegeville, MN: Liturgical Press, 2000.

Rose, Lucy Atkins. *Sharing in the Word: Preaching in the Roundtable Church*. Louisville, KY: Westminster John Knox, 1997.

Genres of Preaching

Evangelization and the Ministry of Preaching

Frank DeSiano

In order to provide some clarity about the connection between evangelization and preaching, in the following essay we will first consider the usage and meaning of the word "evangelization," especially after Vatican II (1962–1965). We will then be able to connect fundamental understandings of evangelization to specific areas of contemporary preaching, e.g., parish mission preaching, retreat preaching, and homiletic preaching. This reflection hopes to enrich insights that can nourish contemporary preachers in Roman Catholic and other Christian traditions.

Defining "Evangelization"

While cognates of "evangelization" were used during Vatican II—mostly as a way to talk about "mission"—Roman Catholic teaching came to more consistent use of this term after the 1974 general synod held under the leadership of Paul VI (d. 1978). The reflections of this synod provided the basis of Paul's 1975 apostolic exhortation *Evangelii Nuntiandi* (*EN*). In that exhortation, the pope used the opening sections to set up the context for a Roman Catholic approach to evangelization. Paul VI was clearly trying to avoid a very narrow concept of the word. He defines evangelization in these words:

> [E]vangelizing means bringing the Good News to all the strata of humanity, and through its influence transforming humanity from within and making it new. . . . The purpose of evangelization is therefore precisely this interior change, and if it had to be expressed in one sentence the best way of stating it would be to say that the Church evangelizes when she seeks to convert, solely through the power of the Message she proclaims, both the personal and collective consciences of people, the activities in which they engage and the lives and concrete milieu which are theirs. (*EN*, no. 18)

The exact meaning of "convert" was not defined in the exhortation because, uniquely and importantly, Paul VI applied evangelization to different dimensions of church ministry. When he elaborated the various beneficiaries of evangelization (*EN*, chap. 5), the beneficiaries were not just "pagans" or "unbelievers" as past usage had assumed. Rather, included in this evangelizing vision were believers with varying levels of commitment: Roman Catholics themselves, other Christians, other believers, as well as nonbelievers. So, depending on the context, "conversion" might mean the spiritual renewal of active believers, an appeal to nonpracticing Roman Catholics, ecumenical and interfaith exchanges, as well as an explicit mission to those who have never heard of Christ or have no belief in God. In this way, Paul VI emphasized dimensions of evangelization that would forever affect preaching, bringing out its evangelizing purposes: conversion, transformation, and having an impact on the world.

John Paul II (d. 2005) introduced the phrase "new evangelization" while visiting Port-au-Prince, Haiti, in March 1983. While speaking to the Latin American episcopal conference (*CELAM*), he spoke about "a commitment, not to re-evangelization, but to a new evangelization, new in ardor, methods and expression" (John Paul II 1983, 662). In addition to this explicit introduction of the term, John Paul II frequently made mention of the "new evangelization" in many subsequent documents during his pontificate. His 1979 apostolic exhortation on catechesis would have the greatest impact on the contemporary usage in Roman Catholicism. In *Catechesi Tradendae* (*CT*), John Paul II introduced the language that imagined faith as an encounter with Jesus Christ. "Accordingly, the definitive aim of catechesis is to put people not only in touch but in communion, in intimacy, with Jesus Christ" (*CT*, no. 5). Later in that document, he stated that it is possible for some Roman Catholics to be catechized but not evangelized in the sense of having heard and responded to the direct message of salvation in Jesus Christ (*CT*, nos. 19–20). Catechesis had to include a dimension of encountering Jesus; in this way, John Paul II made such encounters a ground of Catholic preaching and teaching. Subsequent catechetical documents continued articulating evangelization as personal encounter. The *General Directory for Catechesis* (1997) frequently spoke in language of encounter and conversion, e.g., "The Christian faith is, above all, conversion to Jesus Christ, full and sincere adherence to his person, and the decision to walk in his footsteps" (no. 53).

It was this thread that the Synod on the New Evangelization took up in 2012, noting, "We consider it necessary that there be a Pastoral Plan of Initial Proclamation, teaching a living encounter with Jesus Christ" (Synod of Bishops 2012, no. 9). The synod went on to say: "Furthermore [the New

Evangelization] calls the church to reach out to those who are far from God and the Christian community to invite them to once again hear the Word of God in order to encounter the Lord Jesus in a new and profound way" (Synod of Bishops 2012, no. 5). As a result, evangelization can be understood as a ministry that fosters encountering Jesus. While this means different things to different "audiences"—e.g., whether people are committed to following Jesus, are tangential in following him, have not yet come to know him, or belong to some other Christian communions or faiths—it still serves as the core meaning of evangelization. Consequently, preaching in the genre of evangelization will need to be understood as fostering an encounter with Jesus Christ in such a way that people respond to that encounter through conversion and commitment. By 2012, Paul VI's initial sketch of evangelization in terms of conversion and transformation received the more specific note of personal encounter with Christ.

Pope Francis (b. 1936) brought this usage into his apostolic exhortation *Evangelii Gaudium* (*EG*). He introduces the theme at the beginning of his message: "I invite all Christians, everywhere, at this very moment, to a renewed personal encounter with Jesus Christ, or at least an openness to letting him encounter them; I ask all of you to do this unfailingly each day. No one should think that this invitation is not meant for him or her, since 'no one is excluded from the joy brought by the Lord' " (*EG*, no. 3).

The upshot of these four decades of reflection on evangelization is the understanding that all ministry aims at bringing about or reinforcing a personal encounter with Jesus Christ. This is true whether the ministry is religious education, faith formation, the catechumenal process, Scripture study, or particularly the ministry of preaching. Encountering Jesus means being exposed to deeper dimensions of Christ and his teaching; it also means growing in the experience of conversion as one invites people into discipleship. Implied in this way of elaborating the Christian message is the further point that to encounter Jesus is to invite others to encounter Christ as well, i.e., to become "missionary disciples" (*EG*, no. 120).

In summary, evangelizing preaching aims for conversion or a deeper transformation and seeks to further discipleship by helping people to encounter and respond to Jesus Christ. This, in turn, leads to broader transformation of communities and contexts by the Gospel message.

Preaching that Evangelizes

Some common settings in Roman Catholic life for preaching that have the purpose of evangelizing include mission preaching in parishes, preaching in retreat houses, preaching at sacramental celebrations, and homiletic preaching. Because sacramental/liturgical preaching will be addressed in other parts of this volume (see 146 and 156 below), present emphasis will concern the nonliturgical settings of parish mission and retreats. First, however, we will consider certain elements that pertain to all preaching for evangelization.

Evangelizing preaching arises from particular pastoral elements; it likewise shares certain rhetorical qualities. Reviewing these elements will give direction as we look at various settings for preaching that evangelizes.

The Word of God

The semantic connection between evangelization and *evangelium* (Lat. for "gospel") is a reminder that this genre of preaching springs from engagement with the Scriptures. The preacher reaches into the Scriptures for the essential questions that confront people today. The preacher does this not only with respect for the authentic meanings of the Scripture but also, in particular, for the analogous connections between experiences related in the Bible and experiences of people today. The preacher drills into the scriptural narrative to explore the crises, motives, and points of decision that biblical sources provide; this allows for an elaboration of the concerns that correspond to the lives of the congregation.

Biblical exploration may be broad, for example, reviewing the idea of "covenant" in a range of passages; or it may be particular, such as looking at David's behavior when confronted by Nathan (2 Sam 12:1-13). Inasmuch as the preacher is seeking to elicit initial interest, or decision, or commitment from members of the assembly, attention falls on the personal elements exposed by the reading of Scripture. These personal elements can then be explicitly related to the relationships that Jesus invites people to have with him and his Father in the Holy Spirit, toward others in the gathering, and toward all people through the virtues and acts of service that the Word elicits.

In this regard, Pope Francis suggests a useful method for preachers to use in exploring the Word of God:

> In the presence of God, during a recollected reading of the text, it is good to ask, for example: "Lord, what does this text say *to me*? What is it about my life that you want to change by this text? What troubles me about this text? Why am I not interested in this? Or perhaps: What do I find pleasant in this text? What is it about this word that moves me? What attracts me? Why does it attract me?" (*EG*, no. 153)

Conversion

Evangelizing preaching speaks the idiom of conversion and commitment. Conversion may be "initial" in that it is a response to a fresh or new presentation of God's Good News; or, more likely, it will be a deepening of experiences of conversion already woven into the life of the believer. While broader meanings make conversion seem like a movement from unbelief to belief, or a change from one faith to another, in actuality all Christian life concerns conversion.

Even for Christian denominations that baptize children, conversion is present and always ongoing. Though there may have been no explicit moment of "before and after" that might be identified in a believer's life, believers are constantly making decisions that move them either closer or further in their following of Christ. For example, one cannot really participate in the Eucharist without engaging in signs and actions that show one's explicit following of Jesus. An important part of preaching, from this perspective of conversion, is to help believers see the implications of conversion in ordinary Christian life.

Of course, conversion has to begin with the preacher. Precisely by probing the Word of God, the preacher is confronted by God's Word. By letting the Word lead the reflections of the preacher to deeper conversion, the preacher models conversion for the congregation. As Pope Francis wrote: "Whoever wants to preach must be the first to let the word of God move him deeply and become incarnate in his daily life" (*EG*, no. 150).

Discipleship

Preaching for evangelization also orients itself toward discipleship, that is, the kind of explicit and conscious following of Jesus that informs the whole life of the believer. Like conversion, notions of discipleship do not arise easily for many Roman Catholics and other Christians who think of themselves more passively as parishioners than as active disciples when it comes to their lives of faith.

As evangelizing preaching elaborates the Word of God and calls people to relationship and to conversion, it also leads people to see themselves as followers of Jesus in their personal lives and in their lives as members of the church. This personal following of Jesus often remains implicit and unrecognized even in the lives of active believers.

Disciples, from their baptisms, see themselves as called by God to follow Jesus Christ and sent by the Spirit to be ambassadors of Christ into the world. Discipleship, therefore, refers to both an inner life of spiritual growth and an exterior life of witness, invitation, and service. We previously noted how Pope Francis refers to believers as "missionary disciples" (*EG*, no. 120). As such, preaching for evangelization has to not only evoke a renewed personal encounter with Jesus but also lead the listener to renewed action because of that encounter. That action, flowing from love and service, provides the basis on which people can, authentically and without manipulation, witness to Jesus Christ.

Rhetorical Skills

Because preaching is a rhetorical event (see 200ff. below) done by and between human beings, it necessarily engages the art and skills of the preacher. While gifts come in different ways from God, every preacher needs the fundamental skills to communicate with the congregation. The preacher's language, voice, gestures, and tone will either further the communication event or hinder it. While preaching has nothing to do with entertaining people, it has everything to do with engaging them so as to get and hold their attention. Some preachers dismiss more evangelical preaching styles as "entertainment," but might this not be a way to cover up their own preaching deficiencies? The congregation should not be entertained, but it should also not be bored. Pope Francis states: "Concern for the way we preach is likewise a profoundly spiritual concern. It entails responding to the love of God by putting all our talents and creativity at the service of the mission which he has given us; at the same time, it shows a fine, active love of neighbor by refusing to offer others a product of poor quality" (*EG*, no. 156).

Because of this, preachers have an obligation to develop their rhetorical skills so as to be more transparent instruments of the Word of God. The artistry of the preacher serves the Word, not the ego of the preacher. Effective preachers leave the congregation filled with the meaning of the Word rather than focused on the preacher. Very gifted preachers speak in such a way that their speaking blends with the feeling and thinking of the congregation; the congregation sees itself more clearly through the preacher. Likewise, the preacher understands himself or herself better through the congregation. This seamless interchange and engagement is an ideal for all preachers.

A seamless interchange also implies a rhetorical circle: from preacher to congregation to preacher. Preachers do not stand before their assemblies imposing the Word as if on underlings. Rather, the broad culture and particular context of the assembly (see 233ff. below) frames the preacher's words and approach. The Word becomes flesh; the Word, through preaching, becomes incarnate in the life of the congregation. Few things demonstrate the openness of the Word of God to the "world" as the rhetorical circle that opens listener to the proclamation of the Good News that, in the preaching event, has been mediated to them. As Pope Francis notes: "The preacher also needs to keep his ear to the people and to discover what it is that the faithful need to hear. A preacher has to contemplate the word, but he also has to contemplate his people" (*EG*, no. 154).

Mission Preaching

Mission preaching, particularly in the nineteenth and twentieth centuries, took a distinct turn for Roman Catholics as a result of the reforms of Pope Pius X (d. 1914) and the Second Vatican Council (Dolan 1978). In the nineteenth century and before, the reception of Holy Communion was not frequent. People rarely approached the altar to receive, and more frequent reception of Holy Communion often presumed permission from one's confessor. In this context, mission preaching, often undertaken by various religious congregations, concentrated on proclaiming a message designed to get Catholics to go to confession so that they could receive Communion, something that was a relatively rare event in their lives (see 79 above). Mission preaching paralleled the widespread religious revivals prevalent in America.

The great themes of these classic missions centered on sin, punishment, the possibility of forgiveness, confession, and the more frequent attending of Mass. Mission preachers worked out their sermons with the best artistry at their command and repeated them in parish after parish, with missions that could last a week or more. Often men attended a mission for a week, followed by women the next week. These pre–twentieth-century missions brought out the spiritual dimension of the Tridentine era, with its focus on sin, death, and punishment—emphases that would change in the second half of the twentieth century after Vatican II.

More frequent reception of communion, encouraged by Pius X, brought about more frequency in the sacrament of penance. Vatican II further cultivated a theology of discipleship, bringing about a change of mission themes. Instead of concentrating on prodding Roman Catholics to more frequent confession and communion, missions increasingly concentrated on themes of knowing one's faith, growing in holiness, living one's faith in daily life in the world, and experiencing the presence of God more frequently in the liturgy and beyond. Missions echoed the themes of the four great constitutions

111

of Vatican II: liturgy, the church, revelation, and the church in the world. Mission preachers today sometimes make evangelization an explicit theme of the parish mission. If for a while after Vatican II the practice of annual parish missions decreased, this decline appears to be reversed at present as parish missions become more frequent once again.

The ultimate effect of recent teaching on the new evangelization will mean that mission preachers emphasize those elements that make an explicit invitation to conversion, or deeper conversion, as a result of having encountered Jesus Christ in a powerful way through the experience of mission preaching.

Retreat Preaching

By definition, retreats aim at deepening the faith of relatively active believers. Retreat houses (see 80 above) often recruit participants into these events through invitations sent to parishes; eventually a retreat house builds up a "clientele" who see the retreat as a regular, or annual, event.

Retreats vary in length, from the longer seven days that religious women and men often experience to the extended weekend experience more accessible to laypeople. Most retreats, as the name implies, occur in facilities located away from city centers, often with acres of woods to reinforce the sense of "getting away." Some retreats have specific themes—such as healing or contemplation—and almost all of them cater to particular groups of people, e.g., women or men, young adults, parish ministers, twelve-step groups, or those preparing for Confirmation.

Retreats, like parish missions, can take great liberties with themes because they are not following any particular liturgical or Lectionary cycle. All retreats, however, concentrate on helping retreatants renew their sense of union with God. Times of quiet, common prayer, spiritual sharing, and activities like journaling, are punctuated by celebrations of the Eucharist or reconciliation. Retreat directors have at their disposal a variety of spiritual activities to support the individual experiences of retreatants and amplify the preaching event.

Retreat preaching often consists of talks (or "conferences") extending a half-hour or more, sometimes accompanied by shared conversation. In these contexts preachers develop topics that reinforce themes that build as the days of retreat progress. The tenor of retreat preaching can often be conversational, depending on the number of retreatants, and might employ readings from a spiritual writer along with readings from the Scriptures. Like all forms of preaching for evangelization, retreat preachers are furthering themes of discipleship in the lives of participants.

The Homily

Roman Catholics are exposed much more to homiletic preaching than mission or retreat preaching. Homilies (see 156ff. below) have become an expected feature of worship in Catholic life since Vatican II. That council brought together a range of renewal efforts that effected a shift from Sunday "sermons," which often had nothing to do with the proclaimed Scriptures, to homilies that arose both from the given Lectionary readings as well as the sacramental setting in which the preaching occurs. Homilies are often differentiated in length from the longer sermons which tend to characterize some Protestant (especially more "Evangelical") services. A general Roman Catholic expectation is that a homily at Mass will last less than fifteen minutes; rare is the setting where Sunday homilies exceed thirty minutes.

The Roman Catholic Church has produced various resources (see 26ff. above) to help explicate the nature of the homily. In the United States, the USCCB has produced two documents: *Fulfilled in Your Hearing* (1982) and *Preaching the Mystery of Faith* (2012). In a broader ecclesial platform, Pope Francis devoted a significant part of *EG* to fostering more effective homilies among the clergy.

Unlike mission and retreat preaching, by definition the homily presumes a sacramental context. In the Eucharist, for example, it occurs at the juncture of the two main parts of that liturgy and forms a dynamic union and transition between the Liturgy of the Word (in which the congregation engages the Word of God) and the Liturgy of the Eucharist (in which the congregation joins in the eucharistic prayer and receives Holy Communion). One dynamic has the congregation encountering the Word of God; the other has the congregation participating in the praise that responds to the proclamation of the Word. Homilies at other sacramental moments—e.g., baptism or marriage—relate the hearers to the Good News through the experience of people and the particular sacramental symbols of that particular service.

Homilists preach after the Word of God has been proclaimed, which has already brought some of the key images, questions, invitations, and challenges of God's Word along with the sacramental event, to the attention of the congregation. Every scriptural passage raises crucial questions for a congregation about God's relationship to humankind and humankind's response—particularly as revealed in the hearts of the hearers. Evangelization themes of call, invitation, challenge, and love become unavoidable for the congregation. The homily, then, furthers the purpose of the sacred moment: experience, encounter, and response through conversion.

Conclusion

Preaching, whether in longer forms, as occur in missions and retreats, or in the shorter homiletic form, relates to the new evangelization by responding to its call for encounter and conversion. Evangelization has always been about the Good News of the Gospel in the various forms in which it is articulated. Preaching, whether directed to those fervent in their faith or to seekers, strives to bring people into a clearer awareness of the relationship that God has initiated with humankind and the power of a personal relationship with God when they respond to divine initiative. Conversion has many meanings: not only a response to an initial proclamation of the Gospel but also regular experiences of spiritual growth, of recommitment, of deeper awareness, and the ongoing appropriation of the Paschal Mystery. Preachers are instruments of the Holy Spirit who calls disciples, confirms discipleship, and leads disciples to deeper levels of commitment and growth.

If preachers stand before their hearers, knowing that they are instruments of the Holy Spirit, asking the same kinds of questions and proposing the same kinds of challenges that Jesus placed before his disciples, then they are on the path for preaching in line with the new evangelization.

Bibliography

Burghardt, Walter John. *Preaching: The Art and the Craft*. New York: Paulist Press, 1987.

DeBona, Guerric. *Fulfilled in Our Hearing: History and Method of Christian Preaching*. Mahwah, NJ: Paulist Press, 2005.

Dolan, Jay P. *Catholic Revivalism: The American Experience, 1830–1900*. Notre Dame, IN: University of Notre Dame Press, 1978.

Foley, Edward. *Preaching Basics: A Model and Method*. Chicago: Liturgy Training Publications, 1998.

John Paul II. "The Task of the Latin American Bishop." *Origins* 12 (1983).

Keller, Timothy. *Preaching: Communicating Faith in a Skeptical Age*. New York: Dutton, 2015.

Long, Thomas G. *The Witness of Preaching*. Louisville, KY: Westminster John Knox Press, 2005.

McBride, Alfred. *How to Make Homilies Better, Briefer and Bolder: Tips from a Master Homilist*. Huntington, IN: Our Sunday Visitor, 2007.

Synod of Bishops on the New Evangelization. "Final List of Propositions of Ordinary General Assemblies of the Synod of Bishops, " 2012; http://www .news.va/en/news/final-words-from-the-synod-of-bishops.

Waznak, Robert P. *Sunday after Sunday: Preaching the Homily as a Story*. New York: Paulist Press, 1983.

Biblical Preaching

Dianne Bergant

Biblical preaching can best be understood as a contemporary example of Jesus' own declaration to those present in the synagogue in Nazareth:

> When he came to Nazareth, where he had been brought up, he went to the synagogue on the sabbath day, as was his custom. He stood up to read, and the scroll of the prophet Isaiah was given to him. He unrolled the scroll and found the place where it was written: "The Spirit of the Lord is upon me, because he has anointed me to bring good news to the poor. He has sent me to proclaim release to the captives and recovery of sight to the blind, to let the oppressed go free, to proclaim the year of the Lord's favor." And he rolled up the scroll, gave it back to the attendant, and sat down. The eyes of all in the synagogue were fixed on him. Then he began to say to them, "Today this scripture has been fulfilled in your hearing." (Luke 4:16-21)

Jesus is here appropriating to himself the essence of this passage from Isaiah (61:1-2). The phrase "fulfilled in your hearing" asserts that the promise announced by the earlier prophet has been fulfilled in him.

The phrase "fulfilled in your hearing" continues to have meaning for us today. It contains two very important concepts that influence the way we interpret the Bible for preaching, namely, "fulfilled" and "in your hearing." "Fulfilled" suggests that the present understanding of an aspect of the religious tradition was either incomplete or open to new meaning(s). This in no way challenges the revelatory authority of the biblical tradition. The Bible itself contains abundant evidence of the reinterpretation of earlier traditions. Both ancient Israel and early Christianity brought the religious traditions into dialogue with the realities of the historical moment. Those that were considered basic to the identity of the people were passed down from generation to generation, shaped and reshaped by the specific circumstances of each successive generation, acquired layer upon layer of meaning, and thus developed what has come to be known as the "surplus of meaning." It was this interplay that kept the traditions constant yet ever new.

"In your hearing" implies that the contemporary situation is the place where fulfillment is realized. The manner in which this fulfillment is achieved depends on the method of interpretation employed. Contemporary communication theory has helped us to distinguish three different "worlds" in relation to the text: the literary world created by the text itself (the world within the text); the historical world out of which the text grew (the world behind the text); and the present world of the reader (the world in front of the text). Examination of each "world" yields various insights into the meaning(s) of the text. For example, Jesus cures a man with leprosy of the disease (Matt 8:3). A careful literary reading (the world within the text) shows that Jesus accomplishes this through his touch. One apparent meaning here is that Jesus exercises divine power over disease. Historical study (the world behind the text) tells us that leprosy makes one ritually unclean, and touching one with the disease would make the other unclean as well. Jesus, however, subverts the idea of ritual impurity. His touch did not make him unclean; it made the man with leprosy clean. One apparent meaning is that Jesus embraces those whom society has marginalized. We are left with the question: "What is the meaning for today?" (the world in front of the text). This is the step into biblical preaching.

Reading the Text

Following the insights of this theory of communication, we see that interpretation is more than just the gathering of information about the text (literary criticism) or its earliest settings (historical criticism). It can be defined as an aspect of the world of the reader meeting the powerful world of the text in such a way that the message of the text takes hold of the reader and transforms the thinking of that reader. Interpretation is the unfolding of the message of the text in a new context ("in your hearing"). This step requires knowledge of the contemporary community and its local and global contexts (see 233ff. below). Such knowledge includes: some understanding of present-day social systems and the way they operate in our lives; an informed appreciation of the economic and political realities that shape our local, national, and international societies; and insight into the respective community's *mythos* and *ethos*. Ours is a multiracial, multicultural, multilingual, multiclass, multigenerational community of people of varying genders in an interfaith, postmodern, global ecosystem. These are some of the key dynamics operative in our society, and they can be neither ignored nor minimized. Anyone resolved to do biblical preaching with understanding and integrity will have to brave the demanding implications of this complexity.

The complexity of contemporary reality begets ambiguity. Even the slightest circumstance can change things. What seems appropriate in one situation may be unfit for another. There is a dimension of ambiguity in biblical passages as well. A message that consoles in one circumstance can denounce in another. Therefore, preachers will also have to be able to decide whether the community in which they preach needs to hear a supportive message or a challenging one. For example, the beatitude "Blessed are the meek, for they will inherit the earth" (Matt 5:5) will fill those who are marginal in a society with hope, while those who are privileged might become apprehensive. This passage might be calling them to assist the meek in this endeavor.

Once both the biblical tradition and the contemporary situation of the community have been analyzed, resignification (providing new significance) can be done. This is perhaps the real challenge, and this is where effective biblical preaching occurs or does not. Just what do we do to make a biblical message come alive in a new context? What strategy do we use to resignify the tradition? Faced with this challenge, many people choose a kind of "concordism" that seeks correspondences between real life situations and similar events described in the Scriptures. This approach limits the message of revelation to situations that seem to have parallels in biblical history. It also tends to confuse what happens in the story with the meaning of what happens. Reading the books of Joshua and Judges in this way has frequently been used to justify the occupation of land already inhabited by others. For those who read the Bible in this way, the theme of "promised land" could well engender a sense of self-righteous acquisition rather than hope tempered by the acknowledgment of divine compassion in the face of human infidelity, as it did for early Israel. On the other hand, this kind of reading can also produce noble aspirations. The story of Israel's flight from Egypt recounted in the book of Exodus has both inspired and encouraged those who live under oppressive systems.

Other people seek to resignify by using some type of correlation that is less concerned with similar historical occurrences than with common human experience. This uncritical type of correlation has led some to conclude that the timeless biblical message can answer questions that have plagued people over the ages, regardless of the difference in the social location of the hearer. Following this approach, biblical prescriptions for living in the land are merely repeated, not reinterpreted. Those who choose this method of reading might suggest that the homelessness experienced by so many people today can instill in them a longing for heaven as their true home. This approach has often reinforced forms of homelessness. It has, however, also developed unshakable hope in many people.

Whichever interpretive approach is employed in reading texts, certain principles should be kept in mind. The first is that of "the ambiguity of reality." What is acceptable in one situation may be unacceptable in another. This means that the preacher must have some knowledge of the contours of the world of those hearing the preaching. The second principle insists that we read the biblical passage as a "mirror" that reflects our identity rather than as a set of directives meant as a model for moral behavior. Third, we are directed to seek the action of God in the events described. Although the passage might express anthropocentric concerns, it is really a theological reflection on God working in and through human lives. Finally, only after we have theologized (discovered God's action) should we "moralize" (discover what the action of God is asking of us).

Celebration of Sacraments

There are many settings in which biblical preaching is appropriate. First and foremost is the celebration of the Eucharist (see 156ff. below), where the Liturgy of the Word is an integral part of the ritual. In that context, the purpose of preaching is to open up the religious meaning of assigned passages in their liturgical context so that the synergy of text and context can transform the minds and hearts of the hearers. Strictly speaking, the passages read during the eucharistic celebration are no longer biblical passages. They have been lifted out of their biblical context and placed in another literary context, the Lectionary. Called lections, they are now to be interpreted within this new context, no longer within their original biblical setting. This does not mean that the New Testament now interprets the Old Testament, but that there is an interplay between the religious meaning of all the readings in their liturgical context. This means that what is left out of the original biblical text should be left out of the preaching.

As the Vatican II document *Sacrosanctum Concilium* states, "Sacred scripture is of the greatest importance in the celebration of the liturgy" (*SC*, no. 24); and "The treasures of the bible are to be opened up more lavishly, so that richer fare may be provided for the faithful at the table of God's word" (*SC*, no. 52). It is through regular Lectionary preaching during eucharistic celebrations that the majority of Roman Catholic believers become acquainted with significant portions of the biblical tradition and its ongoing power to shape and reshape religious identity. We are reminded of the importance of such preaching again and again by successive religious leaders. In his first apostolic exhortation, *Evangelii Gaudium* (*EG*), Pope Francis (b. 1936) reiterates this point as he quotes John Paul II's (d. 2005) apostolic letter, *Dies Domini*:

> It is worth remembering that "the liturgical proclamation of the word of God, especially in the eucharistic assembly, is not so much a time for

meditation and catechesis as a dialogue between God and his people, a dialogue in which the great deeds of salvation are proclaimed and the demands of the covenant are continually restated." (*EG*, no. 137)

Underscoring the extraordinary character of such Lectionary preaching, Pope Francis considers it a form of dialogue between God and the believer. It enjoys a place of honor in the Eucharist, for it points to the ultimate moment of dialogue that takes place in sacramental communion. Such preaching becomes both part of the offering made to God during this sacred moment and a meditation on the grace poured out by Christ through the Holy Spirit on those participating in the eucharistic celebration.

Biblical preaching finds a place in the celebration of other sacraments (see 146ff. below) as well. The Rite of Christian Initiation of Adults—which includes the sacraments of baptism, confirmation, and Eucharist—often comes to fruition during the Holy Saturday Vigil. On this occasion, biblical-liturgical preaching not only opens up the meaning of each sacramental moment and describes the power of the grace that flows through them but also situates that sacrament within the all-encompassing mystery of the death and resurrection of Jesus. The celebration of the sacrament of ordination also must take place within the context of the Eucharist. On this occasion, Lectionary preaching can link those ordained with the great sacrament for which they are ordained. Marriage and the anointing of the sick may similarly take place within the Eucharist, though they are often celebrated outside this setting.

The rituals for each sacrament include the reading of some biblical passage. This enables the preacher to lead those present into the realization of the divine mystery about to take place. With baptism, it is an appreciation of divine graciousness that has invited us to be children of God, incorporated into Christ as a new creation; with confirmation, it is the opportunity to ratify one's baptismal commitment and to freely take on the challenges this commitment entails; with Eucharist, it is the privilege of feeding on the body and blood of Christ, accepting the mission to become Christ's presence in the world, thereby anticipating the eternal life that this promises. The bishop's instruction to the candidates for ordination may not flow from a biblical theme, but the eucharistic setting of the celebration of this sacrament includes relevant biblical texts. Readings selected for the celebration of marriage often describe human love as a reflection of divine love, a precious gift to be cherished. Those passages chosen for the anointing of the sick emphasize courage and trust. Those included in the celebration of reconciliation underscore divine compassion and forgiveness. It is clear that biblically rooted preaching is an essential component of sacramental celebrations.

Prayer Services

Prayer services of various kinds are created to mark a variety of occasions. They can be celebratory, rejoicing in accomplishments or commemorating the anniversary of a significant event. They can focus on prayers of petition, asking for assistance in a time of challenge, for deliverance in the face of mortal threat, or for guidance when serious decisions must be made. In such cases, the nature of the event or the character of those involved influence the choice of biblical readings and prayers. Biblical preaching or faith sharing based on those readings are often part of these prayer ceremonies.

One specific kind of prayer service is the wake or memorial vigil. While officially considered an integral part of the Roman Catholic funeral, it is not always considered pastorally essential and many omit it all together. When it is included, the wake takes place between the death of the deceased and the actual funeral. The approved format for such a "Vigil for the Deceased" follows the pattern of introductory rites, the Liturgy of the Word, prayers of intercession, and a concluding rite. In some cases, the people simply recite the Office for the Dead from the Liturgy of the Hours. A service patterned after the Liturgy of the Word presumes that there will be readings from Scripture and subsequent biblical-liturgical preaching, as is found in eucharistic celebrations. While the Office for the Dead consists of psalms and biblical readings, actual preaching is not always included. The occasion of death and the resulting sense of loss and grief, however, often call for words of support and comfort. In this way, biblical preaching could become part of the service. The same is true regarding a wake service patterned after the Liturgy of the Hours. Depending on the psalms and readings chosen, mourners should be able to express their bereavement, their gratitude to God for having been blessed by the deceased's presence in their lives. For some, the wake is really a time to celebrate the quality of life enjoyed by the one now deceased. However a wake is celebrated, the psalms and biblical readings encourage reflection on the religious sentiments expressed therein, and some form of sharing of these sentiments often follows.

The often informal character of the wake allows for a great deal of flexibility and adaptation to the specific situation. Prayers, readings, and preaching are often chosen at the discretion of the presider, preferably in consultation with the family of the deceased. These choices set the character and direction of the biblical preaching and the sharing that might follow.

Retreats and Missions

Since Vatican II (1962–1965), preached biblical retreats in the Roman Catholic Church have grown in popularity. They usually lack the catechetical (see 124ff. below) and mystagogical (see 134ff. below) dimensions found in preaching that occurs as part of sacramental celebrations or the specific focus of above-noted prayer services meant to mark a special event or need. While the latter are meant to be communal experiences, retreats are ordinarily exercises designed to help deepen the individual's spiritual life. This is true even though preaching occurs in a communal setting. The content addressed can be limited to readings from one biblical book, or it might develop religious themes that span several books. It could concentrate on biblical characters chosen as possible models for imitation or on exhortations for righteous living. Here again, flexibility and personal interest determine the passages chosen.

Another phenomenon in which biblical preaching has gained a foothold is the parish mission (see 111f. above). Although the content of the preaching events in such missions might appear to be similar to the retreat, the actual focus and the goal of a parish mission is quite different. Ordinarily led by an outside preacher, the mission is focused on the revitalization and spiritual growth of a single parish. To this end, preachers collaborate with the parish staff so that the actual needs of the community will be addressed and the fruits of the mission will continue to be nurtured by that community long after the mission is finished. An effective mission will ordinarily provide events and exercises for all groups within the parish—young and old, women and men, those actively involved in parish life and those only minimally interested.

Biblical passages chosen for preaching can concentrate on issues such as community building, Christian living, prayer, reception of the sacraments, or the return to the practice of the faith. While many of these issues are also addressed during a preached retreat, there is a significant difference here. The retreat focuses on the enrichment of the spiritual life of individuals; the parish mission focuses on the spiritual development of the individuals as members of a parochial community and so builds up the religious life of the community.

Devotional Practices

Many Roman Catholics felt that Vatican II's renewal erased meaningful devotional practices of the past and did not replace them with new devotions. In their desire to express their faith in comfortable contextual ways, they have revived some of those practices such as Forty Hours Devotion, novenas, and Stations of the Cross. When this has occurred, however, the resulting retrieval is not unchanged. Many "traditional" practices now include a biblical component where there was once only devotional prayer. Sometimes Forty Hours Devotions now include some form of biblical preaching. Since there is only a general format for this ritual—outlined in the USCCB's "Order for the Solemn Exposition of the Holy Eucharist" (1992)—its specific structure and the content of biblical preaching is left to the discretion of the presider in dialogue with those who plan and coordinate the service. The specific needs of the parish, the universal church, the country, or the world can and should be appropriately addressed in this way.

Novenas also lend themselves to various formats. The routine recitation of standard prayers can easily be replaced by short reflections on biblical themes that correspond to the specific focus of the novena. This can also be done with the Way of the Cross, since the stations themselves originated from biblical stories. Here too, short reflections on the biblical scene can replace well-worn prayers.

Conclusion

It is clear that biblical preaching need not be limited to eucharistic celebrations. There are many established religious settings in which Scripture already is or can be incorporated as part of the ceremony. Believers, however, need not be hampered by traditional settings. They can devise new ones. In all of these situations, the creativity of those conducting devotional service comes into play. When this happens, the Word of the Lord might actually be "fulfilled in your hearing."

Bibliography

Ahlgrim, Ryan. *Not as the Scribes: Jesus as a Model for Prophetic Preaching*. Scottdale, PA: Herald Press, 2002.

Bellinger, Karla J. *Connecting Pulpit and Pew: Breaking Open the Conversation about Catholic Preaching*. Collegeville, MN: Liturgical Press, 2014.

Bergant, Dianne. *The Word for Every Season* (Cycle B, Cycle C, Cycle A). New York: Paulist Press, 2008, 2009, 2010.

———. *Preaching the New Lectionary* (Year B, Year C, Year A). Collegeville, MN: Liturgical Press, 1999, 2000, 2001.

Brueggemann, Walter. *Collected Sermons of Walter Brueggemann*, vols. 1 and 2. Louisville, KY: Westminster/John Knox, 2001, 2015.

Skudlarek, William. *The Word in Worship: Preaching in a Liturgical Context*. Nashville, TN: Abingdon, 1981.

Doctrinal and Catechetical Preaching

Michael E. Connors and Ann M. Garrido

One of the most important questions for the Christian preaching ministry is its relationship to the church's official doctrine. The relationship is traditionally a close one, although not without some tensions and possible misunderstandings. In recent years this issue has been pushed to the fore once again.

In the Roman Catholic tradition, Scripture and church doctrine are not separate sources of revelation; rather, they are inseparably intertwined. Scripture mediates the living Word of God and is foundational for the church's preaching. As *Dei Verbum* from Vatican II (1962–1965) noted, "[T]radition and scripture make up a single sacred deposit of the word of God" (*DV*, no. 10). Through various literary genres, the biblical texts articulate the spiritual experiences of Israel and the early Christian community and continue to live—most fully—in the context of worship. Thus, doctrine may be understood as essentially a distillation and refinement of the church's reflection on Scripture, liturgy, and its ecclesial experience. Doctrine emerges over time, in part, from the ongoing preaching and catechesis of the church, as the church reflects more deeply on the meaning of its foundational realities and faces new historical contexts and their challenges.

Likewise, "biblical preaching" (see 116ff. above) and "doctrinal-catechetical preaching" ought not be viewed as two separate genres but rather two faces of the same coin. All the church's preaching is to be grounded in Scripture and all the church's preaching is to be accountable to the wider wisdom of the ecclesial community, a wisdom codified in its doctrinal and creedal formulations and enacted in its liturgical celebrations. Unfortunately, however, "scriptural" and "doctrinal" have become labels sometimes associated with differing goals, emphases, and styles in the preaching act. The history of preaching in the church could be read, in part, as an ongoing effort to preserve the right relationship between its Scriptures and its doctrine.

The Emergence and Purpose of Church Doctrines

It is too often overlooked that the development of the entire doctrinal tradition of Christianity is intimately related to preaching. From its earliest years (see 41ff. above) the church's survival and expansion depended on effective communication. A fundamental claim of emerging Christianity was that God communicates the Divine self to human beings, especially in the incarnate Word of Jesus Christ. Therefore, divine self-revelation can metaphorically be regarded as a speech act. Moreover, the New Testament was written in part as a response to emerging Christianity's need to articulate for itself and others what it had experienced in the Risen Christ. Additionally, as Christianity spread, communities separated by distance and language needed to ensure that the Gospel and its implications were properly and richly understood and communicated. Hence, there emerged a need for coordinating structures—initially residing in the twelve but eventually moving to apostles, charismatic prophets, and eventually bishops. Recognized founders and leaders of local communities also established other communities, deploying similar expressions of faith by means of preaching and the writing of letters. Local churches of different provenances needed some means by which to recognize believers from churches founded by others.

From this perspective, one can grasp the need for coordination and standardization of teaching and practices. In the New Testament, this is perhaps most obvious in the pastoral epistles, as when Paul admonishes Titus, "But as for you, teach what is consistent with sound doctrine" (Titus 2:1). Paul's concern that basic teachings be maintained and guarded is evident in many of his letters, e.g., his heated appeals to the Corinthians and the Galatians. To his coworker Timothy, Paul entrusts the task of pastoral correction: "I urge you . . . to remain in Ephesus so that you may instruct certain people not to teach any different doctrine" (1 Tim 1:3).

Biblical scholar Luke Timothy Johnson underscores certain passages of both Testaments as providing a kind of protodoctrinal form and function. For example, he points to the basic affirmation of Jewish faith—the *Shema*: "Hear, O Israel: The LORD is our God, the LORD alone" (Deut 6:4)—and to the New Testament's repeated affirmation of the Lordship of Jesus Christ (Johnson 2004, 5 and 16). In some passages, Paul summarizes his preaching and teaching in words that clearly indicate a standard, repeated, formalized expression, e.g., "For I handed on to you as of first importance what I in turn had received: that Christ died for our sins in accordance with the scriptures, and that he was buried, and that he was raised on the third day in accordance with the scriptures, and that he appeared to Cephas, then to the twelve" (1 Cor 15:3-5). Johnson notes that "this passage is especially important because it will help form the heart of the eventual Christian creed" (Johnson 2004, 15). Thus, one can see within the New Testament itself the beginnings of the process of clarifying beliefs and regulating teaching, a process that will eventually lead to doctrinal formulation.

Doctrines, consolidated in liturgies and creeds, continued developing in the early centuries of the church in response to pastoral needs. In particular, the great christological doctrines formulated at Nicea (325 CE), Chalcedon (451 CE), and other councils were created not merely to satisfy an intellectual need or political exigency. Rather, these emerged as pastors recognized that differing formulations could shape the prayer and praxis of the church in diverging, even divisive ways. Behind these more broad-ranging struggles to define Christian belief were critical contextual issues about the local community's faith, prayer, enacted spirituality, self-understanding, and mission refracted in its preaching.

The capstone of these early centuries of doctrinal ferment was the development of creeds like the Nicene-Constantinopolitan formulation, which remains in use among nearly all Christian churches today. Johnson identifies five essential functions for this collection of central Christian doctrines (Johnson 2014, 58–64). First, it "narrates the Christian myth" in one compressed, integrated form, from creation to eschatology. It speaks to the biggest questions of life's origins, meaning, and destiny. Second, it "interprets Scripture." The creed and the doctrinal affirmations that comprise it are not "nonscriptural" but drawn from Scripture and contemplations of Scripture's meaning and intent. They provide a community guide to the proper reading of Scripture. Third, the creed "constructs a world," i.e., it provides a kind of imaginative hermeneutical key through which all reality is refracted. This is a key that both opens up an understanding of reality and existence while standing in contrast to other systems of belief. Fourth, the creed "guides Christian practices." This function is more implicit than explicit. The affirmation of a good God who became incarnate to save people will have definitive practical ramifications for how Christians live their lives, pray, spend their time, and use their resources. Lastly, says Johnson, the creed "prepares the worshipping people." The recitation of the creed in Christian worship bridges the transition from the engagement with the biblical-lectionary texts to the table of the Eucharist, orienting the assembly to the meaning, proper celebration, and interconnection of both. It is notable that the so-called Nicene Creed did not find a place in Roman Eucharist until the eleventh century.

Each of these doctrinal and creedal functions has pointed implications for preaching. The liturgical preacher engages scriptural readings and liturgical symbols, prayers, and rituals—then wrestles with their interpretation to open up fresh avenues of meaning for contemporary believers. Other forms of preaching—e.g., catechesis and evangelization (see 105ff. above)—

are yet rooted in and inspired by these central narratives and actions of the faithful community. Preachers need the guidance of the tradition in the Holy Spirit to discharge this ministry effectively. While doctrinal formulations and the creed cannot tell the preacher exactly what to say, since the prescribed texts and rituals generate a plurality of meanings, they are nonetheless among the most important resources at the preacher's disposal.

Some of the erstwhile tension between doctrine and preaching flows from the compressed nature of doctrinal language: a language never intended to be used verbatim from the pulpit, at least not without Scripture, additional explanation, and other supportive forms of rhetoric, images, and illustrations. Doctrinal formulations are generally meant to function in the background of the preaching event, informing and guiding preaching by their cogency, transportability, and communal authority. They cannot, however, bear the full weight of the preacher's responsibility to move minds, hearts, and wills in a particular context.

The Scriptures themselves employ varieties of language, genre, and literary style that often have great poignancy and immediacy for the hearer and provide a wide reach into the human personality, especially in the hands of a skillful preacher. Contrarily, doctrinal language can seem flat and monochromatic, lacking in narrative dynamism, artistry, and the vivid imagery of so much biblical literature. The scriptural character of doctrinal formulations, however, must not be lost from view. In the words of Avery Dulles (d. 2008), "Doctrinal definitions are normally based on a convergent use of many biblical texts, prayerfully read in the tradition of the worshiping church under the light of the Holy Spirit" (Dulles 2006, 24). In a parallel way, William Levada (b. 1936) observed:

> We tend to think of doctrine as something added to Scripture, but in fact doctrines are the result of a cluster of scriptural texts understood in a particular way. . . . When the homilist knows the clusters of texts that surround certain doctrines, then the appearance of these texts in a particular liturgy becomes an occasion for doctrinal teaching that is nonetheless thoroughly scriptural. (Levada 2008, 605)

Doctrine and Scripture are never intended to be viewed in a contrasting light but, rather, as complementary: Scripture is an important source that gives rise to doctrine, and doctrine helps to guide the ongoing interpretation of Scripture.

Patristic scholar John Cavadini describes doctrines this way:

> The doctrine has no value apart from its function of "carrying" this mystery of divine Love so that it can be handed on—so that this handing on or

127

"tradition" may develop and continue. In a way, a doctrine of the faith is like a carrying case, a little suitcase, for Mystery. Doctrines are the normative way of handing on a mystery—they make it so we can pick mysteries up and carry them around and hand them to someone else and know we are handing on this mystery and not some substitute. But in order to hand it on properly the person has to know it contains a mystery, has to have it opened up so that receiving a doctrine means encountering the mystery it carries so that one can be transformed by it. (Cavadini 2012, 26)

The proper use of doctrine from the pulpit, therefore, is not simply to quote the definition or formulation accurately but to "open up the mystery" evoked in the doctrine to hearers. The preacher or catechist must stand behind, in, and in front of the doctrinal formulation, as it were, in order to excavate the scriptural and experiential sources that the church's doctrines enable a local community to engage, embrace, and critique.

Historically, church doctrines have at least two types of utility for the contemporary preacher. First is a kind of delimiting function. Doctrines define the church's faith in abstract terms. A high level of abstraction is helpful to harmonize multiple scriptural sources, to maximize applicability, and especially to define what teaching and believing is out of bounds. For example, that Christian orthodoxy has a high tolerance for paradox is never more evident than in the way Orthodox churches understand the person of Christ, "truly divine and truly human." Preaching or catechesis that emphasizes one of these poles while excluding the other would be regarded as incomplete at best, misleading at worst. Employing a common metaphor, one contemporary theologian describes the function this way: "Perhaps the best way to explain the proper function of doctrines is to think of them as the foul lines on a baseball field" (González 2005, 6). The magisterium umpires the game, and doctrines keep the action within certain bounds, while not dictating in detail how players must play the game.

This negative or disciplinary function of doctrines, however, is not the whole picture. It needs to be complemented by a second, directive or exhortatory, function. Doctrines fertilize the imagination of the preacher, goading her beyond the shallows, to search deeply and prayerfully into the world of the biblical text and its liturgical context in order to unearth contemporary meanings. The doctrinal tradition exhorts the timid preacher to go beyond light inspiration, cheap comfort, or mere moralism into the spiritual treasury, of which the discrete pericope is only one small part, and interpret that text in its proper liturgical context: against the background of the whole Bible and its history of interpretation. In so doing, accountability to church doctrines helps to guard against superficiality, artificiality, and idiosyncrasy in preaching and catechesis. This aspect of doctrine's function is perhaps expressed best by the US Roman Catholic bishops' statement *Preaching the Mystery of Faith*:

> The doctrines of the Church should direct the homilist and ensure that he arrives at and preaches about what is in fact the deepest meaning of Scripture and sacrament for Christian life. For doctrines simply formulate with accuracy what the Church, prompted by the gift of the Spirit, has come to know through the Scriptures proclaimed in the believing assembly and through the sacraments that are celebrated on the foundation of these Scriptures. . . . These doctrines ought to be seamlessly introduced and articulated still today in the course of our liturgical celebrations in order to ensure that by reading the Scriptures and celebrating the Eucharist we understand ever more deeply the essential beliefs of the Church. (PTMOF, 25–26)

Relating Doctrine to Liturgical Preaching

The Roman Catholic Church has often struggled to actualize the nuance of its tradition in the preaching act itself, most especially liturgically. Although the tradition stresses that there should be no distinction between "scriptural" preaching and "doctrinal" preaching, by the start of the twentieth century, the sermon was too often viewed as an optional teaching moment in the midst of the Mass: too frequently set apart from the liturgical rite by a sign of the cross marking the beginning and end of this extraliturgical event. The content was commonly based on some catechetical notion of the preacher rather than engaging the Lectionary texts and their doctrinal resonance.

Vatican II (1962–1965) named the reform and the promotion of the liturgy, including a revision of the role of preaching as integral to the eucharistic rite, as a privileged aspect of the reform. A key to this reform was a renewed recognition of Scripture in liturgy and theology. *Sacrosanctum Concilium (SC)* called for a greatly expanded repertoire of scriptural texts in the Lectionary (*SC*, no. 51) and allowed for the proclamation of these texts to be in the local languages of people for greater comprehension (*SC*, no. 36). Vatican II emphasized that in liturgical preaching, "The primary source . . . should be scripture and liturgy" (*SC*, no. 35) rather than doctrinal sources. Reasserting the importance of the ministry of the Word, the council stated that "the first task of priests as co-workers of the bishops [is] to preach the Gospel of God to all" and spoke of an "indivisible unity" among the Word, the response of faith, and the eucharistic offering (*Presbyterorum Ordinis*

129

[*PO*], no. 4). *SC* clearly envisions doctrinally based instruction as *one* of the roles of liturgical preaching but sets this role within the context of active participation in worship and the elicitation of faith (*SC*, no. 33). Elsewhere, the council also embraced the instructional importance of nonliturgical forms of preaching (e.g., *DV*, no. 24; *Ad Gentes Divinitus* [*AGD*] nos. 2, 15; *Gravissimum Educationis*).

Roman Catholic documents following Vatican II continued to place strong emphasis on the scriptural foundation of preaching—so much so that, unfortunately, they seemed to some to almost remove entirely doctrinal explication of liturgical preaching. Of particular note is *Fulfilled in Your Hearing*. "The homily is not so much *on* the Scriptures as *from* and *through* them" (FIYH, no. 50). It continues: "[T]he goal of the liturgical preacher is not to interpret a text of the Bible (as would be the case in teaching a Scripture class) as much as to draw on the texts of the Bible as they are presented in the lectionary to interpret peoples' lives" (FIYH, no. 52).

Already in FIYH, however, the bishops acknowledged possible concerns about the lack of attention to systematic exposition of doctrine. FIYH discourages didactic sermons disconnected from their scriptural roots and liturgical setting, but that "does not exclude doctrinal instruction and moral exhortation" so long as it is "situated in a broader context, namely, in the recognition of God's active presence in the lives of the people and the praise and thanksgiving that this response elicits" (FIYH, no. 70). At the same time, FIYH considered the possibility of more doctrinally focused preaching *outside* of the liturgy:

> But even though the liturgical homily can incorporate instruction and exhortation, it will not be able to carry the whole weight of the Church's preaching. There will still need to be special times and occasions for preaching that addresses human values in such a way as to dispose the hearers to be open to the Gospel of Jesus Christ, preaching intended to bring the hearers to an inner conversion of heart, and preaching intended to instruct the faithful in matters of doctrine or morality. These three kinds of preaching—sometimes referred to as pre-evangelization, evangelization, and catechesis—can be found today in evangelistic gatherings, the adult catechumenate, youth ministry programs, spiritual renewal programs, Bible study groups and many forms of religious education. (FIYH, no. 72)

Under the papacies of John Paul II (d. 2005) and Benedict XVI (b. 1927), voices concerned about an overall lack of basic catechesis in the post–Vatican II church gained a greater hearing, and the role that liturgical preaching could play to alleviate this concern was brought into question.

Most of the voices of concern were not advocating a return to a purely didactic style of preaching, nor were they departing from the centrality of Scripture. As John Paul II wrote, "The reading of Scripture cannot be replaced by the reading of other texts, however much they may be endowed with undoubted religious and moral values" (John Paul II 1980, no. 10). In *Sacramentum Caritatis* Benedict XVI emphasized that "generic and abstract homilies should be avoided" (*SaCar*, no. 46).

Instead, the worry was that the Sunday eucharistic assembly may be the only point of contact between most Roman Catholics and the wider doctrinal tradition, and that liturgical preaching on the readings of the Lectionary alone might leave hearers with an incomplete exposure to the breadth of the church's teaching. This concern found expression in the writing of John Paul II: "Preaching, centered upon the Bible texts, must then in its own way make it possible to familiarize the faithful with the whole of the mysteries of the faith and the norms of Christian living" (*Catechesi Tradendae* [*CT*], no. 48). This concern becomes most explicit in PTMOF:

> The *Catechism* itself is organized into four "pillars" of Christian life. . . . Over time the homilist, while respecting the unique form and spirit of the Sunday homily, should communicate the full scope of this rich catechetical teaching to his congregation. During the course of the liturgical year it is appropriate to offer the faithful, prudently and on the basis of the three-year Lectionary, "'thematic' homilies treating the great themes of the Christian faith." (PTMOF, nos. 23–24)

Even here, however, the bishops are careful to caution against a purely didactic approach to liturgical preaching: "Doctrine is not meant to be propounded in a homily in the way that it might unfold in a theology classroom or a lecture for an academic audience or even a catechism lesson. The homily is integral to the liturgical act of the Eucharist, and the language and spirit of the homily should fit that context" (PTMOF, no. 23).

Around the time PTMOF was published, a number of efforts were made to connect the Roman Catholic Lectionary with the *Catechism of the Catholic Church* to assure that over a three-year period the major doctrines of the church could be introduced. The bishops sought integration:

> A wedge should not be driven between the proper content and style of the Sunday homily and the teaching of the Church's doctrine. To encounter the living presence of the Risen Christ in the word of the Scriptures and in the Sacrament of his Body and Blood is not incompatible with effective communication of what faith in Christ means for our lives. Without being pedantic, overly abstract, or theoretical, the homilist can effectively spell

out, for example, the connection between Jesus' care for the poor and the Church's social teaching and concern for the common good. (PTMOF, no. 24)

Such efforts again raised concerns that the relationship between Scripture and doctrine in preaching might get out of balance, and that the homily was being viewed more as an opportunity for addressing catechetical deficits than for liturgical prayer and holistic, multidimensional conversion (Lonergan 1972, 237–43).

Pope Francis's (b. 1936) *Evangelii Gaudium* (*EG*) is the most recent document of note for Roman Catholics for contributing to this conversation. While quoting liberally from Vatican II and previous pontiffs, Francis seems primarily concerned not so much about whether doctrine has a role in the preaching of the church but how it is used. Francis favors a highly dialogical tone to preaching, at one point comparing it to "a mother's conversation" (*EG*, nos. 139–41). He continues, "A preaching which would be purely moralistic or doctrinaire, or one which turns into a lecture on biblical exegesis, detracts from this heart-to-heart communication which takes place in the homily and possesses a quasi-sacramental character" (*EG*, no. 142). Francis wants the language used to be "simple, clear, direct, well-adapted" (*EG*, no. 158), serving a positive message that engenders hope (*EG*, no. 159). He further challenges preachers who fixate on one aspect of church teaching at the cost of "a fitting sense of proportion" (*EG*, no. 38) that more accurately reflects the hierarchy of truths: for example, "when we speak more about law than about grace, more about the church than about Christ, more about the Pope than about God's word" (*EG*, no. 38).

Conclusion

The relationship of doctrine to preaching continues to be a point of contention. Although the close connections among Scripture, liturgy, and doctrine have the potential to guide and invigorate the preaching act in numerous ways, the lived experience of the church attests that the relationship has not always been well framed in practice. "It will be my contention that there should be no real opposition between the scriptural/liturgical homily and the doctrinal homily," stated Cardinal Levada at the start of his address to a gathering of US bishops and other preachers in 2008. "But," he immediately acknowledged, "I believe that a certain tension does continue to exist for a variety of reasons" (Levada 2008, 603).

A renewed understanding of the nature and purpose of doctrinal formulations will be essential to these ongoing discussions. Cavadini emphasizes that the "informative" purpose of doctrines cannot be severed from the "formative" power of the mystery that the doctrine attempts to express. He writes:

> The teaching of doctrine often gets a bad name because we conceive of it not as the handing on of formative mysteries, but as simply informative, as merely informational. How often have you heard the phrase, "we have to get beyond the 'mere' teaching of doctrine"? In other words, to the real stuff, the experience, relevance, etc. The hidden premise behind this sentence is that doctrine is mere information and not in some way itself formation. What I say is, we have to get beyond the teaching of doctrine as though it *were* mere information. (Cavadini 2012, 27)

Cavadini suggests that preachers and teachers must do what Augustine (d. 430) was so adept at, namely, "grant 'access' to [the doctrine] by bringing out its formative dimension" (Cavadini 2012, 27). The preaching task is to let the mystery—distilled by doctrine and enacted in the liturgy—speak with its full formative and transformative power.

Bibliography

Cavadini, John C. "On Teaching Christianity." *Church Life* 1, no. 2 (2012).

Dulles, Avery. "Vatican II on the Interpretation of Scripture." *Letter and Spirit* 2 (2006).

González, Justo L. *A Concise History of Christian Doctrine.* Nashville, TN: Abingdon Press, 2005.

John Paul II. Letter *Dominicae Cenae* (On the Mystery and Worship of the Eucharist). February 24, 1980. https://w2.vatican.va/content/john-paul-ii/en/letters/1980/documents/hf_jp-ii_let_19800224_dominicae-cenae.html.

Johnson, Luke Timothy. *The Creed: What Christians Believe and Why It Matters.* New York: Doubleday, 2004.

Levada, William. "The Homilist: Teacher of Faith." *Origins* 37, no. 38 (2008).

Lonergan, Bernard J. F. *Method in Theology.* Minneapolis: Seabury Press, 1972.

Mystagogical Preaching

Catherine Vincie

In contemporary Christianity, mystagogy and mystagogical preaching appear to be new terms and new concepts closely related to the sacraments of initiation. In the Roman Catholic Rite of Christian Initiation of Adults (RCIA), mystagogy is presented as the stage following the celebration of the initiatory sacraments. The ritual describes it as a period of postbaptismal catechesis and as "a time for the community and the neophytes together to grow in deepening their grasp of the paschal mystery and in making it part of their lives through meditation on the Gospel, sharing in the Eucharist, and doing the works of charity" (RCIA, no. 244). Despite mystagogy's recent appearance in the RCIA and the criticism that this is introducing a new and alien term into Christian practice, however, mystagogy and mystagogical preaching have a rich history throughout the entire life of the church, even if some would focus on the bishop mystagogues of the late fourth and fifth centuries as the high point of the tradition (see 51 above).

Although controverted, it is possible to trace the word "mystagogy" to the Greek verb *mueō*, which means to close the lips or to keep silent. By the fifth century BCE, it was virtually always used in a religious context and referred to the process of initiating a person into the sacred realities of the mystery cult in question. Central to the meaning of mystagogy was reflection on the rites that celebrated the mysteries. The mystagogue was the person who led neophytes into the mysteries and into the implications of the mysteries for life. Appropriately, mystagogy was almost always used in relationship to the religious "mysteries" or to Greek words such as *mystērion* (mystery), *mystikos* (mystic), and *mystēs* (priest of the mysteries).

The term *mystērion* appears twenty-eight times in the New Testament, mostly in the Pauline corpus. For Paul, the great *mystērion* was the saving work of God intended from all time and now made visible in Christ Jesus. Jesus himself can be understood as a mystagogue in that he proclaimed through his own life and teachings the mysteries of the reign of God. In his table praxis of sharing meals with outcasts and sinners and in his teachings on the same, he offered a critique of the practices of his time and provided a vision for the eschatological table fellowship offered by God to all peoples.

Mystagogy in the Patristic Period

Although practiced in the mystery cults for at least six hundred years prior to Christianity, mystagogy was embraced in early church practice and reached a high point in the so-called patristic era. Mystagogy eventually was understood as the way pastoral bishops of the fourth and fifth centuries opened up the mysteries of the Christian faith to communities within the context of adult initiation. Through mystagogical preaching or commentaries, bishops such as Ambrose (d. 397), Cyril of Jerusalem (d. 386), John Chrysostom (d. 407), Theodore of Mopsuestia (d. 428), and Cyril of Alexandria (d. 444) led their communities and newest members into the deeper meanings of their initiation rites, either before or after their celebration. Cyril (or John) of Jerusalem famously notes that while he had longed to explain the mysteries of initiation to the baptismal candidates, he delayed on the principle "that seeing is believing . . . calculating that after what you saw on that night I should find you a readier audience now when I am to be your guide" (*Catecheses mystagogicae* 1.1; trans. Stephenson 1970, 153). Ambrose had a similar conviction. Others, such as Theodore of Mopsuestia and John Chrysostom, preached their mystagogical homilies before the celebration of the sacraments. John Chrysostom speaks of his method of teaching the meaning of the rites before their experience "so that you may go from here with knowledge and a more assured faith" (*Catecheses ad illuminandos* 2.12; trans. Yarnold 1972, 162); later in the same homily he says, "It is not without good reason and careful thought that I have explained all these things to you in advance. . . . Even before you actually enjoy them, I wanted you to feel great pleasure as you fly on the wings of hope" (*Catecheses ad illuminandos* 2.28; trans. Yarnold 1972, 170). The focus of these mystagogues was the liturgical rites and their various elements: an exposition of their meanings was accomplished through an exploration of the particular Scriptures that resonated with the symbols and rites of initiation.

The scriptural basis for the meaning of sacrament brings us to the question of methods of biblical interpretation in the patristic practice of mystagogy. The preferred form of biblical interpretation of the early "fathers" was typology, although they also employed allegorical explanation. Simply put, typology regards the linking of events while allegory deals with meanings; typology generally considers concrete stories in Scripture, while allegory tends to be more speculative in the articulation of meaning.

Rooted in the typology of Paul and the Gospel of John, typological biblical interpretation of the church fathers took the two Testaments (Hebrew and Christian) and related them dynamically to one another. Often Hebrew Scriptures were interpreted as types (Gr., *tupos*) or figures of the fullness of salvation revealed in the Christian Scriptures. This was conceived as a pattern of promise and fulfillment. Additionally, Christian Scriptures could be read backward, giving further insight into the events of salvation history witnessed in the Hebrew Scriptures. Typology was an effort to keep the various phases of salvation history in relationship to one another. It could be either commemorative or prophetic. The movement could be from past salvific events to present realities or from present realities to future eschatological fullness.

Ambrose spoke of the cleansing of Naaman the leper in the Jordan (2 Kgs 5:1-14) as a type of Christ's baptism in the Jordan by John (*De Sacramentis* 1.13-15). Cyril (or John) of Jerusalem waxes eloquently on the relationship of Old Testament realities to Christ's fulfillment:

> Pass, pray, from the old to the new, from figure to the reality. There Moses sent by God to Egypt; here Christ sent from the Father into the world. Moses' mission was to lead out from Egypt a persecuted people; Christ's, to rescue all the people of the world who were under the tyranny of sin. (*Catecheses mystagogicae* 1.3; trans. Stephenson 1970, 154)

Theodore of Mopsuestia was famous for his use of the "two ages"—the present age and the age to come—in his typological reading of salvation history.

The church fathers went further than just relating the two Testaments; typology became mystagogy when they self-consciously related the celebration of Christian sacraments to the salvific realities of past, present, or future. This is evident when Ambrose spoke about the superiority of the Christian sacraments over those of the Jews, using the Exodus 14 account of the crossing through the Red Sea as a type of the baptismal washing of Christian initiation.

> What superiority is there over the people of the Jews having passed through the sea [Exod 14: 1-15; John 6:49], that meanwhile we may speak of baptism? Yet the Jews who passed through, all died in the desert. . . . But he who passes through this font does not die but rises." (*De Sacramentis* 1.12; trans. Deferrari 1963, 273)

In exploring the meaning of the sacraments through frameworks of types or figures, the fathers stressed that through participation in the sacraments, one participated in the saving realities acknowledged in the Hebrew Scriptures, in the Christian Scriptures, or promised in the eschaton. Cyril (or John) of Jerusalem said it well, while making the connection between the mysteries of Christ and the experience of baptism for neophytes:

> The strange, the extraordinary thing is that we did not really die [in baptism], nor were we really buried or really crucified; nor did we really rise again: this was figurative and symbolic; yet our salvation was real; and all these he has freely made ours, that by sharing his sufferings in a symbolic enactment we may really and truly gain salvation. (*Catecheses mystagogicae* 2.5; trans. Stephenson 1970, 165)

Others made the link between the present age of the sacraments and the promise of the world to come. Theodore of Mopsuestia wrote:

> Baptism contains the signs of the new birth which will be manifested in reality when you rise from the dead and recover all that death has stolen from you. . . . [N]ow you have faith in Christ our Lord, and while you are waiting for the resurrection you must be content with receiving symbols and signs of it in this awesome sacrament which affords you certainty of sharing in the blessings to come. (*Sermones catecheticis* 3.2; trans. Yarnold 1972, 190)

In both of these last examples, we recognize the development of incipient sacramental theologies.

Mystagogical catechesis and preaching went beyond exploring the rituals and their biblically supported events and meanings; it was concerned with the transforming effects of the sacraments on the believers. It can be said that patristic mystagogy engages at least three elements: (1) the liturgical rites, (2) their theological meaning as found in the Scriptures and tradition, and (3) their consequences for Christian behavior. John Chrysostom spoke of the anointing with chrism as a sign that "you are now a soldier and signed on for a spiritual contest. . . . From that day onwards you will confront [the devil] in battle, and this is why the bishop anoints you as athletes of Christ before leading you into the spiritual arena" (*Catecheses ad illuminandos* 2.22, 23; trans. Yarnold 1972, 166–67). Chrysostom, who is most often associated with a moralistic approach in his catechesis, stressed the behavioral implications in the lives of the neophytes because of their participation in these divine realities. He stated:

> As you step out of the sacred waters and express your resurrection by the act of coming up from them, ask for alliance with him so that you may show great vigilance in guarding what has been given to you, and so be immune

from the tricks of the Enemy. Pray for the peace of the Churches. Intercede for those who are still wandering. Fall on your knees for those who are in sin. . . . And so may we all together, living lives that are in keeping with the grace we have received, be counted worthy to win the eternal indescribable blessings through the grace and loving kindness of our Lord Jesus Christ. (*Catecheses ad illuminandos* 2.29, 31; trans. Yarnold 1972, 170–71)

A fourth element of patristic mystagogy is that the early "fathers" took the cultural and political context of their time into account (see 54ff. above) as they unfolded the meanings of the sacraments and their implications for life. Ambrose, in particular, found Christianity in a very difficult situation in the late fourth century—when becoming a Christian gained social respectability, even prestige. He feared that Christianity was losing its countercultural edge, and so he articulated his mystagogy in conflictual terms with Greco-Roman culture. Christian life was depicted as a battle against the forces of evil. This deliberate treatment of Christian behavior within the mystagogical process met with mixed results. Despite the fathers' warnings and the eloquence of their mystagogical preaching, those who underwent initiation in the mysteries often went back to their previous, sinful lifestyles. Rather than shining as a "light to the nations" (Isa 49:6), Chrysostom found it difficult to distinguish those who had been initiated into the Christian mysteries from those who were not; in the marketplace they all looked and acted the same. His mystagogy is filled with warnings of the irreconcilable relationship between such behavior as swearing, drunkenness, and the shows in the hippodrome and stadiums with Christian faith and practice.

One last point to be made about the church fathers and their mystagogical preaching is the relationship they made between seeing the initiation rites with "normal" eyes and seeing with the "eyes of faith." Ambrose noted that the reason he delayed speaking of the meaning of the rites until after the sacraments was because baptism gives the gift of faith, and it is only with this gift of faith that the full meaning of the sacraments can be understood. For Ambrose, seeing with the eyes of the body reveals the visible; seeing with the eyes of faith reveals the unseen, which is infinitely greater. "You have seen what you were able to see with the eyes of your body, with human perception. . . . Those [things] which are not seen are much greater than those which are seen" (*De Sacramentis* 1.10; trans. Deferrari 1963, 272). At this time the candidate's actual bodily experience of the rites was beyond the purview of these mystagogues, as they were heir to a neoplatonic philosophy that denigrated the body and overvalued the mind and spirit. Attention to the embodied, personal experience of the rites themselves would have to await the post-Reformation period and beyond.

In closing this section on mystagogy in the fourth to fifth centuries, we may say that mystagogy faded from view (although not entirely) for a number of different reasons. Perhaps the primary one was the decline of the adult catechumenate when infant baptism gradually became the norm. As adult baptisms became rarer, the need to explain the rites to the neophytes lessened, if not ceased altogether (although this does not explain why a mystagogical approach could not be employed with other sacraments and rites). A second reason related to the limitations of typological exegesis. While holding the two Testaments in dynamic relationship, typology did not give adequate space for the unique meaning of each Testament. It must also be said that there was a shift in biblical exegesis from typology to allegory, even as one finds allegory more typical of the Alexandrian than the Antiochene church in the patristic period. This allegorical method, which focused on the arbitrary assignment of meanings of a liturgical rite when linked to a biblical text, was taken to new heights in the medieval period in the "explanations of the Mass" (Lat., *explicationes Missae*) and other commentaries on the liturgy. As Enrico Mazza (b. 1940) states, "Allegory has historically been the death of mystagogy" (Mazza 1989, 13). Another explanation for the decline and disappearance of mystagogy was the emerging intellectualization of theology in the medieval period. While the contributions of this theological tradition cannot be denied, nonetheless, Christian formation became poorer for lack of mystagogy. Lastly, as sacramental theology developed within this intellectual tradition, concern for the proper matter and form for the validity of the sacraments overtook concern for the fullness of symbols used in liturgical celebration. A minimalist approach to sacramental symbols became the norm.

Mystagogy in the Medieval and Reformation Periods

As Christianity spread west and north on the European continent, the practice of mystagogy nearly disappeared. The catechists and bishops of the Germanic tribes did not have the intellectual preparation of the patristic fathers and thus were not in a position to teach and preach mystagogically. Remnants of reflection on the rites of initiation were still found, however, in the insistence on knowing and understanding the creed and Our Father, which had been basic parts of the initiation rites for adults. A few priests preached mystagogically, such as the Anglo-Saxon monk Ælfric of Eynsham (d. ca. 1010), and some argue that the artistic tradition of the medieval West as found in cathedrals were actual visual forms of theological reflection often connected to the sacraments. An example would be the capitals on the columns of the great church of Cluny.

The sixteenth-century Reformation was a period when preaching on the sacraments once again reached a high point. Not only knowledge of the faith (particularly that of the creed and Lord's Prayer) became a common concern but also personal appropriation of the faith and its implications in life also became more important. The age of Pietism (seventeenth to nineteenth centuries) attended to personal experience, and this prepared the way for the later twentieth-century turn to experience and to a phenomenological approach to liturgical reflection. Within Roman Catholic circles in the late nineteenth and early twentieth centuries, the church's attention turned once more to the mysteries of the faith (through such figures as Prosper Guéranger [d. 1875] and Odo Casel [d. 1948]) and on the participation in these mysteries through sacramental celebration. This prepared the way for the revival of the adult catechumenate that had been requested in mission lands for several hundred years and finally came to fruition in the liturgical changes of Vatican II.

Mystagogy in the Modern and Postmodern Periods

Why has a mystagogy of the sacraments become once again a viable option for liturgical reform in the life of the church? As changing circumstances of initiation practice, changes in theological method, and changes in biblical interpretation resulted in the loss of mystagogy in the medieval church, so too have changes in these three areas brought mystagogy back into practice in the post–Vatican II era. We also have experienced significant changes in liturgical practices, liturgical studies, theological methods, and in biblical interpretations.

The liturgical reform movement of the nineteenth and twentieth centuries led to the retrieval of the adult catechumenate in the Vatican II liturgical reforms. In fact, it was the need for new kinds of adult formation practices in mission lands in the preceding centuries that pressed the question for a new approach to faith formation and the need for a new rite. Already in 1962, prior to the council, the rite for initiation of adults was modified into a seven-step process to take into account the gradual formation of adult subjects. Following the mandate in *Sacrosanctum Concilium* (*SC*, no. 64) for the revision of the adult catechumenate and its implementation in the Latin edition of the Order for Adult Christian Initiation (1972), mystagogy once again became a reality in the postconciliar church—at least in theory. As indicated earlier in this essay, mystagogy was introduced as a formal period of postinitiation catechesis. Whether we have in fact actually learned how to preach or catechize mystagogically is another matter to which we will return below.

An important change in liturgy and liturgical studies that affected the retrieval of mystagogy was a return to a more maximalist approach to liturgical celebrations. Supported by *SC* (nos. 7, 21, 33, 34, etc.), liturgical symbols gradually have become more fulsome, clear, and directly connected to the realities they signify. Water is becoming more abundant in baptismal washing; oil is used generously in the consecration of a church and altar and in the sacrament of the sick and confirmation; eucharistic bread that looks like bread is becoming valued. Regarding liturgical studies, the interpretation of the liturgy is no longer limited to texts but has expanded to include the entire liturgical act—environment, sound, movement, ritual symbols and actions, persons, etc. This growing sensitivity to the whole liturgical experience will be of importance to the development of mystagogical preaching.

A second change that affected a return to a mystagogical approach to liturgical formation was the change in theology from a more speculative to a more experiential approach. The so-called turn to the subject in the theology of the last half of the twentieth century opened the door to a more pastoral and experiential approach to theology, which is a precondition of contemporary mystagogy. Vatican II's *Gaudium et Spes* (*GS*) supported and enhanced this more pastoral and experiential approach. Karl Rahner (d. 1984), who was closely tied to this "turn to the subject," also reintroduced the term mystagogy into theological discourse (Rahner 1971 [1966]), suggesting that it is necessary to take account of the transcendental experience of the individual for Christian living in a secularized world. Following on his work, developments in political and liberation theologies pressed the question of whose experience counts in theological reflection. South American, Black, Feminist, Womanist, Asian, and African theologies (see 210ff. below) have subsequently emerged, which take into account the social and cultural situation of the adult subject, again providing another element central to mystagogical preaching.

This turn to the subject and to experience was furthered by developments in spirituality that stressed it was not just any experience that was in question but the experience of divine mysteries. Theologians began speaking of the "Paschal Mystery" as a way of designating the essential elements of the Christian life and belief system. The Paschal Mystery became shorthand for speaking of the dying, rising, and ascension of Christ, of Easter, and of the sacraments of baptism-confirmation-Eucharist and of the whole of Christian life. The RCIA explains mystagogy as follows:

> A time for the community and the neophytes together to grow in deepening their grasp of the *paschal mystery* and in making it part of their lives through meditation on the Gospel, sharing in the eucharist, and doing the works of charity. (no. 244, emphasis added)

The ritual order further explains that mystagogy involves a deepening understanding of the mysteries through liturgical experience.

> The neophytes are, as the "mystagogy" suggests, introduced into a fuller and more effective understanding of the mysteries through the Gospel message they have learned and above all through their *experience of the sacraments* they have received. (RCIA, no. 245, emphasis added)

As indicated in RCIA no. 244, quoted above, mystagogy also involves "meditation on the Gospel," and so we turn to the third element that has fostered a return to mystagogy in the present age—the developments in biblical studies and biblical interpretation.

As we look at biblical methods of interpretation in the period immediately before and after Vatican II, we see a similar move from a more speculative to a more experientially based method of interpretation. Efforts in historical-critical studies, literary criticism, and form criticism have all helped enormously to clarify the origins, genres, and understanding of the biblical texts within the context of the ancient world. More recent developments in interpretation theory (hermeneutics), however, have stressed the role as well as the social location of the reader in the interpretation process (see 117 above); reader-response criticism, social-scientific, and liberationist readings have all contributed to an emphasis on the meaning of the text for today and the importance of experience in this exploration. This expanded repertoire of interpretive methods has provided new possibilities for preachers seeking to explore the mysteries of the faith with contemporary neophytes and faith communities.

Mystagogy in the Ministry of Preaching

There is clearly a need once again for Christian formation that is liturgical in its source, tied to the experience of the divine in those rituals, rooted in the faith history of the community as expressed in the Scriptures and tradition, and permeated with implications for Christian living in this postmodern world. Mystagogical preaching is the kind of catechesis that—before, during, or after the sacramental celebrations—enables the neophytes and the whole community to appropriate their experience of the divine through imaginative and insightful reference to the Scriptures and tradition. It is poetic in tone, rather than prosaic; enthusiastic rather than solemn; personal rather than generic. Mystagogy was retrieved in the context of adult initiation but is not limited to the initiation sacraments. Mystagogical preaching can take any liturgical experience (feast, season, ritual act, prayer, etc.) and open the meanings and explore the implications of those experiences. In other words, mystagogy's source is the liturgy in all its diversity, as well as the experience of that multifaceted reality. The mystagogue begins with the question "what did you experience in the liturgy?"

The second question is, "What does your experience mean?" Mystagogy's purpose is to explore the mysteries of faith embedded in the liturgy so that the participants come to understand that they are participating in the realities signified. This kind of interpretation is an act of revelation; the mysteries being celebrated are seen now as part of the reality of the liturgical subject. This is not an intellectual exercise, although it is not without use of reason. It aims at building faith through seeing with the eyes of faith, as Ambrose would have us do. It also aims at engaging the neophyte or community as active liturgical subjects through a holistic approach to their experience. The exploration of meaning comes through dialogue with the Scriptures of both Testaments. The mystagogue is not limited to a typological reading of the Scriptures, although that might be a suitable approach, but in this postconciliar period, all the methods of interpretation indicated above can be utilized with discretion. The mystagogue needs to be imbued with the scriptural witness to the faith and competent with the various means of interpretation.

Scripture does not have to be the only dialogue partner with liturgy. The broader experience of the faith community in what we know as tradition can also be used to good purpose. This is not the same as saying we need more dogmatic preaching (cf. 124ff. above), as some are wont to suggest. It does mean, however, that the evolution of the faith through the lived experience of the community and its theological reflection can be brought to bear on the elements of liturgical celebration. The mystagogue needs to be conversant with the broad range of church teaching and lived experience.

The third movement or question that needs exploration is, "What difference does this make in your life at this time and place?" The ultimate purpose of mystagogy is transformation of life in the light of liturgy, Scripture, and tradition, all aimed at building up the reign of God. The community needs to hear that Christian belonging as accomplished through the initiation sacraments also leads to Christian behavior inside and outside of liturgical spaces. As sacramental theologian Louis-Marie Chauvet (b. 1942) argues, Christian life must be balanced on the three pillars of Scripture, liturgy, and ethics (Chauvet 2001). Here, the mystagogue must be contextually competent, knowing the strengths and weaknesses of the contemporary context and situation. She or he must be able to "name grace" as it appears

143

in our world and to call out prophetically for Christian witness in a world that is also marred by evil and the perceived absence of God.

To enact mystagogy effectively, the mystagogue must know the community well. The liturgical assembly is never a generic group but a particular embodiment of the faith community in a given time and place. It has its own strengths and weaknesses, and the mystagogue must discern where the community needs to grow and where it can celebrate its grace. Beneath all these suggestions lies the belief that mystagogical preaching is a work of the Spirit. The conviction that the church has been given all the gifts and ministries it needs suggests that all the mystagogical preachers of the community, lay or ordained, are empowered by the Spirit to build up the faith of the community and enhance its transformation in Christ.

Bibliography

Chauvet, Louis-Marie. *The Sacraments: The Word of God at the Mercy of the Body*. Collegeville, MN: Liturgical Press, 2001.

Chriszt, Dennis. *Creating an Effective Mystagogy: A Handbook for Catechumenate Leaders*. San Jose, CA: Resource Publications, 2000.

Collins, Mary, and Edward Foley. "Mystagogy: Discerning the Mystery of Faith." In *Commentary on the New Ordo Missae*. Edited by Edward Foley, Mary Collins, John F. Baldovin, and Joanne M. Pierce. Collegeville, MN: Liturgical Press, 2011.

Deferrari, Roy J. *Saint Ambrose: Theological and Dogmatic Works*. Fathers of the Church, vol. 44. Washington, DC: The Catholic University of America Press, 1963.

Finn, Thomas M. *Early Christian Baptism and the Catechumenate*. Vol. 5, *West and East Syria*. Vol. 6, *Italy, North Africa, and Egypt*. Collegeville, MN: Liturgical Press, 1992.

Harmless, William. *Augustine and the Catechumenate*. Revised edition. Collegeville, MN: Liturgical Press, 2014.

Hughes, Kathleen. *Saying Amen: A Mystagogy of the Sacraments*. Chicago: Liturgy Training Publications, 1999.

Mazza, Enrico. *Mystagogy*. New York: Pueblo, 1989.

Rahner, Karl. *Theological Investigations*. Vol. 7, *Further Theology of the Spiritual Life*. Translated by David Bourke. London: Darton, Longman & Todd; New York: Herder and Herder, 1971 [1966].

Regan, David. *Experience the Mystery: Pastoral Possibilities for Christian Mystagogy*. Collegeville, MN: Liturgical Press, 1994.

Riley, H. M. *Christian Initiation: A Comparative Study of the Interpretations of the Baptismal Liturgy in the Mystagogical Writings of Cyril of Jerusalem, John Chrysostom, Theodore of Mopsuestia and Ambrose of Milan.* Washington, DC: The Catholic University of America Press, 1974.

Stephenson, Anthony, trans. *Cyril, Saint Bishop of Jerusalem.* Fathers of the Church, vol. 64. Washington, DC: The Catholic University of America Press, 1970.

Torvend, Samuel. "Preaching the Liturgy: A Social Mystagogy." In *In the Company of Preachers.* Edited by Regina Siegfried and Edward Ruane. Collegeville, MN: Liturgical Press, 1993.

Yarnold, Edward. *The Awe-Inspiring Rites of Initiation: Baptismal Homilies of the Fourth Century.* Collegeville, MN: Liturgical Press, 1970.

Liturgical and Sacramental Preaching

John F. Baldovin

Introduction

A number of years ago, I awoke one morning with a terrible toothache. Of course it was on a Saturday and so I had to seek emergency dental care. The oral surgeon who accommodated me was a very pleasant man. Just as he was about to extract the tooth he asked, "Aren't you the priest who preached at St. Frances Cabrini last Sunday?" I nodded "Yes" and prayed that he had not been turned off, bored, or offended by the homily. The incident was a reminder that there are a number of perils that face the preacher.

This essay is an attempt to reflect on both the perils and the opportunities that attend preaching the sacraments and other devotional and liturgical occasions. My starting point is the presumption that preaching on sacramental or liturgical occasions calls for a very different strategy from preaching a Sunday homily (see 156ff. below). The latter calls (at least ideally) for familiarity with the local assembly and some attempt at what might be called the cumulative effect of preaching. Sacramental occasions are very different in that one can usually presume that the gathered people are for the most part not frequent churchgoers or not Roman Catholics. Admittedly, there are some liturgical events such as eucharistic adoration or "Sunday Celebrations in the Absence of a Priest" that are usually attended by people who go to church more regularly. Nonetheless, most liturgical and sacramental preaching, broadly speaking, differs from the ordinary Sunday homily and from preaching that reflects on the experience of the sacraments, i.e., a form of mystagogical preaching (see 134ff. above).

In this essay I will address a variety of distinctive sacramental or liturgical experiences and describe some of the challenges and opportunities for each.

Baptism

After the reading, the celebrant gives a short homily, explaining to those present the significance of what has been read. His purpose will be to lead

146

them to a deeper understanding of the mystery of baptism and to encourage the parents and godparents to a ready acceptance of the responsibilities which arise from the sacrament. (ICEL 1976, 200 no. 45)

Baptism is a joyous and festive occasion. In the case of infants it can be as much a celebration of birth, new life, and hope for a family as it is a celebration of the Paschal Mystery. Although a certain minimum profession of faith and assurance that the child will be raised a Christian is expected, it is often enough the case that the celebration of a baptism will be a rare occasion of church attendance for the parents and for many relatives and friends. The preacher needs to keep this in mind, not in order to scold or embarrass, but to take advantage of this evangelical opportunity to explain the significance of this beginning of new life in Christ. Thus the preacher can take this opportunity to invite parents, godparents, relatives, and friends to renew their Christian commitment.

In the case of infants I have sometimes written a letter to the child, expressing the importance of baptism. I try to emphasize what a special day this is and how much we hope that he or she will grow to become a good Christian. Of course the immediate recipients are the parents, relatives, and friends, but I also give the parents a copy so that they might share it at an appropriate time in the future with the child.

The unprepared preacher can easily fall into gaffes like praising the glory of some abstract ideal family life without recognizing perhaps that a single parent is presenting the child or that one of the parents is not a Roman Catholic. Even when there are a number of children to be baptized a well-prepared priest or deacon should be able to be sensitive to the diversity of family situations represented.

Preaching at the initiation of adults and children—if of catechetical age this will include confirmation and first Eucharist—will normally be done in the context of the Easter Vigil. The vigil is rich in material for preaching, but certainly the candidates for sacramental initiation need to find a significant place in the homily. They are, as Aidan Kavanagh (d. 2006) used to put it, "living icons of the Risen Christ."

Confirmation

The Bishop then gives a brief homily, by which, shedding light on the readings, he leads, as if by hand, those to be confirmed, their sponsors and parents, and the whole gathering of the faithful to a deeper understanding of the mystery of Confirmation. (ICEL 2013, no. 22)

Confirmation, along with ordinations and the institution of readers and acolytes, is an occasion where a sample homily is provided in the rite itself. The homily explains the gift of the Holy Spirit and the connection between confirmation and baptism in rather abstract terms. It accounts for the fact that bishops are the ordinary ministers of the sacrament but that presbyters may be deputed to celebrate it as well, i.e., in the case of the initiation of adults and children of catechetical age.

The sample homily might be used as a source for preaching at confirmations but surely the age, cultural context (see 233ff. below), and concrete situation of the confirmands need to be taken into account. In any case, the connection between baptism and confirmation—for so long underemphasized in practice—should be stressed. The preacher should avoid the temptation to employ overblown rhetoric in this celebration. There is a delicate balance between preaching this renewed gift of the Spirit and the actual situation in which confirmation might mark some ending (e.g., of religious education) as much as a further step in Christian initiation. The preacher should be aware that theologically it would be problematic to consider confirmation the "culmination" of Christian initiation, since that culmination obviously takes place in one's incorporation into Christ in the Eucharist.

As some dioceses restore the traditional order of initiation—baptism, confirmation, first communion—the preacher will find an excellent opportunity to link confirmation to its "completion" in the celebration of the Eucharist.

Penance

The post–Vatican II provision of two communal rites for the sacrament of penance as well as nonsacramental penance services has given ample opportunity for preaching about sin, forgiveness, penance, and reconciliation. Communal celebrations of penance with individual confession have tended to draw a good number of people to the sacrament.

In situations like these the preacher needs to be aware of the variety of people seeking penance. There are those who frequently take advantage of the sacrament and may be striving to advance in holiness more than to repent of serious sins. There are those who need to confess serious sins. Finally, there are those who have been alienated from the church for one reason or another and need to be welcomed back with open arms.

In my experience, preachers have too often so emphasized God's mercy and love—something essential to be sure—that they have failed to address sin in any serious way. The challenge of preaching penance, which needs to be addressed in Sunday homilies as well, is: (1) to acknowledge the seriousness of sin and our need of forgiveness, (2) to put this in the context of God's mercy, and (3) to do so in such a way that the variety of penitents present can hear the Word of God in such a way as to be able to recognize their own sinfulness and bring their need for healing to God through the ministers of the church.

In an analogous way this kind of invitation also occurs in the first form of the rite of penance designed for individual reconciliation, but the "preaching" in that case is much briefer and more informal.

Anointing of the Sick

This sacrament may be the one with most "growth potential" for the church. The reaction of people who come to communal services of anointing is telling. When given the invitation—although this is admittedly beyond the purview of what the church officially requires for recipients of the sacrament—the vast number of people in the assembly will come forward for healing. This should tell us something about people's need for experiences of healing.

As with the celebration of the first form of sacramental penance for individual reconciliation, the anointing of an individual—for example, before surgery—provides an opportunity for the preacher to address the situation of the sick person briefly in light of the Paschal Mystery and to give the person (ideally along with some family and friends and even health-care staff) comfort and courage in face of an ambiguous future. Of course, the anointing of an individual can also take place in the context of the celebration of the Eucharist, in which case the same strategy might apply but this time at greater length and with a more diverse assembly in mind.

Preaching at a communal anointing is an opportunity and challenge to speak more broadly of human illness and physical and mental suffering in light of the Gospel. The preacher might also want to point out the ministry that the sick persons offer to the community by witnessing faith in the midst of adversity as well as reminding the rest of us of our human frailty.

As with all preaching, preaching for the anointing of the sick should leave the sick persons and the assembly as a whole with a more confident hope in the God of life. As a friend once remarked: "If you cannot interpret everything with hope, then you have no right to call yourself a Christian."

Holy Orders and Ministries

The rites for the ordination of bishops, presbyters (priests), and deacons all prescribe the ordaining bishop as the preacher. Each rite contains a sample homily that the bishops may deliver or adapt. He may also choose to create a homily of his own. This is in contrast to the Church of England, for example, where the person who has given the ordination retreat (at least for deacon and priest candidates) gives the ordination homily. One wonders what it would be like if the Roman Catholic Church provided the option for someone in the order into which the candidate(s) was to be ordained to give the ordination homily.

In any case, we can express the hope that ordination homilies, in addition to exhorting the candidates to fulfill the office they are about to receive and to instructing the assembly about the nature and importance of the order in which candidates are being initiated, might contextualize the ordained ministry in its service to the whole church. After all the *Catechism of the Catholic Church* calls both holy orders and matrimony "Sacraments in Service of the Church's Communion" (CCC, II, ii, 3; cf. CCC, no. 1534). This concern is particularly pertinent in the case of the sample homily given for the ordination of presbyters that is addressed solely to the candidates.

The bishop is also expected to preach at admission to candidacy for holy orders and the installation of readers and acolytes. On the other hand, priests or deacons may preach at the blessing of various parochial ministries, e.g., readers, ministers of communion, and those exercising pastor service. In this case the following directive is given when the blessing takes place at the celebration of the Eucharist: "After the gospel reading, the celebrant in the homily, based on the sacred text and pertinent to the particular place and the people involved, explains the meaning of the celebration" (*Book of Blessings* 1989, no. 1811). In the case of such blessings outside of the Eucharist the following instruction is provided: "As circumstances suggest, the minister may give those present a brief explanation of the biblical text, so that they may understand through faith the meaning of the celebration" (*Book of Blessings* 1989, no. 1821).

Religious Profession and Consecration to Virginity

The rites foresee a number of different situations in which religious profession can occur. In the case of initiation into religious life—whether for women or for men—the preacher is presumed to be the superior of the particular religious congregation. In the case of men, for example, the rite provides the following instruction: "the superior addresses the religious community and the postulants on the meaning of the religious life and the spirit of the institute, or he reads the appropriate chapter of the rule" (*Rite of Religious Profession* 1989, no. 11).

On the other hand, rites for the profession of vows—either temporary or perpetual—are required to take place during the Eucharist. For the profession of perpetual vows for women the following is prescribed: "Those to be professed then sit and listen to the homily or address which should develop the scriptural readings and the theme of religious profession as God's gift and call for the sanctification of those chosen and for the good of the Church and the whole human family" (*Rite of Religious Profession* 1989, no. 56).

Although not foreseen by the rites, one wonders if in the case of women religious or religious brothers the profession itself might take place outside of the context of the Eucharist so that the superior might be able to preach. This would certainly be appropriate in light of the fact that these candidates are being initiated into a particular institute with its own specific charisms and place in the wider church. Such a liturgy might then be followed by the celebration of the Eucharist, or celebrated in the context of the Liturgy of the Hours. In any case, the instruction quoted above seems rather narrow in that it fails to recognize the importance not only of religious life in general but also of religious life within a particular institute. Clearly one size does not fit all. In addition, when preaching from the biblical text and the liturgical rite, preachers must be aware that the Rite of Profession for women religious focuses on "consecration" because the profession prayer for women is taken from the Consecration of Virgins liturgy. That for male religious, on the other hand, focuses on ministry and apostolic work. For women religious with an apostolic charism, this distinction raises significant issues.

In the case of the Consecration to a Life of Virginity for Women Living in the World, the Eucharistic Liturgy is presided over by a bishop. Just as with the rites of ordination, a sample homily is provided. This homily addresses both the people assembled and those who are about to be consecrated and broaches a number of themes, like the church as Christ's Bride and spiritual motherhood. As in the case of ordinations, however, simply to deliver the written homily is certainly a missed opportunity to open up God's Word in light of the present situation and the persons who are actually being consecrated.

Weddings

After the reading of the Gospel, the Priest in the Homily uses the sacred text to expound the mystery of Christian Marriage, the dignity of conjugal love, the grace of the Sacrament, and the responsibilities of married people, keeping in mind, however, the various circumstances of individuals. (ICEL 2013, no. 57)

In this essay I have saved the most challenging liturgies (weddings and funerals) for last. They are challenging because frequently the assembly will consist of Roman Catholics who do not regularly participate in liturgies or have an inadequate grasp of the church's understanding of Christian marriage; or they are challenging because of the presence of participants who are not Roman Catholics, or who have no religious affiliation at all. The official introduction to the rite explicitly addresses this concern:

> Although pastors are ministers of Christ's Gospel for all, they should, nonetheless, direct special attention to those, whether Catholics or non-Catholics, who never or rarely take part in the celebration of Marriage or the Eucharist. This pastoral norm applies in the first place to the spouses themselves. (ICEL 2013, no. 37)

Many of those attending a Roman Catholic wedding are doing so out of courtesy or a sense of obligation. They will have little idea why a Roman Catholic wedding takes place in a church, much less what it means to call marriage a sacrament. Addressing these issues as well as the Scriptures and the circumstances of this particular wedding while being sensitive to the variety of people in the assembly—e.g., the widowed, divorced, those who will never marry for one reason or another—is quite a tall order.

When preparing a couple for marriage, I normally ask each of them to send me a letter (without consulting the other), addressing the following: background, education, employment, history of the relationship, hopes and plans for the future, and any "gaffe alerts" of which I need to be aware. I am usually delighted with their responses, which are invaluable in helping me craft a homily that can speak to them and their families as well as put the wedding in the context of the church's understanding of Christian marriage. I am particularly aware of the need for all to understand that the sacrament may be initiated by the wedding ceremony but that the sacrament itself is the reality of their married love that witnesses God's love and fidelity. This is similar to the sacrament of holy orders, which is initiated by ordination but consists in the bishop's, priest's, or deacon's ministry and life.

While not the place for an extended treatment of this subject, preachers need to be aware that the seven official sacraments of the church bear analogous meanings. We have not been well served by a view that "one receives a sacrament." That attitude grew out of a gradual reification or objectification of the sacraments that many scholars attribute to the Germanization of Christianity in the Early Middle Ages. Recent sacramental theology has tried to recognize sacraments more as activities than as things, better understood as verbs than as nouns. After all, the reality of living the Christian faith is usually a lot messier than the neat definitions we tend to give to aspects of the faith like sacraments.

I have been stressing the challenges involved in preaching at weddings, but it is also important to note that these occasions provide an excellent opportunity for evangelization (see 105ff. above). If the preacher can manage to get the attention of those who may not ordinarily be eager to listen to the Christian message, this may be an ideal time to get them to ask themselves whether there is something to Christian faith after all. One should not, however, underestimate the challenge of overcoming the all-too-popular image that many have of Christianity as merely a series of prohibitions rather than the encounter with the living God made manifest in Jesus Christ. Clearly the church has not been well served by this image but often enough we have only ourselves to blame. Consequently, the preacher would do well to steer clear of issues like the frequent breakup of marriages or communion for the divorced and remarried. Likewise those who are tempted to emphasize Roman Catholic restrictions on those eligible for eucharistic communion would do well to rethink their strategy.

Finally, while this may be the umpteenth wedding homily that the preacher has given, it will be the only one that *this* couple will hear on their wedding day, and so while the preacher could easily be fatigued, he yet needs to make an effort to honor this special occasion. Despite the stress that often accompanies weddings, they can be truly joyous celebrations; it would be ideal if the wedding liturgy could be experienced as joyous as the prandial feast that follows.

Funerals and Vigil Services

A brief homily based on the readings is always given after the gospel reading at the funeral liturgy and may also be given after the readings at the vigil service, but there is never to be a eulogy. Attentive to the grief of those present, the homilist should dwell on God's compassionate love and on the paschal mystery of the Lord, as proclaimed in the Scripture readings. The homilist should also help the members of the assembly to understand that the mystery of God's love and the mystery of Jesus' victorious death and resurrection were present in the life and death of the deceased and that these mysteries are active in their own lives as well. Through the homily members of the family and community should receive consolation and strength to face the death of one of their members with a hope nourished by the saving word of God. Laypersons who preside at the funeral rites give an instruction on the readings." (Order of Christian Funerals 1985, no. 27; cf. no. 141)

This description of the funeral homily is about twice as long as the one found in the General Instruction of the Roman Missal (*IGMR2002*, no. 65), although not as long and detailed as the one found in the Introduction to the Lectionary for Mass (*OLM1981-Pr*, no. 24). I have deliberately quoted it in full since—at least in my experience—many homilists at funerals do not seem to have consulted it. In terms of the Funeral Mass or Vigil at which such a homily is given, it should be noted that the Roman Catholic approach to death has changed considerably with the new rites. One need only consider the elimination of the famous sequence *Dies Irae* (Lat. for "Day of Wrath") to understand that a theology that focused on the (dire) fate of the deceased has shifted to paschal hope and the consolation of the mourners. This shift can easily be discerned in the various Eucharistic Prefaces for the Dead.

Given this shift in theology and spirituality it is perhaps not terribly surprising that preachers veer in the direction of eulogizing the deceased. There is great pressure to turn the funeral in general into a memorial service, but this is clearly not the intent of the official introduction to the rite. The preacher needs to find a way to shed light on the Christian meaning of death and resurrection in the light of God's compassion and the Paschal Mystery. At the same time, of course, it is *this* particular individual whose funeral is being celebrated. Unsurprisingly, this is not such an easy task.

Several other considerations need to be mentioned with regard to the funeral or vigil homily. There is a common tendency to canonize the deceased long before the church has considered any process of "raising him or her to the altars." No matter how admirable an individual might be, we are all sinners in need of God's mercy. The preacher need not dwell extensively on sin, but simply praising the deceased for a devout life is unrealistic. Besides, what does one do when the deceased was clearly a flawed or difficult individual?

Few if any of us really know what to say in the face of death, especially when it is tragic, like the death of a child. It is all the more important, then, to avoid saying things that are well intentioned and meant to be consoling, but theologically questionable, like "God must have wanted another angel in heaven." People say all manner of things in the face of death, but it is particularly unhelpful for the preacher to add comments that make little sense in terms of Christian faith. I have found that sometimes the use of alliteration can work. At the funeral of a nineteen-year-old woman who had committed suicide, I did my best to situate the funeral homily in the context of Christian faith and our confidence in a compassionate God, but I also needed to address the tragic situation directly. Luckily I knew her and the family well and so was able to speak of her as talented, troubled, and treasured—all of which she was.

Lastly, it bears repeating that funerals—like so many other sacramental and liturgical celebrations—are an important evangelical opportunity. One can assume that many in the assembly will be nonpracticing Roman Catholics, Christians from other churches, people of other faiths, or unbelievers. Since the Paschal Mystery is at the heart of the Christian faith, a funeral or vigil service, including the brief remarks at the committal (*Order of Christian Funerals* 1985, nos. 217 and 311), are moments that have profound potential for inviting people to deeper faith or even to faith at all. Needless to say, poor preaching at funerals or the tired repetition of clichés should be avoided; such can even be a hindrance to evangelization.

Conclusion

Little has been said above about cultural and contextual considerations for such preaching, though such are essential: as Bevans notes below (see 233ff.), all preaching is contextual. For example, the official introductions to many of these rites sometimes note that a "brief" homily is to be given, but there are contexts in which a brief homily could be considered at least inappropriate if not insulting. Recently I attended a diaconate ordination for ten men which lasted for two hours. An African confrere commented afterward that the liturgy was at least half as short as it should have been!

All the liturgical services surveyed in this essay are powerful opportunities for sharing and deepening Christian faith, and for leading to that profound and ongoing conversion that is to be expected of all Christians.

Bibliography

Book of Blessings. New York: Catholic Book Publishing Co., 1989.

ICEL. *The Rites of the Catholic Church*. New York: Pueblo, 1976.

Order of Christian Funerals. Washington, DC: ICEL, 1985.

Rite of Religious Profession. Washington, DC: United States Catholic Conference, 1989.

The Homily

Edward Foley

Introduction

The homily is a revered form of preaching in the Christian tradition; one testimony to that fact is the number of times the genre is referenced throughout this volume. As highlighted in the historical essays in part two of this work, however, the term has been variously employed to designate a wide array of preaching forms rendered in different contexts and for different purposes. As is so often the case, the form of a ritual in one epoch or provenance of Christianity does not necessarily correspond to contemporary usage, even though an identical designation is employed. Even today there is wide-ranging opinion about the nature of the homily among Christian preachers: something that marks the discussion within Roman Catholicism as well.

Without repeating the fine historical work already set forth here by my colleagues, it seems useful to summarize something of the complex history of this term and the types of preaching it has referenced throughout Christianity. After this brief historical recap, we will then consider some of the ways contemporary commentators and documents define the homily. This will allow us to propose basic characteristics of the homily, especially as it is defined within Roman Catholicism today, with its many official and canonical prescriptions about this form of preaching. We will also consider the underlying theologies of these characteristics as a way to underscore that the homily is not only a rhetorical exercise but also an enacted form of public theology.

An Historical Review

The Greek word *homilia* only occurs once in the New Testament (1 Cor 15:33), where it means companionship or communication. As Alden Bass notes, the New Testament does not give us many instances of ritual preaching within a worshiping congregation—the combination that will become central to the definition of a homily in succeeding centuries. By the third century, however, the regular occurrence of preaching with established worshiping communities was often designated as a homily (see 53 above). Origen (d. 253–254) is sometimes deputed to be "the father of the Christian homily."

It is by the fourth century that the homiletic act, parallel to that which reemerged after Vatican II, developed its fundamental characteristics. As classically described by Jean Leclercq (d. 1993), the ancient homily could be characterized as "an informal conversation between a pastor of souls and the people entrusted to his care, during a liturgical event, on a biblical text suggested by the liturgy" (Leclercq 1946, 30). He further summarizes that the congregation was composed of largely uneducated believers who needed to be led into a deeper understanding of their faith.

Bass has previously noted that the temptation to rhetorical pretentiousness sometimes jeopardized the conversational style and pastoral purpose of the homily (55–56 above), although key figures such as Augustine of Hippo (d. 430) and Leo the Great (d. 461) maintained the integrity of the genre. The death of Gregory the Great (d. 604) is commonly cited as the end of the patristic period in the West. It may also be employed as a marker for not only the decline of preaching in the West but also the gradual disappearance of the homily from the liturgical event. Thus, the early eighth-century description of the papal Mass (*Ordo Romanus I*) has no indication of preaching after the gospel. On the other hand, the baptismal rite described in *Ordo Romanus XI* does indicate that the deacon preached a homily after the gospel.

The homily largely continued to survive within Western Eucharistic Liturgies through collections of patristic preaching known as homilaries (traditionally addressing the Scriptures, especially the gospel of the day) or sermonaries (ordinarily explaining the sense of the celebration or liturgical season [Martimort 1992, 80]). These were employed by priests and bishops who no longer felt theologically prepared to preach, as well as by deacons who might read a homily if the priest was infirm (Council of Vaison in 529, c. 2). The pastoral efficacy of such texts, however, is questionable, given their "already antiquated theological language" (Grégoire 1992, 1:394).

The Middle Ages was the period in which the homily as an integral act of the liturgy cedes to the topical sermon, functioning as a kind of instructional pause in the middle of the Eucharist. While there was a style of preaching that drew upon biblical texts, this sophisticated form of sermonizing offered a systematic reflection on the text according to some scholastic method and was very distant from the lives of ordinary believers (Join-Lambert 2004, 69). A second type of preaching in a more popular style was more prevalent, but it was not intimately linked to Scripture or the liturgy, as symbolized by the preacher actually leaving the sanctuary to ascend a pulpit in the nave. Eventually this vernacular parenthesis in the Latin liturgy evolved into the "prone" that included announcements, bidding prayers, and various devotional texts. The liturgical disconnection of this type of preaching is underscored by the frequency with which it was moved to before or after Mass. Thus, while shocking, it is not surprising that the Tridentine Roman Missal (1570) makes no mention of preaching in its Order of Mass. While the language of "homily" does surface throughout the ensuing centuries, it seldom if ever reflects a style of preaching intimately connected to the liturgy and its readings. Thus, *The Books of Homilies* (1547)—while heavily referencing Scripture—basically contains instructions on the reformed doctrines of the Church of England.

The genre begins to reappear in the early twentieth century, e.g., a "Christmas Homily" by the US liturgical pioneer Virgil Michel (d. 1938), replete with references to various liturgical texts of the day (Michel 1928). The genre was increasingly revitalized in the years before Vatican II (1962–1965) in the scholarship of people like Jean Leclercq (1946) and Cipriano Vagaggini (1956, 683–84). More practically, in the years leading up to the council the liturgical journal *Worship* began publishing a series of "homily outlines" deeply rooted in the official worship of the Roman Catholic Church (Kittleson 1961, 41–45).

For Roman Catholics and many other Christians, it was Vatican II's *Sacrosanctum Concilium* (*SC*) that both revived and renewed this ancient mode of preaching. Central was its teaching:

> By means of the homily, the mysteries of the faith and the guiding principles of the Christian life are expounded from the sacred text during the course of the liturgical year. The homily is strongly recommended since it forms part of the liturgy itself. In fact, at those Masses which are celebrated on Sundays and holydays of obligation, with the people assisting, it should not be omitted except for serious reason. (*SC*, no. 52)

Defining the Contemporary Homily

While Vatican II revived the homily for a renewed liturgy, it did not simultaneously end the definitional process, and our understanding of the homily has continued to evolve. While pivotal for resurrecting this form, *SC* also introduces some difficulties when it indicates that the purpose of the homily is to explain the readings (*SC*, no. 24), suggesting a somewhat didactic role of the homily and almost exclusively linking it to the Scriptures. On the other hand, in an often underexamined text, *SC* expands our understanding when noting that "by means of the homily, the mysteries of the faith and the guiding principles of the Christian life are expounded from the sacred text during the course of the liturgical year" (*SC*, no. 52). While at first glance "sacred text" could appear to be a synonym for Scripture, the Vatican's first instruction "on the orderly carrying out of the Constitution on the Liturgy" (*Inter Oecumenici* [*IO*]) teaches otherwise, noting that "a homily on the sacred text means an explanation, pertinent to the mystery celebrated and the special needs of the listeners, of some point in either the readings from sacred Scripture or in another text from the Order or Prayer of the day's Mass" (*IO*, no. 54). The current code of canon law (*CIC*) is similar, though it happily avoids the problematic language of "explanation," noting that the homily "is a part of the liturgy itself . . . in the homily the mysteries of faith and the norms of Christian living are to be expounded from the sacred text through the course of the liturgical year" (*CIC*, c. 767 § 1). What all of these documents make clear is that a homily, properly speaking, can only be offered by an ordained cleric. While documents often refer to the homily as restricted to priests and deacons, it is first and foremost within the purview of bishops to offer homilies.

Few instructions on the homily have been more influential in English-speaking North America than the 1982 publication *Fulfilled in Your Hearing* (FIYH). This landmark text, widely employed in training preachers in the United States, makes multiple contributions: its emphasis on the need for preachers to listen to and engage people's experiences in preparing to preach (FIYH, nos. 4, 12, 18, 21, etc.); its essential understanding of the homily as an interpretive act for the sake of people's lived experience (FIYH, nos. 13, 44–46, 69 and 81); its strong emphasis on engagement with the Scriptures both in the preparation for preaching and the homiletic act itself (FIYH, nos. 25–30); the emphasis on the integral relationship of the homily to the liturgy (FIYH, no. 61); and its proposal of a method of homily preparation (FIYH, nos. 78–101), including its unique emphasis on creating a homily preparation group involving members of the congregation (FIYH, nos. 106–8).

When it comes to defining the homily, however, FIYH does not seem to embrace the renewed homiletic image emerging from *SC* but seems to reiterate a patristic homiletic model with Scripture as its sole core. It defines the homily as a "scriptural interpretation of human existence which enables the community to recognize God's active presence, to respond to that presence in faith through liturgical word and gesture, and beyond the liturgical assembly, through a life lived in conformity with the Gospel" (FIYH, no. 81). This definition does not share the broadened vision of "sacred texts" articulated by *SC* and ensuing documents. In particular, FIYH does not take the broader liturgical action as a source for the homily. This is something the US Roman Catholic Bishops do in an expansive way, even beyond the vision of *IO*, noting: "By means of the homily, the mysteries of the faith and the guiding principles of Christian living are expounded, most often from the Scriptures proclaimed but also from the other texts *and rites of the liturgy*" (emphasis added, Bishops' Committee on the Liturgy 2003, no. 92). FIYH is more one-sided, as capsulized in its statement: "Just as a homily flows out of the Scriptures of the liturgy of the Word, so it should flow into the prayers and actions of the liturgy of the eucharist which follows" (FIYH, no. 100). It never recognizes that the homily flows out of the Eucharistic Liturgy as well.

In the decades following FIYH, various authors and sources gave more or less emphasis to the roles of Scripture and the liturgy as homiletic resources. Presbyterian Donald Stake (b. 1935) notes that "Roman Catholics generally use this term [homily] for sermon, while Protestants opt for the word 'sermon.' The two words mean the same thing, namely, the proclamation of the Word" (Stake 1992, 93). Roman Catholic Kevin Irwin (b. 1946) seems to agree when he notes that "the homily is an interpretation of the Scriptures in order that their anamnetic character can be unleashed in contemporary ecclesial settings" (Irwin 1994, 13). Episcopal scholar Charles L. Rice (b. 1936), however, balances the scriptural with the liturgical when describing the homily as "a comment on the connection of one or more of the texts to the liturgical occasion [rendering it] 'liturgy-friendly.' " He concludes that the homily "must rely on the liturgical occasion for its power" (Rice 1991, 86).

The Roman Catholic bishops in the United States issued a follow-up document to FIYH in 2013, *Preaching the Mystery of Faith* (PTMOF). While the document emphasizes that the homily is integral to the liturgical event (PTMOF, no. 17), in the spirit of FIYH it plays down the role of the liturgy as a source of the homily, noting that the Lectionary readings are "the prime source of the homily" (PTMOF, no. 18). It reduces the other "sacred texts" to possible illustrations of the biblical text. In this regard, it also seems to put the liturgical texts on the same level as the *Catechism of the Catholic Church* or other church documents (PTMOF, no. 18), which seems to undercut the liturgy as *theologia prima* (Lat. for "first theology").

Another subtle shift in the definition of the homily in PTMOF is its increasingly exclusive definition as an element of the Eucharist, and not other liturgies of the Roman Catholic Church. If one reviews the revised sacramental rites after Vatican II, the designation "homily" is not restricted to preaching at the Eucharist. For example, a homily is prescribed as the form of preaching that occurs in the "Rite for Celebrating Marriage Outside Mass" (no. 42). The "Rite of Baptism for Children," primarily designed as a ritual occurring outside of Eucharist, similarly notes that after the reading, the presider offers "a short homily" (no. 45). The General Instruction of the Liturgy of the Hours notes that at morning and evening prayer, in celebrations with congregations, a short homily may follow the reading (no. 47). Even the "Rite of Eucharistic Exposition and Benediction" notes that during the exposition of the sacrament, there should be scriptural readings "with a homily or brief exhortations" (no. 95). As canonist Patrick Lagges has insightfully noted, contemporary documents of the Roman Catholic Church increasingly narrow the definition of the homily to a type of preaching that occurs only in the Eucharist (271 below). This narrowing was, in some ways, heralded by FIYH that only considered the homily in the Sunday's eucharistic assembly.

In view of these developments and the apparent pendulum swings between emphasizing the homiletic act as more a scriptural interpretation or considering it as having its foundations in the liturgical event, this author defines the homily as:

> [A] ritual conversation between God and the liturgical assembly, that announces God's reign as revealed in Jesus Christ through the mediation of a preacher, who offers a credible and imaginative interpretation for Christian living, in dialogue with the lives of the faithful, that draws upon the whole of the liturgy—especially the lectionary texts—in the context of a particular community at a prescribed moment of their shared life.

Characteristics of a Homily

While each homily is a unique occurrence, one can generalize that there are basic characteristics of a homily from a Roman Catholic perspective. Because of the extensive official teaching and law defining the homily for Roman Catholics, these characteristics may or may not translate well into other Christian traditions.

The Homily Is a Liturgical Act

To suggest that the first and central characteristic of a homily is that it is liturgical may appear to be stating the obvious. On the other hand, there have been periods in the history recounted above when the preaching *in* the liturgy was not *of* the liturgy and appeared as a pause or parenthesis especially in the Eucharist. The homily, however, is not only in but essentially of the liturgy, which means that such preaching itself is a liturgical event. There are multiple practical and theological consequences of this assertion. From a practical perspective, an authentic homily needs to be in dialogue with the whole of the liturgical context. Besides the Lectionary, which we will consider below, that includes the primary texts, ritual actions, and theologies of a given liturgy. This homilizing is inherently mystagogical (see 134ff. above). Homilizing at weddings, for example, needs to take into account not only the chosen readings for the day but also the exchange of vows and rings and the underlying theologies of those actions that recognize that the couple are the ministers of the sacrament to each other.

Recognizing the homily as an integral liturgical element also theologically underscores that it is not simply a communication between the preacher and an audience. *SC* clearly teaches that liturgy is an action of Christ, head and members (*SC*, no. 7). Thus the homily as well must be an encounter between Christ and the faithful. Members of the assembly are not the objects of such preaching, but subjects of the homiletic event with Christ, just as they are subjects of the whole of the liturgy with Christ. Pope Francis (b. 1936) underscores this point in *Evangelii Gaudium* when he speaks about the dialogue between God and God's people and recognizes that the homily requires an "intermediary" (*EG*, no. 143) to enable this dialogue.

The Homily Is Rooted in the Lectionary

As noted by Dianne Bergant (116f. above), there are multiple forms of biblical preaching. The homily is a particular genre of liturgical preaching that is not simply biblical or scriptural, but rooted in the Lectionary. As Bergant and Fragomeni have noted elsewhere,

> The Lectionary is a unique genre of ecclesial literature. It is part of the liturgical canon. . . . The Lectionary, while not identical to the Bible, is drawn from its contents, providing a kind of narrative infrastructure for celebration of the Liturgical Year. The Lectionary is drawn from sacred Scripture by selecting passages from the biblical material (decontextualizing) and then places these readings within a new literary and liturgical context (recontextualizing), thus creating a new ecclesial genre. This recontextualization of former biblical material calls for a new way of interpretation, one that takes into consideration the liturgical character and setting of the Lectionary readings. (Bergant and Fragomeni 2001, vii)

It is the juxtaposition of the three readings along with the psalm in the liturgical context that gives the homily its particular dynamic. The interplay of a first reading, chosen to echo some central thematic of the gospel reading, adjacent to a semicontinuous second reading and a recrafted responsorial psalm can be daunting but also energizes the homiletic event. Those who choose to employ a narrative lectionary, with its four-year cycle of readings of a single biblical text from the Old or New Testament, as well as those who select their own text for preaching would not be engaging in homilizing from the perspective of this lectionary principle.

It is notable that the selection of texts for the Roman Catholic Lectionary—and the Common Lectionary that was modeled on it—are largely determined by the cycle of the liturgical year and the intersecting sanctoral cycle. Fritz West calls this "the Catholic Principle," or a practice in which the season and celebration set the texts of the readings. On the other hand, when texts are employed to determine the season or celebration, West deems this the "Protestant Principle" (West 1997, 47–52). Thus, the very structure of the Lectionary is saturated with nonbiblical elements such as the nature and rhythms of the liturgical year and reiterates the primary characteristic noted above, that the homily is a liturgical act.

The Homily Is a Rhetorical Event

Just as the liturgy is not a book or text but an experience, so the homily is not merely words on a page but an event. While a prepared text is ordinarily helpful in this form of preaching, properly speaking the homily is not the text but a rhetorical performance. As Lucy Lind Hogan explains, rhetoric is the "planned and strategic use of symbols, language and discourse . . . to influence and persuade" (200 below). Since liturgy is an action that Christ does (Head and members) then the rhetorical task here is not primarily to persuade the assembly to agree with the preacher but to persuade them to encounter Christ in both the liturgy of the church and, just as important, in what Karl Rahner (d. 1984) called the liturgy of the world.

While a homily can be instructional, it is not fundamentally a catechetical act, biblical exegesis, or a way to supply the assembly with a set of injunctions that they should observe in their lives. Rather, like the New Testament parables, it is intended to be an engaging conversation requiring the active participation of the hearers so that they might experience the surprising revelation of God's reign in their own lives. Because the homily is persuading people into encountering Christ—into loving God, other, and self as Jesus modeled in his earthly ministry—there is a clear place for poetic, lyrical, and nondiscursive language in the homily. Reminiscent of ancient preaching from the East that wed poetry together with theology (see 57 above), today's reimagined homily is more about moving hearts than informing intellects. Jesus consistently achieved this through his parables, and storytelling in parabolic mode is a particularly apt mode for homilizing. In *EG* Pope Francis notes that "proclaiming Christ means showing that to believe in and to follow him is not only something right and true, but also something beautiful, capable of filling life with new splendor and profound joy, even in the midst of difficulties" (*EG*, no. 167). While employing the idioms and speech of the local community, the homily is yet an art form that is to reflect the very beauty of God.

The Homily Is an Act of Public Theology

While clearly an ecclesial event, intended to help enable a life-giving encounter between Jesus Christ and the baptized, in this digital age of growing religious pluriformity and disaffection, it seems appropriate to consider the homily in a more centrifugal mode as also an act of public theology. Public theology as envisioned by Christian theologians at the end of the twentieth century is not designed to win converts to a particular church or bolster the public standing of some denomination (see 180ff. below). Rather, as Duncan Forrester opines, public theology is a kind of theological speech,

> which claims to point to publicly accessible truth [and] to contribute to public discussion by witnessing to a truth [that] is relevant to what is going on in the world and to the pressing issues facing peoples and societies today. . . . It offers convictions, challenges and insights derived from the tradition. . . . Public theology is thus confessional and evangelical. It has a gospel to share, good news to proclaim. Public theology attends to the Bible and the tradition of faith at the same time as it attempts to discern the signs of the times and understand what is going on in the light of the gospel. (Forrester 2001, 129–30)

This is a nuanced attempt to recalibrate the homily as more than "insider speech" and recover something of its missiological and evangelizing trajectory. Such seems important in this era when the number of disaffected Roman Catholics, religiously unaffiliated and those who identify as agnostics is growing at a rapid rate. Whether they are guests at some wedding, funeral, or other liturgical event, or they happen to run across digital snippets of a homily delivered by a visiting pope or other prominent cleric, the homily as public theology presumes that the church can contribute to the common good; it embodies the conviction that we have something of value to say even to those who do not align themselves with our faith tradition. Converting these "overhearers" of the Word to our way of believing is not the goal. Rather, it is engaging them as what Pope Francis called "precious allies" in broader societal commitments "to defending human dignity, in building peaceful coexistence between peoples and in protecting creation" (*EG*, no. 257).

Conclusion

The style, purpose, and content of the homily has undergone many variations over the centuries. This evolution will undoubtedly continue. At the same time, at least for Roman Catholics, the magisterial teaching and pastoral instincts of Vatican II have irrevocably revitalized and renewed this ancient form, planting it dead center in the middle of liturgical worship. In some ways it could be considered the crown jewel of Roman Catholic preaching, an art form to be studied, nurtured, and practiced with great humility and reverence.

Bibliography

Bergant, Dianne, with Richard Fragomeni. *Preaching the New Lectionary*. Vol. 1, *Year A*. Collegeville, MN: Liturgical Press, 2001.

Bishops' Committee on the Liturgy. *Introduction to the Order of Mass*. Washington, DC: United States Conference of Catholic Bishops, 2003.

Grégoire, Réginald. "Homily." In *Encyclopedia of the Early Church*. Edited by Angelo di Berardino. New York: Oxford University Press, 1992.

Irwin, Kevin. *Context and Text: Method in Liturgical Theology*. Collegeville, MN: Liturgical Press, 1994.

Join-Lambert, Arnaud. "Du sermon à l'homélie. Nouvelles questions théologiques et pastorals." *Novelle Revue Théologique* 126 (2004).

Kittleson, James F. "Homily Outlines." *Worship* 36, no. 1 (1961).

Leclercq, Jean. "Le sermon, act liturgique." *La Maison-Dieu* 8 (1946).

Martimort, Aimé George. *Les Lectures Liturgiques et leurs Livres*. Typologie des sources du Moyen Âge Occidental 64. Turnhout: Brepols, 1992.

Michel, Virgil. "A Christmas Homily." *Orate Fratres* 3, no. 2 (1928).

Rice, Charles L. *The Embodied Word: Preaching as Art and Liturgy*. Minneapolis: Fortress Press, 1991.

Stake, Donald Wilson. *The ABCs of Worship: A Concise Dictionary*. Louisville, KY: Westminster-John Knox Press, 1992.

West, Fritz. *Scripture and Memory: The Ecumenical Hermeneutic of the Three-Year Lectionaries*. Collegeville, MN: Liturgical Press, 1997.

Vagaggini, Cipriano. *Il senso teologico della liturgia*. Rome: Paoline, 1956.

Contemporary Perspectives on Preaching

Narrative Preaching and Narrative Reciprocity

Herbert Anderson

The context for preaching today is replete with troubling issues that disrupt the common good, infect the human spirit, and effect widespread irrational suffering. Racial disdain, religious intolerance, unjust economic systems, pervasive violence on both sides of the law, isolating technology, agonizing sagas of migration, terrified souls, unchecked greed, and apathy about the climate crisis are among the present social issues confronting the preacher. How is one to preach in such a time of social disequilibrium? How does the preacher declare God's narrative of compassion, justice, and mercy in ways that connect with people whose storyline of struggle and disorder seems so far from the story of God's intent for humankind?

In another chapter in this volume, Jorge Presmanes outlines one approach to prophetic preaching for our time that identifies with God's *pathos*, struggles *with* the hearers, avoids *naïve* certainty, and proclaims a "divine-centered narrative" (see 210ff. below). The preacher's task is to discern what is of God and what is alien to God's intent. Homilies that critique social injustice and challenge people of faith to responsible ethical action need to avoid "simplistic answers to complex social issues that undermine God's narrative" (211 below). As Presmanes envisions it, God's narrative provides the content and vision for prophetic preaching but not the form.

Narrative preaching provides another way to address the complexities of a globalized world. What distinguishes narrative preaching is the form as well as the content of the homily. The dynamics of a good story—movement, purpose, climax, and outcome held together by a plot—determine the form and define the characteristics of narrative preaching. A good story is intriguing because of the tension carried by a plot; narrative preaching is no different. Rather, in the latter the hearer is drawn into the tension created by the ambiguity of a major life crisis, some discrepancy in the biblical narrative itself, the tension between a biblical text and a human dilemma, or some human conflict in which survival depends on discovering

God's vision for living. The hearer is invited to participate in the preacher's effort to resolve the disequilibrium or ambiguity that is articulated in the homiletical plot.

The Homiletical Plot

Although preaching has always presumed to connect the biblical narrative and daily living, narrative preaching, as an identifiable method, emerged in the last quarter of the twentieth century. It was a corrective to the prevailing preaching style that was didactic, deductive, doctrinal, and logical: sometimes described as an "army of pompous phrases moving over the landscape in search of an idea." At a time of social and political upheaval—at least in the United States—the preaching art was in crisis. Three points and a poem did not persuade. Nor was a hodgepodge of sentimental anecdotes sufficiently compelling. Dialogue sermons remained monologues. Around 1980, story preaching crystallized a turn toward interpreting the biblical story that had been part of Christian preaching since the early church. What developed under the banner of narrative preaching transformed story preaching into a homiletical method that remains relevant today.

While Fred Craddock (d. 2015), Richard Jensen (d. 2014), David Buttrick (b. 1927), and Charles L. Rice (b. 1936) were writing about the "new homiletics," Eugene Lowry's (b. 1933) proposal that "the homiletical plot" is the central feature of effective preaching established him as the primogenitor of narrative preaching (Lowry 1980, 2001).

The listener is invited into a narrative that begins "once upon a time," or "as the story goes," or as Jesus said, "A certain man had two sons." Immediately, we want to know what happens. The narrative homily may begin with an imaginative question for which there is no obvious answer. It is critical that the narrative preacher convey at the beginning that the resolution is unknown.

Ambiguity and resolution—essential pillars of narrative preaching—are themselves in tension. The parabolic nature of narrative preaching resists the temptation to tidy up complex biblical texts and ambiguous human situations.

> The homiletical plot must catch people in the depths of the awful discrepancies of their world—social and personal. . . . Sometimes it appears that there is no redemptive answer to the human predicament. That is the bind felt as ambiguity by people—and this is the discrepancy that is the central question in every sermon. (Lowry 2001, 25)

After identifying the disequilibrium, the preacher analyzes the discrepancy, discloses some clue to the eventual resolution, declares the Gospel promise, and anticipates possible consequences. The Gospel of Jesus Christ provides the general contours of a homiletical plot resolution: the specific redeeming word for each particular context comes from the intersection between divine and human mystery.

The Origins of Narrative Preaching

Three factors influenced this emerging preaching perspective. Philosophical theologian Stephen Crites's essay "The Narrative Quality of Experience" (1971) is often credited with introducing the idea that we understand our life as story. According to Crites, narrative is the ubiquitous form of human awareness. It gives distinctive shape and significance to the sometimes random events and encounters that enter human consciousness and then locates them in a temporal and narrative manner.

Human experience is structured in time and narrative. There are beginnings and endings that shape our life in time. We comprehend our temporal lives not as random or disconnected events but in terms of story. We think in stories in order to weave together into a coherent whole the unending succession of people and events, joys and sorrows, challenges and success that fill our days. The stories we tell—whether human or divine, mythic or parabolic—make sense of experience, connect past-present-future in an orderly way, construct meaning, establish and confirm our identity, and communicate that identity to others. The narratives we fashion out of our lives are necessary for constructing the identities we inhabit and the worlds that sustain us.

Narrative preaching is a logical extension of storied living because stories are so central to human living. It seeks to weave together stories of God and people into a meaningful framework that sustains and challenges believers for faithful living. Narrative preaching helps people find their place in the religious narrative and discover connections to God's story in the human saga. The divine tale narrates God's relentless longing for relationship with ordinary folk. The human narrative recounts our desires for God and our perennial difficulties of living fully in God's presence. This contribution of narrative preaching hinges on a lively interaction between human and divine stories.

The recovery of the biblical narrative is at the heart of narrative preaching. Christian identity is grounded in salvation history, moving from creation and fall through redemption to new creation. To be a Christian is to live in that story. Stretching over many centuries, this sacred history details God's invitation to people to move from bondage to freedom, darkness to light, and death to life. With the exception of African American preaching, the biblical narrative had been eclipsed by Enlightenment trends in which "the text was raided for some discursive theme" (Eslinger 2002, 57). When a homily is constructed around themes abstracted from the divine narrative or reflections from faith's wisdom, the beginning point is already disconnected from the contemporary human dilemma.

When narrative preaching connects God's incarnate mystery with the mystery of being human in all its joy and sorrow, then the depth of human darkness is illuminated with the very depth of God. Charles Gerkin clarifies: "The biblical story of God is thus the story of an active, purposing, covenanting, promising, and redeeming God who has always had and continues to have a stake in whatever takes place in God's world" (Gerkin 1986, 48). Narrative preaching enables hearers to see and be formed by the images, metaphors, and stories that reflect an expanded vision of the world and of God's activity in human affairs. Preachers are more likely to do this well when they live with both feet planted firmly in midair, daily trafficking in mysteries of God and the human journey.

Narratives that connect discreet events into enlarging patterns of meaning are themselves interpretations of those events rather than direct representations of objective external reality. The power of narrative, according to Paul Ricoeur (d. 2005), is the capacity to integrate multiple and scattered events into a whole and complete story (Ricoeur 1984). The resulting narrative fiction reconfigures temporal experience and makes it more intelligible and accessible to reality than direct description. It is nonetheless an interpretation.

The narrative approach depends on three interrelated assumptions about the nature of reality: (1) reality is socially constructed over time and in time; (2) reality is constituted largely through language and metaphorical speech; and (3) these socially constituted realities are organized and maintained through narrative. People make sense of their lives through the stories they fashion and the cultural-contextual narratives into which they are born. To be a person is to live in a narrative web with many stories, subplots, contradictions, and surprise endings. Consequently, all ministry—preaching in particular—is about listening to and linking stories, weaving and interpreting stories, attending to our own, and inviting others to write and rewrite the stories of their lives. This requires that narrative preachers learn to think in stories. Richard A. Jensen developed the theme of "thinking in story" in response to the challenges of a postliterate age. Learning to think in stories "is one of the keys to effective preaching in our time" (Jensen, 1993, 10).

Since narrative preaching is inescapably dialectical—holding in tension divine and human mysteries—it requires both humility and imagination. Standing habitually in the presence of God, and in the messiness of the human story, allows preachers to speak a holy word of hope and grace to people who live in terror and judgment. It matters not where we begin; what matters is that we move back and forth between tales of divinity and humanity, attending to the intersection of Holy Wisdom with incarnate tales of pain and joy.

Not long before his death, Chicago's Cardinal Joseph Bernardin (d. 1996) gave an address to a gathering of clergy in which he talked about the religious leader as a "doctor of the soul" (Bernardin 1995). The priest stands on the horizon between God and the world, Bernardin said, as a bearer of the mysteries of God. In actions and speech, the transformative images, stories, and tableaux of the Christian saga are held up for people to see and hear. Preaching is a particular ministerial moment when those entrusted with the sacred symbols are expected to make them speak grace and hope to people whose lives are often filled with distress. To do this, Bernardin instructed preachers to be in habitual contact with the mystery, standing stubbornly in the presence of God.

Anglican theologian Urban Holmes (d. 1981) made a parallel observation about attending to the human story. The priest, he said, is a "living symbol joining the mystery of the abyss to the everyday world of people. . . . To preach well is to illumine the darkness of our personal depths from the depths of God's meaning" (Holmes 1978, 97). Birth and betrayal, friendship and failure, rejection and reconciliation, the terror of contingency and the bliss of the beloved are all avenues to God. There are strategies and techniques for critically correlating human and divine stories, but this is more likely to happen effectively when such correlating becomes a habitus in the preacher's soul.

Narrative Reciprocity and Narrative Preaching

Narrative preaching regards tales of the Creator and creatures with equal seriousness. The malady of perceived human insignificance is overturned when people understand how their stories are part of the larger drama of God's journey with them. Because the divine narrative in Scripture is a shockingly honest chronicle of unbridled passion, remarkable births, sibling rivalry, military heroics, political intrigue, and the complex dynamics of family living, it not only reveals God's relentless love for the world but also validates the human struggle to live faithfully in that love. Hearing the biblical narrative is like listening again to familiar family stories and still being amazed that a narrative of such flawed folk could lead to exceptional family gatherings where we are welcomed and fed.

Narrative reciprocity as the interactive weaving of the human and divine—locating our story in God's and simultaneously linking God's with our very human stories—finds convergence for Christians in Jesus Christ, the consummate mediation of the divine and human. Thus, narrative preaching is incarnational to the extent that it embodies divine and human narration reciprocally; it is incarnational when it traffics in the mysterious depth of human and divine narratives. In this incarnational mode, such preaching does not regard either the divine or human narrative as primary but insists on reciprocity between both. Thus, narrative preaching is incarnational because it emerges in simultaneous proximity to humanity and divinity. A particular Roman Catholic expression of this reciprocity is the so-called sacramental imagination, i.e., the conviction that God is disclosed in the objects, events, and stories of everyday life.

Preaching that links tales of the Holy and the human takes seriously a fundamental human need for recognition and validation. Incarnation is God's validation of humankind; nothing that is human is foreign to God. Validation occurs when hearers recognize something of their lives in the chronicle of God's people throughout history. Validation is itself good news. *Narrative reciprocity* validates human experience by using divine words and images that diminish isolation and confirm human identity. Moreover, honest stories of revelation create open space in which believers can explore their uncertainties and doubt.

The initial purpose of narrative preaching was to reinvigorate the biblical imagination and invite people of faith to rediscover the disclosive power of biblical narrative. That purpose remains. Although there are multiple ways to maintain contact with the divine mystery, the biblical narrative is primary. The disclosive power of the Bible presses us to see what we might prefer to ignore in our lives and invites us to discover alternative visions for whatever traps us and saps us of life. Narrative in general—and the biblical narrative in particular—is world-disclosing and world-making. Biblical texts have the power to change attitudes, behavior, and perceptions. Simultaneously, the possibility of human transformation increases when the preacher stays close to the human story. Moreover, our stories are transformed when they point beyond themselves to transcending narratives and are open to the all-embracing story of God (Anderson and Foley, 1998).

Narrative reciprocity is at the center of narrative preaching. Critically correlating human and divine narratives allows us to hear our own narrative confirmed and then retold with new clarity and possibility. In addition to reinvigorating and fostering a lively reciprocity between divine and human mysteries, such preaching has the potential to address a critical contemporary issue: the lack of empathic imagination in a world of growing diversity.

Fostering Empathic Imagination through Narrative Preaching

Some have observed that the absence of empathic imagination is at the heart of modern human travail. Although people may have the capacity to imagine themselves as someone else or feel or see what others feel or see, they choose not to do it. Instead, many flee from difference to the sameness and safety of gated communities or tribalized gatherings; others propose building high borders to keep out the undesirable. In a world that has become more diverse and interconnected than many people can tolerate, preaching needs to enable hearers to transcend their own frameworks and see with new eyes and expanded empathic imaginations. Narrative preaching is an appropriate, even necessary response to the present context because it invites hearers to participate in a world larger than their own.

Fear of the "other" often accompanies the proximity of difference. Richard Kearney (b. 1954) has suggested that modern genocides and atrocities presuppose a failure of narrative imagination. If, however, we possess narrative empathy—enabling us to see the world from the other's point of view—killing another is more difficult. Ethnocentrism also breeds violence toward the other. As long as my world is *the* world, the other is an enemy to be feared and maybe eliminated. If, however, we can imagine the suffering of others and recognize the other as oneself, such an *empathic imagination* may reverse our apprehension of difference and open us to new ways of seeing and being in which God's narrative of justice and equality triumphs over narratives of bigotry and injustice (Kearney 2002, 139–40).

The absence of empathy is not the only issue. The parabolic question from Jesus about neighborliness (Luke 10:25-37) is also critical for our time. Being neighborly on a shrinking globe in which diversity marks our neighborhoods and our families—not simply some distant shore—requires a willingness to engage worlds of difference with empathic imagination on a daily basis. Narrative preaching not only expands the world of the hearer by making absent things and unfamiliar stories present but also fosters empathic imagination by linking concrete tales of faithfulness and struggle with equally concrete human stories that comprise God's narrative. Rehearsing our stories in connection with the biblical and other stories of God refines truth through an expanding empathic imagination.

If the aim of the homily is an invitation to encounter—to "come and see Jesus" and then see the neighbor with new eyes—narrative preaching is a noncoercive way to encourage such a transformative encounter. When the preacher says "imagine that" or "the story is told," the narrative approach invites hearers to imagine a situation radically different from their own and enter the world of others through a godly lens. Stories alter us by transporting us to other times and contexts where we can experience things dissimilarly, so to expand our view of the world and in turn embrace the surrounding diversity (Kearney 2002, 137). Stories of God and in God open a space where we can reflect on our own narrations without being pushed or persuaded in one direction or another. That is both the risk and the gift of narrative preaching. It invites us to be coconspirators with the parable of God in Jesus who eternally opened unimagined spaces.

Fashioning a Narrative Homily

On our best days of sermon preparation, there is often a moment in the midst of unfocused reflection or "wandering thoughtfulness" when an image or dilemma emerges to focus the preacher's attention. It is often a discrepancy of some kind in the divine narrative or between God's story and the human story that generates tension. A narrative homily begins with the preacher's disequilibrium about a biblical text or faith matter or a public crisis, about a sudden death or amazing wedding. Eventually that tension generates a question for reflection and a plot that creates movement in the homily toward resolution.

The five stages in Lowry's "homiletical loop" provide a framework for fashioning a narrative homily. The formulation of the ambiguous into a question or a statement is the first and, perhaps, most critical aspect in preparing such a homily. For example, a homily I experienced on the baptism of Jesus included a parishioner's story about interviewing a serial killer as part of her job. It began with this statement, repeated throughout the sermon: "It's when you know who you are that the trouble begins." A sermon preached after Christmas in an African American parish about the flight of the holy family into Egypt began with this statement repeated several times: "Most people don't get no daddy like this." A woman fashioning a homily on the sacrifice of Isaac (Gen 22:1-19) explored overlooked details of the story from a woman's perspective: "Did Sarah wonder why the servants were loading wood on the donkey's back? Did Sarah kiss Isaac goodbye?" The aim is to upset the equilibrium in the listener so that something is at stake in listening to the homily (Lowry 2001, 22–38). The effectiveness of the narrative homily ironically depends on articulating the ambiguity clearly and creatively at the outset without revealing a resolution.

The second stage—analyzing the discrepancy—is the longest part of the homily and probably the most demanding in preparation. There are at least two essential dimensions of this homiletic moment and its preparation: (1) the stories told must be honest and sufficiently complex to sustain the exploration of the ambiguity or tension in the homiletic plot; and (2) the preparation must include the preacher being attentive to possible biases in story selection based on social location. The tension in the homily is constructed through the preacher's determination to leave no stone unturned or rabbit hole unexamined. In other settings, this might be understood as a "thick description" of the situation. The narrative homily about Sarah's take on the trip of Abraham and Isaac up the mountain raises questions about familiar collaboration; the flight into Egypt includes honest analysis of the failures of fathers. The temptation both in the homily and the preparation is to rush to resolution. The preacher needs the grace to live with ambiguity and uncertainty—if only for a little while—so that the analysis is as deep as the truth revealed.

The third stage in Lowry's homiletical loop releases part of the tension that has been building in the homily (and maybe in the preparation) by disclosing some clue to the resolution of the ambiguity: "It is often the case that the clue making understandable the issue at stake comes as a surprise. It is not quite what one expected and arrives from where you were not looking. And *it turns things upside down*. . . . Things can never be seen in the same old way" (Lowry 2001, 54). Sometimes the reversal begins with an awareness that the resolution of the tension is itself part of the problem. Persistence and the capacity to tolerate ambiguity promotes deep analysis: the willingness to think outside the box and be surprised helps in uncovering a "clue." One famous preacher readied the hearers for the radical grace in the parable of the *waiting parent* (Luke 15:11-32) by asking, "Are you really in favor of parties for prodigals?" Careful analysis of the conditional nature of most interactions in US society is a prelude to the critical clue that the Gospel of grace is not necessarily continuous with human experience.

Once the clue to the resolution of the tension has been articulated, the listeners are often primed to hear good news. As with many aspects of ministry, timing is critical. Careful analysis has revealed that every humanly devised way to resolve the tension is a dead end. Building the tension initiated by the homiletical plot through the first three stages of the sermon prepares the way "that when the gospel is then proclaimed it is *effective*—that is, it does what it says, and *is* that to which it points" (Lowry 2001,

77). The preacher's temptation, one that this method seeks to avoid, is to declare the Gospel's promise before it can be heard effectively.

Disciplined diagnosis of the plot during sermon preparation is a key to avoiding premature good news. Homilies conclude by "anticipating the consequences" of the liberating Gospel. If the announced good news has a parabolic turn or unexpected response to the human struggle, it is well to anticipate possible outcomes of Gospel living before hearers are commissioned into the world to love and serve the Lord.

A Concluding Thought

The liberating promise of the narrative perspective is that if our lives are socially constructed, they may also be reconstructed. We are never trapped in the narratives we construct; it is always possible to renarrate our lives in another way. Storytelling is an act of hope—even defiance—because it carries within it transforming power. Proclaiming our stories and connecting them to biblical and other stories of God refines truth through expansion rather than constriction. When retelling the story is done imaginatively around an engaging plot, the listener is invited to enter into a process of refurbishing the divine narrative with questions from experience and refashioning human stories with insights from revelation. Given the storied nature of the Bible and daily living, it is not surprising that from the early fathers of the church to the present, pastors and teachers have sought in various ways to fuse divine and human stories.

Preaching from a narrative perspective helps folk generate new language and new interpretive lenses, thus generating new truths by retelling their story in relation to God's story. It also enhances empathic imagination by expanding our awareness of every "other" held in the mercy of the eternal one. Narrative preaching, however, is not a "one size fits all" mode of preaching. There are times a preacher needs to exegete, analyze, correct, exhort, or teach. The narrative perspective does not provide all the resources for invigorating sociopolitical change or instigating moral formation. Yet, for this age in which life is increasingly regarded as episodic and disequilibrium reigns, ambiguity is shunned as weakness and the stranger is deemed dangerous, narrative preaching is a worthy option and maybe even a necessary habitus in the preacher's journey into the mystery.

Bibliography

Anderson, Herbert, and Edward Foley. *Mighty Stories, Dangerous Rituals: Weaving Together the Human and the Divine*. San Francisco: Jossey-Bass, 1998.

Bernardin, Joseph. "Priest: Religious Leaders, Doctors of the Soul." Twenty-Seventh Annual NFPC Convention. San Diego, 1998.

Eslinger, Richard L. *Narrative & Imagination: Preaching the Worlds That Shape Us*. Minneapolis: Fortress Press, 2002.

Gerkin, Charles. *Widening the Horizons: Pastoral Responses to a Fragmented Society*. Philadelphia: Westminster, 1986.

Holmes, Urban. *The Priest in Community: Exploring the Roots of Ministry*. New York: Seabury Press, 1978.

Jensen, Richard A. *Thinking in Story: Preaching in a Post-Literate Age*. Lima, OH: CSS Publishing Co., 1993.

Kearney, Richard. *On Stories*. London-New York: Routledge, 2002.

Lowry, Eugene. *The Homiletic Plot: The Sermon as Narrative Art Form*. Atlanta, GA: John Knox, 1980.

———. *The Homiletic Plot: The Sermon as Narrative Art Form*. Expanded Edition. Louisville, KY: Westminster John Knox, 2001.

Preaching as Public Theology

William T. Ditewig

This essay endeavors to describe three related areas. Considered first is the nature of "public theology" itself, followed by a consideration of public theology as a consistent element of preaching and theology throughout the Christian tradition. Finally, we will note several characteristics of such preaching as public theology.

Defining Public Theology

Before turning to the idea of preaching as public theology, one must first come to grips with the concept of public theology itself. As a relatively recent term, there is still no standard or universally accepted definition for it, and its use varies greatly from author to author. Martin Marty (b. 1928) is often credited with the development of the term, as he reflected on the nature of "civil religion" in the United States. Responding to Robert Bellah's (d. 2013) concept of civil religion (Bellah 1967), Marty turned to Benjamin Franklin's (d. 1790) notion of the need for "public religion" in American society. Marty preferred the term "public church," which he defined as "a family of apostolic churches with Jesus Christ at the center . . . that are especially sensitive to the *res publica*, the public order that surrounds and includes people of faith" (Marty 1981, 3). This public church engages in public theology, defined by Marty as the attempt "to interpret the life of a people in the light of a transcendent reference" (Marty 1981, 16). He explains that this interpretation is not restricted to particular "churches," or even people of faith, "but the pluralism of peoples with whom the language of the church is engaged in a larger way" (Marty 1981, 16). Bernard Lonergan (d. 1984), while not specifically naming public theology, has famously described all theology as "mediating between a cultural matrix and the significance and role of religion in that matrix" (Lonergan 1971, xi). It is easy to find resonance here between Marty and Lonergan, situating as they do the entire project of theology within a much wider cultural-contextual matrix.

From the perspective of contemporary civil society, it is not unusual that this term emerged in the postwar Western world of the late 1940s and 1950s. During this time of rebuilding out of the chaos of war, frequent public service announcements were heard on radio and television in the United States—many prepared by political leaders as well as popular entertainers—reminding audiences that the highest ideals of the nation were reflected in religious observance (cf. 91 above). Therefore, people were encouraged to "go to the church or synagogue of your choice" as regularly as possible. Religion itself, regardless of denominational differences, was considered a vital component of a healthy, well-ordered civil society.

More recently, Scott Paeth observed in his study of public theology and social theory in the writings of Jürgen Moltmann (b. 1926) that "public theology strives to uncover the theological issues that underlie human culture. . . . As theology it is an interpretive and constructive project emerging from the experience and faith of particular religious communions in an attempt to reveal the general public relevance of the theological truth of which it speaks" (Paeth 2008, 3).

While public theology is a relatively new term, its roots are deep within the Christian tradition. After all, when attempting to speak of God (Gr., *theos* + *logos*) the theologian must ultimately engage in discussing the impact theological claims make on the human family and its responsibilities toward all of God's creation. Even the traditional Western division of the theological enterprise between dogmatic theology and moral theology speaks to the interpenetration of the divine with the human, of the Creator with creation, of faith with resultant action. In response to God's gracious self-revelation, believers respond through *metanoia* (Gr. for "a change of mind") with lives forever transformed. This transformation finds concrete expression through the specific ways in which the believer now lives in relationship with God and God's creation. The famous passage from the Letter of James comes to mind:

> What good is it, my brothers and sisters, if you say you have faith but do not have works? Can faith save you? If a brother or sister is naked and lacks daily food, and one of you says to them, "Go in peace; keep warm and eat your fill," and yet you do not supply their bodily needs, what is the good of that? So faith by itself, if it has no works, is dead. (Jas 2:14-17)

Christians, who are to be known by their love (John 13:35), must walk the walk as well as talk the talk. A Roman Catholic bishop was once asked, "How many of the people to be helped by this program are Catholic?" His response: "We're not doing it because they are Catholic but because we are."

Thus, while the term public theology may be relatively new, its underlying reality and implications are not. At least in a general sense, all theologizing that is authentically Christian is public in that it has a profound and potentially transformative impact on all of God's creation. Therefore, it is quite easy to recognize that public theology—and preaching as a form of public theologizing—perdures throughout the entire Christian tradition.

Public Theology: Preaching throughout the Tradition

In one of the most dramatic and "public" passages about Jesus in the New Testament, Jesus stands and gives one of the shortest and most powerful sermons ever delivered.

> "The Spirit of the Lord is upon me, because he has anointed me to bring good news to the poor. He has sent me to proclaim release to the captives and recovery of sight to the blind, to let the oppressed go free, to proclaim the year of the Lord's favor." And he rolled up the scroll, gave it back to the attendant, and sat down. The eyes of all in the synagogue were fixed on him. Then he began to say to them, "Today this scripture has been fulfilled in your hearing." (Luke 4:18-21)

Throughout his life and ministry, Jesus was a public theologian whose words both affected those around him and effected change, not only in his own followers but also in the larger society. In the temple, he was presented with the coin used to pay the tax and asked whether it was lawful to pay the tax or not. Notice that he was being asked about the legality of the action—not strictly a spiritual question. Jesus responded that both the divine and secular should be honored: "Render to Caesar the things that are Caesar's, and to God the things that are God's" (Mark 12:17). Clearly, Jesus was operating within the "cultural matrix" described by Lonergan. Even during his passion and death, we find Christ-as-public-theologian in his interaction with the Roman governor Pilate, challenging him: "You would have no power over me unless it had been given you from above" (John 19:11).

Jesus' followers have continued this pattern throughout history. Consider only a few examples from the tradition. Justin Martyr (d. 165) wrote apologetic works addressed to Roman emperors and the Roman senate for the expressed purpose of demonstrating the respectability of Christianity in the philosophical currency of the day. Some scholars have suggested that even the apologetic form used by Justin was unique, in that he took what had been an administrative and legal procedure of the empire to petition for a legal remedy and transformed it into a vehicle for expressing Christian beliefs (Parvis 2008, 53–61).

Ambrose (d. 397), like other leading bishops in the post-Constantinian era, publicly criticized civil leadership over issues of rights and privilege. Consider a portion of just one sermon by John Chrysostom (d. 407), the patriarch of Constantinople:

> Ships are built, sailors and pilots engaged, sails spread and the sea crossed, wife and children and home left behind, barbarian lands traversed and the trader's life exposed to a thousand dangers—what for? So that you may trick out the leather of your boots with silk laces. What could be more mad? . . . Your chief concern as you walk through the public places is that you should not soil your boots with mud or dust. Will you let your soul thus grovel while you are taking care of your boots? Boots are made to be dirtied: if you can't bear it, take them off and wear them on your head. You laugh!—I am weeping at your folly. (Attwater 1959, 62–63)

Alcuin of York (d. 804) is another example of an outstanding public theologian. In his life he was deacon and abbot, writer and ambassador and—perhaps most profoundly—an educator. Friend and tutor of Charlemagne (d. 814) and his children and head of the court school, Alcuin's influence was felt throughout academia, church, and civil governance (Depreux and Judic 2004). Other figures who might also be reckoned as public theologians range from Thomas Becket (d. 1170) and Thomas More (d. 1535) to Bartolomé de Las Casas (d. 1566). In the United States we could certainly include Jonathan Edwards (d. 1758), who thought deeply and communicated clearly about what it meant to be both a citizen and a believer. In the twentieth century, one can point to theologians such as the Jesuit John Courtney Murray, and his work on the role of religion in public life, and Dr. Martin Luther King Jr., who embodied courageous public engagement of Christian principles of human rights and justice with modern American public and political life.

Within the Roman Catholic tradition, one can consider Vatican II (1962–1965) as a prime example of how the Roman Catholic Church envisions the relationship of the people of God to the contemporary world: the council was public theologizing on a grand, even global scale. Called by Pope John XXIII (d. 1963) in view of the slaughters, violence, wars, and destruction of the first half of the twentieth century, the council confronted multiple issues, using a basic schema developed by Cardinal Suenens (d. 1996) of Belgium and adopted by John XXIII: issues were to be considered from the perspective of *ad intra* (as they pertain to the internal life of the church) and then *ad extra* (how they pertain to the engagement of the church with the wider world). Consider just one famous passage from the capstone document of the council, *Gaudium et Spes* (GS). It describes the church as

> at once "a visible organization and a spiritual community," [which] travels the same journey as all of humanity and shares the same earthly lot with the world: it is to be a leaven, as it were, of the soul of human society in its renewal by Christ and transformed into the family of God. (*GS*, no. 40)

More recently, we can ponder the ministry of Pope Francis (b. 1936), who is perhaps one of the most provocative examples of a contemporary preacher and church leader as public theologian. Building solidly on the teaching of Vatican II and his predecessors—especially John XXIII and Paul VI (d. 1978)—Francis offers a number of principles to be kept in mind concerning preaching as public theology.

For example, in *Evangelii Gaudium* (EG), the pope frequently cites his predecessor Paul VI:

> Consequently, an evangelizer must never look like someone who has just come back from a funeral! Let us recover and deepen our enthusiasm. . . . "And may the world of our time, which is searching, sometimes with anguish, sometimes with hope, be enabled to receive the good news not from evangelizers who are dejected, discouraged, impatient or anxious, but from ministers of the Gospel whose lives glow with fervor, who have first received the joy of Christ." (*EG*, no. 10; citing *EN*, no. 75)

In this document Francis also offers a lengthy section on the development of the homily (*EG*, nos. 135–59); equally important, however, is the section that follows, in which he teaches about "the social dimension of evangelization." Nowhere is "preaching as public theology" more apparent in his writings. "The kerygma has a clear social content," he writes. "At the very heart of the Gospel is life in community and engagement with others." The pope speaks of an "inseparable bond" between our acceptance of the message of salvation and the resulting obligation for "genuine fraternal love" for others (*EG*, no. 179). He cautions that while Scripture is clear on this point, there is a risk that we might take its message for granted,

> without necessarily ensuring that it has a real effect on our lives and in our communities. How dangerous and harmful this is, for it makes us lose our amazement, our excitement and our zeal for living the Gospel of fraternity and justice! . . . By her very nature the Church is missionary; she abounds in effective charity and a compassion which understands, assists and promotes. (*EG*, no. 179)

Here, the pope highlights a thread running through the entire fabric of the tradition, linking the mission Jesus articulated in that synagogue so long ago to the mission of the church today. As many contemporary missiologists recognize, "[I]t is not the church of God that has a mission in the world, but the God of mission who has a church in the world" (Dearborn 1997, 2).

Characteristics of Preaching as Public Theology

Why do we preach? This fundamental question needs to be posed to all forms of preaching, in every venue. When we offer reflections during retreats, missions, ecumenical gatherings, prayer services: why do we preach? What is it that the preacher is seeking? By means of exhortation, challenge, teaching, inspiration, and all the other tools available to the preacher, it seems that there is one goal that remains fundamental throughout this ministry: to help the community (including the preacher) encounter God and to be transformed through the encounter. Furthermore, that transformed disciple then extends God's message to the wider world. German theologian Herbert Vorgrimler (d. 2014) once wrote that "the liturgy must have concrete consequences in the world with all its needs, and that work in the world that is done in the spirit of charity has a spiritual dimension" (Vorgrimler 1992, 270). Certainly what is true of the liturgy in general would be true as well of preaching that is not only "in" but also "of" the liturgy (see 161f. above); furthermore, "extra-liturgical" preaching strives for the same goal of "concrete consequences."

What does "preaching as public theology" look like? What are the "contexts" in which such preaching takes place? Later on in this volume, Stephen Bevans considers context as encompassing four basic aspects: (1) individual and social experience; (2) culture; (3) an individual's or community's social location; and (4) the dynamics of social change (see 233 below). It is the task of theology to engage these aspects of our individual and collective lives, and preaching is a privileged moment for such engagement. Within this contextual matrix, therefore, certain characteristics of preaching as public theology suggest themselves. The following lists of these is indicative, not exhaustive, and hopefully stimulates further discussion and reflection on the topic.

Acting in Imitation of Christ

The first principle of a contemporary Christian understanding of preaching as public theology is its very christological foundation, with the profound ramifications this demands. First, the Christian proclaims that Jesus, the Christ and the Word of God, is Lord. This Lordship, however, is characterized and expressed through *kenosis* (Gr.): that divine self-emptying which John Paul II once described as "a grand and mysterious truth for the human mind, which finds it inconceivable that suffering and death can express a love which gives itself and seeks nothing in return" (John Paul II, *Fides et Ratio*, no. 93). Authority, following Christ, is not "lording over" others; authentic authority is found in emptying oneself on behalf of others. The preacher not only echoes Christ's words but also calls herself and others to follow the example of Jesus. John Paul II even referred to the need for a greater understanding of God's *kenosis* as "the prime commitment of theology" (John Paul II, *Fides et Ratio*, no. 93).

The public implications of this christological foundation are profound. A love that "gives itself and seeks nothing in return" is a dangerous love: it is a love without borders, without exception, and without exclusion. Jesus himself assumed that risk, and as Lutheran pastor Dietrich Bonhoeffer (d. 1945) noted in his classic *The Cost of Discipleship* (Bonhoeffer 2015), the price of that risk can be high. A kenotic love, always focused on the needs of others, frequently serves as a critique of societies and institutions whose motives are not similarly oriented. Furthermore, a kenotic love breaks down barriers and is not restricted to ecclesial or cultural or political categories. Paul's famous challenge that "there is no longer Jew or Greek, there is no longer slave or free, there is no longer male and female; for all of you are one in Christ Jesus" (Gal 3:28) captures this reality. Following Christ, then, the Christian preacher not only echoes Christ's words but also assumes the public risks of Christian discipleship.

Christian preaching finds its source in the great mysteries of God's love and frequently in what is commonly referred to as "the public ministry" of Jesus. Just as Jesus engaged with his own followers, the religious and political figures of his day, and the needs of all he encountered, so now the Christian preacher evokes a contemporary encounter with that same publicly transformative Christ in the present context. Preaching is public theology in no small measure because the Christian preacher proclaims the virtues, values, and vision of the public Christ to the world.

Preaching the Tradition

There is a tendency among some today, especially within consumeristic societies like the United States, to reduce religion to one commodity among many. Religion, with its accompanying paraphernalia, provides one more field of objects available to those who desire them. The tangible elements of symbolic discourse risk being emptied of their richness, depth, and beauty. The commodification of religion divorces the symbolic from its authentic grounding, or what Vincent Miller calls its "semantic mass" (Miller 2005, 72). The effective Christian preacher, throughout the tradition, has been one who helps restore that vital connection between the actual experiences of people with their most deeply held beliefs, values, and hopes. Such preaching presumes a preacher who is conversant with the contemporary realities of the community yet also able to plumb the symbolic depths of that community.

One of the most beautifully rendered descriptions of this is found in Thomas Cahill's *How the Irish Saved Civilization*. In describing the ministry of Patrick, he writes:

> In becoming an Irishman, Patrick wedded his world to theirs, his faith to their life. . . . Patrick found a way of swimming down to the depths of the Irish psyche and warming and transforming Irish imagination—making it more humane and more noble while keeping it Irish. No longer would baptismal water be the only effective sign of a new life in God. New life was everywhere in rank abundance, and all of God's creation was good. (Cahill 1995, 191)

This is the task of the preacher as public theologian: to engage the current "cultural matrix" while remaining grounded in the breadth of the Christian tradition. The scope of this tradition, of this community of faith, extends far beyond the immediate gathering of some of the faithful in one particular time and place; it is grounded in the incarnation, the public ministry of Jesus, and indeed the Paschal Mystery itself. It extends through the witness of the early disciples, and on through the countless generations of believers who constitute our living faith tradition. This tradition is handed on in multiple ways: from parents to children, from teachers to students, through schools, councils, catechisms, and countless other ways. Public theologizing by Christians recognizes that there is a central core to the living *kerygma* (Gr. for "preaching") that has been proclaimed through the centuries. At the same time that these creedal beliefs are communicated, they are also renewed

> in language intelligible to each generation, [responding] to the perennial questions which people ask about this present life and the life to come, and about the relationship of the one to the other. We must therefore recognize and understand the world in which we live, its explanations, its longings, and its often dramatic characteristics. (*GS*, no. 4)

The Community of Faith and the "Earthly City"

Every day, headlines remind us that we are living in a world that is a suffering and dangerous place. All people, including people of faith, struggle to find meaning and solutions to the tragedies around us. It is one thing to proclaim the inherent dignity of the human person in principle while at the same time realizing that the contingent, imperfect, and often sinful realities of life threaten that dignity through the horrors of war, terrorism, mass shootings, capital punishment, famine, and disease. What can people of faith do to respond, to challenge, and to transform the world?

Earlier, we cited Paeth's description of public theology "as an interpretive and constructive project emerging from the experience and faith of particular religious communions in an attempt to reveal the general public relevance of the theological truth of which it speaks" (181 above). Within the broader catholic tradition there is a sustained recognition of the essential goodness of creation that, although its human participants have been marred by sin, is nonetheless capable of renewal and transformation. The constant refrain in Genesis 1—that God declared creation to be good—underscores this fundamental truth. Aware of this framework, authentic catholic preaching demands that this essential goodness be recognized and affirmed. It also means that such preaching is essentially hopeful.

As noted previously, Vatican II considered the church a kind of "leaven" in and even "the soul of human society" (*GS*, no. 40). The bishops continued in this vein when they taught that the church "heals and elevates the dignity of the human person" and "through each of its members and its community as a whole it can help to make the human family and its history still more human" (*GS*, no. 40).

Pope Francis captures this conciliar insight when he notes that "an authentic faith—which is never comfortable or completely personal—always involves a deep desire to change the world, to transmit values, to leave this earth somehow better than we found it" (*EG*, no. 183). These words capture a pivotal element of public theology, namely, that the community of faith has something to say to all, not just to its own members. Public theology is a mode of the "leavening" that the community of faith can provide to society as a whole.

Consequently, preaching as public theology must grapple with the essentially public nature of the church itself. This means, among other things, that preachers wrestle with the very public dimensions of four pivotal practices that we have traditionally lifted up as central to our Christian identity: worship (Gr., *leitourgia*), witness (Gr., *martyria*), service (Gr., *diakonia*), and especially a union of values and the preciousness of relationships (Gr., *koinonia*). Preaching as a form of public theology recognizes and nurtures this connectedness between the community's prayer and praise, witness to the Paschal Mystery of Christ, the self-sacrificial service of others, and the unrelenting commitment to sustain the cohesion of the body. Such preaching reflects as well a shared responsibility for the world that transcends all denominational, religious, and spiritual lines. God's brooding spirit that led Jesus into his public ministry is freely offered to all. Preaching, in its myriad forms, acknowledges this gift and so prods us into spiritual collaboration with all of creation in the ongoing transformation of the world.

Bibliography

Attwater, Donald. *St. John Chrysostom: Pastor and Preacher*. London: Harvill Press, 1959.

Bellah, Robert. "Civil Religion in America." *Daedalus* 96, no. 1 (1967).

Bonhoeffer, Dietrich. *The Cost of Discipleship*. London: SCM Press, 2015 [1937].

Cahill, Thomas. *How the Irish Saved Civilization*. New York: Nan A. Talese, Doubleday, 1995.

Dearborn, Tim. *Beyond Duty: A Passion for Christ, a Heart for Mission*. Monrovia, CA: MARC, 1997.

Depreux, Philippe, and Bruno Judic, eds. *Alcuin: De York à Tours: Écriture, pouvoir et réseaux dans l'Éurope du haut moyen* âge. *Annales de Bretagne et des pays de l'ouest* 111:3. Rennes-Tours: Presses Universitaires de Rennes, 2004.

Foley, Edward. "Liturgy as Public Theology." *Studia Liturgica* 38, no. 1 (2008): 31–52.

John Paul II. Encyclical Letter *Fides et Ratio* (On the Relationship between Faith and Reason). September 14, 1998. http://w2.vatican.va/content /john-paul-ii/en/encyclicals/documents/hf_jp-ii_enc_14091998_fides -et-ratio.html.

Lonergan, Bernard. *Method in Theology*. Toronto: University of Toronto Press, 1971.

Marty, Martin. *The Public Church*. New York: Crossroad, 1981.

Miller, Vincent. *Consuming Religion: Christian Faith and Practice in a Consumer Culture*. New York: Continuum, 2005.

Paeth, Scott. *Exodus Church and Civil Society: Public Theology and Social Theory in the Work of Jürgen Moltmann*. London and New York: Routledge, 2008.

Parvis, Paul. "Justin Martyr." *The Expository Times* 120, no. 2 (2008).

Vorgrimler, Herbert. *Sacramental Theology*. Translated by Linda M. Maloney. Collegeville, MN: Liturgical Press, 1992.

Imagination and Preaching

David J. Lose

Near the beginning of George Bernard Shaw's (d. 1950) play *Saint Joan*, the title character, Joan of Arc, seeks backing for her crusade against the English. She has come to Robert de Braidicourt, a military squire, to solicit his support for her campaign. In the course of Robert's questions about her intentions, Joan reveals that she hears voices directing her moves. In fact, Joan had been instructed to come to petition Robert by one such voice. The squire is taken aback: "How do you mean? Voices?" "I hear voices telling me what to do," Joan replies, adding, "They come from God." Robert is unconvinced: "They come from your imagination." To which Joan answers, "Of course. That is how messages of God come to us" (Shaw 1924, 59).

The scene sheds light on an important, though often overlooked, element of the life of faith. While it is easy to assume that faith is primarily about knowledge, whether of the Scriptures or the tradition or about an experience of God's presence, it is also very much about imagination. For whatever knowledge or experience one may possess, one still has to *imagine* the difference the Christian faith makes, the world it assumes, the actions it demands, and the kind of life it invites. Imagination is, in this sense, central to the life of faith and a crucial means, as Joan asserts, by which God's presence is mediated to us. Along these lines, theologian Garrett Green (b. 1941) has suggested imagination as the primary "point of contact" between God and humanity, a proposal that transcends the typical dichotomy between natural theology and divine revelation (Green 1989, 40).

Recognizing intuitively the connection between faith and imagination, many preachers assume that the imagination plays an important role in their sermons to invite hearers to a deeper encounter with the divine. Yet despite this nearly universal acclamation, preachers differ greatly in their conception and use of imagination. Indeed, the history of imagination's role in preaching is both complex and varied. While most have honored it, and a few mistrusted it, it may be that almost all have underestimated it. To explore this possibility, it will help to divide this inquiry into three parts, corresponding to three distinct ways preachers have viewed and

190

employed imagination in preaching: imagination as device, as practice, and as competency. While these dimensions are not at all mutually exclusive, homileticians usually tend to emphasize one of them as central to the role imagination plays in preaching.

Imagination as Device

The history of preaching seems dominated by the conviction that imagination is a device and faculty by which preachers can conceive and share their sermons more effectively, ultimately aiming to implant their message securely into the hearts and minds of their hearers. Whether consciously or unconsciously, preachers borrow this understanding of imagination from the field of classical rhetoric (see 201ff. below) that has, from at least the time of Augustine (d. 430), profoundly influenced Christian proclamation.

Noting the deplorable quality of the preaching and teaching of his priests, Augustine determined to write a book instructing those under his care in how to interpret Scriptures correctly and teach those interpretations effectively. The result was his *On Christian Doctrine* (Lat., *De Doctrina Christiana*), which many argue represents the first textbook in Christian homiletics. Despite Augustine's contention that he was not simply restating the rules of rhetoric he taught before his conversion to Christianity (Augustine 1958, 118), most of what Augustine has to say about preaching and teaching is influenced heavily by the Roman rhetorician and political philosopher Marcus Tullius Cicero (d. 43 BCE). Cicero, who believed that the key to republican government was the politician's ability to move an audience through effective oratory, averred that imagination plays a pivotal role in all human endeavors, but most especially in rhetoric. Understood as the persuasive arrangement of logical arguments designed to inform, delight, and move the hearer, rhetoric both springs forth from the human imagination as well as employs the imagination to convince hearers by taking abstract ideas and making them concrete, on the one hand, or inspiring the hearer through the use and creative juxtaposition of images, on the other (Kennedy 1980, 114 and 256).

Cicero, Augustine, and other classical orators borrow this conviction in turn from Aristotle (d. 322 BCE), who viewed the imagination as a bridge between thinking and the senses, providing the soul access to the external world by mediating between the activity of the mind and our sensorial perceptions of the material world (Flory 1996, 147). Similarly, rhetoric itself—driven by and employing the imagination—stands between logical thought and action, providing the orator with the capacity not only to inform hearers but also to move them to action.

In all these ways, imagination is both faculty and device: the faculty by which we conceive of an argument that may touch and shape our hearers' consciousness and the device by which we inspire, delight, and move the will of our hearers by giving ideas more tangible shape so that they may impress themselves—almost physically—onto the psyche of those listening. Imagination, from this point of view, is therefore absolutely crucial to persuasive speech. Little wonder, then, that most of the textbooks written on preaching over the better part of the last two millennia first extol the virtues of the imagination and then go on to describe sources of and methods for nurturing a preacher's creativity. Stressing that preaching is as much art as science, the typical homiletics text invites preachers to immerse themselves in literature, plays, and, more recently, movies and music to ponder how artists across the ages engage and move the imagination of their hearers.

In addition to offering advice on nurturing the imagination, however, most preaching guides also provide instruction on the proper use of the imagination, and it is this counsel that illumines the shortcoming of this approach. This is because whatever Aristotle's influence on developing a positive view of imagination, classical rhetoricians and later Christian preachers had difficulty escaping a view of the imagination that was far more mundane, typified by the teacher of Aristotle, Plato (d. 347). In Plato's view, imagination did not exist in its own right but rather was a mixture of our senses and our opinions. While it certainly made communication of ideas easier, it was nevertheless only a vehicle for rational thought, not the idea itself. For this reason, imagination was not only optional—something of a luxury for the lazy mind—but also could ultimately lead us away from what we truly wanted to know, i.e., the basic idea or eternal Form that we should be seeking (Flory 1996, 147).

In the realm of Christian proclamation, this more Platonic suspicion expresses itself in the almost ubiquitous warning to preachers to avoid an excess of imagination lest our creativity outshine or even undercut our message. John Broadus (d. 1895), whose *On the Preparation and Delivery of Sermons* served as a primary textbook from the late nineteenth century through much of the twentieth, typifies this ambivalence by distinguishing between imagination and fancy. Describing imagination as "indispensable" and as a "wonder worker," Broadus writes, "Piles of bricks and lumber and sand are as much a house as the mere piling up of thoughts will constitute a discourse. The builder of palace or cabin works by constructive imagination: and it is the same faculty that builds a speech" (Broadus (1979, 224). This is imagination as indispensable faculty. Further, according to Broadus and following the logic of classical rhetoric, the imagination also functions as a critical device, enabling "the preacher to clothe ideas in familiar and revealing imagery" (Broadus 1979, 225).

Despite this high praise, however, Broadus also warns against "fancy," that is, a form of imagination not tied to reality and ungoverned by the rules of reason but employed instead to manipulate the thoughts and emotions of others. Unmoored from the logic and consistency of the rational mind, fancy is at best superficial and at worst distorts the original message to serve its own manipulative and self-aggrandizing ends (Broadus 1979, 223). Preachers may resort to fancy to impress or manipulate their audience, but doing so inevitably leads people away from the Gospel: either inviting undue attention to the creative and rhetorical brilliance of the preacher or immersing hearers in the superficial image rather than leading them to the deeper truth of the message.

This concern for the abuse of imagination illumines the tendency of homileticians who adopt the assumptions of classic rhetoric to slide from valuing imagination as an indispensable and innate faculty to treating it as a useful, but rather neutral, and even amoral, device. While imagination can invent interesting ways to organize one's material, capture the attention of one's audience, or adorn one's speeches and sermons with penetrating images, the heart of the matter is not imagination but the idea itself from which the use of imagination dare not detract. Imagination, in other words, is an indispensable device because, and only in so far as, it serves to lift up the central idea of the sermon.

Imagination as Practice

When H. Grady Davis (d. 1975) contended that "a sermon should be like a tree . . . a living organism . . . with deep roots" (Davis 1958, 15), he reinvigorated the more Aristotelian view of imagination as indivisible from the ideas it brings to expression. The contrast between Broadus's construction metaphor of "piles of bricks and lumber and sand" that imagination pulls together and Davis's organic imagery of a tree that springs forth from the ground to sprout and grow in indeterminate but organized direction is telling. In the former, imagination is something that is applied to give preexistent ideas a useful form, while in the latter there simply can be no division between thought and form, and imagination is the faculty that recognizes and embodies that unity. As Davis writes in his opening line, "Life appears in the union of substance and form," and then continues:

> Every thought likewise comes in some form. We cannot have a thought without its form. Quite correctly we say that a thought "takes shape"

193

> or "is formed" in our minds. The thought must take form in order to be
> recognized for what it is, and it certainly has to take form in order to be
> expressed. (Davis 1958, 1)

This relentless commitment to the unity of thought and form restores imagination from serving merely as a device to a primary faculty and it lays the groundwork to recognize that preachers are not called simply to *use* imagination to engage their hearers or adorn their messages but rather to *be* imaginative in the fullest sense, perceiving the traces of God's presence in everyday life and illustrating for their hearers what the life of faith looks like. Barbara Brown Taylor (b. 1951) describes this imaginative work as being a "detective of divinity" and places it at the heart of the preaching life (Taylor 1993, 15). Imagination, in this sense, is a practice, a pattern of living and seeing, even a way of being in the world.

In recent years, homileticians have distinguished among a variety of different kinds of imagination, each which invites a distinct kind of practice. In his book, *Imagining a Sermon*, Thomas Troeger (b. 1945) describes a "conventional imagination" as encompassing the images and patterns of thought we have inherited by being part of a living faith tradition. It includes the sermons we've heard, favorite hymns, familiar biblical passages, images from the stained-glass windows in the sanctuary, the rhythms and words of the liturgy, and more (Troeger 1990, 128). Preachers are invited to practice paying attention to this dimension of imagination because it is the primary means by which we are invited out of our myriad responsibilities and tasks and drawn into the common story of God's activity through the ages. Similarly, Mary Catherine Hilkert (b. 1948) identifies the value of developing a "sacramental imagination" that lifts up the incarnational presence of God in all creation (Hilkert 1997).

In both of these views, a central part of the preacher's task is to tell the biblical and Christian narrative vividly enough so that hearers can imagine the claims of Scripture as a genuine possibility. Preachers practice a conventional and sacramental imagination by first noticing and then drawing out rich biblical images, retelling the congregation's faith stories, employing the poetry of the hymns and liturgy of the church, and reminding people of the promises of the sacraments. This is done in order to take the often disparate persons and experiences gathered together on any given Sunday and weave them together into a faith community joined by the shared story of God's ongoing commitment to love, bless, and save the world. In this sense, a conventional and sacramental imagination is a communal imagination, the shared vision of a world sanctified by God, and for this reason it is an integral part of preaching.

While a conventional and sacramental imagination is necessary, however, it is not sufficient. The church's imagination of God and the life of faith has always been expressed in and through the images, languages, and values of a particular time and place. It cannot be otherwise. Yet no culture or context perceives all of God, and all cultures and contexts at times err in their imagination, perceiving something of the grace and goodness of God but also distorting elements of God's work through the lens of their own prejudices and limitations. For this reason, preachers are invited to practice a conventional and sacramental imagination anchored in their faith tradition but to do so with sensitivity and, indeed, with a critical eye to note the gaps or distortions of the particular conventions of their community and tradition.

An important corrective to a conventional imagination is what is often called a prophetic or visionary imagination, where preachers are invited to look beyond the past or current reality of the faith community to what it might be and, indeed, to what God is calling it to be. Rooted in the prophetic tradition (cf. 210ff. below) that unfailingly beckons Israel to live more fully into its identity as God's people, chosen, called, and commissioned to be a blessing to the world, the prophetic imagination holds up the vision of God's passionate commitment to and concern for all of God's people—especially those who are poor or oppressed—in order to provide a mirror and measure of the current state of the church.

Preachers who stand in the line of Israel's prophets recognize that God's dreams for people are regularly domesticated or co-opted by the powers that be, leading at times even a church to allow its conventional imagination to be warped by the voices of the dominant cultural context. For this reason, prophetic or visionary preaching that tells the story of God's redemptive and revolutionary work requires what Walter Brueggemann (b. 1933) describes as "an enormous act of imagination" in order to step into God's pathos for God's people and experience God's anger over injustice. This calls Christians to transcend the limited imagination of the age and be infused instead by God's vision of peace and justice for all (Brueggemann 2012, 13).

The practice of a prophetic imagination requires not only a close reading of Scripture, and particularly the Hebrew prophets and the teachings of Jesus, but also a dual identification: first with God and God's concern for the world, and second with those left behind or outside of society's material blessings. Motivated by the disparity between God's intentions and humanity's actions, a prophetic imagination often first sounds the note of judgment, the natural consequence of God's commitment to justice. Prophetic rebuke is rarely effective, however, if not accompanied by the visionary imagination of the world God offers us and invites us to embrace and enact. As Leonora Tubbs Tisdale (b. 1951) writes, prophetic imagination at its best "invites us to envision the new day God intends and to discern how God would creatively use us to help bring that day to completion" (Tisdale 2010, 5). The challenge for preachers, therefore, is to practice attending both to the heartbreaking poignancy of those beloved by God but overlooked by society and, simultaneously, to the stunning beauty of God's vision of a world of equity, wholeness, and peace that invites our engagement and participation.

Standing between a conventional imagination of the tradition and the visionary imagination of the prophets is a third, and in many ways more quotidian, imagination that enables preachers to speak regularly into the homes and hearts of those sitting in the pew. Named "empathetic imagination" by Fred Craddock (d. 2015), it requires preachers to move beyond their own experience in order to imagine the questions, needs, and reactions of their people. In his widely read text *Preaching*, Craddock suggests that preachers make it a practice to focus on one or two facets of the human condition in each sermon. That element may be "facing surgery," "being fourteen years old," "fired from one's position," or "feeling alone," but the goal is the same: to ground our preaching in the everyday realities of the people to whom we preach. An empathetic imagination pushes preachers to ask what their sermons will sound like to persons in various conditions and, perhaps more important, to inquire what their people need to hear from the biblical witness to help them sense God's Word addressed to them in their particular circumstances (Craddock 2010, 97).

While the practice of empathetic imagination—because it is employed so frequently—may seem rather ordinary, it is anything but mundane. In fact, empathetic imagination is key to crafting a sermon that resonates with hearers, allowing them to imagine themselves in the sermon and thereby believe that the message of good news announced from the pulpit has the capacity to shape their lives. It also invites preachers to bridge the tendency to speak either to the elements of congregational life (the domain of conventional imagination) or more global concerns and larger issues (often the thrust of prophetic imagination) in order to touch upon the "middle ground" where people spend most of their lives—e.g., relationships, personal and familial challenges, and pressures at work, school, or in the local community, etc. The practice of empathetic imagination, therefore, requires a commitment to walking with people in their everyday lives; it is essential to preaching that conveys not merely information about the Christian faith but an invitation to the abundant life God offers in Christ.

Imagination as Competency

While most Christian preachers of the second half of the twentieth century were schooled in the necessity of adopting imagination as a practice by which to offer their hearers a vision of the Christian faith that is relevant and compelling, more recent theologians and homileticians have asked whether such a conception of imagination is sufficient to the challenges of the day. Christianity, these theologians argue, is itself an *act* of imagination, a way of viewing, even constructing, the world that invites a variety of options for living that are otherwise unavailable.

George Lindbeck's (b. 1923) *The Nature of Doctrine* heralded this turn. According to Lindbeck, Christianity—indeed all religions—are neither merely dogmatic propositions to be adopted or rejected nor symbolic representations of eternal truth to be translated and transmitted. Rather, Christianity offers its adherents a cultural and linguistic world of signs and rules that are simultaneously self-referential, in that they create a seamless picture of the world, and profoundly productive, in that they set the terms on which life is experienced and lived (Lindbeck 1984, 33). When one becomes a Christian, therefore, one doesn't merely obtain more information about Jesus or tap into a great religious tradition; rather, one adopts a particular way of seeing the world that cannot be proved true (or false) outside of the experience of those living within and sharing the Christian imagination of God, the world, and each other.

From this point of view, while imagination can certainly be an effective device by which to animate preaching, and while preachers should absolutely cultivate, practice, and employ imagination in the preparation of their sermons, neither of these is sufficient to equip contemporary believers with a distinctly Christian imagination in a decidedly post-Christian world. The major shift in emphasis in such a conception of the role of imagination in preaching is from the preacher to the hearer. That is, the measure of success of the preacher is not how effectively he or she employs imagination but rather how rich, abundant, and three-dimensional an imagination the congregation develops and can employ over time. Imagination is, therefore, no longer viewed as either a device or practice but is understood instead to be a competence, the ability of the hearer to imagine and act within the cultural-linguistic world projected by the biblical narrative.

Charles Campbell (b. 1954) describes this goal as nurturing in hearers a "typological" or "figural" imagination" that allows them to connect persons and events from disparate times. In short, it is the kind of imagination that enables Christians to see themselves in the biblical story and the biblical story being played out all around them. It is not sufficient that only the preacher exercise this kind of imagination. Rather, preachers seek through their sermon to develop in their hearers a more competent and robust biblical imagination through their regular participation in the faith community that creates living options by which they can live in the world: "People learn to do figural 'improvisation' not as a hermeneutical or homiletical technique, but through immersion in Scripture, participation in the liturgical practices of the church and engagement in the alternative politics of the community of faith" (Campbell 1997, 257).

Before they can be delighted or persuaded, Christian hearers must first be able to imagine the truth of the faith and the way of life it offers. Then they must, through practice, gain the capacity and competence to see the world through the lens of the biblical narrative and act according to the norms of the Christian faith. The hallmark of rich, capable, and imaginative preaching, from this point of view, is not that the preacher can display an inventive or creative imagination in interpreting and preaching the texts but, rather, that the hearers become over time more competent at imagining the world as the biblical narrative describes it.

Conclusion

"The faithful imagination," Garrett Green writes near the end of his influential book *Imagining God*, "enables us to hear the melody of revelation" in both Scripture and everyday life. Preaching, from this point of view, is the act of "singing the scriptural melody so that others may learn to hear and enjoy it and to join in its singing" (Green 1989, 151). Or, as Dolan Hubbard (b. 1949) says of African American sermons, when preachers invite their hearers into the biblical story, they "create a world" that is available in and through the imagination (Hubbard 1996, 4). When hearers are caught up into that world, a world infused by the divine vision and permeated by the song of the Christian faith, they are transformed in body, mind, and spirit. Indeed, they encounter the presence of the living and holy God because, as Joan of Arc rightly testifies, God speaks to us through the imagination.

Bibliography

Augustine. *On Christian Doctrine*. Translated by D. W. Robertson. Upper Saddle River, NJ: Prentice Hall, 1958.

Broadus, John A. *On the Preparation and Delivery of Sermons*. 4th ed. New York: Harper and Row, 1979 [1870].

Brueggemann, Walter. *The Practice of Prophetic Imagination*. Minneapolis: Fortress Press, 2012.

Campbell, Charles L. *Preaching Jesus: New Directors for Homiletics in Hans Frei's Postliberal Theology*. Grand Rapids, MI: Eerdmans, 1997.

Craddock, Fred. *Preaching*. Nashville, TN: Abingdon Press, 2010.

Davis, H. Grady. *Design for Preaching*. Philadelphia: Fortress Press, 1958.

Flory, Dan. "Stoic Psychology, Classical Rhetoric, and Theories of Imagination in Western Philosophy." In *Philosophy and Rhetoric* 29, no. 2 (1996).

Green, Garrett. *Imagining God*. San Francisco: Harper and Row, 1989.

Hilkert, Mary Catherine. *Naming Grace: Preaching and the Sacramental Imagination*. New York: Continuum, 1997.

Hubbard, Dolan. *The Sermon and the African American Literary Imagination*. Columbia: University of Missouri Press, 1996.

Kennedy, George A. *Classical Rhetoric and Its Christian and Secular Tradition*. Chapel Hill: University of North Carolina, 1980.

Lindbeck, George. *The Nature of Doctrine: Religion and Theology in a Post-Liberal Age*. Philadelphia: Westminster Press, 1984.

Shaw, George Bernard. *Saint Joan*. New York: Penguin Classics, 2001.

Taylor, Barbara Brown. *The Preaching Life*. Boston: Cowley Publications, 1983.

Tisdale, Leonora Tubbs. *Prophetic Preaching: A Pastoral Approach*. Louisville, KY: Westminster John Knox Press, 2010.

Troeger, Thomas H. *Imagining a Sermon*. Nashville, TN: Abingdon Press, 1990.

Rhetorical Approaches to Preaching

Lucy Lind Hogan

Upon his conversion, Augustine (d. 430) resolved "that I should withdraw the service of my tongue from the market of speechifying . . . the citizens of Milan would have to provide another word-peddler for their students" (Augustine 1997, 210 and 218). If this renowned teacher of rhetoric and doctor of the church saw that the life of faith and peddling words were incompatible, why should we include an essay on the rhetorical approach in a handbook for preachers? The reason is that, as soon as the preacher considers what to say, how to say it, for whom, when, where, why, and what the preacher hopes that the listeners will take away from the sermon, the preacher is taking a rhetorical approach. Years after his conversion, the bishop Augustine came to admit the need for his preachers to learn the art of rhetoric, for they were putting their charges to sleep—a topic to which we will return later. Therefore, preachers should make their rhetorical analysis and decisions wisely and thoughtfully, informed by centuries of reflection on the task.

We do not need to return to the fifth century to hear rhetoric disparaged. Open any newspaper or listen to the news and sooner or later you will be reminded that a politician is offering only empty rhetoric. People are suspicious of rhetoric, thinking that the speaker is playing word games, deceiving listeners with "purple prose." Therefore, it is important to have a good working definition of rhetoric.

Rhetoric is not empty or shallow speech. It is not necessarily manipulative or coercive, although it definitely can be misused. Rhetoric is the planned and strategic use of symbols, language, and discourse—both spoken and written—to influence and persuade. Karlyn Kohrs Campbell observes that with rhetoric, we "overcome the obstacles in a given situation with a specific audience on a given issue to achieve a particular end" (Campbell 1996, 9). Rhetoric, as contemporary rhetoricians have come to understand, is a way of knowing.

We seek to persuade all of the time. It may be as trivial as asking someone to accompany us to lunch, or it may be as monumental as asking someone to marry. While in the latter, one may actually make use of rhetorical insights and skills, the purview of rhetoric has generally been restricted to public speaking and the written, published word. What are the structures or language of an argument that one must consider in order to render it successful? For Aristotle (d. 322 BCE) the definition of rhetoric was discovering and identifying "all available means of persuasion."

Rhetoric through the Ages

Athenian democracy and its legal system are the foundation of classical Western rhetoric. A crucial attribute of being a citizen was the ability to deliver a speech. Numerous precursors to the blossoming of Greek rhetoric occurred, but it is with Aristotle that rhetoric flourished. In *On Rhetoric* Aristotle develops his program for dealing with persuasion in particular cases, as opposed to dialectics that deals with general cases. Aristotle says this about rhetoric: "Let rhetoric be [defined as] an ability, in each case, to see the available means of persuasion" (*On Rhetoric* 1.2; trans. Kennedy 1991, 36). A speech is given to a particular group at a particular time for a particular purpose.

Aristotle describes two different means of persuasion: nonartistic and artistic. Nonartistic proofs are those that are not invented by the speaker: laws, witnesses, and contracts. More important are the artistic proofs developed by the speaker: *ethos*, *pathos*, and *logos*. Aristotle argues that the *ethos*—the character, knowledge, and trust that the listener has in the speaker—is essential to the success of the speech. *Pathos* is the emotional state of the listeners that is cultivated by the speaker. If a politician urges approval of a particular action, such as the move toward war, feelings of anger or fear must be aroused. Finally, the speaker must develop logical arguments or *logos*, based on evidence persuasive to the listeners and "probability." We will return to the importance of probability or contingency shortly.

Aristotle's identification of the different types of speeches and the various proofs became part of the core of the rhetorical tradition. For the other significant classical traditions, we must turn from Athens to Rome. The famous orator Cicero (d. 43 BCE) wrote several works on rhetoric. He describes the pattern of rhetorical subjects by which the men of Rome were trained. These subjects have come to be identified as the canons or rules of rhetoric: the steps a speaker takes to prepare a speech.

The first step is *inventio* or invention, which is the discovery and development of the arguments, illustrations, and examples that will be the content of the speech. Once the content is determined, the speaker must then decide on an orderly, appropriate, and engaging arrangement. The term for this second canon is *dispositio*, language drawn from the military concerning how a leader arranges and dispatches his warriors.

The third canon of rhetoric is *elocutio*. While we may be familiar with the later schools of elocution, the third canon for Cicero dealt with the issues and questions of style. Would a speech be written and delivered in a grand style or very plain style? What language choices could be made? What tropes and figures of speech might be employed?

Memoria is the fourth canon. There is some debate as to whether memory meant simply memorizing one's speech, or whether it also included the importance of having an expansive memory of all of those previously noted "available means of persuasion." Either way, memory received little attention in most handbooks.

The final canon is delivery or *pronuntiatio*. Like memory, delivery also received little attention over the centuries, despite the fact that according to the Greek orator Demosthenes (d. 322 BCE), the most important part of rhetoric was "delivery, delivery, delivery" (Quintilian *Institutio* 11.3.6; trans. Butler 1922, 245). Unfortunately, this continues to be one of the most ignored of the canons. Since the advent of the microphone and sound system, most preachers feel that this canon "has been covered." Demosthenes would no doubt disagree.

We cannot leave this discussion of Roman rhetoric—and Cicero in particular—without noting the admonition he gives in his work the *Orator*. According to Cicero, the principle duties of the orator are to teach, to delight, and to move or stir the listeners to action or judgment (*De Oratore* 2.115). It is Cicero's observation that becomes crucial as we move into a discussion of Christian rhetoric.

As noted above, many early leaders of the church were not only suspicious of but also rejected rhetoric. In addition to being a pagan enterprise, rhetoric focused on human skills, logic and arguments, and the pursuit of human rather than divine truths. The irony of this rejection by church fathers is that many of them were trained rhetoricians and teachers. Therefore, it is with great eloquence that Tertullian (d. before 240) asks his important rhetorical question, "What indeed has Athens to do with Jerusalem?" The answer implied in Tertullian's rhetorical question was obviously to be nothing. Ironically, for many centuries those in the church would have "nothing" to do with rhetoric. As soon as he embraced his conversion, for example, Augustine wrote a letter resigning from his post as teacher of rhetoric, a "word peddler."

Tertullian's "Jerusalem," or an emerging Judaeo-Christian understanding of revelation, depended on the Scriptures and the prophetic utterance that often opened with, "Thus saith the Lord." The prophet-preacher was the mouthpiece for the divine, and the prophet-preacher's primary preparatory task was to listen and read. Following his conversion and ordination, Augustine made that sacred turn toward direct revelation and away from pagan Hellenistic rationalism. Shortly after he became bishop of Hippo, Augustine wrote *De Doctrina Christiana* as a guide for reading and interpreting the Scriptures.

Early in the prologue of the work, Augustine addresses the concerns of those who believe in direct revelation, those "who exult in divine assistance and who glory in being able to understand and treat the sacred books without precepts of the kind which I have undertaken" (Augustine 1958, 4). Augustine admitted that there were those individuals who were able to hear and learn the Scriptures without the need of human assistance. He also recognized, however, that most people needed someone to teach them to read; they needed human instruction. He wanted to claim that instruction in preaching could be done humbly without stepping in the way of the Holy Spirit. Having argued for the importance of human teachers, Augustine provides his "precepts" for reading Scriptures: "There are two things necessary to the treatment of the Scriptures, a way of discovering those things which are to be understood, and a way of teaching what we have learned" (Augustine 1958, 7). Books 1, 2, and 3 are devoted to these two "necessary" things.

Included in Augustine's duties as bishop was attending the services of his priests and listening to them preach or "teach what [they] have learned" about the Scriptures. Augustine came to understand that, while direct revelation might assist the preacher in "discovering those things which are to be understood" (Augustine 1958, 117), it did not appear to help them in their teaching and preaching. So, in 426 Augustine undertook to add a fourth and final book to *De Doctrina Christiana* in order to "say a few things concerning teaching" (Augustine 1958, 118). He found that too many of his preachers were "sluggish, cold, and somnolent" (Augustine 1958, 118). In other words, his priests were putting their listeners, and maybe even their bishop, to sleep.

In the opening of book 4, Augustine assures his readers, "I must thwart the expectation of those readers who think that I shall give the rules of rhetoric here which I learned and taught in the secular schools" (Augustine 1958, 118). Yet, what follows proves to be just that, the foundation of an approach to Christian rhetoric, although he did not actually identify a difference between Christian and classical rhetoric. Augustine is concerned that his preachers are boring their listeners while those secular speakers, trained in rhetoric "ardently exhort [their listeners], moving them by their speech so that they terrify, sadden, and exhilarate them" (Augustine 1958, 118).

Using Scripture as examples of eloquence, Augustine then steps into his old role as a teacher of rhetoric in order to help preachers learn the rules that will enable them to "speak in such a way that he teaches, delights, and moves" (Augustine 1958, 136). Here, Augustine is quoting Cicero. And he continues to quote a "certain eloquent man. . . . 'To teach is a necessity, to please is a sweetness, to persuade is a victory'" (Augustine 1958, 136).

In laying out the steps toward eloquence in the service of the Gospel in the Holy Spirit, Augustine provided the church with a truce, if you will, between Athens and Jerusalem: a truce that would hold until the twentieth century.

Recovering from a Barth Attack

Reflecting on the church fathers and their rejection of pagan rhetoric, we must recognize that Augustine's compromise was somewhat tenuous. Yet it held for centuries, and homiletics continued to be a significant part of rhetorical education. In the twentieth century, however, as there was a renaissance of the importance of rhetoric, Protestant homiletics suffered from what Thomas Long has described as "a fatal Barth attack" (Long 1993, 174). Karl Barth (d. 1968), a Swiss theologian in the Reformed tradition, resurrected the ancient arguments that rhetoric and persuasion shifted the focus away from God to human reason. Consequently, many in the Reformed tradition once again rejected the rhetorical approach.

Rhetoric can certainly be abused. Orators and preachers can manipulate their listeners. For every manipulative public speaker, however, there are an equal number of women and men who have taken to the podium and pulpit to bring about justice. In spite of the objections raised by some homileticians and theologians, contemporary rhetorical theory has much to offer the preacher today. Therefore it is crucial to remember the Latin maxim *abusus non tollit usum* ("abuse does not eliminate use"), which was an important element of Augustine's approach.

In the 1960s and 1970s, the political ferment in the West gave rise to new ways of thinking about rhetoric. No longer were scholars content with merely rehearsing classical rhetorical theories and teaching students to be "good men speaking well." Classical rhetoric had emphasized the contingent, public, persuasive, and contextual nature of the event (Lucaites and Condit 1999, 4). Scholars urged a much broader understanding of rhetoric. While they did not want to reject the classical theories, they sought to demonstrate that rhetoric is ubiquitous. Rhetoric is how we come to know, it is epistemic. It is how we argue for and present what we would like to understand as the truth. Rhetoric, therefore, appears not only in the forum, the court, or the pulpit but also in multiple other arenas. Whether we are asking a jury for a guilty verdict, urging a nation to war, or presenting a new understanding of the role of genetics, we are employing rhetoric. Moving far beyond the classical understanding of "a good man speaking well," philosopher and literary critic Kenneth Burke understands rhetoric not as what we say but who we are. He argued that we use language or rhetoric because "man [*sic*] is the symbol-using (symbol-making, symbol-misusing) animal" (Burke 1966, 16). We are rhetorical beings. We utilize symbols to urge people to do something because we are symbol-using beings.

Jeffrey Maciejewski locates a similar argument in theology. Grounding his argument in Thomas Aquinas's (d. 1274) philosophy of human nature, Maciejewski seeks to "forge an ontological connection between rhetoric and human nature" (Maciejewski 2014, 1). Rhetoric and persuasion are "innately human."

Elements of a Rhetorical Approach

Rhetoric would seem to be constitutive of who we are. The question is not whether we will use rhetoric—we will. As Maciejewski believes Aquinas demonstrated, persuasion is in our very nature. Therefore, the question is how well, faithfully, and respectfully we will use rhetoric and persuasion.

Among the many significant changes initiated by Vatican II (1962–1965) was a return to homilies closer to those of the early church. Robert Waznak describes the renewed homily as one that "placed primary emphasis on the biblical, liturgical, and kerygmatic." Waznak argues that *Fulfilled in Your Hearing* (FIYH) "offered the most creative understanding of the liturgical homily" (Waznak 1998, 9). FIYH examines four aspects of the homily: the assembly, the preacher, the homily, and homiletic method. We might argue that what FIYH explores are none other than elements of the rhetorical approach. In the final section of this article, we will briefly explore these various elements.

The Assembly: Grounded in a Context

A sermon, homily, or speech is written for a particular group of people in a particular place at a particular time. FIYH—with its specific focus on the homily—begins with the assembly. An important dimension of the rhetorical approach is exegeting the congregation and its context. In order to prepare the arguments (Gr., *logos*), or find what will move the congregation (Gr., *pathos*), FIYH stressed the preachers need to know "what a congregation needs, wants, or is able to hear" (FIYH, no. 11). One must know both the history of a congregation and what is important to them.

Asking questions and listening, therefore, are important elements of the rhetorical approach. One must discover not only the superficial demographics—e.g., is it a younger or older congregation? what is its economic and racial makeup?—but also the more deeply held theological and cultural values. Through listening, the preacher will discover that even a congregation that seems quite homogenous is in reality quite diverse.

The broader context must also be explored. The preacher must be aware of the ways that the cultural context exerts its influence. Christians live by many calendars; the liturgical year is only one of them. Work, school, sports, and civic holidays all shape the lives of those who come through our doors. Likewise, current events may and should have a profound effect on the shaping of the sermon. While Karl Barth may not have approved of the rhetorical approach, he yet came to regret that he had drawn such a sharp divide between the sermon solely focused on the biblical message and life during the rest of the week. He came to understand that the preacher must prepare the sermon with the Bible in one hand and the newspaper (or smart phone) in the other. If, for example, a crisis has occurred, people come to hear God's Word in that difficult moment.

The Preacher and Ethos

Aristotle observed that the character of the speaker (Gr., *ethos*) was a crucial element of the speech. Although FIYH begins with the assembly, it argues that the preacher is equally important, identified as a "mediator of meaning . . . representing both the community and the Lord" (FIYH, no. 20). Yet, even before the preacher opens his or her mouth to speak, those sitting and watching wonder: Who is this person? Does he know what he is talking about? Does she care about me and have my best interest at heart? Is this a person of faith? Does this person know what my life is like—my questions and my concerns? *Ethos* is the persuasive quality of the preacher and it is developed in a number of ways both internally and externally.

Ethos is developed internally in the message. It can be as complex as developing thoughtful arguments that are intelligently crafted, or as simple as pronouncing words (especially people's names) correctly. Speaking incorrectly about something with which the preacher is not familiar could cause the listener to wonder what else is incorrect in the sermon. For example, an uninformed excursus on fishing could prompt the fishing experts in the assembly to wonder if the preacher also misunderstood the Gospel. *Ethos* is also established externally. An alb and stole inform the listeners that the preacher has the authority to preach.

The preacher brings experiences, knowledge, and faith to the preaching moment. The preacher also brings prejudices and shortcomings. An important element of the rhetorical approach, therefore, is to come to know and recognize both one's gifts as well as limitations so that one may make sure that those blind spots do not sabotage one's message.

The Homily: All Available Means

The Bible in one hand—or Lectionary in homiletic preaching—is essential for the preacher. Careful exegesis becomes the cornerstone of the message. Vatican II urged preachers to recognize and recover the centrality of the Scriptures in the homily (see 27 above). Through the interpretation of the Scriptures and the liturgy, the preacher, the "mediator of meaning," helps the assembly hear and understand God's Word spoken anew to them.

Exegesis and interpretation, however, are not the end. As Aristotle encouraged, the orator must find all available means of persuading the listeners. Illustrations, poetry, and stories help the message come alive and connect with the listeners. They help to make the abstract concrete, allowing people to form pictures and images in their minds.

Crucial also is how the preacher speaks about her- or himself. It is appropriate to speak about oneself, but it must be done sparingly, and the preacher must quickly move from focusing on oneself to including the listeners. The sermon should not be about all the wonderful things the preacher has done. It is also important not to share an issue or crisis the preacher is experiencing. The congregation is not a support group for the preacher. Therefore, the preacher must also ask why he or she is sharing some information; what purpose does it serve in the sermon?

Preaching Method: Putting It Together

Once the preacher has discovered all of those "available means" the task remains to discover how many of them and in what order to present them. Arrangement or form is essential to the sermon, an active not neutral participant. While the simplest understanding of arrangement is introduction, body, and conclusion—or tell them what you are going to say, say it, and tell them what you said—how we put together the pieces can draw in the listeners or confuse them. Like a musician or composer, the preacher should develop a broad repertoire of preaching forms for presenting the message.

The preacher must know not only what to say but also how to say it; she or he must find the right words. For centuries the focus of rhetoric was only on style and figures of speech. From this perspective one only turned to rhetoric after an argument was formulated. That turn was for finding the right language for communicating the argument eloquently and persuasively. While contemporary rhetoricians now understand rhetoric as applying to both the content and the presentation, an important part of rhetoric continues to be finding the right words.

Matching the language choices to the listeners is central if understanding is to occur. The preacher must learn to speak the language of the community. Even if the preacher and the congregation are speaking the same language, there will still be local particularities. The preacher must also recognize that the technical theological language learned in seminary may not be familiar to the listeners. It does not mean that they cannot be brought into the sermon, but it does mean that the preacher cannot assume that the listeners will know them. In that vein, Pope Francis (b. 1936) noted: "The greatest risk for a preacher is that he [*sic*] becomes so accustomed to his own language that he thinks that everyone else naturally understands and uses it. If we wish to adapt to people's language and to reach them with God's word, we need to share in their lives and pay loving attention to them" (*EG*, no. 158).

Finally, the preacher gives voice to the words, which requires paying attention to the delivery. If the listeners cannot hear or cannot understand what is being communicated, the preaching is for naught. Unfortunately, too many speakers today think that the need for projection, articulation, and breath control are all unnecessary because of amplification and sound systems. Nothing could be further from the truth. The preacher must learn how to perform the sermon, to make it come alive, to give flesh and life to the word. That includes practicing it out loud (see 23 above).

The Rhetorical Approach: A Way of Life

As was noted earlier, rhetoric, persuasion, and preaching are not just what one does, it is who one is (see 205 above). Therefore, the preacher must devote his or her life to the enterprise in and out of the study. James Wallace observes, "To nourish the hearts of others includes tending to one's own" (Wallace 2002, 175). The preacher, he urges, must be one who loves words, loves the Scriptures, loves people, and before anything else loves Jesus

Christ. Jesus feeds the preacher and in turn sends the preacher forth to feed the beloved people of God. The rhetorical approach becomes a way of life.

Bibliography

Aristotle. *On Rhetoric: A Theory of Civic Discourse*. Translated by George Kennedy. New York: Oxford University Press, 1991.

Augustine. *On Christian Doctrine*. Translated by D. W. Robertson. Upper Saddle River, NJ: Prentice Hall, 1958.

———. *The Confessions*. Translated by Maria Boulding. Hyde Park, NY: New City Press, 1997.

Burke, Kenneth. "Definition of Man." In *Language as Symbolic Action: Essays on Life, Literature, and Method*. Berkeley: University of California Press, 1966.

Campbell, Karlyn Kohrs. *The Rhetorical Act*. Belmont, CA: Wadsworth Publishing Co, 1996.

Edwards, O. C. *A History of Preaching*. Nashville, TN: Abingdon Press, 2004.

Hogan, Lucy Lind, and Robert Reid. *Connecting with the Congregation: Rhetoric and the Art of Preaching*. Nashville, TN: Abingdon Press, 1999.

Kennedy, George A. *Classical Rhetoric and Its Christian and Secular Tradition*. Chapel Hill: University of North Carolina Press, 1980.

Long, Thomas. "And How Shall They Hear?" In *Listening to the Word: Studies in Honor of Fred B. Craddock*. Edited by Gail R. O'Day and Thomas G. Long. Nashville, TN: Abingdon Press, 1993.

Lucaites, John Louis, and Celeste Michelle Condit. Introduction to *Contemporary Rhetorical Theory: A Reader*. Edited by John Louis Lucaites, Celeste Michelle Condit, and Sally Caudill. New York: Guilford Press, 1999.

Maciejewski, Jeffrey J. *Thomas Aquinas on Persuasion: Action, Ends, and Natural Rhetoric*. Lanham, MD: Lexington Books, 2014.

Quintilian. *The Institutio Oratoria of Quintilian Books 10–13*. Translated by H. E. Butler. Cambridge, MA: Harvard University Press, 1922.

Sloane, Thomas O., ed. *Encyclopedia of Rhetoric*. Oxford: Oxford University Press, 2001.

Wallace, James A. *Preaching to the Hungers of the Heart*. Collegeville, MN: Liturgical Press, 2002.

Waznak, Robert P. *An Introduction to the Homily*. Collegeville, MN: Liturgical Press, 1998.

Prophetic Preaching

Jorge Presmanes

Borrowing from his predecessor John Paul II (d. 2005), Pope Francis (b. 1936) defines preaching in terms of a dialogue between God and God's people (*Evangelii Gaudium* [*EG*], no. 11). Prophetic preaching is also dialogue between God and people, except that it is based on divine anger at the injustice that perpetuates human and environmental suffering of the oppressed. This pathos of God feels intensely, suffers with the suffering, consoles the inconsolable, rails against injustice, identifies with the oppressed, and loves illimitably. It is this God of pathos that calls the prophetic preacher to proclaim God's immeasurable compassion for all but especially for the poor and the oppressed.

Out of compassion for humanity, God called the prophets of the Hebrew Scriptures who were quick to reject that call with a panoply of excuses: "I'm too young," "I don't have the words," "I'm too sinful," and the like. Today those called by God to preach the prophetic word may, like prophets of old, reject the call with similar excuses. Yet those who empathize with God's pathos eventually will accept the mission with passionate conviction. Abraham Heschel (d. 1972) claims that the motive present in the mind of the prophet is always sympathy with God's own pathos:

> Prophetic sympathy is a response to transcendent sensibility. It is not, like love, an attraction to the divine Being, but the assimilation of the prophet's emotional life to the divine, an assimilation of function, not of being. The emotional experience of the prophet becomes the focal point for the prophet's understanding of God. He lives not only his personal life, but also the life of God. The prophet hears God's voice and feels His heart. He tries to impart the pathos of the message together with its logos. As an imparter his soul overflows, speaking as he does out of the fullness of his sympathy. (Heschel 1962, 26)

The prophetic word flows from the preacher's participation in divine life and prompts the preacher to engage critically the dominant social forces that are in conflict with God's compassion, justice, and love.

210

Motivated by empathy with God's pathos, the prophetic word is, as Walter Brueggemann (b. 1933) asserts, "an enormous act of imagination" (Brueggemann 2012, 13). The preacher must prayerfully discern competing imaginations. On the one hand is an imagination that is centered on God as "character and agent," on the other hand there is the "dominant imagination that predictably assimilates God into its powerful socio-political claims" (Brueggemann 2012, 27). Thus prophetic preachers stand in history discerning what is of God in their time and place and what is antithetical to the divine narrative. This discernment is certainly not a facile venture but, on the contrary, is one that requires prayerful and critical reflection.

Preaching that is the fruit of critical discernment avoids simplistic answers to complex social issues that undermine God's narrative. Moreover, the complexity of this discernment is much more challenging when the preacher is part of a dominant group whose narrative the preacher is called to confront. In their book *The Liturgy That Does Justice*, James Empereur (b. 1933) and Christopher Kiesling (d. 1986) caution prophetic preachers to be self-critical in their preaching:

> Prophetic preachers who proclaim the demands of biblical justice to others must be less concerned to preach *to* them than to struggle *with* their congregation. The bearers of the message of justice cannot prescind from the complexities of global problems. We need less naïve certainty and more struggling reflection in the pulpit. This is not to say that preachers cannot be clear, make use of dramatic images, or call for responsible action. But the rhetoric must be matched with thoughtful questioning and some agony of searching. (Empereur and Kiesling 1990, 12)

Prophetic preachers from affluent congregations should also avoid the temptation of projecting their guilt onto their hearers. No one individual is responsible for oppressive social constructs, and feeling personally guilty about such things is counterproductive to the active and concrete effort to change death-dealing structures that perpetuate human and environmental suffering. In the middle of the twentieth-century, voices that had been silenced by the dominant narrative prophetically challenged the status quo in both church and society. In the remainder of this chapter, I will explore some liberationist theologies of preaching from historical contexts marked by injustice and oppression. In an abridged fashion, I will present contributions that liberationist theologies have made to the Christian tradition, highlighting elements of these contextual theologies of proclamation that advance the study and praxis of prophetic preaching.

Latin American Liberationist Preaching

Bred in the bone of the colonial structures that favored the dominant social narrative, the church in the New World demonstrated a systematic "preferential option" for the powerful. Conversely, in the middle of the twentieth century, a grassroots ecclesial community movement (Sp., *comunidades eclesiales de base*) flourished first in Brazil and then throughout Latin America. These communities became not only the *locus* for the development of Latin American liberation theology but also of grassroots liberationist preaching. I briefly focus on two important points here: first, liberationist prophetic preaching in Latin America is primarily carried out by poor laypeople within an ecclesiology of "communion and participation"; and second, the preaching is developed in the context of a liberating hermeneutic that unabashedly favors the poor and sees faith and discipleship uniquely tied to seeking justice for the oppressed in the here and now.

The prophetic preaching of the poor of Latin America has been primarily heralded by lay members of the *comunidades eclesiales de base*. They preach from their ecclesial membership in communities of "communion and participation." Brazilian theologian Marcello Azevedo (d. 2010) explains this model of church:

> Communion (*koinonia*) is essential for effectiveness and credibility of the faith-community, whose life is to profess and bear witness, announce and denounce, and establish love and justice among human beings in the framework of truth and freedom. Participation is the commitment of all, with their differing personalities and vocations, to build and serve the community (*diaconia*) and to construct a society that dovetails with the postulates of faith in all their reach. (Azevedo 1987, 194)

All members share a communion of faith and mission and they offer their Spirit-given charisms to the service of the community. Those who have the gift of preaching preach. Yet the preaching is never the work of an individual but is a communal process of analyzing their situation of oppression in light of the Word of God. Through this process, the oppressed "discover the causes of their oppression, organize themselves into movements, and act in coordinated fashion" (Boff and Boff 1987, 5).

These faith communities adopted the *see-judge-act* method of Joseph Cardijn's (d. 1967) Young Christian Worker Movement. In the *first mediation* (see), awareness of their own oppression leads the poor to ask a fundamental question: "Is it God's will that we should suffer in such fashion?" The answer is, "Of course not." The logical follow-up question is: "If it isn't God's will then whose will is it?" To answer this vital question social analysis is used to determine the root causes of their oppression.

In the *second mediation* (judge) the community engages the Word of God with a hermeneutic of suspicion that asserts that the tradition has not only silenced their voices but also that God's Word has been co-opted to oppress them. In partnership with the membership of the community, the liberationist preacher reflects on God's Word with a hermeneutical bias in favor of the poor. In other words, the liberationist preacher engages the "scriptures bearing the whole weight of the problems, the sorrows, and hopes of the poor, seeking light and inspiration from the divine word" (Boff and Boff 1987, 32).

The *third mediation* (act) is the preaching event. Here, the preacher unveils the liberating biblical interpretation carried out by the previous mediation. The God who is unveiled in the preaching is irrevocably committed to the liberation of the oppressed. Because this God of pathos abhors the suffering of the poor, liberationist preaching demands with urgency concrete action on behalf of justice. These three mediations illustrate the threefold process of liberationist preaching: denouncing the cause of the oppression, proclaiming a compassionate God of pathos who is in solidarity with the oppressed, and calling for structural changes in the social order and the church that will make the lives of the poor better.

Prophetic Preaching in the African American Church

W. E. B. DuBois (d. 1963) documents the tragedy that the "Negro church antedates the Negro home" (DuBois 1999, 330). This church, born in slave quarters, backwoods, and swamps, was often called a "hush house." These were secret places where the slaves gathered to pray and hear a preached Christianity different from that of the white preacher whose service they were forced to attend. The white preacher's message reminded the slave that the Bible exhorted them to be obedient to their masters. He would often preach that it was the devil that put thoughts of freedom in their mind. At the "hush house," however, the preacher would voice God's pathos that, out of compassion, had freed the Hebrew slaves from Pharaoh's grip and desired their freedom.

From the time of the hush houses to today, the African American church and its preaching have been highly political. The African American preacher, wrote DuBois, is the "unique personality developed by the Negro on American soil." DuBois defined him as a "leader, a politician, an orator, a 'boss,' an intriguer, an idealist" (DuBois 1999, 326). James Cone (b. 1938) claims that authentic Black preaching is prophetic because the preacher "speaks God's truth to the people." "The sermon," says Cone, "is a prophetic oration wherein the preacher 'tells it like it is' according to the divine Spirit who speaks through him or her" (Cone 1999, 22).

African American prophetic preaching is grounded in a threefold pneumatology. First, only the Holy Spirit can summon a believer to the ministry of preaching divine truth. Second, the preaching event is the work of the Spirit active in the heart of the preacher whose job is to juxtapose God's narrative with the context of Black people's lives. Third, the Spirit verifies the call and words of the preacher in the "logical praxis which proceeds from the spoken word" (Cone 1999, 23). The praxis that authenticates Spirit-driven preaching is the preacher's work on behalf of justice for the poor and those marginalized by a society burdened with the sins of racism and "white privilege."

Through the power of the Spirit, Black prophetic preaching, according to Carlyle Stewart (b. 1951), is at once the balm of Gilead and an ointment that stings before it heals. He writes:

> Black preaching . . . has healed lives, brought families together, comforted the afflicted, and afflicted the comforted, been a catalyst for cultural, spiritual, and social freedom, and black institution building, served as a force for the creative transformation of black communities, institutions, and the personal lives of African American people. (Stewart 1997, 22)

This creative transformation flows from the hope-filled eschatological imagination of African American preaching. "I have a dream," the Black preacher asserts, that God's narrative of justice and equality will triumph over the narrative of bigotry and racism. Because it is God's Word that the prophet pronounces, the hearer is prompted by the Spirit to march forward in the struggle for justice with the conviction that God's promises will be fulfilled.

Feminist, Womanist, and *Mujerista* Preaching

After her encounter with the risen Christ and following his instruction, Mary Magdalene went and announced to the disciples, "I have seen the Lord." These five words, in a sense, can be imagined as the beginning of the church's preaching ministry. Today, women stand in church pulpits and preach from a wide variety of ecclesial contexts.

The prevailing method in feminist theology is *critique-recovery-reconstruction* (Carr 1993, 8–13), which is mirrored in feminist prophetic preaching. The starting point of feminist preaching is the oppression of women in society and church that is rooted in patriarchy and androcentric bias that systematically marginalizes and silences women's voices (*critique*) (Hilkert 1997, 174). The preacher likewise engages the Bible, its historical interpretation, and the other elements of the tradition from the hermeneutics of women's experience (*recovery*). The feminist prophetic preacher then "draws on women's historical experience, women's lives and activities in the past in a variety of contexts . . . to recover the memory of women whose stories have been ignored" (Hilkert 1997, 174). In other words, this movement calls the preacher to gain new insights and wisdom from the overlooked and unconscious perspectives that have been marred by biblical interpretations and theological discourse dominated by men. The final movement in this method is the preaching event itself that enriches the community with interpretations of Scripture and the faith tradition that are liberating not only for women but also for all people and all of God's creation (*reconstruction*).

Mary Donovan Turner (b. 1949) and Mary Lin Hudson (b. 1955) describe feminist preaching as that which brings forth God's Word "in her own distinctive, authentic, authoritative, resistant, and relational voice, born of spirit and experience of one's own god-likeness" (Turner and Hudson 2014, 99). Feminist prophetic preaching not only gives women voice; it also gives God a woman's voice. The preacher, however, must be careful not to confuse God being woman-like with God being feminine-like. This is a pitfall into which both well-intentioned men and women preachers can fall. This type of dualism which attributes both "feminine" and "masculine" characteristics to God the "Father" can perpetuate a patriarchal understanding of God that propagates the marginalization of women in church and society. Analogically speaking, the feminist prophetic preacher proclaims God as female (as well as male) while avoiding gender stereotypes and dualisms. Elizabeth Johnson (b. 1941) explains:

> Women reflect God not only as mothering, nurturing, and compassionate, although certainly that, but also powerful, taking initiative, creating-redeeming-saving, wrathful against injustice, in solidarity with the poor, struggling against and sometimes victorious over the powers of this world. Reorienting the imagination at a basic level, these female images open up insight into the maternal passion, fierce protectiveness, zeal for justice, healing power, inclusive hospitality, liberating will, and nonhierarchical, all-pervading relationality that characterize divine love. (Johnson 2007, 109)

Feminist preaching proclaims a God who is both loving Mother and benevolent Father whose grace is freely offered to all.

215

Integral and inclusive to feminist theologies are interpretations done from the prism of the experience of women of color. "Womanist" and *mujerista* theologies and preaching are two such perspectives that begin with the experience of non-European American women. The former springs from the experience of African American women and the latter from the experience of US Latinas. Both of these embrace the feminist critique of patriarchy and androcentric structures and language, yet they also critique the marginalization created by European and North American communities of women and men. At the heart of the womanist and *mujerista* theology is the struggle experienced by African American women (Williams 1993) and *la lucha* (Sp. for "the struggle") of poor Latinas (Isasi-Díaz 1993).

Katie Cannon (b. 1950) contends that womanist preaching operates within the critical awareness of the "negative and derogatory female portraiture in Black preaching" (Cannon 1995, 119). Moreover, Cannon argues that womanist preaching builds on what she calls the genius of Black preaching but must perform a critical analysis of it for the "genre is both sacred and profane, active and passive, life-giving and death-dealing" (Cannon 1995, 120). Womanist prophetic preaching is concerned with the removal of pejorative language and images of women encountered in Black preaching. It also emphasizes liberating praxis in church and society. "A Womanist orientation toward prophetic preaching is a critical hermeneutic and homiletic framework that broadens the conversation about preaching beyond sermonic content to include the audience and the context" (Allen 2012, 388). Womanist preaching theory not only critiques the treatment of women in Black preaching but also demands that Black women's experience of struggle be brought to theological reflection and named in the pulpits of African American churches.

Mujerista theology and its correlative preaching proclaim a God who is ever at the side of poor Latinas in their daily *lucha*. This form of prophetic preaching sheds light on the Jesus who continues to walk with Latinas each day "hidden in, with, and under our suffering," leading them to resurrection and abundant life day by day (Vargas 2007, 274). *Mujerista* preaching names this intimate affinity that poor Latinas have with God. Ada María Isasi-Díaz (d. 2012) writes about this relationship: "We argue with God, barter with God, get upset with God, are grateful and recompense God, use endearing terms for God. This intimate relationship with the divine is what is at the heart of our *comunidad de fe*" (Sp. for "community of faith"; Isasi-Díaz 1993, 139).

Another goal in *mujerista* preaching is to raise the consciousness of Latinas about the structures in Hispanic cultures and societies that oppress them and to call forth liberative praxes through new ecclesial and social constructs. This preaching denounces the patriarchal structures of the North Atlantic societies "that plays into the hands of the dominant forces of society . . . to repress and exploit us" (Isasi-Díaz 1992, 106). Consonant with the God of pathos's preferential concern for the poor, *mujerista* preaching calls for concrete action in the church and society to eradicate the injustices that perpetuate the oppression of poor women of color.

Latinoa Prophetic Preaching

The hermeneutic circle of *see-judge-act* that frames much Latin American liberation theology is inculturated in US Hispanic contexts. While to the south it has focused primarily on economic factors, in US Hispanic contexts the hermeneutic engages issues of identity politics, racism, sexism, xenophobia, and the systematic exclusion of Hispanics in the church and society. Here, I focus on preaching in relationship to three factors addressed in the prophetic imagination of Hispanic communities: the xenophobic exclusion of Latinoas in ecclesial and social structures, the experience of otherness and exile that marks the lives of many Hispanics, and a Latinoa understanding of the self that challenges the dominant culture's "modern-liberal" notion of subjectivity.

Prophetic Latinoa preaching condemns the xenophobic exclusion of Hispanics in North America. Roman Catholic bishops and other Christian leaders have prophetically denounced unjust social structures that marginalize Latinoas and discriminatory immigration policies that cause extraordinary suffering for many Hispanic families. Church leaders have proclaimed a God of pathos who was a stranger and was welcomed, not deported. They have fought for just immigration policy and promoted the participation of Hispanics in political processes. Likewise, Latinoa preachers and their communities have called for inclusion in the church similar to what ecclesial leadership has called for in society. They have challenged the neocolonial state of affairs in many church structures dominated by a powerful Euro-American minority that silences the majority church membership that is poor and of color. Yet the prophetic stance of the Latino community and its preaching names God as one who, in Jesus, chose to identify not with the rich and powerful but with those who have no power and have been rejected and marginalized by a privileged elite.

The lived reality of many Latinoa in the United States is marked by otherness whereby one is a stranger in the country where one resides and even in one's country of heritage or origin. Fernando Segovia (b. 1948) defines this experience of exile as a "very paradoxical and alienating situation involving a continuous twofold existence as permanent strangers or aliens, as permanent 'others' " (Segovia 1995, 62). If this dual exile is internalized by the individual, it can lead to radical otherness that destroys. On the other hand, being "other" can be transmuted from oppression to liberation if it leads to identity and voice. "From such a voice," Segovia writes, "emerges a profound commitment not to overwhelm or override the other but rather to acknowledge it, value it, engage it—a theology of mixture and otherness, a hermeneutics of otherness and engagement" (Segovia 1995, 67). For the Hispanic whose life is marked by otherness and exile, prophetic preaching can acknowledge and engage alienating experience and name God's presence within it, which in turn can transform the listener's internalized oppression into liberating consciousness.

Finally, prophetic preaching in the Hispanic community challenges the understanding of the self that pervades dominant perspectives of modern-liberal culture. In North America, the prevailing understanding of the self is an autonomous individual. Roberto Goizueta (b. 1954) argues that for Latinoa anthropology, there is "no such thing as an isolated individual." Moreover, he says that the person is a collective embodiment of his or her relationships. In other words, when one encounters a person, he or she encounters the person's "parents, relatives, friends, community . . . as well as the God who created" the person and the earth that nourishes humanity (Goizueta 1995, 50).

Latinoa prophetic preaching denounces the dominant modern liberal individualist perspective that leads to isolation from God and from each other and, in its most destructive manifestation, is partially responsible for the marginalization of the other and for oppressive structures in society. The Latinoa prophetic preacher thus heralds a communion with God that participates in a universal communion of brothers and sisters made in the image and likeness of the divine communion we call Trinity.

Conclusion

The call to communion with God and each other is the common denominator of the prophetic word proclaimed by the prophets of old and our time. In this essay I have employed Pope Francis's definition of preaching as a dialogue between God and God's people, with the divine dialogue partner as the God of pathos who identifies with and loves all, but especially those who suffer. Those who accept God's call to preach the prophetic word do so out of empathy with God's pathos. The prophet suffers with God when God's narrative of peace, justice, and love is subverted by a dominant and oppressive narrative in society that co-opts God for its own means. God uses prophets to proclaim a divine-centered narrative in order to thwart the narrative that uses God for its own sociopolitical gains.

Prophetic preaching challenges history and arises from divine anger against injustice that perpetuates human and environmental suffering. Through the contextual theologies that demarcate prophetic preaching, I have outlined various hermeneutics of suspicion. While the historical contexts of oppression differ in these perspectives, all share a method in preaching that critiques the causes of oppression in its historical context. Moreover, prophetic approaches reread the Bible, its historical interpretation, and other elements of the tradition to find new insights and wisdom. Finally, the prophetic preacher speaks the emancipating truth of God's Word and calls for concrete action on behalf of justice in the world.

Bibliography

Allen, Donna. "Womanists as Prophetic Preachers." *Review & Expositor* 109, no. 3 (2012).

Azevedo, Marcello. *Basic Ecclesial Communities*. Washington, DC: Georgetown University Press, 1987.

Boff, Leonardo, and Clodovis Boff. *Introducing Liberation Theology*. Maryknoll, NY: Orbis Books, 1987.

Brueggemann, Walter. *The Prophetic Imagination: Preaching an Emancipating Word*. Minneapolis: Fortress Press, 2012.

Cannon, Katie. *Katie's Canon*. New York: Continuum, 1995.

Carr, Anne. "The New Vision of Feminist Theology: Method." In *Freeing Theology: The Essentials of Theology in Feminist Perspective*. Edited by Catherine LaCugna. San Francisco: Harper, 1993.

Cone, James. *Speaking the Truth*. Maryknoll, NY: Orbis Books, 1999.

DuBois, W. E. B. "Of the Faith of the Fathers." In *African American Religious History: A Documentary Witness*. Edited by Milton Sernett. Durham, NC: Duke University Press.

Empereur, James, and Christopher Kiesling. *The Liturgy That Does Justice*. Wilmington, DE: Michael Glazier, 1990.

Goizueta, Roberto. *Caminemos Con Jesús*. Maryknoll, NY: Orbis Books, 1995.

Heschel, Abraham. *The Prophets*. New York: Harper & Row, 1962.

Hilkert, Mary Catherine. *Naming Grace: Preaching and the Sacramental Imagination*. New York: Continuum, 1997.

Isasi-Díaz, Ada María. "*Mujeristas*: Who We Are and What We Are About." *Journal of Feminist Studies in Religion* 8, no. 1 (1992).

————. *En la Lucha*. Minneapolis: Fortress Press, 1993.

Johnson, Elizabeth. *Quest for the Living God*. New York: Continuum, 2007.

Segovia, Fernando. "Toward a Hermeneutics of the Diaspora: Hermeneutics of Otherness and Engagement." In *Reading from This Place*. Edited by Fernando Segovia. Minneapolis: Fortress Press, 1995.

Stewart, Carlyle. *Joy Songs, Trumpet Blasts, and Hallelujah Shouts*. Lima, OH: CSS Publishing, 1997.

Turner, Mary Donovan, and Mary Lin Hudson. *Saved from Silence: Finding Women's Voice in Preaching*. St. Louis: Lukas Park Books, 2014.

Williams, Delores. *Sisters in the Wilderness*. Maryknoll, NY: Orbis Books, 1993.

Vargas, Alicia. "The Construction of Latina Christology: An Invitation to Dialogue." *Currents in Theology and Mission* 34, no. 4 (2007).

The "New Hermeneutics"

Mary Margaret Pazdan

Hermeneutics, or the art of interpretation (Gk., *hermeneia*), began with Plato (d. 347) and continues through the present century. In analyzing Plato, James M. Robinson distinguishes three traditional forms of the word: (1) the *speech* of the poets who spoke for the gods, (2) *written discourse*, and (3) *commentary* and *translation*. *Commentary* as interpretation and *translation* as carrying over meaning "from one culture, age or situation to another" are important considerations in the past two centuries (Williams 1974, 619). In addition to Greek thought, Anthony C. Thiselton describes early rabbinic writing as another source for hermeneutics. Rabbi Hillel (about 30 BCE) developed *Seven Rules of Interpretation* (Thiselton 2009, 2). In early Christian thought Augustine of Hippo (d. 430) wrote biblical commentaries and the first instructional book for homiletics (*De Doctrina Christiana*, 4.)

Robert Kysar observes that before the influence of Friedrich Schleiermacher (d. 1834) "hermeneutics was simply the science of interpretation . . . of literary documents." Schleiermacher extended hermeneutics to include the process of understanding the texts (Kysar 1969, 216).

This essay considers contemporary contributions to hermeneutics that developed in the twentieth century with roots in the nineteenth century. Sometimes biblical and homiletic instructors and students use "exegesis" and "hermeneutics" interchangeably; often there is a separation. This article clarifies the differences.

The New Hermeneutics

The roots of the "New Hermeneutics" are located in the Romanticist hermeneutical tradition of Friedrich Schleiermacher, Wilhelm Dilthey (d. 1911), and Rudolph Bultmann (d. 1976). Schleiermacher did not consider that the grammatical-historical approach of the historical-critical method was sufficient to bridge the historical gap between the author and the interpreter. Carl Braaten, commenting on Schleiermacher's addition, notes that he introduced "a psychological interpretation . . . by an imaginative reproduction of the creative art by which the work was originally produced" (Braaten 1965, 222).

While Dilthey recognized Schleiermacher's work, he understood that "historical events in the past have to be as expressions of historical, personal life" (Braaten 1965, 222). Dilthey contributed two insights. First, interpretation and its objects are historically conditioned. Second, "life" is the common denominator between an interpreter and objects. Thiselton summarizes, "The interpreter is to 'relive' (Ger., *nacherleben*) the other's experience by stepping out of his or her shoes and exercising 'sympathy' (Ger., *Hineinversetzen*) or 'transposition'" (Thiselton 2009, 163).

Bultmann agreed with Schleiermacher and Dilthey about their presuppositions concerning the historical relationship between the author and the interpreter. He further added two questions about the language of the New Testament and what constitutes a genuine hermeneutical principle. Bultmann was convinced that the mythological language of the New Testament misrepresented human existence and faith. Paul Ricoeur (d. 2005) comments on his process of demythologizing:

> What he demythologizes is the cosmological form in primitive preaching. In fact, the conception of a world composed of three stories—heaven, earth, and hell—and peopled with supernatural powers which descend down here from up there is purely and simply eliminated, as out of date, by modern science and modern technology as well as by how man represents ethical and political responsibility. Everything that partakes of this vision of the world in the fundamental representation of the events of salvation is from now on void. (Ricoeur 1980, "Preface to Bultmann")

Paul J. Achtemeier confirms that for Bultmann, the mythic language "distort[s] the true subject matter of faith by objectifying it" (Achtemeier 1966, 102).

Bultmann also argued that a preunderstanding of faith must accompany the interpreter to ask the right questions of the New Testament. "[O]nly the one vitally engaged in the faith, one for whom questions of faith are existential concerns can understand and interpret the text" (Achtemeier 1966, 103–4). Braaten critiques this existential interpretation as the only hermeneutical principle. He asserts that the life of Jesus "and everything in the New Testament that transgress the framework of existentialist anthropology is considered as theologoumena in the questionable form of myth" (Braaten 1965, 224–25).

The creators of the "New Hermeneutics" are Ernst Fuchs (d. 1983) and Gerhard Ebeling (d. 2001). Ebeling asked, "What is the relationship of exegesis, as the concrete process of interpretation, to hermeneutics, as the explicit or implicit grasping of the ultimate conditions for understanding?" (Ebeling 1964, 34). Understanding takes place through the "linguisticality of human existence" (Achtemeier 1966, 105). Ebeling and Fuchs turned to the hermeneutical function of speech since language is the "very quintessence of human life" by which human beings understand themselves and the world in which they live (Kysar 1969, 216).

"Word-event" (Fuchs) or "language-event" (Ebeling) means "the occurrence of authentic expression in which being is exposed" (Kysar 1969, 217). They posit a relationship of the individual to the New Testament text in terms of existential becoming. The question of the self is central to the exclusion of everything else. Unlike Bultmann and his stance on believing, they describe the only reality as being human and being honest in front of the text. The Gospel does not presume faith but that we be pointed toward it (Achtemeier 1966, 104). For Fuchs, "faith [is] the achievement of true self-hood through the abandonment of the attempt to justify one's own existence. . . . If faith seeks to base itself on historical fact rather than on that continuing encounter with God within existence, such historical fact may lead faith away from its true task: the becoming self" (Achtemeier 1966, 114). Therefore, Jesus' death and resurrection have secondary importance compared to Jesus' words and teaching. As a founder of the "Second Quest for the Historical Jesus," Fuchs was especially involved with establishing authentic criteria for Jesus' sayings and teachings.

For Fuchs and Ebeling, everything is language. God's communication occurs through language. Only language mediates grace "because it functions as it ought to function as language, in creating unity, acceptance and rest" (Achtemeier 1966, 104). All theology is caught up in language and its interpreters. Their anthropological convictions are their theology.

The "New Hermeneutics" has many critics that question language as the only hermeneutic of reality. They wonder if the "self" is the only principle for understanding the New Testament. To say that the death and resurrection of Jesus are linguistic factors is to reduce the kerygma to words without any historicity. According to Fuchs, "The significance of Jesus is dissolved into words: It is the parables not the resurrection, 'which in reality resist death. They lead into eternal life.' Jesus' death is therefore 'a point where our daily life intersects with the death of Jesus' because our daily life has to do with death'" (Achtemeier 1966, 116). While the "New Hermeneutics" was important in the 1960s, Thiselton concludes, "[It] has generally lost much of its attention and interest, especially since the Heideggerian notion of language has been recognized as one-sided and its overgeneralized concept of 'speech-event' does not fully match the sophisticated theory of John Searle . . . and others" (Thiselton 2009, 191). For Thiselton and others, "[T]he movement seems largely to have burned itself out" (Thiselton 2009, 56).

Schleiermacher, Dilthey, Bultmann, Fuchs, and Ebeling contributed to biblical interpretation in different modalities. While they preferred an existential approach to preaching, they did not develop a method. According to Nancy Lammers Gross (2002, 73), a two-step model gradually developed for homiletics that is still used today. First, "understanding" (Ger., *Verstehen*) a text is using exegesis for textual meaning. Second, the homilist offers the assembly a homily, the "explanation" (Ger., *Eklären*).

Paul Ricoeur

When we explore the contributions of Paul Ricoeur, we find a scholar in whose extraordinary corpus are principles for interpretation and preaching. Although Ricoeur did not consider himself either an exegete or homilist, he admitted, "I stand in the position of a listener to Christian preaching: I assume that this speaking is meaningful, that it is worthy of consideration, and that examining it may accompany and guide the transfer from the text to life where it will verify itself fully" (Ricoeur 1979, 215).

The two-step model of "understanding" and "explanation" is too limited for Ricoeur. "Understanding" is not located in the exegetical task of the historical-critical method that reconstructs authorial intention and community. To the contrary, "[T]he text . . . is the paradigm of the distanciation in all communication" (Ricoeur 1973, 130).

Ricoeur describes three levels of *distanciation*. First, "[W]riting makes the text autonomous in relation to the intention of the author. . . . In short, it belongs to a text to decontextualize itself as much from a sociological point of view as from a psychological one and to be able to recontexualize itself in new contexts. The act of reading accomplishes the latter." Second, in regard to the audience, "[W]hereas the vis-à-vis is given in advance by the colloquy itself in the dialogical situation written discourse is open to an audience virtually understood as made up of whoever knows how to read." Third, "The functioning of the reference is profoundly altered when it is no longer possible to show the thing about which we are speaking as belonging to the common situation of the partners in the dialogue" (Ricoeur 1973, 133). The distanciation from author, situation, and audience fosters wide horizons for interpretation. For Ricoeur, "[T]his capacity of the text to mean more than any one interpreter can grasp at any one time is referred to as a surplus of meaning" (Gross 1992, 156).

Since Ricoeur finds that "understanding" (Ger., *Verstehen*) a text does not belong in the exegetical process of the historical-critical method, he suggests engaging a text through three steps:

*First Naivet*é. When a preacher turns to the text itself, e.g., a gospel pericope, she brings specific worldviews, experiences, social location, and pre-understandings to the text. It is a noncritical reading, a first naiveté. In reading the text several times, however, a dialogue often ensues. The preacher asks questions and makes guesses. The text asks questions too. Ricoeur states,

> The text is like a musical score and the reader like the orchestra conductor who obeys the instructions of the notation. Consequently to understand, is not merely to repeat the speech event in a similar event, it is to generate a new event beginning from the text in which the initial event has been objectified. In other words, we have to guess the meaning of the text because the author's intention is beyond our reach. (Ricoeur 1976, 75)

The context of the *first naiveté* can be Christian prayer, such as meditation or *lectio divina*. Here, the Holy Spirit encourages the preacher to let the pericope wash over body, mind, and spirit. Questions and dialogue with the text continue.

Critical Inquiry. Next, the preacher engages in "explanation" (Ger., *Eklären*). There is an opportunity to "analyze critical, analytical, exegetical methods . . . to begin checking the validity of the guesses" (Gross 1992, 197). Here, the preacher experiences the three levels of distanciation. Ricoeur declares, "Understanding is entirely mediated by the whole of explanatory procedures which precede it and accompany it" (Dorairaj 2000, 406). The preacher can clarify the context of *Eklären* by reviewing questions that arise from the text. By separating them according to a particular textual world, i.e., behind the text, of the text, and before the text (see 117 above), the preacher finds direction for the research (Schneiders 1999, 97–169).

*Second Naivet*é. For Ricoeur, the dialectic between understanding as guessing and explanation as validation becomes an *appropriation*. It is

> the actualization of meaning for someone. . . . What has to be appropriated is the meaning of the text itself, conceived in a dynamic way as the direction of thought opened up by the text. In other words, what has to be appropriated is nothing other than the power of disclosing a world that constitutes the reference of the text. (Ricoeur 1976, 92)

Where is the meaning of the text located? "It is neither behind the text as the presumed author, nor in the text as its structure, but unfolded in front of it" (Ricoeur 1979, 217). Ricoeur emphasizes the importance of *appropriation*:

"Interpretation is completed as appropriation when reading yields something like an event, an event of discourse, which is an event in the present moment. As appropriation, interpretation becomes an event" (Ricoeur, 1976, 92). "Interpretation" as "event" suggests that proclamation is the final step of hermeneutics. Ricoeur's distinctive contribution to "understanding" and "explanation" is not a linear progression, rather preachers discover that it is a spiral between *first naiveté* and *critical inquiry* until the proclamation (*second naiveté*) emerges.

Mimesis (Gr. for "imitation") is another important concept for Ricoeur. Lance B. Pape presents his analysis of a narrative by describing Ricoeur's three-part mimetic structure. *Mimesis* is "the universal, poetic activity through which humans struggle to make sense of their temporal existence. . . . [T]ime becomes human time to the extent that it is narrated; conversely, narrative is meaningful only insofar as it portrays or gives shape to temporal, human experience" (Pape 2013, 91).

Mimesis₁ means:

> [W]e come to every narrative with a readiness to see our own lives as a story, indeed with some vague sense of our lives as already an inchoate narrative. . . . [M]*imesis₂* designates the characteristics of a narrative text as a composition. . . . It is not simply the mimicking of human action but the creative reworking of incidents into an intelligible whole . . . [*mimesis₃*] designates the dimension of *mimetic* activity related to reading and corresponds to Ricoeur's general account of hermeneutical appropriation of poetic discourse. (Pape 2013, 94–96)

Pape develops *mimesis* further than Ricoeur. His argumentation is convincing: "[T]he preacher's engagement with the biblical text during sermon preparation can be grasped in three mimetic moments." Pape also proposes "the preached sermon in the hearing of *the* church will reflect three mimetic moments" (Pape 2013, 123–24).

Mary Catherine Hilkert also describes Ricoeur's *mimesis* for effective narrative preaching by using an analysis of the Emmaus story. Here, there is "the threefold pattern of prefiguration of past human experience [mimesis-1], configuration of the human story in light of the divine plot of the story of Jesus [mimesis-2], and refiguration of imagination and life through the ongoing process of conversion [mimesis-3]" (Hilkert 1997, 93–94). When Pape and Hilkert describe the three-part mimetic structure, echoes of *first naiveté*, *critical inquiry*, and *second naiveté* resound.

Likewise, *testimony* and *witness* are important concepts for Ricoeur in his understanding of the Bible. He develops not only a broad spectrum of testimony but also what happens when one testifies (Ricoeur 1979, 435–61). Testimony is "a dual relation: there is the one who testifies and the one who hears the testimony. The witness has seen, but the one who receives his testimony has not seen but hears. It is only by hearing the testimony that he can believe or not in the reality of the facts that the witness reports" (Ricoeur 1979, 439).

In his analysis of Isaiah 43:8-13, Ricoeur highlights the prophetic aspects of testimony: First, the witness is not just anyone who comes forward; rather, God sends the witness. Second, the witness testifies "about the radical, global meaning of human experience." Third, the testimony is oriented toward proclamation. "It is for all people that one people is witness." Fourth, the witness "implies a total engagement not only of words but of acts and, in the extreme, in the sacrifice of a life" (Ricoeur 1979, 445).

In his analysis of the New Testament, Ricoeur specifies the importance of the " 'confessional' kernel of testimony [as] certainly the center around which the rest gravitates. The confession that Jesus is the Christ constitutes testimony par excellence" (Ricoeur 1979, 447). He also describes eyewitness testimony: "[T]he witness is witness to things that have happened. We can think of the case of recording Christian preaching in the categories of story, as narration about things said and done by Jesus of Nazareth, as proceeding from this intention of binding confession-testimony to narration-testimony" (Ricoeur 1979, 447).

From his understanding of the Bible, Ricoeur identifies the importance of testimony as a double hermeneutic: "It gives to interpretation a content to be interpreted [and] it calls for an interpretation" (Ricoeur 1979, 454). By linking testimony and witness in his analysis of the Bible, Ricoeur lays the foundation for the hermeneutical process. In the *first naiveté*, the preacher encounters the testimony of the witness in a pericope. In the *critical inquiry*, the preacher expands understanding of the pericope. In the *second naiveté* or *appropriation*, the preacher testifies to the witness of the Gospel.

Conclusion

This essay presents a few considerations of hermeneutics from Plato to the twenty-first century. In particular, it considers the roots of the "New Hermeneutics" in the contributions of Friedrich Schleiermacher, Wilhelm Dilthey, and Rudolph Bultmann as well as what Ernest Fuchs and Gerhard Ebeling offer as founders of the movement. In this history, Dilthey, Bultmann, Fuchs, and Ebeling move the question of hermeneutics from exegesis of the author and community to questions about the text itself. Dilthey recognized the historical conditioning of the text and its interpreters. Bultmann demythologized the text to speak to contemporary readers. Fuchs and Ebeling focused on the power of the text in that its language connected to the "linguisticality of human existence." Nancy Lammers Gross notes that a homiletical model gradually developed from their work. The homilist uses exegesis for textual "understanding" (*Verstehen*) and offers "explanation" (*Eklären*) as a homily for the assembly.

Paul Ricoeur does not consider himself as an exegete or homilist. As a Christian believer he listens to the sermon and hopes it is life-giving to the community. His work in the philosophy of language and interpretation theory provides three contributions to homiletic theory and praxis. First is his biblical hermeneutics. His understanding of a text as written discourse opens it up to a surplus of meaning. His theory of triple *distanciation* also offers possibilities for preachers. Since "understanding" a text is "to generate a new event," Ricoeur offers a spiral hermeneutical process, namely, *first naiveté, critical inquiry*, and *second naiveté* (appropriation). Second is a structure for the preaching. He develops a three-part *mimetic* movement. This dynamic construction offers preachers opportunities to move from their personal social location to a proclamation for the assembly. Third is his "focus and function of preaching." His biblical and philosophical work on *testimony* and *witness* offers preachers new understanding of biblical texts as well as praxis.

Jacob D. Myers sees an integral connection "between Ricoeur's work and the contemporary preacher in the West: both are seeking answers to the deepest questions of what it means to be (before God and others in 'just institutions') and to find words to render a sufficient answer" (Myers 2013, 218).

Anna Carter Florence affirms, "God is not altogether hidden and silent, God is manifest in this world; God can be seen and known, here and now. God breaks into human lives and reflections and gives us an *experience* of the divine. And when this happens, we testify to it! . . . God calls us to testify" (Florence 2009, 63–64).

Bibliography

Achtemeier, Paul J. "How Adequate Is the New Hermeneutic?" *Theology Today* 23, no. 1 (1966).

Braaten, Carl E. "How New Is the New Hermeneutic?" *Theology Today* 22, no. 2 (1965).

Dorairaj, A. Joseph. "Ricoeur's Hermeneutics of the Text." *Indian Philosophical Quarterly* 37, no. 4 (2000).

Ebeling, Gerhard. "The New Hermeneutics and the Early Luther." *Theology Today* 21, no. 1 (1964).

Farris, Stephen. "Hermeneutics." In *The Interpreter's Handbook of Preaching*. Edited by Paul Scott Wilson. Louisville, KY: Abingdon Press, 2008.

Florence, Anna Carter. *Preaching as Testimony*. Louisville, KY: Westminster John Knox, 2007.

Gross, Nancy Lammers. *If You Cannot Preach Like Paul. . . .* Grand Rapids, MI: Eerdmans, 2002.

———. "A Re-examination of Recent Homiletical Theories in Light of the Hermeneutical Theory of Paul Ricoeur." PhD diss., Princeton Theological Seminary, 1992.

Hilkert, Mary Catherine. *Naming Grace: Preaching and the Sacramental Imagination*. New York: Continuum, 1997.

Kysar, Robert. "Demythologizing the New Hermeneutic Theology." *Journal of the American Academy of Religion* 37, no. 3 (1969).

Myers, Jacob D. "'Preaching Philosophy': The Kerygmatic Thrust of Paul Ricoeur's Philosophy and Its Contributions to Homiletics." *Literature and Philosophy* 27, no. 2 (2013).

Pape, Lance B. *The Scandal of Having Something to Say: Ricoeur and the Possibility of Postliberal Preaching*. Waco, TX: Baylor, 2013.

Ricoeur, Paul. "Chapter 1: Preface to Bultmann." In *Essays on Biblical Interpretation*. http://www.convencionbautista.com/yahoo_site_admin/assets/docs/Ricoeur_Paul_-_Essays_on_biblical_interpretation.155205058.pdf.

———. "The Hermeneutical Function of Distanciation." *Philosophy Today* 17, no. 2 (1973).

———. "The Hermeneutics of Testimony." *Anglican Theological Review* 61, no. 4 (1979).

———. *Interpretation Theory: Discourse and the Surplus of Meaning*. Fort Worth: Texas Christian University Press, 1976.

———. "Naming God." *Union Seminary Quarterly Review* 34, no. 4 (1979).

Schneiders, Sandra M. *The Revelatory Text: Interpreting the New Testament as Sacred Scripture*. 2nd ed. Collegeville, MN: Liturgical Press, 1999.

Thiselton, Anthony C. *Hermeneutics: An Introduction*. Grand Rapids, MI: Eerdmans, 2009.

Williams, Michael E. "Religious Education and the Hermeneutical Task." *Religious Education* 74, no. 6 (1979).

Contemporary Issues in Preaching

Contextual Preaching

Stephen Bevans and Ricky Manalo

The purpose of this essay is to provide a primer on the wider lens of contextual theology and suggest how this lens has implications for preaching. Specifically, "contextual preaching"—our preferred term—moves beyond the immediate boundaries of cultural location when the preacher takes into account four aspects of context: (1) the individual and social experiences of the preacher and the worshipers; (2) the cultural systems of meaning and interconnected values, customs, and practices that emerge from and are expressed by members of particular cultural groups; (3) the various "social locations" or identity/ies of the preacher and the worshipers; and (4) the ebb and flow of social change that continually transpires among worshipers, the worship event, and the larger world. After setting the context for preaching, the second half of this essay will provide useful pastoral examples and resources with the aim of developing contextual competence for preachers.

Contextual Theology and Contextual Preaching

There never has been just "theology" or "theologizing," but only "contextual theology" and "contextual theologizing." Theologians have concluded that theologizing today needs to honor the centrality of experience in human religious existence. Thus what has always been an implicit inclusion of experience now has become conscious and intentional. Theology, therefore, needs to be a reflection-in-faith that is a mutually illuminating and critical dialogue between the experience of the past in Scripture and tradition and the experience of the present in daily life—in other words, a dialogue between "text" and "context."

Theology done in context happens in many ways: as simple people ask deep questions and share faith; as poets marvel over glimpses of transcendence in ordinary life; as scholars meet together in conferences or write books and articles; as pastors prepare couples for marriage or parents for baptism; as congregations celebrate Eucharist in movement and song. Perhaps, however, where such theologizing might be done most frequently and consciously is in the pulpit, when preachers preach, as preachers prepare to preach, or when they assess their preaching in its aftermath. Preaching is a theological act, and authentic catholic preaching is a contextual act, the product of a dialogue between the scriptural-liturgical texts and a congregation's context.

Just as there is no such thing as "theology" but only "contextual theology," so there is no such thing as "preaching." There is only "contextual preaching." Only preaching that makes an effort to communicate to real people in real situations is preaching that is worthy of the name. It is not enough, writes Pope Francis (b. 1936), to "contemplate the word." A good preacher is one who contemplates the people, who has "an ear to the people" (*Evangelii Gaudium* [*EG*], no. 154). It is never a matter of *not* preaching in context. Rather, it is always a matter of what context one preaches out of and/or preaches to. A "default context" might be the culture or family background of the preacher, or the preacher's theological preferences or personal interests or passions (e.g., pro-life, social justice, music, or sports). That there is a context is not the issue. What is important is the discernment of what the context *is* by a conscious, intentional recognition of it as one prepares, delivers, or assesses a homily.

What Is Context?

As noted above, we prefer the term "contextual preaching." This is because we prefer the term "contextualization" or "contextual theology" to the term "inculturation." While "inculturation" has become the standard way of describing the process of including human experience in the act of theologizing among Roman Catholics, we are persuaded that paying homage to a wider range of human experience in theology is actually a much more comprehensive practice. According to Hervé Carrier, the term "inculturation" goes back to the 1930s (Carrier 1989, 89). It appeared in papal teaching for the first time in 1979 (*Catechesi Tradendae* [*CT*], no. 53). British missionary and anthropologist Aylward Shorter finds the term particularly useful and wrote a classic book on the topic (Shorter 1988). It appeared in John Paul II's (d. 2005) mission encyclical *Redemptoris Missio* (*RM*, nos. 25, 52–54), and in Francis's *EG* (nos. 116 and 122). Stephen Bevans has argued that the term "context" is a much broader and therefore much more useful term (Bevans 2002, 26–27). Thus, "contextual preaching" assumes a much wider focus, certainly including culture and all its elements but going beyond it to many other aspects of experience in which members of a particular congregation are participating.

Context has at least four major aspects to it. All of these may be present and operative in a particular congregation within which a preacher preaches, or only one or the other of them might be operative. As the preacher prepares, delivers, and assesses the preaching, however, she or he might use these four aspects as a kind of checklist.

First, there is individual and social experience. By "individual experience" we mean things that might be happening or have happened to individuals in the congregation, or what might even be happening or have happened to the preachers themselves. If preachers have "an ear to the people" they might know of members of the congregation that have experienced deaths in their family recently, or couples who have been struggling in their marriages, or who are celebrating the births of children or grandchildren. Preachers might have recently had significant pastoral encounters with others that have been transforming in some way, or preachers might draw on an experience of reading a poem or novel, or watching a film. By "social experience" we mean events or trends that people in a particular community, a wider area like a diocese or country, or the entire world have experienced. A brutal storm that has devastated a neighborhood, the sudden death of a teenager in a traffic accident, a worldwide phenomenon like climate change, the popularity of a song or a movie—all these are contexts out of which or within which a preacher might address her or his preaching.

Second, there is culture—in all of its complexity. Clifford Geertz (d. 2006) has famously described culture as a "system of inherited conceptions expressed in symbolic forms by means of which people communicate, perpetuate, and develop their knowledge about and their attitudes toward life" (Geertz 1973, 89). Thus a culture is like a web of interconnected values, customs, practices, kinship relations, and the like, creating the "world" in which people live. Robert Schreiter (b. 1947) speaks of this understanding as an "integrated" approach to culture and goes on to speak also of "global" concepts of culture wherein a worldview or meaning structure is not so much inherited as constructed, often as a way of addressing a power imbalance (Schreiter 1997, 46–61). Various ethnic cultures in the United States emerge in this way—for example, Latinoa or Asian American cultures are hybridities that have developed across what would ordinarily be distinct cultural lines (e.g., Mexican and Peruvian or Chinese and Korean). Contextual preaching connects the texts of the liturgy to the languages, practices, customs, and burning interests of the various cultural groups in the Christian assembly.

Third, and somewhat associated with these more "postmodern" (Arbuckle 2010, 1–18) understandings of culture, context consists of the various "social locations" of the men and women gathered for worship. By this we mean the various generations of the congregation—baby boomers, generation X, millennials—or the social location of race or gender or economic status. Depending on one's social location one will hear the message of the Gospel differently. Depending on the preacher's social location, she or he will hear the text differently and needs to take this into account vis-à-vis members of the assembly of different ages, education, generations, or race.

Fourth, context is about movements of social change. No context is static, and even traditional cultures are always undergoing change. We preach in a context of globalization, for good or for ill. We preach in a context of ecological crisis and climate change. We preach in a world that is struggling with new understandings of sexuality, with economic upturns and downturns, with drastic changes in population due to global migration and immigration, resulting in a multicultural society or multicultural liturgical assemblies. Technology has revolutionized the world in the last thirty or so years since the introduction of the personal computer, the advent of the cellular phone, Skype, Facetime, texting, and blogging (see 254ff. below). Our preaching needs to address these "new Areopagi" as John Paul II called them (*RM*, no. 37).

Preaching in Context

Like effective theologizing, the most effective preaching has always been done from within and in dialogue with particular contexts. In the New Testament, Jesus' preaching addressed his audience's daily concerns and was full of references to the Scriptures that Jews of his day knew so well (e.g., Matt 5:21, 27, 31; 8:4; 11:10; 13:14-15; Mark 12:26-27; Luke 11:29-32), current events (e.g., Luke 13:1-5), and folksy examples from daily life (e.g., Mark 4:1-34; Luke 15:1-10). Peter's powerful sermon in Acts of the Apostles (2:14-36) is a primary example of such contextual preaching: he addresses the crowd's immediate concern (its suspicion that he and the others were drunk!), he speaks within the context of Jewish culture (it was made up of Jews and proselytes from many nations), and he boldly announces the Good News of Jesus' Lordship, again with words that would challenge his audience with language they could understand.

How might preachers today continue to engage in this tradition of contextual preaching? Bevans has provided a set of models for engaging in contextual theology that can also prove helpful for discerning how preaching might be done in particular contexts as well. He names six models of contextual theology: the translation model, the anthropological model, the praxis model, the synthetic model, the transcendental model, and the countercultural model. Bevans understands models as "a kind of pattern or template that offers a way of performing a task. . . . [They are] streamlined, *artificially constructed* ways of thinking. . . . However, when we discern a pattern in the way a number of theologians proceed in doing theology, we might find it *useful* to identify that pattern so we can use it in similar situations" (Bevans 2009, 168). These models are to be understood as complementary to one another or inclusive. For example, in preaching, one might start with a translation model (details below) by adapting the meaning of a scriptural passage to a particular cultural context but, at another point, employ the countercultural model as a means to challenge a sociocultural practice that the scriptural passage critiques or denounces. Further, the models represent a dialogical process of basic attitudes that the preacher may have toward the past (Scripture and tradition) and/or the present context, i.e., "what is happening in one's personal or communal life, one's cultural reality, one's social location—or in the process of change in one's culture or in our world" (Bevans 2009, 169). For contextual preaching to be most effective, preachers have to consider the contexts in which they preach and then discern which model or complementing models might be used. Based on Bevans's work, we will now relate his six models to contextual preaching.

The Translation Model

A translation model for preaching presupposes that there is an inherent theological content that needs to be preserved while the preacher proceeds to translate this content into other languages, symbols, or cultural terms that are familiar to the people of the local worship community. The preacher first locates the essence of the content (e.g., the meaning of the scriptural reading or an official church teaching) and, then, through a more creative or idiomatic method, clothes the essence of this content "with the trappings of the culture or context into which one is translating" (Bevans 2009, 173). Thus, the content of the Christian message is taken seriously, but this content, while remaining preserved, receives a more accessible interpretation for the benefit of the listeners.

An example of this form of preaching can be found in Acts 17:16-31 (see 48ff. above). During his time in Athens, Paul preached in the synagogues and marketplaces and debated with Epicureans and Stoic philosophers. Distressed over the city's idol worship of "the unknown God" (17:23), Paul eventually preached at the Areopagus (the city's high court) in the language and cultural imagery that is familiar with his Greek listeners. At one point, he even quoted the Greek poets Epimenides of Knossos (sixth or seventh century BCE) and Aratus of Soli (d. 240 BCE) in his attempt to highlight a more personal relationship between God and them.

The Anthropological Model

While the primary concern of the translation model may be the preservation of the Christian tradition, the primary concern of the anthropological model is the preservation of the cultural identity and the worship context: the *context* of the community is more important than the *content* of Scripture or tradition. This does not mean Scripture and tradition are not taken seriously as they are still considered normative components, "but they are—like any theological expression of God's presence among us—thoroughly culturally conditioned, and as such are incomplete" (Bevans 2009, 175). The story of the Canaanite (Matt 15:21-28) or Syrophoenician woman (Mark 7:24-30) illustrates this model. Here, the non-Jewish woman's conversation with Jesus challenges Jesus' attitude toward her by expanding his cultural horizon beyond his own Jewish biases.

Preachers who might employ this model often spend considerable time studying or becoming immersed within the local context of the worshiping community. In so doing, "the warp and woof of the people's lives in their experiences, cultures, and identities" are safeguarded while the preacher provides "fresh perspectives on Christianity" (Bevans 2009, 176).

One example of this style of preaching comes from María Luisa Iglesias who suggests that preachers participate in regular gatherings of small Christian communities such as RENEW and the Cursillo (Iglesias 2000, 65). The preacher would not only learn about the cultural values of the local people but also maintain continuous engagement with the ebb and flow of social changes. She proposes:

> Imagine a preacher who participates in such a small Christian community. [The preacher] engages laborers who gather with others around a chipped kitchen table and listens to them explain how the word of God has impacted their lives and how they struggle to live this word daily. "Preaching" as a conversation or a sharing of faith has begun. Everyone in the small community speaks and is therefore a "preacher." And everyone is also a listener. The wise official preacher uses this participation in the Sunday homily to choose a theme or highlight from scripture, draws on illustrations or applications from the group, even borrows phrases or vocabulary. [The preacher] knows that the homily will reach his community because it is drawn from the heart of the same community. (Igliesias 2000, 68)

The Praxis Model

There may be circumstances when a preacher wishes to call the congregation to a particular action. The praxis model draws inspiration from theologies of liberation (e.g., Latin America, feminist, and African American) in which one's reflection on an injustice leads to prophetic action (see 210ff. above). Yet as a model for preaching, this may also be employed in any context in which the community is invited to choose, to proclaim, to evangelize in the light of the texts on which, or the occasion or situation in which, the preacher is preaching. Further, Scripture and tradition are viewed as both sources and models of God's ongoing revelation to these circumstances; hence, another name for this model is the "situational model."

Among the many examples one might cite is that of the great African American preacher and civil rights leader Dr. Martin Luther King Jr., renowned for his eloquent, deeply biblical, yet always contextual preaching in the civil rights and anti-Vietnam War movement. Richard Lischer described King's form of preaching as "Movement preaching," in which "every sermon presented the possibility of a focused response. Because every sermon was an expression of God's solidarity with the Movement, there was always something its hearers could do, hope, or suffer in harmony with this new Way God had unleashed in the South" (Lischer 1989, 180).

The Synthetic Model

As stated earlier, these models are not meant to be exclusive of one another. For this reason, a fourth model for contextual preaching is the synthetic model, in which the preacher intentionally combines the translation and anthropological models with the praxis model, while holding both of these models in dialogue with other cultural identities and contextual theologies within and among worship participants. Because the focus is on the dynamic process of dialogue and interchange, one may also call this an "analogical model." In worship contexts, the preacher is presumed to be aware of the context and then proceeds to translate Scripture and tradition in light of this context on the one hand and the praxis implications that may emerge as a result of this synthesis on the other hand.

A homily by Chicago Archbishop Blase Cupich (b. 1949) on the Second Sunday of Advent might provide an example of the synthetic model at work. It was a time when the nation was watching the daily demonstrations in Ferguson, Missouri, following the shooting by a white police officer of an eighteen-year-old African American male named Michael Brown. Cupich focused on the first reading (Isa 40:1-5, 9-11) and the gospel (Mark 1:1-8), and explained that in the Roman culture, within which Mark was writing, "gospel" meant the solemn proclamation of the "good news" of another Roman victory, proclaimed in the city as the victorious general was entering in triumph. Cupich said that Mark begins his gospel with a reference to this practice, but the Gospel he proclaims is of Jesus Christ, first witnessed to by John in the desert. It is a Gospel of the triumph over the enemy of sin that slithers into the deserts of our lives, often unexpectedly, and so it is a triumph that we can only enjoy if we lift our hands, so to speak, in a gesture of openness and vulnerability to God's grace. Focusing on the image of raised hands, the archbishop spoke of others today who seem to be lifting their hands in frustration at their own defenselessness and powerlessness: after Brown's shooting, many protesters raised their hands in a "don't shoot" gesture to the police. He then called the congregation to join in solidarity with them in their protest. After the prayer of the faithful, Cupich said, he would raise his hands in silence for some moments, and he invited the entire congregation to join him in that action. The Gospel needs not only to be proclaimed and accepted but also lived out in solidarity and service to others. The incidents at Ferguson were never explicitly mentioned, but Cupich skillfully translated the Gospel message by putting it in dialogue with contemporary experience and called for symbolic and concrete action.

The Transcendental Model

The transcendental model draws its inspiration from Immanuel Kant (d. 1804) and his "transcendental method" but is not meant to refer to a model that "points beyond itself," as the term "transcendence" suggests. Rather, this model places emphasis on the centrality of the "subject," that is, the human person in the act of knowing: "one only 'knows' when one has weighed all the evidence and come to a personal judgment of the truth" (Bevans 2009, 182). In worship contexts, preachers place value in their own context—their personal experiences, culture, and social location—for it is here that one encounters God that leads to the awareness of a wider truth. Bevans explains, "The deeper one goes into oneself and finds one's own identity as a believer and a unique subject with *these* experiences, *this* culture and *this* social location, the more my expression of faith helps others to discover their own authenticity as a believer and cultural subject" (Bevans 2009, 183–84).

In preaching, this model is made explicit when the preacher shares her own personal stories and reflections of lived experiences with the hope that others would find resonance with her experiences. This generative process may deepen levels of credibility and trust between preacher and listener, while still remaining faithful to both Scripture and tradition.

An example of this contextual model could be found in the preaching style of Fr. Kirk Ullery, the pastor of Our Lady of Lourdes Church, San Francisco, during a Sunday Mass on 8 October 1995. As recounted by liturgical ethnographer Mary McGann (McGann 2004, 122), Fr. Kirk began his preaching to this African American congregation by recounting his own experience, just three days before, of sleeping in Golden Gate Park among the homeless people. Being of European descent, he eventually admits his past racist attitudes ("I was born a racist."), his growing up in Pennsylvania ("All my playmates were white!"), his time living in New York in the 1950s where he first encountered black Catholic students, and his years in college and in the army. "It was [only gradually, slowly] that people / / broke / / my white / / heart." Following this last powerful statement, McGann describes the impact Fr. Kirk's stories have on the congregation: "Speaking deliberately, Father Kirk turns full circle, looking first at the choir seated behind him, then returning his gaze to the rest of the congregation. All eyes were focused on him, the room hushed by the power of his honesty. I could hear tears welling up inside me—tears of recognition, tears of empathy, tears of healing" (McGann 2004, 122).

The Countercultural Model

Unlike the previous five models that viewed context with somewhat positive lenses—while still maintaining that certain aspects of the context may need to be perfected or healed—the countercultural model views context through more suspicious eyes, to the extent that aspects of the context become a hindrance to the Gospel message. Countercultural themes can be found throughout Scripture and the church's tradition: e.g., "Do not love the world or the things in the world" (1 John 2:15); "Do not be conformed to this world, but be transformed by the renewing of your minds, so that you may discern what is the will of God—what is good and acceptable and perfect" (Rom 12:2); and Tertullian's (d. before 240) warning of cultural trappings that could obscure the Gospel (e.g., his *De Spectaculis*). As a model for preaching, the preacher first recognizes the validity of the Christian narrative that emerges from Scripture and tradition, and then uses this lens "to interpret, engage, unmask, and challenge the experience of the present, the context of individual and social experience, human culture, social location, and the dynamics of social change" (Bevans 2009, 186).

241

A homily of Pope Francis, addressed to the clergy, religious, and semi-narians of the Philippines on 16 January 2015 is a good example of this contextual model. Following his introduction in which he referenced the Gospel (John 21:15-17), Francis set the tone that primarily challenged those present to build a just and redeemed world order: "We are called to be 'ambassadors for Christ' (2 Cor 5:20). . . . We proclaim the joy of the Gospel. For the Gospel is the promise of God's grace, which alone can bring wholeness and healing to our broken world. *It can inspire the building of a truly just and redeemed social order*" (emphasis added; Francis 2015). This countercultural thread is woven throughout the entirety of the homily, urging bishops "to acknowledge and combat the causes of the deeply rooted inequality and injustice which mark the face of Filipino society, plainly contradicting the teaching of Christ." To the priests and members of religious communities, he warned of "a certain materialism which can creep into our lives and compromise the witness we offer. Only by becoming poor ourselves, by stripping away our complacency, will we be able to identify with the least of our brothers and sisters." He ended his homily with a petition that "the reconciling love of Christ penetrate ever more fully into the fabric of Filipino society and . . . to the farthest reaches of the world."

Conclusion

Francis writes how preachers "must be bold enough to discover new signs and new symbols, new flesh to embody and communicate the word, and different forms of beauty which are valued in different contextual settings, including those unconventional modes of beauty which may mean little to the evangelizers [read: "preachers"], yet prove attractive for others" (*EG*, no. 167). Such "new signs and symbols" will emerge as preachers commit themselves to discern them within the concrete context in which they preach. Contextual preaching, we contend, is not an option but a pastoral imperative.

Bibliography

Arbuckle, Gerald A. *Culture, Inculturation, and Theologians: A Postmodern Critique*. Collegeville, MN: Liturgical Press, 2010.

Bevans, Stephen. *An Introduction to Theology in Global Perspective*. Maryknoll, NY: Orbis Books, 2009.

———. *Models of Contextual Theology*. Rev. and expanded ed. Maryknoll, NY: Orbis Books, 2002.

Carrier, Hervé. *Gospel Message and Human Cultures*. Pittsburgh, PA: Duquesne University Press, 1989.

Francis. "Homily at Manila Cathedral." January 16, 2015. http://m.ncregister .com/blog/edward-pentin/full-texts-of-popes-homily-at-cathedral-in -manila-address-to-diplomats#.VdiEIEVWlss.

Geertz, Clifford. *The Interpretation of Cultures*. New York: Basic Books, 1973.

Iglesias, María Luisa. "Participative Preaching: Laity as Co-Authors of the Homily." In *Preaching and Culture in Latino Congregations*. Edited by Kenneth G. Davis and Jorge L. Presmanes. Chicago: Liturgy Training Publications, 2000.

Lischer, Richard. "The Word That Moves: The Preaching of Martin Luther King, Jr." *Theology Today* 46, no. 2 (1989).

McGann, Mary E. *A Precious Fountain*. Collegeville, MN: Liturgical Press, 2004.

Schreiter, Robert. *The New Catholicity: Theology between the Global and Local*. Maryknoll, NY: Orbis Books, 1997.

Shorter, Aylward. *Towards a Theology of Inculturation*. Maryknoll, NY: Orbis Books, 1988.

Ecumenical and Interfaith Preaching

Barbara K. Lundblad and Margaret Moers Wenig

Introduction

A Roman Catholic clergyman, woman religious, or layperson might be invited to preach in a synagogue, a multifaith gathering in honor of a national holiday, at a public rally against some injustice, or at a celebratory baccalaureate service. In such settings a preacher would hopefully use only texts and images that the various groups present shared in common, omitting what was particular to the preacher's own faith tradition. In his famous "I Have a Dream" "sermon" (28 August 1963), Dr. Martin Luther King Jr. (d. 1968) quoted the Declaration of Independence and "My Country 'Tis of Thee." From Scripture he proclaimed verses only from Amos and Isaiah, not Matthew or Paul; he mentioned "The Lord" but never Jesus. Similarly, when a rabbi speaks in a church or at a multifaith gathering she would hopefully omit all that is particularistic to Judaism from her sermon. That is the "easy" kind of interreligious preaching, focusing on the universal or "the lowest common denominator." Some might say that King's "I Have a Dream" speech was not a sermon at all, for it did not proclaim salvation through the crucified and risen Christ.

Then there are situations when the Roman Catholic homiletician on his own turf, might think that he does not have to worry about excluding or offending anyone until he discovers that the in-laws and children of the deceased's first wife are Jewish or that the grandmother of the bride is a survivor of the Shoah, and then he quickly edits his sermon. On Sunday mornings in churches around the world there are worshipers who have Protestant, Muslim, Jewish, or Hindu spouses, grandchildren, friends, or neighbors. What parishioners hear in church can affect how they think about and relate to such neighbors, friends, and extended family members. As Dianne Bergant notes, "Ours is a multiracial, multicultural, multilingual, multiclass, multigenerational community of women and men in an interfaith, postmodern, global ecosystem. These are the dynamics that are operative in our society and they can be neither ignored nor minimized" (117 above).

244

All preaching is interfaith preaching. Integrity demands that what we preach when speaking *to* people of other faiths aligns with what we say when speaking in our own settings *about* people of other faiths. Integrity demands that what we communicate from the pulpit explicitly and implicitly aligns with what we communicate in casual conversation overtly or by innuendo. Integrity also demands that what we say from the pulpit or at a party aligns with how we act and how we live. Our words and deeds ought to be a reflection of what we truly believe. At its core this chapter is about what we believe about people whose faiths are different from our own. Since beliefs are influenced both by the teachings of faith traditions and by personal experiences we will address both teachings and experiences that help to form one's belief about people of other faiths, specifically Jews. Finally, the chapter will examine two sermons delivered by Christians for Christians and the messages those sermons convey about Jews.

Teachings

Beginning with Vatican II's *Declaration on the Relation of the Church with Non-Christian Religions* (*Nostra Aetate*, 1965) and continuing with documents such as *Notes on the Correct Way to Present the Jews and Judaism in Preaching and Catechesis in the Roman Catholic Church* (Commission for Religious Relations with the Jews, 1985), the Catholic Church began to adopt what Mary Boys identifies as six key themes in relationship to Judaism: (1) repudiation of the charge of deicide, (2) repudiation of anti-Semitism, (3) repentance in regard to the Shoah, (4) recognition of the State of Israel [and subsequently Palestine], (5) rejection of proselytizing, and (6) a review of teaching about Jews and Judaism (Boys 2000, 248).

Pope Francis (b. 1936) has furthered Christian-Jewish relationships by rejecting a supersessionist view of Christianity and suggesting that Judaism and Christianity have equal claims to an understanding of the Word of God:

> Even with our different [Christian and Jewish] perspectives we confess one God, Creator of the Universe and Lord of history. And he, in his infinite goodness and wisdom, always blesses our commitment to dialogue. The Christian confessions find their unity in Christ; Judaism finds its unity in the Torah. Christians believe that Jesus Christ is the Word of God made flesh in the world; for Jews the Word of God is present above all in the Torah. Both faith traditions find their foundation in the One God, the God of the Covenant, who reveals himself through his Word. In seeking a right attitude towards God, Christians turn to Christ as the fount of new life, and Jews to the teaching of the Torah. (Francis, 30 June 2015)

According to Francis, Christianity has not replaced God's covenant with the Jewish people, for "with regard to the Jews . . . 'the gifts and the call of God are irrevocable'" (Francis, 24 June 2013).

Experiences

Why would this pope make such bold statements? Perhaps because as Archbishop Bergoglio in Argentina he, Rabbi Abraham Skorka, and another rabbi became friends, study partners, and teachers. "As friends, we enjoyed each other's company, we were all enriched through encounter and dialogue, and we welcomed each other, and this helped all of us grow as people and as believers" (Francis, 24 June 2013). The fruits of their friendship, of their "significant moments of sharing on a spiritual level" (Francis, 26 May 2014) and of Bergoglio's multiple visits to synagogues extend far beyond the book he and Skorka coauthored (Francis and Skorka, 2013 [2010]). These fruits continue to nourish the pope's teaching and preaching.

The authors of this chapter enjoyed a similar experience of collaboration, dialogue, and friendship. In tight financial straits, the Lutheran and Reform Jewish congregations we served in northern Manhattan shared a building for almost two decades (Barbara's congregation as the landlord and Maggie's as the tenant). Our congregations worshiped together on Thanksgiving and Martin Luther King Day—sometimes with Pentecostals or Seventh Day Adventists—and shared a Passover seder. We co-led a group for interfaith couples, co-taught a course for both congregations on the history, calendar, liturgy, and beliefs of Judaism and Christianity, co-taught an exploration of Jewish and Christian commentary on the binding of Isaac, celebrated milestones in each other's congregations and in each other's lives, co-officiated at the funeral of a newborn whose Jewish mother and Christian father had not decided in which faith their child would be raised, and we became fast friends. Barbara came to Rosh Hashanah and Yom Kippur services and Maggie attended worship services on Christmas Eve and during Holy Week. Along the way we also visited each other's services on Sabbaths and Sundays. No documents or books we read about each other's religious traditions had more impact than these encounters.

We are hardly alone in our experience. Two participants in Catholic-Jewish dialogue expressed the effect that dialogue had on their thinking. Julie Collins wrote:

> The Colloquium was a profoundly religious experience; it drew its participants into the boundlessness of the Divine. It challenged participants to move beyond the narrow limits in which they confine the Holy One, to

acknowledge in their heart of hearts that God, the Mother and Father of us all, has many children. With each of them, and each branch of the larger family, God has a specific and precious relationship. (Boys 2000, 277–78)

John Merkle reflected:

[Dialogue] forced me to realize that Christianity must never be the *object* of my faith but the *means* by which I express my faith in God. I became convinced that genuine faith in God demands a relativizing of one's own faith, that faith in God is incompatible with the absolutizing of anything other than God, including a cherished tradition that exists to foster faith in God. (Boys 2000, 277, emphasis added)

Two Sermons

During his 2015 visit to the United States, Pope Francis preached at a Mass in New York's Madison Square Garden. Here are a few pertinent excerpts from that homily:

We are in Madison Square Garden, a place synonymous with this city. This is the site of important athletic, artistic and musical events attracting people not only from this city, but from the whole world. In this place, which represents both the variety and the common interests of so many different people, we have listened to the words: "The people who walked in darkness have seen a great light" (Is 9:1).

The people who walked—caught up in their activities and routines, amid their successes and failures, their worries and expectations—have seen a great light. The people who walked—with all their joys and hopes, their disappointments and regrets—have seen a great light.

In every age, the People of God are called to contemplate this light. A light for the nations, as the elderly Simeon joyfully expressed it. A light meant to shine on every corner of this city, on our fellow citizens, on every part of our lives.

"The people who walked in darkness have seen a great light." One special quality of God's people is their ability to see, to contemplate, even in "moments of darkness," the light which Christ brings. God's faithful people can see, discern and contemplate his living presence in the midst of life, in the midst of the city. Together with the prophet Isaiah, we can say: The people who walk, breathe and live in the midst of smog, have seen a great light, have experienced a breath of fresh air.

Living in a big city is not always easy. A multicultural context presents many complex challenges. Yet big cities are a reminder of the hidden riches present in our world: in the diversity of its cultures, traditions and historical experiences. In the variety of its languages, costumes and cuisine. Big cities bring together all the different ways which we human beings have discovered to express the meaning of life, wherever we may be.

But big cities also conceal the faces of all those people who don't appear to belong, or are second-class citizens. . . . These people stand at the edges of our great avenues, in our streets, in deafening anonymity. They become part of an urban landscape which is more and more taken for granted, in our eyes, and especially in our hearts.

Knowing that Jesus still walks our streets, that he is part of the lives of his people, that he is involved with us in one vast history of salvation, fills us with hope. A hope which liberates us from the forces pushing us to isolation and lack of concern for the lives of others, for the life of our city. A hope which is unafraid of involvement, which acts as a leaven wherever we happen to live and work. A hope which makes us see, even in the midst of smog, the presence of God as he continues to walk the streets of our city. Because God is in the city.

What is it like, this light traveling through our streets? How do we encounter God, who lives with us amid the smog of our cities? How do we encounter Jesus, alive and at work in the daily life of our multicultural cities?

The prophet Isaiah can guide us in this process of "learning to see." He speaks of the light which is Jesus. And now he presents Jesus to us as "Wonderful Counselor, the Mighty God, the Everlasting Father, the Prince of Peace." In this way, he introduces us to the life of the Son, so that his life can be our life.

[The sermon then focuses on each of Isaiah's titles to encourage people to see light in the midst of the city.]

God is living in our cities. The Church is living in our cities. God and the Church living in our cities want to be like yeast in the dough, to relate to everyone, to stand at everyone's side, proclaiming the marvels of the Wonderful Counselor, the Mighty God, the Eternal Father, the Prince of Peace. "The people who walked in darkness have seen a great light." And we, as Christians, are witnesses to this.

Although this homily was preached at a Roman Catholic Mass and proclaims the role Jesus can play in people's lives and in the life of the city, it does not preclude the possibility that there might also be *other* ways in which the light of God is manifest. This sermon affirms "all the different ways which we human beings have discovered to express the meaning of life, wherever we may be."

Jews believe that God has "called us to righteousness, taken us by the hand to keep us as a covenant people, a light to the nations" (Isa 42:6), to bring about the very same redemption of humankind the pope so poignantly describes. The Jewish coauthor of this article has no trouble believing that God has sent many lights to the world, Jesus and Jews among them. She suspects that Pope Francis agrees, for in his address to the General Assembly of the United Nations he credited achievements of that body with being "lights which help to dispel the darkness of the disorder caused by unrestrained ambitions and collective forms of selfishness." He concludes with an assurance of

> my support and my prayers, and the support and prayers of all the faithful of the Catholic Church, that this institution, all its member states, and each of its officials, will always render an effective service to mankind, a service respectful of diversity and capable of bringing out, for sake of the common good, the best in each people and in every individual. (Francis, 28 September 2015).

The Lutheran coauthor of this essay is a frequent preacher on the radio program "The Protestant Hour," now called "Day 1." In one of her sermons she explores what it means to experience the closeness of God's Word expressed in Deuteronomy 6. She moves from the story of older Jewish women learning Hebrew to Luther's translating the Bible into German and the story of Helen Keller seeing the connection between water and word. By the end of the sermon she gently invites people to experience God's closeness through new language.

> Every Wednesday at 2:30 they gather around the table. Six Jewish women . . . all except the rabbi over sixty years old. They have come, not to clean the kitchen or to embroider names on the Seder table cloth—though they have done those things many times. On Wednesdays they come to learn Hebrew.
>
> They come because when they were children, girls were not taught Hebrew alongside boys. So now these women cannot read the Torah in the Sabbath service. They must trust phonetic spelling on the prayer book's page, words they have learned to pronounce, but cannot actually read. Slowly, they read around the circle, saying the ancient letters aloud. Writing the words right to left, always right to left.
>
> Why would someone do such a thing at sixty-five? All those years of Sabbath services, years of Passover seders and candle blessings, without reading a word of Hebrew. Why now? I cannot speak for them. . . . I only sit in their circle, learning beside them. But my guess is that something inside them longed to read the words for themselves. They have been invited to write the word on the doorposts of their lives.
>
> [The preacher goes on to talk about Luther translating the Bible into German and tells the story of Helen Keller discovering the connection between the word being tapped into her palm and the water gushing from the pump.]

The connection changes everything. . . . The connection between word and self is at the same time a connection always larger . . . between Helen and her teacher, one human being to another.

Yet there is another connection even bigger when the word that is touched is the word we call "God's word." Our ancestors in the faith stood in awe before this holy word of God. . . . But they knew also that this word was near.

These words which I command you this day shall be upon your heart. And you shall teach them diligently to your children, and shall talk of them when you sit in your house, and when you walk by the way, and when you lie down, and when you rise. And you shall bind them as a sign upon your hand, and they shall be as frontlets between your eyes. And you shall write them on the doorposts of your house and on your gates.

This word is so close that it is bound on our hands and between our eyes. We must write it on our gates and on our doorposts to ensure that we never go out or in without seeing the word of God there. On my street I watch the Jewish children running in and out to play, reaching up to touch the mezuzah on the doorframe. Touching it quickly, but touching it every time.

The longing to touch God's word is very deep. . . . What does it mean when women hear a new word, not spoken before? "You shall be called sons and daughters of God." Daughters. A woman who has never heard her gender, her experience, her story will begin to see the connection between her life and God's word.

Such work is not a passing fancy, nor a fad: such work is the work of faithfulness. It is taken on because we are a people who believe the word of God is near, not far off. It must be written on OUR doorposts, on our gates, even on our hands and between our eyes. . . . We are translating slowly, speaking words we had not dared to speak before, speaking of God who is both mother and father. . . . God who longed to be so near that the Word became flesh and dwelt among us. To believe such a mystery is to believe the word is living, always pouring into our palms. . . . Until we make the connection between God's word and our own lives . . . and our doorposts will never be the same. (Lundblad 2001, 82–88)

In this sermon, Barbara subtly explains the longing for new language by those whose lives are not yet reflected in liturgies and hymns. As she does this, she also honors some of the gifts she's received from her Jewish neighbors. She shows Jews as real people, not caricatures—people she lives among, people for whom she has empathy and appreciation. She does not disparage the Jews she describes nor imply that their rituals of lighting candles or touching mezuzahs are silly or empty or unnecessary. On the contrary, she holds up the elderly Jewish women learning Hebrew and the Jewish children touching their mezuzahs as they cross their thresholds, as models of faithfulness. She does not refrain from saying that the Word became flesh in Jesus, yet she also portrays the word as being quite tangible in the form of the mezuzah and the Hebrew language.

Barbara considers Krister Stendahl to be one of her mentors in the Lutheran family of Christians. In his scholarly writing on Paul and the Jews and his advocacy for religious tolerance as bishop of Stockholm, he called Christians to see religious pluralism as a gift rather than a threat. In 2007 Yehezkel Laudau interviewed Stendahl for the *Harvard Divinity School Bulletin*:

> [Stendahl] was my New Testament professor. I still consider him my "Christian rebbe." We have stayed in touch, as friends and colleagues, over three decades. After I moved to Israel in 1978, I saw him whenever he and his wife, Brita, came to Jerusalem. . . . Once more we see the significance of friendship for interfaith understanding. When Laudau asked him about leadership, Stendahl gives an answer related to interfaith dialogue:
>
> I would apply the same rules for good leadership that I often do for effective interfaith dialogue: let the other define herself (don't think you know the other without listening); compare equal to equal (not my positive qualities to the negative ones of the other); and find beauty in the other so as to develop "holy envy." (Laudau 2007)

While a central focus of this essay has been Roman Catholic attitudes toward Jews and Judaism, Stendahl's three-point advice applies to all interreligious preaching:

1. Let the other define herself: don't think you know the other without listening.
2. Compare equal to equal—not my positive qualities to the negative ones of the other.
3. Find beauty in the other so as to develop "holy envy."

Such guidelines apply to our preaching about other religions, including Muslims:

> [A]s stated clearly in *Nostra Aetate*, recent papal teaching and statements of episcopal conferences, Catholics are called to respect Muslims. An emphasis on peace and patience together with the encouragement to foster good relations with local Muslims is crucial, therefore, when preaching about Islam in any context. (United States Catholic Conference of Bishops 2012, no. 41)

Why engage in interfaith dialogue, why encounter the other as a dear friend, why consider all of our sermons to be interfaith sermons? While violence and revenge and incitements to more violence are voiced by leaders in the Middle East, as well as in Europe and the United States, we recall these words from Pope Francis: "Mutual understanding of our spiritual heritage, appreciation for what we have in common and respect in matters on which we disagree: all these can help to guide us to a closer relationship, an intention which we put in God's hands. Together, we can make a great contribution to the cause of peace" (Francis, 26 May 2014).

Bibliography

Allen, Ronald J., and Clark M. Williamson. *Preaching the Letters without Dismissing the Law: A Lectionary Commentary*. Louisville, KY, and London: Westminster John Knox, 2006.

———. *Preaching the Gospels without Blaming the Jews: A Lectionary Commentary*. Louisville, KY, and London: Westminster John Knox, 2004.

Bishop's Committee on the Liturgy. *God's Mercy Endures Forever: Guidelines on the Presentation of Jews and Judaism in Catholic Preaching*. Washington, DC: USCCB, 1988.

Boys, Mary C. *Redeeming Our Sacred Story: The Death of Jesus and Relations between Jews and Christians*. Mahwah, NJ: Paulist Press, 2013.

———. *Has God Only One Blessing? Judaism as a Source of Christian Self-Understanding*. Mahwah, NJ: Paulist Press, 2000.

Commission for Religious Relations with the Jews. *Notes on the Correct Way to Present the Jews and Judaism in Preaching and Catechesis in the Roman Catholic Church*. March 6, 1982. http://www.vatican.va/roman_curia/pontifical_councils/chrstuni/relations-jews-docs/rc_pc_chrstuni_doc_19820306_jews-judaism_en.html.

Francis. "Address to United Nations General Assembly." September 28, 2015. http://w2.vatican.va/content/francesco/en/speeches/2015/september/documents/papa-francesco_20150925_onu-visita.html.

———. Homily. Madison Square Garden, New York. September 25, 2015. https://w2.vatican.va/content/francesco/en/homilies/2015/documents/papa-francesco_20150925_usa-omelia-nyc.html.

———. "Address of His Holiness Pope Francis to Members of the International Jewish Committee on Interreligious Consultations." June 30, 2015. https://w2.vatican.va/content/francesco/en/speeches/2015/june/documents/papa-francesco_20150630_iccj.html.

———. May 26, 2014. "Courtesy Visit to the Two Chief Rabbis of Israel." Heichal Shlomo Center, Jerusalem. Online at https://w2.vatican.va/content/francesco/en/speeches/2014/may/documents/papa

-francesco_20140526_terra-santa-visita-rabbini-israele.html - 13k - 2014-05-26.

———. "Address of His Holiness Pope Francis to Members of the International Jewish Committee on Interreligious Consultations." June 24, 2013. https://w2.vatican.va/content/francesco/en/speeches/2013/june /documents/papa-francesco_20130624_international-jewish-committee .html.

Francis, and Abraham Skorka. *On Heaven and Earth: Pope Francis on Faith, Family and the Church in the Twenty-First Century.* New York: Image, 2010 [repr. 2013].

Henderson, J. Frank. "An Alternative Lectionary for Lent, Good Friday, Eastertide and Advent: Respecting Jews and Judaism, Revisioning Church, Refocusing Liturgical Seasons." www.jfrankhenderson.com (revised 2005).

Laudau, Yehezkel. "An Interview with Krister Stendahl." *Harvard Divinity School Bulletin* 35, no. 1 (2007).

Lundblad, Barbara. *Transforming the Stone: Preaching through Resistance to Change.* Nashville, TN: Abingdon Press, 2001.

Salmon, Marilyn J. *Preaching without Contempt: Overcoming Unintended Anti-Judaism.* Minneapolis: Fortress Press, 2006.

United States Conference of Catholic Bishops. *Preaching the Mystery of Faith: The Sunday Homily.* Washington, DC: USCCB, 2012.

Webb, Joseph M. *Preaching and the Challenge of Pluralism.* St. Louis: Chalice Press, 1998.

Preaching in a Digital Age

Anthony Collamati, Richard Vosko, and Alex Zenthoefer

During the Vatican's first radio broadcast, Senator Guglielmo Marconi (d. 1937) had the honor of introducing Pope Pius XI (d. 1939). As one of the early inventors of radio, Marconi was asked to build a station for the church on Vatican Hill. By 1931 construction was complete, and Marconi prepared his audience for an unprecedented event. He explained in English that for the first time in history, a pope's voice would be heard at the same moment around the world.

The radio address was a milestone in technology's ever-expanding ability to navigate time and space. Nine years after this first radio broadcast Fulton J. Sheen led the first televised religious program on Easter Sunday in New York (see 89ff. above). Parishes that were promoting local TV broadcasts in the 1950s are now programming the content of their own YouTube channels. Similarly, almost every public appearance of the pope can be live-streamed in high definition video on mobile devices—complemented by a bevy of Facebook pages, Instagram accounts, podcasts, playlists, and e-books.

The Roman Catholic Church has moved relatively quickly in adopting these new technologies. Early on it voiced sustained opposition to some media—particularly film, a resistance that persisted from the silent film era through a 1958 ban on film projections during the liturgy. Vatican II (1962–1965), however, ushered in an era of prudent acceptance of new communication methods, including a papal Twitter account in 2012. Pope Benedict XVI (b. 1927) captured this cautious optimism in a message delivered on World Communications Day in 2011. Recognizing that the internet had instigated a "period of vast cultural transformation," he underscored the promise of digital networks. "This means of spreading information and knowledge," he said, "is giving birth to a new way of learning and thinking, with unprecedented opportunities for establishing relationships and building fellowship" (Benedict XVI, 2011).

Given this potential of new media—and the announcements every few months of new "must-have" devices, expanded features, and updated apps—preachers and other religious leaders interested in using the most effective means of communication at their disposal are faced with the difficult question: "What ought we to do?" How might technology feasibly be integrated with the resources, traditions, and fluencies of a local or even universal church? Where might the Gospel message be found, for example, on Snapchat?

Such questions could prompt an "arms race" mentality, in which the metric of success is calculated according to the number of active new media accounts. Some are tempted to dismiss or reject completely technologies that emerged after the heyday of their generation. Still others desire a catered menu, which organizes and enumerates the many available digital services so that they might select à *la carte* a collection of communication styles that best suits their preferences.

When making such decisions about media and technology, it is advisable to pause momentarily and reflect on the fundamental nature of these terms that have become inflated over the years with so many hopes and anxieties. The noted media theorist Marshall McLuhan (d. 1980) famously tried to provoke this kind of critical pause with his seemingly paradoxical statement, "the medium is the message" (McLuhan 1994, 7). Taken conservatively, the line challenges us to consider how meaning changes based on the medium through which it is communicated; for example, how "I love you" texted on a phone carries an entirely different resonance than "I love you" spoken in person or written in rose petals. Tools, materials, and contexts alter the rhetorical situation. They transform content.

"Technology" as a term, and close relative of "media," stems from the Greek *techne*. In antiquity it referred to a specific form of knowledge that was created during artistic production. Aristotle (d. 322 BCE) offers the example of a flutist whose playing demonstrates substantial knowledge (Aristotle 2000, 312). This Greek framing of *techne* becomes important to French philosopher Bernard Stiegler (b. 1952), who uses it to situate his definition of human *techne* or "technics." For Stiegler, technics describe the sense-making activities that humans use to transfer meaning from their "interior milieu" or inner thoughts into their "exterior milieu" or physical environment (Stiegler 1998, 55). A carpenter's hands and hammer, therefore, become a technology that impresses an idea of "chair" into a piece of wood. The flute would also count as a technology, as it vibrates into the air notes that derive from the player's internal rhythm. Even a preacher's voice echoing over the congregation becomes a technology, each syllable enunciating a new signal into the room. The same holds true for a dancer's movements or an architect's drafting—all of these would be for Stiegler "technics" or practices and tools (technologies) for projecting ourselves onto the world. In Stiegler's terms, technics is a defining characteristic of being human.

Thus, a more provocative interpretation of McLuhan's "the medium is the message" becomes clear. Not only does the medium affect the messages it carries but also, in Stiegler's estimation, society pays far too much attention to the content a medium produces. The words spoken, the text written, or the movie filmed consumes popular interest. McLuhan called for a reversal, a move from questions of "what" media produce to investigations of "how" they communicate. For example, rather than examining the notes on the Facebook page of someone who has died, we might instead question how this posting of condolences changes the expression and reception of grief.

The focus on "how" media function was intimately connected to McLuhan's own faith life. His conversion to Roman Catholicism later in his career made him a regular figure at daily Mass. There, he noted an extraordinary transformation of the liturgy even before the reforms of Vatican II. Surprisingly, he dates it at the introduction of the microphone. McLuhan found that the solitary meditative space, which he once enjoyed at a discrete distance from the presider's recitations in Latin, disappeared under the amplified signal of loudspeakers. What had once been an almost chant-like murmur became clear and forceful, as if the priest was engaged in a personal dialogue with him. He makes the somewhat bold claim that this shift from physical projection to electronic projection of the spoken word served as the catalyst for the use of the vernacular during liturgy. The microphone emphasized the necessity of being heard by the congregation and being understood. It is difficult to validate such a theory; anecdotes of increased microphone sales to churches after the council could simply have been the result of lower cost or greater familiarity with the technology. Still, McLuhan's assertions are worth noting as a reminder that choices in *techne* bear consequences. He was fond of saying that every extension which media grant to our capacities (such as the ability to extend one's voice across a vast space) comes simultaneously with a type of amputation. Loss attends every gain. Whereas the microphone increased clarity, heightened a sense of proximity within the congregation, and suggested the possibility that everyone's voice might be equally heard within a church, it also detracted from a sense of private space, the availability of personal reflection, and—in McLuhan's estimation—the architecture of existing churches: built around the acoustics of the human voice and meant to magnify perceptions of distance, place, and space (McLuhan 1999, 110). His plea in all of this is to be more thoughtful of the *effects* of media—how they transform meaning, how they influence behavior, and how they reconfigure our perception.

If McLuhan's invitation to focus on effects offers a strategy to those searching for a foothold in the dramatic shifts of digital culture, how does one go about attending to these effects? A number of approaches hold promise, but two seem especially useful to those in positions of ministry and leadership. The first comes from another seminal figure in media studies, Harold Innis (d. 1952), one of McLuhan's foremost influences. Beginning his career as an economist, Innis studied the history of some of Canada's natural resources or "staples" like the fur trade. He became fascinated by how the material makeup of a nation's media influenced its efficiency and organization. His subsequent work broadened this scope to communication styles of history's most prominent empires and institutions. He proposed that the longevity and success of a society was in large part attributable to the media they used to negotiate time and space. Just as the Vatican's first radio address transcended longstanding challenges to reaching audiences across great distances, so too did the invention of papyrus, parchment, and paper present new communication opportunities for their respective societies. Innis classified these media into two types. Light media, like paper, were aligned with conquests of space and could be easily reproduced and transported. On the other hand, durable media, like stone tablets, were aligned with time and far more permanent (albeit more difficult to produce). In Innis's estimation, light media have historically been favored by societies needing to assert military control over broad regions. Ancient Romans, he claimed, were able to administer their empire through the affordability of papyrus, which could be procured inexpensively and used to disseminate information to distant lands. Conversely, durable media have been much more helpful to religious societies looking to organize and exercise spiritual authority. Monastic scribes, for example, took painstaking effort to copy manuscripts on parchment, safeguarding the wisdom of past ages and consolidating knowledge into future centers of learning. Innis's takeaway is that sustained prosperity requires a balance of both durable and light media (Innis 2007, 159–60).

In terms of the present age, it is clear that the internet has initiated a boom in light, portable media. Voices around the world continuously update newsfeeds on Twitter, family members thousands of miles apart chat in video streams on Skype, and mobile users share images with hundreds if not thousands of followers. Longstanding monopolies of knowledge have broken down and rendered information much more accessible to a wider audience. This abundance, while meriting praise and optimism, is also indicative of a relative lack: the scales have shifted away from more durable and permanent media. Following Innis's argument, this imbalance would signal a dearth of spiritual channels and expressions in the popular media landscape.

The charge for current religious leaders, therefore, is not necessarily to condemn light media but rather to seek out ways to enrich the church's longstanding traditions and resources in durable media. With Stiegler's and McLuhan's broader approaches to technology and communications in mind, a worthy aim would be to consider how the church might celebrate the technics and media in which it is so fluent: the great architectural spaces for worship and community; the sacramental symbols of water, fire, oil, and incense; the liturgical rites of movement and song; the rich iconography of church history; the practices of meditation and prayer; the oral tradition of proclamation and fellowship. How might these media be put in renewed service of people missing more durable modes of communication and the spiritual growth which they facilitate?

This reassessment of the church's own durable media and fluencies is one way of responding to McLuhan's plea to think more expansively of media's effects. A second would be to reflect on how the church historically has used media in its ministry. Eileen Crowley offers a helpful overview of this history in *Liturgical Art for a Media Culture*. In it, she identifies a number of uses for technology in religious practice. The first and perhaps most evident is evangelization (see 105ff. above). The effort to disseminate religious messages to persuade believers and nonbelievers alike has drawn a host of technologies, from magic lantern shows during the Reformation to cinematic, audiovisual light shows in modern megachurches. Crowley points out that evangelical and "growth-oriented" denominations tend to focus their resources on this particular use of media and have far outpaced the majority of Roman Catholic parishes. A second role for media has been liturgical renewal that, while popular in the first two decades after Vatican II, lost its impetus in the late 1980s (Crowley 2007, 28). Furthermore, the ecclesial content that is produced today tends to lag significantly behind the professional, creative industries in terms of practices and applications (Crowley 2007, 32).

One use that Crowley implies more than analyzes is media as a locus for pastoral intervention. Emerging technics are in need of guidance, leadership, and spiritual care. The "vast cultural transformation" that Benedict identified has changed not only "the way we communicate, but communication itself" (Benedict XVI 2011). Human technics have been reconfigured and with them, everyday behaviors and perceptions. The adoption of portable, light media has been so accelerated that there has been little time for reflection and analysis. In the midst of frequent upgrades some prominent voices have tried calling attention to digital technology's effects on the mysteries and phenomena of being human. Sherry Turkle has discussed the ways in which empathy and intimacy are diminished outside of face-to-face conversations (Turkle 2015). Jaron Lanier has speculated about encroachments on privacy and financial security when online services continually exchange their resources for users' information and creative output (Lanier 2011). Jonathan Crary has written about the impact on memory and individuality as networked societies enter a 24/7 work cycle (Crary 2014). These are just a few examples, and whether or not one agrees with their critiques, they are evidence of a growing movement that questions the adaptations society has made to integrate networked technologies into daily practice.

Media and Evangelization

In the Roman Catholic Church the new evangelization is understood as a calling to deepen one's faith, believe in the Gospel, and then proclaim it to others (see 105ff. above). The homily is one important vehicle for such evangelizing. Astute preachers and pastoral leaders use all available instruments to reach as many people as possible with a fresh interpretation of the Gospel. Pope Francis (b. 1936), like his predecessor Benedict XVI, uses Twitter (@Pontifex) to send brief messages daily. The Twiplomacy Study (2015) reported that while President Barack Obama (b. 1961) may be the most followed world leader, Pope Francis—with accounts in nine languages—is the most influential, judging by how often his messages are retweeted.

Why are social media services important venues for evangelization? The shift in the religious behavior of people offers at least one compelling reason. Tracked by different organizations, including the Center for Applied Research in the Apostolate and the Pew Research Center, findings indicate that people are increasingly disassociating themselves from the religions of their childhood. The number of affiliated regular churchgoers is declining in the United States and abroad, while the number of unaffiliated, nonbelievers, and atheists is rising.

According to a study by the Pew Center, 29 percent of millennials (born between 1977 and 1992) are unaffiliated (Pew Center, 2014). Eighty-six percent say they believe in God but only 58 percent are certain that God exists. According to this survey 81 percent of them are on Facebook. Although employing Facebook is no guarantee that pastoral leaders and preachers will connect with these young adults, it can be a significant way to reach them.

The post-millennials (also generation Z or pluralists) represent the generation born after 1997. The social networks of this young age group are the most diverse in terms of race, sexual orientation, genders, economic status, and spiritual or religious beliefs. Time will tell if this "iGeneration" will become disenchanted with the religion in which they were raised, if they were raised in one at all.

The pastoral instructions of popes, bishops, and religious leaders in the Roman Catholic Church have expressed concern about these documented shifts. Communication from recent popes invites the church to heed the call to a new evangelization. They have summoned the church and its leadership to proclaim the person of Jesus Christ in ways that can be attractive; at the same time they challenge habitual assumptions. Documents from the Pontifical Commission on Social Communications such as *Communio et Progressio* (1971) and *Aetatis Novae* (1992) as well as the themes for the World Communications Days since 2002 have either pointed to or stressed the important role that the internet and social media can play in the work of evangelization. Rethinking traditional forms of evangelization such as preaching in the digital age is the challenge.

Social networking services can help pastoral teams and homilists in their ministries as evangelizers in achieving a variety of different goals:

Preparing for preaching. The internet is a boon to those looking for fresh material, insights, and models in the process of preaching preparation. Schools of theology and divinity schools send out weekly scriptural reflections or exegetical guides on readings for the coming Sunday. Many preachers have taken to blogging and populate the internet with sermon outlines, illustrations, and even full-blown homilies. Texts and articles on preaching are available through multiple outlets such as the American Theological Library Association (ATLA.com), and dynamic preaching exemplars can sometimes be found on YouTube.com. Most helpful are sprawling digital commons such as Textweek.Com that draw together hundreds of links for sermonic browsing and borrowing.

Publishing homilies. Innumerable platforms are available for sharing homilies and other evangelizing materials. These include Facebook.com, Linkedin.com, and Twitter.com. Blogging platforms can also be used for posting homilies, such as WordPress.com or Blogpot.com. Digitally recorded homilies can be uploaded on YouTube.com or Vimeo.com. Sites such as Podomatic.com enable preachers to disseminate their preaching as podcasts. Communities interested in live-streaming video services—a contemporary twist on televised Masses—can engage a company such as Ustream.tv. Many congregations are establishing their own websites, which among other things can also archive homilies.

Getting Feedback. There are multiple ways that preachers can get feedback on their preaching or continue conversations with parishioners about topics raised in a homily. Parish chat rooms are a possibility, as well as many of the social media platforms noted above. More systematically, organizations could employ a site like SurveyMonkey.com for designing, disseminating, and analyzing surveys about past preaching events, or soliciting ideas for future preaching. Communication platforms such as Skype.com could allow preachers to receive feedback from peers on sermon ideas or brainstorm ideas for the coming Sunday or feast.

Connecting with people. Weekly paper bulletins or seasonal publications are slowly giving way to electronic newsletter services like ConstantContact.com and MailChimp.com. A more geographically appropriate platform is NextDoor.com, a private social network designed for neighborhoods. Territorial parishes might find this resource useful in connecting with members who are geographically close. Some communities are creating their own parish app for staying connected to their members. A service such as Parishapps.com from Our Sunday Visitor is directed explicitly at Roman Catholic parishes. More broadly, given the many parish consolidations that have occurred in Roman Catholic dioceses, live streaming technologies could be employed to connect satellite churches to a local parish, or even cathedral, for key worship events such as Triduum.

There are certainly challenges to engaging the digital world for preaching. Maintaining a website or parish app, streaming liturgies, archiving homilies, or hosting a feedback chat room could be a full-time job. It is not unusual for larger congregations to establish an information technology (IT) department. While preachers do not have to assume responsibilities for these many aspects of a digital presence, the more their digital fluency the more effectively these new technologies can become. Lastly, some of these programs do require subscriptions or other fees. Budgeting for these services will require advance planning. Local businesses who sponsor the weekly bulletin will be just as eager to advertise online where links to their companies will be just a click away. Gradually moving away from light media such as paper is a sensitive and laudable environmental action.

Media in the Preaching Event

Employing media while preaching offers another opportunity to render a homily more accessible and intelligible. Although worship is not essentially a time for entertainment—although hopefully it is enjoyable—studies suggest that attention spans of adults can be relatively short and even shorter for the young. It can be difficult for even the best preachers to keep everyone's attention during a homily. Notable is the rise in reported cases of attention deficit hyperactivity disorder—the Centers for Disease

Control and Prevention (CDC 2014) project it affects over 11 percent of all children. Educators maintain that learners of every age absorb and retain more information when they hear it and see it at the same time.

Preachers understand that a well-chosen visual aid can help get a point across. In this digital age, preachers are invited to rethink their use of images not only as a visual aid to complement a spoken point but also as a potentially transformative element capable of articulating a point or dimension that speech alone is unable to capture. Media projection will not make a bad sermon good, but it can make a good sermon better.

Although projecting still slides is yet the norm, flashing videos or clips on the screen can make a sermon more accessible. Some software to achieve these purposes is specifically marketed for the worship environment, e.g., through EasyWorship.com and WorshipHouseMedia.com. Of course, such videos are not a substitute for proclaiming the Word of God and should not displace it. Rather, they are intended to help the assembly make more dynamic connections between God's Word and their own lives.

It is critical that everyone in the church can see what is projected. In long, narrow churches monitors may have to be installed along the length of the nave. In more centralized worship seating plans, two or three well-placed screens will suffice. Some churches are designed where one enormous projection surface runs along the back wall of the chancel or sanctuary serving as a kind of contemporary ever-changing reredos.

The dynamic technologies required to support worship preaching can be very expensive. They also require a steep learning curve for the preacher and the technicians so that such digitally enhanced preaching becomes a seamless part of worship.

Conclusion

New and wondrous innovations inevitably lie ahead, each one replete with its own conveniences and concerns. In the face of this future, Benedict invites Christians to participate "confidently and with an informed and responsible creativity" (Benedict XVI 2011) in these new digital networks. The journey to this conscientious and thoughtful agency with technology, however, is neither an easy nor a clear one. There is no app for bearing witness online to the sacred mystery of other human beings; no map for the incarnation of grace in video games. The opportunity for pastoral work in this area ought to be greeted with enthusiasm by the preachers and other religious leaders. Certainly the need for guidance and attentive care of our technical and mediated lives will only increase. Here is where the new ministries of new media will emerge.

Bibliography

Aristotle's Politics. Translated by Benjamin Jowett. Mineola, NY: Dover, 2000.

Benedict XVI. *Truth, Proclamation and Authenticity of Life in the Digital Age*. January 24, 2011. http://w2.vatican.va/content/benedict-xvi/en /messages/communications/documents/hf_ben-xvi_mes_20110124 _45th-world-communications-day.html.

Centers for Disease Control and Prevention. "ADD by the Numbers: Facts, Statistics, and You." http://www.healthline.com/health/adhd /facts-statistics-infographic.

Crary, Jonathan. *24/7*. London: Verso, 2014.

Crowley, Eileen D. *Liturgical Art for a Media Culture*. Collegeville, MN: Liturgical Press, 2007.

Gould, Meredith. *The Social Media Gospel: Sharing the Good News in New Ways*. Collegeville, MN: Liturgical Press, 2013.

Innis, Harold. *Empire and Communications*. Victoria, Canada: Press Porcépic, 1986.

Lanier, Jaron. *You Are Not a Gadget*. New York: Vintage, 2011.

McLuhan, Marshall. *Understanding Media: The Extensions of Man*. Cambridge, MA: MIT Press, 1994 [1964].

———. *The Medium and the Light: Reflections on Religion*. Toronto: Stoddart, 1999.

Pew Center. "Millennials in Adulthood: Detached from Institutions, Networked with Friends." March 7, 2014. http://www.pewsocialtrends.org/2014 /03/07/millennials-in-adulthood/.

Stiegler, Bernard. *Technics and Time, 1: The Fault of Epimetheus*. Translated by Richard Beardsworth and George Collins. Stanford, CA: Stanford University Press, 1998.

Turkle, Sherry. *Reclaiming Conversation: The Power of Talk in a Digital Age*. New York: Penguin, 2015.

Twiplomacy Study. 2015. http://twiplomacy.com/blog/twiplomacy-study -2015/.

Vosko, Richard. "Liturgical Technology, Social Media and the Green Church." *Liturgical Ministry* 20 (2011).

Zenthoefer, Alex J. "The Networked Preacher: Using New Media in the New Evangelization." DMin thesis, Aquinas Institute, 2014.

Zsupan-Jerome, Daniella. *Connected toward Communion: The Church and Social Communication in the Digital Age*. Collegeville, MN: Liturgical Press, 2014.

Charism and Order in Preaching

Patricia Parachini and Patrick Lagges

For many contemporary Roman Catholics attending Sunday worship, the quality of the homily is an important measure of their satisfaction or dissatisfaction with the entire liturgy. Walking out of church after participation in a Eucharistic Liturgy, it is not uncommon to hear comments about the homily, especially if the preaching was notably good or poor. With great animation, those talking about what they heard, speak almost dogmatically: "That was an excellent homily!" "He spoke as if he were talking directly to me." "I wish he would stop talking about himself and preach on the gospel of the day." "Does he ever consider our needs—the needs of the folk in the pews?"

Some who are unfamiliar with Roman Catholic practice or teaching may not be aware of the new importance given to preaching in Roman Catholic worship since Vatican II (1962–1965). Liturgical practice has been strongly influenced by the theology of *Sacrosanctum Concilium* (*SC*), which understands the relationship of the Liturgy of the Word and the Liturgy of the Eucharist as two tables not unlike movements of a symphony: each aspect together forming the whole of the liturgical celebration. Scholars such as Yves Congar (d. 1995), whose writings influenced the development of *SC*, highlighted this intimate connection, noting that the Word gives meaning to the sacrament and sacrament gives flesh to the Word. Because of this new emphasis on the Liturgy of the Word as an integral component of the liturgy, the homily received new attention, described by some as the bridge connecting the Liturgy of the Word with the Liturgy of the Eucharist (see 156 above).

The fact that liturgical preaching assumed a new significance in Roman Catholic worship after Vatican II raised new questions about the nature of preaching and who should be doing this preaching not only in the liturgy but also in other contexts. Questions such as: Why is preaching limited to ordained men? What is lost when women and nonordained men do not preach at worship? What is the basis for the mandate to preach? In the US church, particularly in the Midwest and the Northwest, interest in these questions peaked in the 1980s and seems to be on the rise again today.

In what follows, we will first look at preaching as a charism. Approaching preaching as a charism can reframe these questions and provide an impetus for looking in a new way at what constitutes suitability for the preaching ministry. We will examine some of the multiple meanings of charism and then consider the implications of each for the preaching ministry. Next, we will examine canon law and other documents that shed light on church order and support the centrality of the preaching ministry in the church. Finally, we will suggest a direction for the future to ensure that the preaching ministry is renewed and strengthened so that the people of God will be nourished and motivated to announce the Gospel in their own contexts.

Charism

In a groundbreaking article, Sandra Schneiders (b. 1936) examines the various threads that together formed the tapestry of the preaching ministry in the early church. She carefully addresses the authority of the church to regulate church life and order and at the same time highlights the role of the Holy Spirit in bringing forth new gifts for the communities of faith. She notes that "the early Church had a profound sense of the liberty of the Holy Spirit to do new things" (Schneiders 1983, 70). The charisms of the Spirit led the way. Schneiders presents clear evidence of preaching by women, especially in her examination of the epistles, and recognizes this early period in the church as the planting of seeds for the blossoming of the charism of preaching by the faithful to enrich the life of the church.

Charism (Gr., *charisma*) has multiple meanings. Even a common internet source helps us grasp something of the breadth of this term, which it alternately defines as: "1. . . . a divinely conferred gift or power. 2. A spiritual power or personal quality that gives an individual influence or authority over large numbers of people. 3. The special virtue of an office, function, position, etc., that confers or is thought to confer on the person holding it an unusual ability for leadership, worthiness of veneration, or the like" (dictionary.com 2015). Considering these commonly defined dimensions of charism could broaden our consideration of preaching, especially that done by Roman Catholic laity by viewing it as an authentic mandate, rather than as an exception or theoretical possibility.

Divinely Conferred Power or Gift

In considering charism as a divinely conferred gift or power, one could posit that baptism is the basis of the divinely conferred gift or power to preach. Baptism, as the first of three sacraments of initiation into the Christian community, is the grounding of all ministry for both laity and the ordained. As Susan Wood reminds us, "[B]aptism initiates a person as a member of the community, and ministry arises from the community" (Wood 2003, 17). Baptism calls the baptized to participate in Christ's ministry, often described in terms of his threefold mission as priest, prophet, and king. Baptism calls us to preach—to proclaim God's saving act in Christ—in all that we do. Paul Philibert speaks of this priesthood of the faithful as being "shaped and expressed in terms of the three 'missions' or tasks of prophecy, pastoral concern and liturgy or worship" (Philibert 2005, 74). This emphasizes not only the right but also the responsibility of Christians to participate in the threefold mission of Christ by virtue of their baptism. With specific reference to preaching, Mary Collins (b. 1935) notes "that it is in holy baptism that the Church can recognize the radical capacity and the fundamental imperative for the preaching ministry" (Collins 1983, 113–14).

Preaching, considered in the broadest sense as announcing the Gospel, is mandated of all Christian disciples. This is true whether it is in a one-to-one setting such as spiritual direction, in small group faith sharing, or in a more public forum such as liturgical, catechetical, or retreat preaching. Perhaps one's preaching is exercised primarily and most effectively in the living out of daily life with a deep concern for the needs of others, especially the poor and marginalized.

A Spiritual Power or Personal Gift

This second meaning is likely the one most people associate with the word "charism." We often experience those who are truly charismatic, capable of drawing people in and having tremendous influence on others. Their words are powerful and their magnetic presence attracts large groups of followers. Many have great depth and invite others into that same depth. Consider a favorite teacher and how much she influenced you, perhaps leading you to a ministry or career. Or on a wider scale, think about Pope John Paul II (d. 2005) or Pope Francis (b. 1936) and consider the influence they have exerted, not only on Roman Catholics but also on people of all faiths and no faith, on world leaders and the marginalized in society.

Such seems to be the kind of preachers we also need in our churches today: people who have gifts for communicating what they believe; for connecting with those who are listening; for capturing the imagination of the young; for helping us make sense out of things that are difficult and challenging or hard to grasp; and who can invite us to follow the way of Jesus.

Drawing from people with these qualities could further broaden the pool of voices we ordinarily hear and represent differences in gender, race, ethnicity, or ecclesial status. Such fresh voices could generate new life and energy in our churches. Effective preaching from the many voices that constitute us as church could provide some antidote to one consistent complaint from Roman Catholic congregations today: the poor quality of preaching.

The Special Virtue of an Office, Function, or Position

The US bishops' 2005 document, *Co-Workers in the Vineyard of the Lord* (CVL), offers a vision of lay ecclesial ministry that speaks to this third meaning of charism. "The call to lay ecclesial ministry adds a particular focus to the Christian discipleship expected of all the baptized. Their call, however, should not foster an elitism that places lay ecclesial ministers above or outside the laity" (CVL, no. 26).

There are many ways the preaching ministry could be enriched by establishing a "ministry of preaching" as an official function of Roman Catholic laity throughout the United States. This would not create a hierarchy among laity but rather ensure the establishment of preaching by laity as a valid ecclesial ministry carried out by those with the appropriate competencies. Appropriate formation and education would be required for this ministry, as for other lay ecclesial ministries, such as pastoral associate or hospital chaplain.

Considering preaching by laypersons as a charism in this third sense, implies that, rather than having an occasional opportunity for preaching, those formed and prepared for this ministry, would exercise it regularly in a specific congregation, in collaboration with the clergy who preach in that congregation. Together, these ministers could provide rich and effective preaching that nourishes the life of the faithful and invites them to the full participation in the mission of Christ.

Preaching and Church Order

As noted above, preaching was a function of charism, not order, in the early church (52ff. above). It was only gradually that the charism of preaching was joined to the sacrament of orders, although in the most recent legislation they have been separated once again. Suffice it to say, there were a number of historical reasons for this happening, not all of which were theological.

By the time of the 1917 Code of Canon Law (*CIC*), preaching was seen as the duty of the Roman Pontiff, bishops, pastors, and other clerics to whom the bishop gave the faculty to preach. The exercise of preaching was seen as a "faculty," which meant that it could only be given to a cleric. Canon 1342 of the 1917 *CIC* states that it was forbidden for the laity, even religious, to preach in churches.

The teaching of Vatican II changed the way the church regarded lay-persons and the apostolate. Prior to Vatican II, the apostolate belonged to the hierarchy. Laity could participate in the apostolate of the hierarchy, but they had no apostolate of their own. In *Apostolicam actuositatem* (*AA*), the church began to speak of an apostolate that belonged to the laity by virtue of their baptism and confirmation, stating that "it is by the Lord himself that they are assigned to the apostolate" (*AA*, no. 3). This meant that apos-tolic works were no longer tied to the sacrament of orders or the exclusive provenance of the hierarchy. *AA* was not a "stand alone" statement, since the apostolate of the laity is also discussed in the dogmatic constitutions *Lumen Gentium* (*LG*) and *SC* and the decrees on instruments of social com-munication, ecumenism, bishops, Christian education, missionary activity, and priestly life. Actually the term "apostolate of the laity" had become so ingrained in the council documents that a proposal to change the title of *AA* to "The Participation of the Laity in the Mission of the Church" was defeated.

Recognizing that the apostolate belonged to the laity by virtue of their baptism and confirmation did not mean that the works of the apostolate could be exercised without any reference to the hierarchical nature of the Roman Catholic Church. The hierarchy was still tasked with the respon-sibility of ensuring that apostolic activity was organized, directed, and coordinated in a unified manner.

This created an opening for the development of canon 766 of the 1983 *CIC*. As with most developing concepts, the canon was somewhat permis-sive and somewhat restrictive. First and foremost, it allowed for laypersons to be permitted to preach under certain circumstances. This means that it was not a right in itself. The layperson could not claim a right to preach, as a bishop, priest, or deacon could. On the other hand, he or she could be permitted to preach under certain circumstances.

The law wisely did not seek to specify what necessity would require a lay preacher or what might make lay preaching advantageous to the church. It left that to the decision of the conferences of bishops, who would have a better sense of what was needed and advantageous in their territories.

Indeed, numerous conferences have established legislation regarding lay preaching. The Canadian Roman Catholic bishops allow the diocesan bishop to make such a determination: (1) when there is no priest or deacon conversant in the language of the people, (2) when the Liturgy of the Word is celebrated in the absence of a priest or deacon, (3) when preaching is part of a seminarian's formation program, (4) when there are special circumstances, or (5) whenever the diocesan bishop judges it opportune. No mention is made of when the preaching can take place. This is similar to the decree of the Roman Catholic bishops of New Zealand, Nigeria, and South Africa. The Roman Catholic bishops of England and Wales stipulate that any lay preaching during the Eucharist must take place after the post-Communion prayer, except as permitted by the Directory for Masses with Children (DMC). This is similar to the requirements of the bishops of India, while the bishops of the United States state, "Preaching by the lay faithful may not take place within the celebration of the Eucharist at the moment reserved for the homily" (USCCB 2001).

Although the US Roman Catholic bishops make no mention of the DMC, they do allow the bishop to make decisions as to when lay preaching would be pastorally appropriate, stating:

> If necessity requires it in certain circumstances or it seems useful in particular cases, the diocesan bishop can admit lay faithful to preach, to offer spiritual conferences or give instructions in churches, oratories or other sacred places within his diocese, when he judges it to be to the spiritual advantage of the faithful. (USCCB 2001)

In order to assist the bishop in making such a decision, the decree mentions the following circumstances which might suggest permission could be given for a layperson to preach: "the absence or shortage of clergy, particular language requirements, or the demonstrated expertise or experience of the lay faithful concerned" (USCCB 2001). This opens up a number of possibilities. It seems, however, that the US legislation on the place in the liturgy where laypeople may be permitted to preach equates preaching with homily, which is not accurate since the homily is only one type of preaching.

Preaching the Word of God

In general, the *CIC* does not provide definitions: law prefers description to definition. Thus, there is no canonical definition of what constitutes "preaching" in the Roman Catholic Church. There are just several examples of preaching given, with an introduction as to who has been entrusted with this function of preaching. These reflect the historical development of associating preaching with jurisdiction, rather than with charism. After identifying those whose principal function in the church is the proclamation of the

Word and who, therefore, have a right to preach (whom the law specifies as bishops, priests, and deacons), the 1983 *CIC* specifically mentions preaching by laypersons. Canon 766 states: "Lay persons can be permitted to preach in a church or oratory, if necessity requires it in certain circumstances or it seems advantageous in particular cases, according to the prescripts of the conference of bishops."

The canons that deal directly with preaching can be found in Book 3: "The Teaching Function of the Church." This book speaks of the church's teaching charism under five major categories: The Ministry of the Divine Word (cc. 756–80), The Missionary Action of the Church (cc. 781–91), Catholic Education (cc. 793–821), Instruments of Social Communication and Books in Particular (cc. 822–32), and a final canon on who is obliged to make a Profession of Faith (c. 833).

The Ministry of the Divine Word is divided into two principal actions: The Preaching of the Word of God (cc. 762–72) and Catechetical Instruction (cc. 763–80). It is the former action that will be the subject of our present discussion.

The *CIC* likes to describe things in an orderly fashion. Thus it introduces the subject of the ministry of the Divine Word as being entrusted first of all to the Roman Pontiff and the college of bishops but then explains that in his individual diocese, the diocesan bishop is "the moderator of the entire ministry of the word within it" (c. 756). How he moderates it is not spelled out in detail, since it will be up to each bishop to determine that for his diocese. *Whom* he moderates it with, however, is spelled out in the subsequent canons. The language is important here, since some of the canons state who can exercise the ministry of the Word by *right*, and who can exercise it by *permission*. The difference is significant, at least in canonical terms, because it indicates who *must* be allowed to do something, and who *can* be allowed to do something. In general, the "must" list is much more circumscribed; the "can" list provides for much more leeway.

Those who have the ministry of the Word as their proper function are the presbyters and deacons of the diocese (c. 757). In addition, the bishop can call on "members of institutes of consecrated life . . . as a help in proclaiming the gospel" (c. 758). There is no distinction made here between institutes of men or of women. The bishop, however, is bound to respect the charism of each institute, so he can only call on them for help, not demand that they fulfill this function. Similarly, the bishop and the presbyters can also count on the cooperation of all the lay members of the Christian faithful, since they "are witnesses of the gospel message by word and the example of a Christian life" (c. 759). It should be noted that it is not just the bishops who can call on the laity to cooperate in the ministry of the Word; presbyters can also ask for such cooperation. These canons are a good example of the principle of subsidiarity, where each decision is made at the appropriate level.

The Homily

In looking at the canons, it is clear that the homily (see 156ff. above) is but one species of preaching. The canons refer to other types of preaching that take place: spiritual exercises, sacred missions, other forms of preaching adapted to the needs of the people, preaching to those who do not have access to ordinary pastoral care, and preaching to nonbelievers. There is also preaching that is associated with the *Book of Blessings*, the Order of Christian Funerals, and with various other rites when they are not celebrated within the context of a Eucharistic Liturgy (see 146ff. above). Thus it would be a mistake to characterize all preaching as a homily.

In recent documents, the homily is described more and more precisely. Canon 767.1 describes the homily as being "preeminent" among all the forms of preaching, and as being part of the liturgy itself. While some ritual books use the language of homily for the type of preaching done at sacraments such as baptism or marriage, the term seems to be more and more restricted. Specifically, the homily is increasingly understood as the type of preaching that is done by the one who presides at the Eucharist, although the task can be given to a deacon or another priest by way of exception. It is also described as part of the liturgical action and is to explain the mysteries of the faith and the norms of Christian living according to the sacred text (which could either be the scriptural readings or the other texts of the liturgy).

The description considers who is preaching and what is being preached, and not when the preaching occurs. The *Institutio Generalis Missalis Romani (IGMR2002)* places the homily in the Order of Mass as occurring after the gospel, but that only indicates where, if there is a homily, it ought to be given in the liturgy. It does not necessarily guarantee that the preaching after the gospel is actually homiletic preaching. Thus, when the presider or another bishop, priest, or deacon preaches on the sacred texts, explaining the mysteries of faith and the norms of Christian living, it is considered a homily. The same persons could give an address after the reading of the gospel on the finances of the parish, or on a special collection, or on the bishop's appeal, and it would not be a homily, since it does not contain what the law says a homily must contain: an explanation of the mysteries of the faith or the norms of Christian living, derived from the sacred texts.

The current legislation and teaching specifies who can preach a homily. Bishops, priests, and deacons have been entrusted with this ministry through their ordination. In a sense, they have a "right" to preach a homily. The Pontifical Council for Legislative Texts has stated that this right cannot be delegated to those who are not clerics, and that no one other than a cleric can be given the faculty to preach a homily. This, however, does not mean that only a bishop, priest, or deacon can preach at a Eucharistic Liturgy. The terms "delegation" and "faculty" are technical canonical terms that refer to designating someone who already has the right to do something the authority to carry it out. In the current legislation, laypersons do not have a right to preach. But that does not mean that they cannot be given permission to preach. In some of the decrees that were passed by various conferences of bishops, it was left to the determination of the diocesan bishop who would be permitted to preach, apart from those who have a right to do so. This would represent a healthy subsidiarity in the church, since the local bishop would be in a better position to judge when such preaching is necessary.

Thus, it seems that there could be four different types of preaching that can be done during a Eucharistic Liturgy. The first is a homily, which is preached by the presider or another bishop, priest, or deacon designated by the presider, and that deals with the mysteries of the faith or the norms for Christian living, based on the sacred texts. The second is preaching that is done by the presider or another bishop, priest, or deacon designated by the presider that deals with matters other than those derived from the sacred texts and the mystery being celebrated. The third is preaching done by someone other than a bishop, priest, or deacon, derived from the sacred texts or the mystery being celebrated. And the fourth would be preaching done by someone other than a bishop, priest, or deacon, not derived from the sacred texts or the mystery being celebrated (such as missionary appeals, finance reports, etc.).

Because these are liturgical actions, they have to respect the action of the liturgy as indicated in *SC*. There is a time in the liturgy for preaching, which occurs within the ebb and flow of the liturgy itself. To direct preaching to be done at a different time would interrupt the flow of the liturgy and create an experience that limps along, perhaps following the prescriptions of the law but not being faithful to the spirit of the liturgy.

Recent Developments

In his apostolic exhortation, *Evangelii Gaudium (EG)*, Pope Francis moves the subject of preaching even further than *CIC*. In his extensive treatment of the homily (*EG*, nos. 135–59), the Holy Father describes the homily more in terms of charism than jurisdiction. He makes a number of points about those who preach to the Christian community, repeating over and over again that it always has the Spirit as its foundation. Describing preaching as "the same way a mother speaks to her child," Pope Francis states that "the same Spirit who inspired the Gospels and who acts in the Church, also inspires the preacher to hear the faith of God's people and to find the right way to preach at each Eucharist" (*EG*, no. 139).

Furthermore, he speaks of the preacher as the one who "must know the heart of his community" (*EG*, no. 137), who is adept at "hearing the faith of people and knowing what must be said" (*EG*, no. 139), who imitates the Lord who "truly enjoys talking with his people" by striving "to communicate that same enjoyment to his listeners"(*EG*, no. 141), who represents "an enrichment which does not consist in objects, but in persons who share themselves in dialog" (*EG*, no. 142), who joins loving hearts: the hearts of the Lord and his people (*EG*, no. 143), who is able to keep "an ear to people" and discover what the faithful need to hear (*EG*, no. 154), who speaks a language the people can understand (*EG*, no. 158), and who speaks a message that is positive, offering hope, pointing to the future, and does not leave people trapped in negativity (*EG*, no. 159). These are not jurisdictional terms but charismatic ones. While it might be possible to say that these charisms should reside in those who preside over a liturgical assembly, it may also be true that the Spirit has given these gifts to others in the assembly, since the Spirit is the one who "inspires the preacher to hear the faith of God's people and to find the right way to preach at each Eucharist" (*EG*, no. 139).

Conclusion

Despite its long presence in one form or another since the early church, preaching by the laity seems to lack real support in the contemporary Roman Catholic Church. Lay preaching has been overlooked or considered no longer an acceptable practice by some in leadership, despite the US bishops' guidelines that permit lay preaching in certain circumstances. In addition, laypersons already mandated to preach in Roman Catholic congregations and who are presently preaching throughout the country, have experienced ambivalence about their mandate and desire greater clarity as well as support. There is an urgency to begin to develop processes and programs to ensure the appropriate formation and education of present and future lay preachers, since at the present time it is sporadic and lacks a coherent approach. Examples of laypersons who are preaching regularly in different settings include: parish life administrators who preach at Word services or communion services in the absence of a priest; retreat leaders who preach retreats and, at times, during the Eucharistic Liturgy in place of the presider; laypersons who preach at vigil services for the dead; and those who preach on occasion at liturgical or other prayer services on college campuses or Catholic high schools.

Other chapters of this book address related questions that need to be brought into the discussion about how we can enhance the preaching ministry and who is suitable to preach. Suffice it to say here that raising up a variety of voices, including both lay and ordained, to preach in Roman Catholic communities of faith, can enhance the ability of listeners to both hear and heed the Word of God preached in the midst of the assembly, whether it be a liturgy or another forum where the people of God gather. In addition, regular preaching by laypersons who are mandated to preach as lay ecclesial ministers, together with ordained preachers, could underscore the mandate of all the baptized called to preach—to announce the good news unceasingly in whatever context they live and work.

It is one and the same Holy Spirit who guides the church as we try to maintain a creative tension between charism and order, keeping in mind the needs of the people whom we are called to serve. Reframing the questions about lay preaching in terms of charism *and* fresh interpretations of Canon Law in light of the needs of God's people can help us to plan creatively for the future and honor what is best in our tradition.

Bibliography

Collins, Mary. "The Baptismal Roots of the Preaching Ministry." In *Preaching and the Non-Ordained*. Edited by Nadine Foley. Collegeville, MN: Liturgical Press, 1983.

Dictionary.com. http://dictionary.reference.com/browse/charism?s=t.

Philibert, Paul. *Priesthood of the Faithful*. Collegeville, MN: Liturgical Press, 2005.

Schneiders, Sandra. "New Testament Foundations for Preaching by the Non-Ordained." In *Preaching and the Non-Ordained*. Edited by Nadine Foley. Collegeville, MN: Liturgical Press, 1983.

USCCB. "Canon 766—Lay Preaching." November 14, 2001. http://usccb .org/beliefs-and-teachings/what-we-believe/canon-law/complemen tary-norms/canon-766-lay-preaching.cfm#.

Wood, Susan. *Ordering the Baptismal Priesthood: Theologies of Lay and Ordained Ministry*. Collegeville, MN: Liturgical Press, 2003.

Preaching and Catholic Social Teaching

John Carr

Introduction

I don't preach homilies; I listen to them. Yet I have spent decades sharing Catholic social teaching (CST) and helping the church act on its social mission. I believe the most important setting for sharing the Gospel call to justice and peace and the church's social teaching is not at the Bishops' Conference, on Capitol Hill, or in a homeless shelter. Rather, it is gathering in a eucharistic assembly to hear the Word of God. It is in the homily that most Roman Catholics will hear—or not hear—the connection of the Eucharist and the Scriptures to our call to be "salt, light, and leaven" (Matt 5:13-16; 13:33).

Sharing the social dimensions of our faith is one of the privileges and joys of catholic preaching. Done well, this should bring life, substance, and dynamism to preaching. If preachers do not reflect the biblical call to "choose life" (Deut 30:19), to care for the "least of these" (Matt 25:34-46), to "hunger and thirst for justice," and to become "peacemakers" (Matt 5:1-12), then the preaching is not truly and fully catholic. US Catholic bishops clearly outlined this task:

> Preaching that reflects the social dimensions of the gospel is indispensable. Priests should not and need not impose an agenda on the liturgy to preach about justice. Rather, we urge those who preach not to ignore the regular opportunities provided by the liturgy to connect our faith and our everyday lives, to share biblical values on justice and peace. Week after week, day after day, the lectionary calls the community to reflect on the scriptural message of justice and peace. The pulpit is not a partisan rostrum and to try to make it one would be a mistake, but preaching that ignores the social dimensions of our faith does not truly reflect the gospel of Jesus Christ. (USCCB 1996, 9)

Today we have a preacher and pastor who offers a stunning example of how to "preach the just word." Pope Francis (b. 1936) does this every day in his simple ways and powerful words. He preaches the just word in his modest daily homilies at Casa Santa Marta and his televised sermons at elaborate papal liturgies. He shares the Gospel message as he speaks to millions in his journeys around the world, in his exhortation *Evangelii Gaudium* (*EG*) and in countless other statements.

The power of Francis's preaching comes not only from what he says but also from what he does; not only from how he says it but also from how he lives it out. He is a living parable of the love of Christ, the mercy of God and the joy of the Gospel. He does not speak often about the "principles" of CST but constantly calls us to practice them in our individual and ecclesial lives. By his words and example, by whom he comforts and whom he challenges, Francis defines and enacts these principles in action and calls us to do the same.

Francis has offered specific directions and suggestions for how to preach, devoting a major section of *EG* (nos. 135–44) to very concrete guidance for those who prepare and deliver homilies. His vision is that a "homily can actually be an intense and happy experience of the Spirit, a consoling encounter with God's word, a constant source of renewal and growth" (*EG*, no. 135). Sharing the social dimensions of the Scriptures and catholic faith and the social calling and responsibilities of followers of Jesus should be at the heart of this experience.

The Social Mission and Message of Preachers

The church's social mission is not optional but integral for Christians, especially those who preach. It is a mistake to treat this simply as an ideological option or personal preference. According to the *Compendium of the Social Doctrine of the Church*,

> The priest should make known the social teaching of the Church and foster in the members of his community an awareness of their right and duty to be active subjects of this doctrine. Through the celebration of the Sacraments, especially Eucharist and Reconciliation, the priest helps the faithful live their social commitment. . . . He should animate pastoral action in the social field, giving particular attention to the formation and spiritual accompaniment of lay Christians engaged in social and political life. (Pontifical Council for Justice and Peace 2004, no. 539)

This calling can be one of the most challenging, satisfying, and life-giving dimensions of ministry. Clergy not serious about the social dimensions of ministry or preaching fail a fundamental test. The ordained may express this dimension of their vocation in different ways, as long as it is integral and not optional. This important dimension of ministry is most often expressed not in extraordinary acts of witness but in the ordinary tasks of prayer and leadership, forming and guiding the community, acting as citizen and neighbor, and especially in preaching.

The links between preaching and CST have to be anchored in the larger social mission of the church and the broader understanding of preaching presented in this volume. Preaching the principles of CST divorced from the broader mission, ministry, and teaching of the church is likely to be not only ineffective but also counterproductive.

The core of this pastoral obligation is found in Jesus' citation from Isaiah as he began his public life in Nazareth: "The Spirit of the Lord is upon me, because he has anointed me to bring good news to the poor. He has sent me to proclaim release to the captives and recovery of sight to the blind, to let the oppressed go free" (Luke 4:18). Jesus chose this passage to communicate to his family and friends his mission on earth, declaring, "Today this scripture has been fulfilled in your hearing" (Luke 4:21). It is also the mission and message of preachers today.

Preachers need to ask: How do we bring "good news to the poor" in an economy that leaves so many behind, a nation with enormous gaps between rich and poor? How does my preaching "bring release to captives" when so many are imprisoned or held captive by injustice or addiction? How does my ministry "bring recovery of sight" to those blinded by indifference, selfishness, prejudice, or ideology? How does preaching "let the oppressed go free" from hunger or homelessness, fear or despair, poverty, or oppression?

Placing the social mission and message at the center of preaching and Christian life is not a diversion from the Gospel and catholic faith but a privileged expression of them. This message is as old as Genesis, where we hear that God is the Creator and we are to care for all creation (e.g., Gen 2:15). It is as clear as the Hebrew prophets who insisted that the moral measure of the community was how the widows, orphans, and strangers were treated (Zech 7:10). It is as stark as Jesus' description of the Last Judgment where those who serve the hungry, the thirsty, and the imprisoned are saved because in caring for them, we care for Christ (Matt 5:1-12).

Through the centuries, the church has sought to proclaim and teach these scriptural mandates. Especially over the last 125 years, the Roman Catholic Church has sought to express and apply these biblical requirements through more than fifteen papal encyclicals, extending from Leo XIII's (d. 1903) *Rerum Novarum* (1891) to Francis's *Laudato Si* (2015). These papal letters addressed a wide range of challenges, e.g., workers and the industrial revolution, war and peace, human rights and economic justice, respect for human life, and care for creation. John Paul II (d. 2005) insisted that CST is real doctrine offering principles for reflection, criteria for judgment, and guidelines for action. These core ideas have been articulated in many places and ways, including the *Catechism of the Catholic Church* and the *Compendium of the Social Doctrine of the Church*.

The most helpful and accessible summary is the *Seven Themes of Catholic Social Teaching* (USCCB 2005). When the US bishops adopted their pastoral Letter *Economic Justice for All* (1986), one bishop strongly supported the letter, but he didn't really know how to use it since it was ninety pages long. He purportedly said, "If we could find a way to fit this on a holy card we could really deliver the message." These seven themes are the "holy card" version of CST:

Life and Dignity of the Human Person: The Catholic Church proclaims that human life is sacred and that the dignity of the human person is the foundation of a moral vision for society. This belief is the foundation of all the principles of our social teaching. In our society, human life is under direct attack from abortion and euthanasia. The value of human life is being threatened by cloning, embryonic stem cell research, and the use of the death penalty. The intentional targeting of civilians in war or terrorist attacks is always wrong. Catholic teaching also calls on us to work to avoid war. Nations must protect the right to life by finding increasingly effective ways to prevent conflicts and resolve them by peaceful means. We believe that every person is precious, that people are more important than things, and that the measure of every institution is whether it threatens or enhances the life and dignity of the human person.

Call to Family, Community, and Participation: The person is not only sacred but also social. How we organize our society—in economics and politics, in law and policy—directly affects human dignity and the capacity of individuals to grow in community. Marriage and the family are the central social institutions that must be supported and strengthened, not undermined. We believe people have a right and a duty to participate in society, seeking together the common good and well-being of all, especially the poor and vulnerable.

Rights and Responsibilities: The Catholic tradition teaches that human dignity can be protected and a healthy community can be achieved only if human rights are protected and responsibilities are met. Therefore, every person has a fundamental right to life and a right to those things required for human decency. Corresponding to these rights are duties and responsibilities—to one another, to our families, and to the larger society.

Option for the Poor and Vulnerable: A basic moral test is how our most vulnerable members are faring. In a society marred by deepening divisions between rich and poor, our tradition recalls the story of the Last

Judgment (Matt 25:31-46) and instructs us to put the needs of the poor and vulnerable first.

The Dignity of Work and the Rights of Workers: The economy must serve people, not the other way around. Work is more than a way to make a living; it is a form of continuing participation in God's creation. If the dignity of work is to be protected, then the basic rights of workers must be respected—the right to productive work, to decent and fair wages, to the organization and joining of unions, to private property, and to economic initiative.

Solidarity: We are one human family, whatever our national, racial, ethnic, economic, and ideological differences. We are our brothers' and sisters' keepers, wherever they may be. Loving our neighbor has global dimensions in a shrinking world. At the core of the virtue of solidarity is the pursuit of justice and peace. Pope Paul VI taught that "if you want peace, work for justice." The Gospel calls us to be peacemakers. Our love for all our sisters and brothers demands that we promote peace in a world surrounded by violence and conflict.

Care for God's Creation: We show our respect for the Creator by our stewardship of creation. Care for the earth is not just an Earth Day slogan; it is a requirement of our faith. We are called to protect people and the planet, living our faith in relationship with all of God's creation. This environmental challenge has fundamental moral and ethical dimensions that cannot be ignored.

These themes are more complicated and nuanced than "What would Jesus do?" They are politically incorrect and do not fit the ideological agendas or partisan platforms of US public life, focused as they are on the needs of the poor and vulnerable, not the priorities of the rich and powerful. These are powerful moral ideas that can *both* deliver the truths of our faith *and* grab the attention of parishioners. Preaching on CST responds directly to the issues many cite as they transfer their loyalty to another religious institution or opt for religious nonaffiliation. In an age of anger and frustration with public and economic life, preaching that extends beyond politics and ideology can be refreshing and enlightening.

Sharing the church's message of social justice speaks directly to the hearts and minds of many millennials. They are becoming "nones" at record rates, but data documents their passion for issues of justice and the plight of the oppressed. CST can be an invitational bridge to young people and others on the edges of our faith communities.

In CST, the most important and repeated word is "and." The tradition of CST is powerful in part because it makes connections between key values often separated in our society and world. Part of the preacher's task is to make these connections, to lift up the "and": human life *and* dignity; human rights *and* responsibilities; the dignity of work *and* the rights of workers; solidarity *and* subsidiarity; practicing charity *and* pursuing justice.

These are not new themes but ones anchored in powerful biblical foundations, reflecting both a unique tradition of thinking and acting and providing a different way of reflecting on our lives and the world. The core message is that a catholic faith is profoundly social. As Francis insists, "An authentic faith, which is never comfortable or completely personal, always involves a deep desire to change the world, to transmit values, to leave this earth somehow better that we found it" (*EG*, no. 150).

Directions and Dangers when Preaching CST

While my life's work has been sharing and engaging the principles of CST, my perspectives on preaching come largely from listening to homilies with my family in my parish. Preaching weekend after weekend in the same community is one of the most challenging tasks in our church. Yet, I don't think our expectations are too high; we don't expect St. Paul or Pope Francis. We do hope homilies will help us understand the Word of God and apply to our lives. We hope they will encourage and guide us to live our faith every day. Preparation and thoughtfulness are required; eloquence and brilliance are optional.

In *EG*, Francis offers pages of concrete guidance for those who prepare and deliver homilies. He believes homilies should *not* be:

> dull (no. 11), doctrinal (no. 35), confined (no. 49), abstract (nos. 142 and 157), ugly (cf. nos. 36 and 142), obsessive (no. 49), out of contact with the local context (nos. 29, 45 and 143), heartless (no. 139), essentially entertaining (no. 138), judgmental (no. 172), tortured (cf. no. 44), bureaucratic and inhospitable (no. 63), pessimistic (cf. no. 85), ostentatious (no. 95), rigid (no. 45), avuncular (cf. no. 139), self-centered (cf. no. 158), monologic (no. 137), long (no. 138), heartless (no. 138), disconnected from God's Word (no. 146), inauthentic (no. 150), negative (no. 159), oppressive (nos. 187ff.), and disengaged from society (nos. 238ff.). (Foley 2015)

While not as comprehensive, here are a dozen other directions and potential dangers for those who seek to preach CST:

1. Integrate, Don't Isolate CST.

The wisdom and power of CST should be woven into homilies in ways that reflect the Lectionary readings and connect to people's lives. The Lectionary offers ample opportunities to connect faith and life and to reference CST. Throughout the liturgical calendar and the Lectionary cycles, preachers will find readings that require focusing on our obligations to defend life, protect the poor, act with solidarity, and pursue peace. I am not a big advocate of "social justice homilies," which can appear to impose an agenda on the liturgy and worshiping community. Yet there are times when texts and contexts suggest— even demand—a homily that lifts up a specific theme of CST. In these cases, a preacher is not adding an external factor but truly proclaiming the Gospel.

Some of these occasions flow directly from the Lectionary readings. Another motivation may be compelling local or global events that demand sharing the church's principles and putting our values into practice. Natural disasters summon talk about charity and solidarity. Racial or ethnic conflict in a community, choices about war and peace, impending legislation on protecting unborn children, or ending the death penalty compels a homilist to share the principles of our faith and moral criteria for finding the best ways forward.

2. Listen Well in Order to Preach Well

Before preachers proclaim, they need to listen. They need to know Scriptures, church teaching, *and* their people. As Francis wrote, "The preacher . . . needs to keep his ear to the people and to discover what it is that the faithful need to hear. A preacher has to contemplate the word, but he also has to contemplate his people" (*EG*, no. 154). Thus pastors and preachers need to have the "smell of the sheep" (*EG*, no. 24), i.e., be close to their people, not distant; a part of their lives, not isolated observers who offer guidance from afar.

Preaching needs to reflect the diversity of our church and respond to the context of particular faith communities. An African American parish with a history of struggle and vibrant worship requires preaching that differs from a relatively affluent and comfortable white suburban parish. Hispanic communities of faith may require not only preaching in Spanish but also responsiveness to their contexts. Diverse communities require distinctive styles and messages from preachers as they proclaim the same Gospel.

3. Share the "Secret"

"CST is our best-kept secret" is an overworked cliché. If true, it is an indictment, not a clever talking point. If the principles of CST are "secrets," it is because they have not been studied and taught in our formation programs, colleges, and seminaries. It is especially important to share the "secret" in preaching, because the only way most Roman Catholics will be in on the secret is if CST regularly finds its way into the preaching. Parishioners like myself want homilies that offer substance and encouragement. We welcome stories, ideas, and challenges that call us to make a difference and live out our faith. In a divided nation and a hurting world, our people and congregations need this "secret" more than ever. This is truly central to Francis's "Joy of the Gospel."

Sharing the secret does not require outlining the seven themes in seven weeks or quoting encyclicals in sermons. Rather, it means offering the ideas at the heart of our social tradition as a lens, a faithful way of looking at our world and lives. By sharing the secret, we empower Christians to ponder life through the eyes of faith and discover concrete ways to follow Jesus in the choices we make.

4. Good Questions Are More Effective than Right Answers

CST does not offer easy answers to complicated questions. The sanctuary is not a lecture hall and the pulpit is not the place for solving complicated problems. Frequently, effective preachers offer good questions more than great answers. Sharing the Word of God and explaining what the church teaches provide parishioners tools they need to answer challenging questions.

Over 130 times in the gospels, Jesus poses questions to his listeners, e.g., who is my neighbor (Luke 10:36)? CST also suggests distinctive questions, e.g., how do we: protect human life and dignity; promote family life and the common good; care for God's creation; work for a more just economy? Posing questions without offering easy answers invites hearers to be actors and engage in the search for their own answers.

5. It's "Good News"

Gospel is literally "good news" and homilies ought to sound like it. I often heard Harry Fagan (d. 1992) say that no one likes "a grim do-gooder." Francis warns us about becoming "sourpusses" and "Christians who act like Good Friday without Easter" (*EG* 85). In life and in preaching, the lament of "ain't it awful" is not motivating or empowering. "We can do better" calls us to action, not hand-wringing. As Francis notes:

> [A] good homily is . . . positive. It is not so much concerned with pointing out what shouldn't be done, but with suggesting what we can do better.
> . . . [I]f it does draw attention to something negative, it will also attempt to

point to a positive and attractive value, lest it remain mired in complaints, laments, criticisms and reproaches. (*EG*, no. 85)

It is sometimes useful to suggest ways that individuals or groups can respond to concerns raised in the texts or contexts and addressed in a homily. Sharing CST should promote social action. This can range from prayer and fasting to donating time or treasure, from legislative advocacy to seriously studying CST as a path to problem solving. Part of the "good news" is coming together to practice what CST teaches about human life and dignity, justice, and peace.

6. Encourage Everyday Christianity

A pivotal element for connecting preaching and CST is promoting "everyday Christianity." Preaching should support and enable the baptized to live their faith as parents and siblings, consumers and investors, citizens and voters. The challenge is to be "salt of the earth," "light of the world," and societal "leaven" in ways large and small. A few will serve in impoverished areas or run for elected office, but Christians must find ways to practice charity, justice, and solidarity in their own lives. Such preaching consistently reminds worshipers that a living faith is much more than a weekend obligation. The Eucharist is not a refuge but a launching pad, as we pray "your kingdom come, your will be done on earth as it is in heaven."

7. Special Effort for Special Celebrations

Preaching at weddings and funerals for people the clergy barely know is daunting. Yet, these offer distinctive opportunities for evangelization. Such homilies can not only provide people ritual consolation or sacramental affirmations but also spotlight social dimensions of their faith. Preachers can underscore that marriage is not only a contract between two people but also a call to service and to extend their love to the world.

I may be one of the few who like "special collections," partly because I have seen firsthand the amazing work of beneficiaries such as Catholic Relief Services. Such collections offer particular opportunities to preach on stewardship, to remind us that we are part of a global community, and to push the boundaries of charity, solidarity, and justice.

8. Preach by Example

Francis reminds us that people prefer to "listen to witnesses" (*EG*, no. 118). Authentic authority is earned, not claimed or assumed. Consistency between what a preacher says and how he or she lives is crucial; thus the purported advice of Francis of Assisi (d. 1226): "Preach always: use words, if necessary." Obviously words are necessary for preaching, but they lack credibility unless they are accompanied by personal integrity, ethical consistency, and loving service.

Preaching on human dignity, rights of workers, priority for the poor, and care for creation will lack credibility if these values are not reflected in the policies, priorities, and practices of our parishes and other institutions. We cannot preach against racism, ethnic discrimination, hostility to immigrants, and mistreatment of people with disabilities if our communities do not welcome in word and deed the dignity and rights of all. Preachers must demonstrate particular respect for the leadership and voices of women if they wish to be heard by the full community.

9. Promote Faithful Citizenship

Francis has declared, "Responsible citizenship is a virtue, and participation in political life is a moral obligation" (*EG*, no. 178)—a position echoed in the teaching of the USCCB. There is no more challenging, intimidating, or potentially explosive area for preachers than preaching about faithful citizenship in a divided nation and sometimes polarized church.

The task of the church and its preachers, according to Benedict XVI (b. 1927) is "to help form consciences in political life and to stimulate greater insight into the authentic requirements of justice . . . as well as greater readiness to act accordingly" (Benedict 2005, no. 28). Preachers should remind voters that their choices should reflect more than what party they prefer, what ideology they embrace, or how their economic interests will be affected, but rather how the "least of these" are treated.

Preachers should follow the directions outlined in the USCCB's *Forming Consciences for Faithful Citizenship*; they should be "political, but not partisan." Preachers who consistently share the principles of CST will challenge the consciences of all. The political arena is where crucial choices are made about life and death, war and peace, who gets left behind, and who moves ahead. Preachers cannot be cheerleaders for any party, champions of any candidate, or apologists for any administration. Similarly, preaching in election times should be "principled but not ideological." It is not telling people whom to vote for or against but offering the church's teaching and biblical values to help form consciences so that the baptized can participate fully and faithfully in political life.

11. Watch Your Language

Making preaching personal is important; pronouns are important here. When preachers say "you" need to do this, I can feel like I am being lectured. "We" is the better way forward. We share common challenges to live out our faith. CST has its own language that can get in the way of the message. "Subsidiarity" is not in spell check. Many terms, such as "marginalized," "peripheries," "just war," and "proportionality," are vague if not incomprehensible. They need to be replaced by more accessible language.

12. Build Bridges

There is a mistaken notion that preachers who take CST seriously will inevitably divide a local community. Sometimes that happens; more often preachers who integrate the principles of CST can build bridges. Effective and positive preaching can link diverse elements of our faith and community by lifting up the "and" at the heart of CST. Preaching can connect the defense of the unborn *and* the undocumented, advocacy of human rights *and* responsibility, care for creation *and* community organizing, prayer *and* action, charity *and* justice.

Preachers cannot be chaplains to factions, pitting one group against others. Instead, they need to remind us that we are in this together, one family of faith—with differing gifts, priorities, and passions—but united by faith in Christ.

Conclusion

In 2001, I participated in a "Preaching the Just Word" retreat in New York that included a visit to Ground Zero shortly after 9/11. It was an overwhelming experience. Twice everything stopped while they brought out human remains. One participant said to me, "What we were talking about last night—respect for human life, justice, solidarity, peacemaking—are the ways we will overcome this hate, this horror." Referring to my work at the USCCB, he said, "The work you do is more important than ever." I responded, "Father, the work *you* do in your parish and pulpit to proclaim the Good News and share those ideas is more important than ever."

I continue to believe that the preacher's gift and responsibility to share the Gospel and the wisdom of CST is "more important than ever."

Bibliography

Benedict XVI. *Deus Caritas Est* (God Is Love). http://w2.vatican.va/content/benedict-xvi/en/encyclicals/documents/hf_ben-xvi_enc_20051225_deus-caritas-est.html.

Burghardt, Walter J. *Preaching the Just Word*. New Haven, CT: Yale University Press, 1998.

Davis, Kenneth G., and Leopoldo Perez. *Preaching the Teaching: Hispanics, Homiletics, and Catholic Social Justice Doctrine*. Scranton, PA: University of Scranton Press, 2005.

Donahue, John R. *Seek Justice That You May Live: Reflections and Resources on the Bible and Social Justice*. Mahwah, NJ: Paulist Press, 2014.

Foley, Edward. "The Homily in the context of *Evangelii Gaudium*." *Pray Tell* (blog). August 13, 2014. http://www.praytellblog.com/index.php/2014/08/13/the-homily-in-the-context-of-evangelii-gaudium/.

Himes, Kenneth R. *Modern Catholic Social Teachings: Commentaries and Interpretations*. Washington, DC: Georgetown University Press, 2015.

Massaro, Thomas. *Living Justice: Catholic Social Teaching in Action*. Lanham, MD: Rowman & Littlefield, 2015.

McKenna, Kevin E. *A Concise Guide to Catholic Social Teaching*. Notre Dame, IN: Ave Maria Press, 2013.

Reinert, James M. *Preaching the Social Doctrine of the Church in the Mass*. Vols. 1–3. Vatican City: Libreria Editrice Vaticana, 2011.

USCCB. *Communities of Salt and Light: Reflections on the Social Mission of the Church*. Washington, DC: USCCB, 1994.

USCCB. "Seven Themes of Catholic Social Teaching." http://www.usccb.org/beliefs-and-teachings/what-we-believe/catholic-social-teaching/seven-themes-of-catholic-social-teaching.cfm.

The Ecumenical Contributions of Roman Catholic Preaching

Craig Alan Satterlee and Gregory Heille

A Protestant Perspective

An outdated stereotype describes Protestants as people of the Word—*Sola Scriptura* (Lat. for "Scripture alone")—and Roman Catholics as people of liturgy and the sacraments—*source and summit*. Since Vatican II (1962–1965), a more hopeful appraisal celebrates the convergence of the ecumenical church as Protestants invite Roman Catholics deeper into the Word and Roman Catholics invite Protestants deeper into sacrament. Things are rarely this simple. As we let go of stereotypes, even hopeful ones, the ecumenical church finds itself blessed by the ways a Roman Catholic understanding of preaching opens up the treasures of the Bible more lavishly, "so that a richer fare may be provided for the faithful at the table of God's word" (*Sacrosanctum Concilium* [*SC*], no. 51). Among its many ecumenical contributions to preaching, the Roman Catholic approach opens the treasure of Scripture more lavishly by expanding Scripture's context, transforming Scripture from something interpreted to interpreter, and enlivening traditional study. These gifts to preaching were not absent from the ecumenical church. Nevertheless, the Roman Catholic Church's attention to preaching the last fifty years clarified, emboldened, and deepened them.

Expanding Scripture's Context

Preaching in many Christian traditions expounds Scripture's original context and applies Scripture to the current context (see 117 above), even as it overlooks or discounts the context in which most people read and hear the Bible, i.e., the liturgy or worship. Many Protestants and their preachers understand Scripture as a book, an ancient document or a text that provides the truth of God and Christ. This document must be interpreted and explained in a way that the people, aided by grace or the Holy Spirit, accept or agree to the biblical text by an act of will. The goal of preaching is that the truth of Scripture is correctly explained and understood. The worship service either calls on the Holy Spirit to bring illumination or reinforces the message of the sermon.

Roman Catholic preaching teaches the whole church that Scripture's most immediate and accessible context is not the canon or even the book in which a passage is found. If Scripture has any privileged context for our people, it is especially the liturgy where they hear Scripture proclaimed and the sermon preached. Rather than a document, Scripture is our family story being told—the story of God ending the old and beginning the new, putting to death and raising to life, bringing light out of darkness, speech out of silence, and hope out of despair. Rather than contained in a book, Scripture is God speaking God's promise—actually pronouncing, declaring, and giving new life. The goal of preaching is that people experience this new life, most especially in the Eucharist. Rather than expounding and applying Scripture's original context and meaning to the assembly, preaching flows out of the readings and the other "sacred texts" of the liturgy and leads the assembly into the liturgical action that follows. As the Roman Catholic bishops stated in *Fulfilled in Your Hearing*, "The homily is not so much *on* the Scriptures as *from* and *through* them" (FIYH, no. 20). In subsequent years, this insight was nuanced to recognize that within Roman Catholic preaching, there are other "sacred texts" as well that can inspire preaching (see 159 above).

This approach to Scripture is nowhere more evident than in the widespread acceptance of the Revised Common Lectionary, which is adopted and adapted from the Roman Catholic Lectionary for Mass. The Lectionary causes the church to read Scripture differently (see 119 above). The Lectionary exposes Christians to more of the Bible by providing a three-year cycle that includes an Old Testament, psalm, epistle, and gospel reading for each Sunday and festival. While the Lectionary is certainly not exhaustive in terms of the canon, it requires assemblies and preachers to hear and consider passages they would not when preachers select the sermon text.

The Lectionary removes Scripture readings from their canonical, literary, and historical contexts and places them in the context of the liturgical year and the other readings. The context of readings is not the books in which they are found but the Sundays, feasts, and seasons of the liturgical year on which they are read, the liturgy of the day, and the assembly at prayer (West 1997, 30). Many Christians, for example, do not identify the context of the Servant Songs with third Isaiah as readily as they do with Holy Week. In so doing, they unquestionably identify the textually unnamed and historically unidentified servant as Jesus. Even more striking, when read on

Christmas Eve, Isaiah 9:6 is unmistakably about Jesus, regardless of what the verse's original context says.

One way the Lectionary readies the assembly to experience new life in the sacraments is by providing many readings that include food and water images, which in the context of worship accumulate sacramental associations not found in their historical context. Read and heard in the context of worship, for example, accounts of Jesus' table fellowship take on a heightened eucharistic dimension—for many confined to the Last Supper narratives in the gospels—that shapes eucharistic hospitality and practice in many denominations.

As these examples make plain, when Christians gather for worship, Scripture's ultimate and most immediate point of reference (because of the liturgical context) is Jesus Christ—the Word, the Truth, and the Life. The liturgical year and the assigned readings from Scripture, together with the other texts assigned to the day, enable the church to reflect on different dimensions of God's gift of salvation in Jesus Christ in the course of the year. By proclaiming the Bible, the Old Testament as well as the New through the memory of our salvation, Christians participate in the gift Jesus gave those disciples on the road to Emmaus (Luke 24:13ff). There he taught that everything written about him in the law of Moses, the prophets, and the psalms must be fulfilled; he opened the disciples' minds to understand the Scriptures in terms of the Messiah suffering and rising from the dead on the third day; and that repentance and forgiveness of sins will be proclaimed in his name to all nations, beginning from Jerusalem.

Scripture as Interpreter

With this Christ-centered hermeneutic, Roman Catholics embrace Scripture (along with the sacred texts encompassing the whole of the liturgy, see 36) as key for interpreting human existence, the world in all its complexities, and the church's life and mission, rather than a document to be explained and accepted. That Scripture is interpreter of life rather than a document to be applied to life is a gift to the whole church. FIYH, a document widely read ecumenically, defines the homily as "a scriptural interpretation of human existence which enables a community to recognize God's active presence, to respond to that presence in faith through liturgical word and gesture, and beyond the liturgical assembly, through a life lived in conformity with the Gospel" (FIYH, no. 81). For many in the ecumenical church, it is important to distinguish between Scripture as interpreter, in which preaching orients us in the cross and resurrection of Jesus Christ, and

Scripture as judge, in which the preacher hands down doctrinal and moral absolutes. By embracing Scripture as interpreter, preachers claim their role as "mediator of meaning" (FIYH, no. 12).

To use Scripture as our interpreter requires preachers to move from saying what the text says to doing what the text does. In that vein, Pope Francis (b. 1936) reflects,

> If a text was written to console, it should not be used to correct errors; if it was written as an exhortation, it should not be employed to teach doctrine; if it was written to teach something about God, it should not be used to expound various theological opinions; if it was written as a summons to praise or missionary outreach, let us not use it to talk about the latest news (*Evangelii Gaudium* [*EG*], no. 146).

The challenge is to proclaim Scripture in keeping with the Gospel, without "weaken[ing] the distinct and specific emphasis of a text which we are called to preach" (*EG*, no. 148). Here, we find resonances with the Lutheran understanding of a "canon within the canon," which is Jesus Christ. We measure the books of the Bible first and foremost by how they relate to and proclaim the life and ministry of Jesus.

Mystagogical preaching (see 134ff. above) is an obvious example of Scripture in its liturgical context, serving as interpretive key rather than being interpreted. Mystagogical preaching can be justifiably described as thematic because the topic of this preaching does not emerge directly from assigned passages but the occasion of bringing the newly initiated deeply into the grace and meaning of the sacraments. Nevertheless, Scripture is integral to mystagogy as preachers describe the sacraments primarily, though not exclusively, in terms of scriptural stories, images, admonitions, and segments of psalms. In addition to preaching, this approach is evident in prayers said over water, bread, and wine. As Scripture is a primary interpretive key for the sacraments, so—from a Roman Catholic perspective—the sacraments are primary interpretive keys to the Scriptures. Together both Word and worship, Scripture and sacraments are fundamental interpretive keys for all of Christian living.

Enlivening Study

To embrace Scripture as a key interpreter of human existence required preachers and, indeed, the church to expand and enliven our ways of studying it. As the Pontifical Biblical Commission asserts,

> Exegetes may have a distinctive role in the interpretation of the Bible but they do not exercise a monopoly. This activity within the church has aspects

which go beyond the academic analysis of texts. The church, indeed, does not regard the Bible simply as a collection of historical documents dealing with its own origins; it receives the Bible as word of God, addressed both to itself and to the entire world at the present time. This conviction, stemming from the faith, leads in turn to the work of actualizing and inculturating the biblical message, as well as to various uses of the inspired text in liturgy, in "lectio divina," in pastoral ministry and in the ecumenical movement. . . . While actualization allows the Bible to remain fruitful at different periods, inculturation in a corresponding way looks to the diversity of place. (Pontifical Biblical Commission 1994, 520 and 521)

Biblical scholarship, which seeks to identify the meaning(s) of a particular text and to teach the Bible as an end in itself, is simply insufficient. While faithful preaching seeks to use the insights of biblical scholars, it recognizes that scholarship, regardless of how careful and well-crafted, is incapable of determining the meaning(s) of the text for a particular people gathered for worship at a particular time and place. Rather than reading Scripture from the primary perspective of the historical-critical method, for example, preachers can use Scripture "to interpret peoples' lives in such a way that they will be able to celebrate Eucharist—or be reconciled with God and one another, or be baptized into the Body of Christ, depending on the particular liturgy that is being celebrated" (FIYH, 52).

This is hardly a call to abandon serious study. In *EG*, Pope Francis instructs that preachers are required to give their "entire attention" to the biblical text, "which needs to be the basis of our preaching"; the Word must be venerated and studied "with the greatest care and a holy fear lest we distort it" (*EG*, no. 146). Serious study is coupled with patience as we wait on the Spirit, setting aside distractions so that we can be truly open to God, and cultivating love for God who desires to speak to us, the Scripture through which God will speak, and the people to whom we share what we have heard.

Approaching Scripture in this way requires that, above all else, preachers are prayerful as they remain open to the Lord's voice in the Scriptures, the other sacred texts, the whole of the liturgy and in the events of our daily lives and the experience of our brothers and sisters (FIYH, no. 20). We are not talking about prayer alongside study. Rather, prayer is the very heart of the study, with the goal that the Word of God in the Scriptures is not only understood but also "interiorized" (FIYH, no. 23). While preachers throughout the ecumenical church agree that prayer is essential to sermon preparation, our petition continues to be that the Holy Spirit will assist us to study faithfully and well.

Roman Catholic preaching teaches that attentively listening to the Scripture, the other sacred texts, the whole of the liturgy, and the people is perhaps the form of prayer most appropriate to the spirituality of the preacher. Preachers pray over the sacred texts seeking the "fire of the Holy Spirit to kindle the *now* meaning in our hearts" (FIYH, no. 21). We pray that God will open the heart of the assembly, so that God's Word falls on receptive ears. Rather than a task of ministry, preaching becomes a primary spiritual discipline and sermon preparation a form of prayer, particularly for the preacher but also for the assembly, as together—in the words of Pope Francis—we strive to "be the first to let the word of God move [us] deeply and become incarnate in [our] daily life" (*EG*, no. 15).

A Roman Catholic Perspective

Pondering what the Roman Catholic Church has given to a reenvisioned understanding of preaching and the ecumenical ministry of the Word over the past fifty years could constitute a volume by itself. One window into that contribution might be achieved by considering the contributions of Vatican II (1962–1965) and those of Popes Paul VI (d. 1978), John Paul II (d. 2005), Benedict XVI (b. 1927), and Francis.

Responding to John XXIII's (d. 1963) invitation to open the church's windows to the modern age, Vatican II issued as its first document *SC*. In a stunning passage, that council asserted, "The liturgy is the summit toward which the activity of the church is directed; it is also the source from which all its power flows" (*SC*, no. 10). Combined with other statements, such as "Sacred scripture is of the greatest importance in the celebration of the liturgy" (*SC*, no. 24) and "In liturgical celebrations, a more ample, more varied, and more suitable selection of readings from sacred scripture should be restored" (*SC*, no. 35), *SC* represented a convergence of the deepest ecclesial instincts of Roman Catholics for sacramentality reflected in the Liturgy of the Eucharist and of Protestants for the Liturgy of the Word.

In another powerful sentence, *SC* observed: "It is very much the wish of the church that all the faithful should be led to take that full, conscious, and active part in liturgical celebrations which is demanded by the very nature of the liturgy" (*SC*, no. 14). This new accent on the constitutive role of the faithful as a worshiping assembly led to deep reflection on baptism, which in turn led, by 1972, to the reappropriation of ancient rites of Christian initiation, in which catechesis itself was reenvisioned as an ecclesial process presuming full, conscious, and active participation.

Catechesis and Evangelization

In the liturgical reforms of the 1960s and 1970s, Roman Catholics re-learned the fundamental interconnectedness of baptism, confirmation, and Eucharist in Christian life. We learned that the faithful begin their eucharistic journey in baptism, a journey confirmed in a life of discipleship. Disciples emerge from the baptismal font into a life symbolized by the liturgical movement between Word and sacrament, their life of discipleship calling them to full participation in the body of Christ and the in-breaking of God's reign.

In 1965, the opening of Vatican II's *Gaudium et Spes* (*GS*) caught the world's attention by stating: "The joys and the hopes, the grief and anguish of the people of our time, especially of those who are poor or afflicted, are the joys and hopes, the grief and anguish of the followers of Christ as well. Nothing that is genuinely human fails to find an echo in their hearts" (*GS*, no. 1).

This statement found an ecumenical echo in the 1982 seminal document of the World Council of Churches, "Baptism, Eucharist, and Ministry":

> The Church is called to proclaim and prefigure the Kingdom of God. It accomplishes this by announcing the Gospel to the world and by its very existence as the body of Christ. In Jesus the Kingdom of God came among us. . . . Living in this communion with God, all members of the Church are called to confess their faith and to give account of their hope. They are to identify with the joys and sufferings of all people as they seek to witness in caring love. The members of Christ's body are to struggle with the oppressed towards that freedom and dignity promised with the coming of the Kingdom. This mission needs to be carried out in varying political, social and cultural contexts. (World Council of Churches 1982, no. 4)

These statements—with their emphases on signs of the times, good news to the poor, baptismal witness and solidarity, and the promises of the reign of God—helped delineate a pathway that led the Roman Catholic Church from emphasizing conscious participation in the liturgy, to a catechetical embrace of the mission of the baptized, and a renewed understanding of evangelization (see 105ff. above).

On the tenth anniversary of the closing of Vatican II, Paul VI issued an apostolic exhortation in which he asserted: "The split between the Gospel and culture is without a doubt the drama of our time, just as it was of other times. Therefore every effort must be made to ensure a full evangelization of culture, or more correctly of cultures. They have to be regenerated by an encounter with the Gospel" (*Evangelii Nuntiandi* [*EN*], no. 20).

In his 1979 apostolic exhortation on catechesis, John Paul II aligned himself with Paul VI, saying, "We can say of catechesis, as well as of evangelization in general, that it is called to bring the power of the Gospel into the very heart of culture and cultures" (*Catechesi Tradendae* [*CT*], no. 53). We cannot, however, say quite the same of the bishops of the United States when they issued FIYH. While this significant document beautifully presented the preacher as a mediator of meaning through the Scriptures in the context of the liturgical assembly, it missed a timely opportunity to discuss the homily vis-à-vis the newly emergent theme of evangelization. This, along with the previously noted lack of attention to preaching in light of the breadth of sacred texts embedded in the liturgy, was a significant deficit of this landmark document. The 1983 revision of the Code of Canon Law (*CIC*) did not miss this opportunity when it synthesized the gains made by Vatican II and Paul VI, noting, "All the Christian faithful have the duty and right to work so that the divine message of salvation more and more reaches all people in every age and every land" (*CIC*, c. 211).

Also in 1983, acknowledging five hundred years of evangelization of the Americas, John Paul II spoke to the Latin American bishops in Port-au-Prince, Haiti, saying, "The commemoration of the half millennium of evangelization will gain its full energy if it is a commitment, not to re-evangelize but to a New Evangelization, new in its ardor, methods and expression" (John Paul II 1983, no. 9).

Evangelical Testimony

John Paul II spoke frequently about this new evangelization. In a 1990 encyclical on the church's missionary mandate, he also spoke about evangelical witness: "People today put more trust in witnesses than in teachers, in experience than in teaching, and in life action than in theories. . . . The evangelical witness which the world finds most appealing is that of concern for people, and of charity toward the poor, the weak and those who suffer" (*Redemptoris Missio* [*RM*], no. 42).

Benedict XVI made a further contribution to a post–Vatican II understanding of the ministry of the Word when, in his apostolic exhortation following the 2008 synod of Roman Catholic bishops on the Word of God, he spoke of the performative character of the Word: "The relationship between word and sacramental gesture is the liturgical expression of God's activity in the history of salvation through the *performative character* of the word itself. In salvation history there is no separation between what God *says* and what he [*sic*] *does*" (*Verbum Domini* [*VD*], no. 53).

The contributions of his predecessors prepared the stage for Pope Francis's call to all the baptized to be missionary disciples. Building on work begun by Benedict XVI, Francis issued his first encyclical on faith in 2013 (*Lumen Fidei*, Lat. for "Light of Faith"), in which he called on all the faithful to move from the dispositions of faith to an active stance of discipleship. In this evangelical vision we are called by faith and sent by virtue of the sacraments of initiation to testify with our lives to what we have heard and seen and touched in Christ (1 John 1:1). This, of course, is the overarching message of Francis's apostolic exhortation *EG*.

What preaching is to the liturgy, testimony is to discipleship. Since Vatican II, the Roman Catholic Church has been appropriating preaching as a full, conscious, and active participation in the Word of God—especially in the liturgy, the *summit and source* of ecclesial life. At this juncture in our implementation of that council it seems we are being called to practice testimony as a full, conscious, and active participation in the Word of God in the life of discipleship. We testify to what we have heard and seen and touched in Christ, giving life to faith in one another and actively and fully participating together in God's saving and transforming work. We preach with our lives, in word and by acts of accompaniment. In Christ, we are heard, seen, and touched—and so, in turn, we are called as missionary disciples to hear, see, and touch: being sent as evangelists to speak the joy of the Gospel, the Good News of Jesus Christ. This is the liturgy of life of which the Eucharist is summit and source.

Gospel-Actualizing Community

In *EG* Francis declares that all the baptized are missionary disciples and evangelizers (*EG*, nos. 119–21). Just as Vatican II called us to full, conscious, and active participation in the liturgy, so now the Vatican II church calls us to full, conscious, and active discipleship. Discipleship dynamically expresses faith in both word and action in the multiple communities and relationships that comprise Christian life. When discipleship is at its best, the worshiping assembly rehearses the reign of God in *preaching* and *sacramental action*; the community passes on the tradition through *catechesis* and *initiation*; the institutional church is inculturated through *evangelization* and *mission*; and persons and communities engage in transforming encounter through *testimony* and *accompaniment*. In each phase of ecclesial life the ministry of the Word issues a participative call to faith-filled action. In this inherently sacramental vision, Christians of every denomination are called to be Gospel-actualized and Gospel-actualizing in the church and in the world.

Bibliography

John Paul II. "Opening Address of the Nineteenth General Assembly of CELAM, Port-au-Prince, Haiti." *L'Osservatore Romano*, English edition, 16:780 (1983).

Pontifical Biblical Commission. "The Interpretation of the Bible in the Church." *Origins* 23, no. 29 (January 6, 1994).

West, Fritz. *Scripture and Memory: The Ecumenical Hermeneutic of the Three Year Lectionaries*. Collegeville, MN: Liturgical Press, 1997.

World Council of Churches. "Baptism, Eucharist, and Ministry." Faith and Order Paper no. 111 (1982).

Contributors

Herbert Anderson is a Lutheran pastor (retired) and professor emeritus of pastoral theology at Catholic Theological Union, Chicago.

John Baldovin, SJ, is professor of historical and liturgical theology at the Boston College School of Theology and Ministry.

Alden Lee Bass is an assistant professor of theology at Saint Louis University.

Dianne Bergant, CSA, is the Carroll Stuhlmueller, CP, Distinguished Professor Emerita of Old Testament Studies at Catholic Theological Union, Chicago.

Stephen Bevans is a presbyter in the missionary congregation of the Society of the Divine Word (SVD) and professor of mission and culture, emeritus, at Catholic Theological Union, Chicago.

Robert Bireley, SJ, is professor emeritus of history at Loyola University Chicago.

John Carr is the director of the Initiative on Catholic Social Thought and Public Life at Georgetown University, Washington, DC.

Anthony Collamati is assistant professor of new media studies at Alma College, Michigan.

Michael E. Connors, CSC, is director of the John S. Marten Program in Homiletics and Liturgics in the Department of Theology at the University of Notre Dame, Indiana.

Guerric DeBona, OSB, is professor of homiletics at Saint Meinrad Seminary and School of Theology, Indiana.

Frank DeSiano, a Paulist, is president of Paulist Evangelization Ministries, a nationally known preacher, writer, and frequent presenter for catechists and clergy.

William Ditewig is a deacon of the Archdiocese of Washington, DC, executive professor of theology at Santa Clara University and director of faith formation, diaconate and pastoral planning for the Diocese of Monterey in California.

Con Foley is pastor at Christ the Prince of Peace Parish, Weybridge, England, and lecturer in homiletics at St. John's Seminary, Wonersh, England.

Edward Foley, Capuchin, is the Duns Scotus Professor of Spirituality and ordinary professor of liturgy and music at Catholic Theological Union, Chicago.

Richard N. Fragomeni, presbyter of the Diocese of Albany, New York, is ordinary professor of liturgy and preaching at Catholic Theological Union, Chicago, and rector of the Shrine of Our Lady of Pompeii, an Italian American spiritual center in the Archdiocese of Chicago.

Ann Garrido is associate professor of homiletics at Aquinas Institute of Theology and former director of the school's doctorate of ministry in preaching program.

Gregory Heille, OP, is professor of homiletics and academic dean at Aquinas Institute of Theology, St. Louis, and promoter of preaching for the Dominican Central Province.

Lucy Lind Hogan, a priest in the Episcopal Church, is Hugh Latimer Elderdice Professor of Preaching and Worship at Wesley Theological Seminary, Washington, DC.

Patrick R. Lagges, JCD, a presbyter and former judicial vicar for the Archdiocese of Chicago, is director of the Hesburgh Sabbatical Program at Catholic Theological Union and chaplain at Calvert House, the Catholic Center at the University of Chicago.

David J. Lose is president of the Lutheran Theological Seminary at Philadelphia and author of *Preaching at the Crossroads* (2013).

Barbara Lundblad is the Joe R. Engle Professor of Preaching Emerita at Union Theological Seminary in New York City, now living in Minneapolis.

Ricky Manalo is a Paulist priest, liturgical composer, and adjunct lecturer of liturgy, music, and culture at Santa Clara University in Santa Clara, California.

Robert F. Morneau is auxiliary bishop emeritus of Green Bay and pastor of Resurrection Parish in Green Bay, Wisconsin.

Carolyn Muessig is professor of medieval religion in the Department of Religion and Theology, University of Bristol, England.

vanThanh Nguyen, SVD, is the Francis X. Ford, M. M., Professor of Catholic Missiology and associate professor of New Testament studies at Catholic Theological Union, Chicago.

Mary Margaret Pazdan, a Dominican of Sinsinawa, Wisconsin, is professor emerita of biblical studies, Aquinas Institute of Theology, and promoter of preaching for her congregation.

Patricia Parachini, a Sister of the Holy Names, is a pastoral theologian, spiritual director, and writer, presently ministering in multiple contexts.

Jorge Presmanes, a Dominican friar, is professor of theology and director of the Institute for Hispanic/Latino Theology and Ministry at Barry University in Miami.

Timothy Radcliffe, a Dominican friar based in Blackfriars, England, is former Master of the Order of Preachers and a councillor of the Pontifical Council for Justice and Peace.

Craig Alan Satterlee, PhD, is bishop of the North West Lower Michigan Synod of the Evangelical Lutheran Church in America.

Catherine Vincie, currently councillor for the Religious of the Sacred Heart of Mary, was professor of sacramental and liturgical theology at the Aquinas Institute of Theology in St. Louis.

James A. Wallace, CSsR, currently director of San Alfonso Retreat House in Long Branch, New Jersey, was previously professor of preaching at Washington Theological Union in Washington, DC.

Margaret Moers Wenig is rabbi emerita of Beth Am, The People's Temple, and instructor in liturgy and homiletics at Hebrew Union College-Jewish Institute of Religion in New York.

Alex Zenthoefer is pastor of Annunciation of the Lord Parish and vocation director for the Diocese of Evansville, Indiana.

Index

Abraham a Santa Clara, *see* Megerle, Johann

Achtemeier, Paul, 222f., 228

Active participation, 15, 76, 85, 97, 129f., 163, 267, 292f., 295; *also see* Assembly

Ad Gentes Divinitus, xxiii, 100, 130

Admonitio Generalis, 63

Advent, xx, 74, 75, 76, 78, 80, 83, 239

Aetatis Novae, 260; *also see* Communication

Affect, affections, 3, 11, 16; emotion, emotional, xvi, 71, 82, 193, 201, 210; *also see* Anger, *Hilaritas*, Joy, Pathos

African, 56, 141, 155; *also see* Augustine, Conferences of Roman Catholic Bishops (Nigeria)

African American preaching, 172, 176, 198, 213ff., 239, 241, 281; *also see* Martin Luther King, Womanist theology

Alan of Lille, 62

Alcuin of York, St., 183

Alexandria, 56, 59, 135, 139

Allegory, allegorical, 59, 135, 139

Alphonsus Liguori, St., 82

Ambiguity, ambiguous, 3, 11, 117f., 149, 169f., 176ff.

Ambo, *see* Architecture

Ambrose, St., 51, 56, 58, 135f., 138, 143, 183

Amplification, *see* Projection (vocal)

Analogy, 11, 239

Androcentricism, 215f.

Anger, 201; God's anger, 195, 210

Announcements, 84, 158

Annunciation, 59, 67

Anointing of the Sick, 31, 120, 149

Anti-Catholic preaching, 84, 86, 90, 92; *also see* Polemics

Anti-Protestant preaching, 77f.; *also see* Polemics

Anti-Semitism, 69, 91, 245; *also see* Polemics

Apocalyptic preachers, 74

Apologetics, 26, 86, 89f., 182, 284; *also see* Catholic Action, Evidence Guilds, Justin Martyr, Polemics, *Postils*, Boniface Spanke

Applause, xi, 55; *also see* Claque

Apse, *see* Architecture

Aratus of Soli, 48, 238

Architecture, 256; ambo, 31; apse, 55; baptistery, 55; basilica, 51, 55; *cathedra*, 55; living rooms, 90, 97; *martyria*, 55; meeting hall, 51, 55; outdoor preaching, 67f., 76, 79; pulpit, xii, xvi, 16, 51, 54, 56, 68, 74, 76, 80, 81, 127, 128, 158, 196, 204, 205, 211, 214, 216, 234, 245, 275, 282, 285; sanctuary, 158, 194, 262, 282

Areopagus, 41, 47, 49, 237; new Areopagi, 236

Aristotle, *see* Rhetoric

Armenian, *see* Languages for preaching

Ars praedicandi, 34, 75

Art, 7, 8, 9, 17, 21, 36, 49; of accompaniment, 101; of exegesis, 51; of interpretation, 221, 222; of preaching, ix, x, 3, 10, 11, 16, 20, 23, 33, 41, 59, 88, 110, 164, 165, 170, 192; of rhetoric, 14, 21, 95, 200

Assembly, 12, 19, 36, 52ff., 85, 119, 126,

129, 131, 146, 150, 153, 159, 161, 224, 228, 273, 274, 275, 288, 292, 294; as subjects in preaching, 162, 163, 161; context and diversity of assembly, 35, 41, 56, 65, 70, 99, 100, 110, 117, 144, 149, 152, 155, 205f., 235f.; educated, 55f., 75; engagement in preaching, 50, 85, 87, 95ff., 99, 108, 147, 207, 289, 295; uneducated, 29, 157; *also see* Applause, Audience, Language for preaching

Athanasius, St., 59; Ps.-Athanasius, 56

Athens, 47f., 56, 201, 202, 204, 237; *also see* Areopagus

Atkinson, O'Brien, 87, 92

Audio divina, 20; *also see Lectio divina* and *Visio divina*

Audience, xii, 43, 48f., 55ff., 70, 75, 76, 90, 91, 107, 131, 135, 162, 181, 191, 193, 200, 216, 224, 236, 254, 257; *also see* Assembly

Augustine, St., x, xii, xvf., xix, 4, 9, 14, 24, 51, 55ff., 62, 80, 133, 157, 191, 200, 202f.; catechetical homilies, 58; collected sermons, 65; *Confessiones* (Confessions), 5, 6, 56, 209; *De Doctrina Christiana*, 14, 24, 59f., 95, 191, 198, 203f., 209, 221; *De Oratore*, 14; feast of, 69; style of preaching, xvi, 57

Augustinians, 65, 81

Authority, Jesus preaching with, 41; laity's authority to preach, 63f., 265ff., 271ff.; loss of authority, xiv, 101f.; of preacher, xix, 186, 207; of Scripture, xxi, 53, 116; to preach, 63, 264ff.; posture of, 55; spiritual, 257; women's authority to preach, 64; *also see* Canon law, Faculty, Hildegard of Bingen, Laity, Right to preach, Women

Ave Maria (Hail Mary), 69, 76

Azevedo, Marcello, 212, 219

Baby boomers, 236

Baltimore, 86; catechism, 26, 37, 89; councils and synods of, 84

Baptism, 15, 36, 56, 120, 135, 137ff., 141, 148, 233, 292; as goal of preaching, 58; infant, 139; of Jesus, 136, 176; preaching at, 113, 146f., 157, 161, 271; root of ministry and preaching, 14, 109, 265f., 268, 293; *also see* Initiation, Mystagogy, Rite of Christian Initiation of Adults

Baptized, xvii, 26, 58; 86, 95, 164, 283, 284, 293; as evangelizers and missionaries, 96, 98, 266, 267, 295; as preachers, 96, 294; *also see* Assembly, Laity

Bartolomé de Las Casas, 183

Basil, St., 51, 55, 59

Beauduin, Lambert, 85

Beauty, 22, 36, 56, 187, 242, 251; of God, 164, 196

Beguines, 66, 69; *also see* Nuns

Bellah, Robert, 6, 180, 189

Benedict XVI, Pope, xvii, xxv, 31f., 33, 97, 130, 131, 254, 258f., 262f., 284, 286, 292, 294f.; *also see Sacramentum Caritatis*

Benedictines, 63, 64, 67; *also see* Lambert Beauduin, Hildegard of Bingen, Virgil Michael and Boniface Spanke

Benediction of the Blessed Sacrament, 79f., 161; *also see* Forty Hours

Berger, Peter, 6

Bernanos, Georges, 6

Bernard of Clairvaux, St., 65, 67f.

Bernardin, Joseph Cardinal, 173

Bernardino of Feltre, 69

Bernardino of Siena, St., xi, 68, 69, 70

Bible, *see* Scripture

Bilingual preaching, 65f.; *also see* Multilingual preaching, Trilingual preaching

Bishops, x, xii, 28, 56, 90, 125, 139,
148, 149, 188, 217, 242, 267, 278; as
preachers, 54, 56, 59, 60, 68, 74, 80,
82, 150, 157, 159, 183, 267, 272; reg-
ulating preaching, 268ff., 272, 273;
teaching on preaching, 3, 29, 31, 75,
98, 106f., 129ff., 135, 160, 251, 260,
275, 288, 294
Black preaching, *see* African American
preaching
Blogging, 236, 260
Blondel, Maurice, 6
Boff, Clovis and Leonardo, 212, 213,
219
Bonaventure, St., 65, 66, 71
Bonhoeffer, Dietrich, 186, 189
Bossuet, Jacques Bénigne, 80, 82
Bourdaloue, Louis, 80, 82
Boys, Mary, 245, 247, 252
Braaten, Carl, 221f., 118
Brazil, 212
Breton *cantiques,* 79
Breton, *see* Languages for Preaching
Brilioth, Yngve, 60, 61
Broadus, John A., 96, 192f., 198
Brueggemann, Walter, 123, 195, 199,
211, 219
Buchinger, Michael, 78
Buechner, Frederick, 6
Bultmann, Rudolph, 221ff., 227f.
Buttrick, David, 170

Caesarius of Arles, 51, 57, 60
Calendar, *see* Liturgical year
Cannon, Katie, 216, 219
Canon law, xxiii, 267ff.; 1917 code, 84;
1983 code, 96, 159
Canons regular, 63
Capella, Andreu, 82
Cardijn, Joseph, 212f., 217
Carolingian reform, 63, 65, 69
Carrier, Hervé, 234, 243
Carroll, John, 84

Casel, Odo, 140
Catechesis, catechetics, 33, 37, 58, 79,
84, 87, 89, 106, 120, 124ff., 142, 163,
270, 292; and evangelization, 293ff.;
catechetical homilies/lectures of
Andreu Capella, 82, of Augustine,
58, of Chrysostom, 135, 137f., of
Cyril, 58, 135, 136, 137, of Theodore
of Mopsuestia, 137; catechetical
preaching, 15, 32, 34, 60, 62, 82, 122,
266; mystagogical catechesis, 32,
134, 137, 140; *also see Catechesi Tradendae,* Education, Mystagogy
Catechesi Tradendae, xxiii, 106, 131, 234,
294
Catechism, 78, 79, 131, 187; of Peter
Canisius, 82; of the Catholic
Church, xxiii, 15, 32, 34, 37, 96,
131, 150, 160, 278; of the Coun-
cil of Trent, 82; *also see* Baltimore
Catechism
Catechumen, catechumenate, 55, 107,
130, 139, 140; Mass of the Catechu-
mens, 27
Caterina Vigri, 67, 73
Catha, Willa, 6
Cathars, 64
Cathedra, see Architecture
Catholic Action, 90; Catholic Action
groups, 85, 86
Catholic Hour, 90; *also see* Fulton J.
Sheen
Catholic social teaching, ix, 91, 275ff.
Catholic University of America, xxiii,
89, 93
Cavadini, John, 127f., 132f.
Cervantes, 10
Chalcedon, Council of, 126
Charism, charismatic, 52, 151, 212,
264ff.; charismatic preaching, 67;
charismatic prophecy, 53, 125; *also
see* Holy Spirit
Charlemagne, 65, 183

Charles Borromeo, St., 75, 78

Charles IV of Bohemia, King, 64

Chat rooms, 260, 261

Chauvet, Louis Marie, 36f., 143f.

Cheering, *see* Applause

Chidwick, John, 88, 93

Christmas, 66, 67, 158, 176, 246, 289

Chronos, 22

Cicero, *see* Rhetoric

Cisneros, Sandra, 6

City, 53, 237, 240; preaching about/in, 47, 54, 55, 56, 69, 76, 77, 80, 81, 86, 98, 189, 237, 247ff.; *also see* Athens, Evidence Guilds, New York City, Paris, Rome

Civil unrest, preaching in times of, 70; *also see,* Disaster, Terrorism

Claque, xii, 55

Code of Canon Law, *see* Canon Law

Codex Iuris Canonici, see Canon Law

Cohen, Leonard, 10

Collins, Mary, 144, 266, 274

Columbanus, St., 63

Communication, xiii, xvi, 52, 125, 156, 192, 224; in twenty-first century, xii, xiii, 254ff.; God's, 223; mass, 74, 92; nonverbal, 10; preaching as, 9, 22, 29, 51, 74, 110, 131, 132, 162; social, 268, 270; theories of, 97, 117, 255ff.; *also see Aetatis Novae, Communio et Progressio,* Digital Age, Internet, McLuhan, Media, Podcast, Radio, Skype, Snapchat, Technology, Television, Twitter, Video

Communio et Progressio, 260; *also see* Communication

Communion, 19f., 150, 212; Christian communions, 107, 181, 188; first communion, 148; Holy Communion, 31, 79f., 85, 88, 111, 113, 120; ministers of, 150; of saints, 20; priest's, 26; restrictions on, 153; services, 274; under one species, 78;

with God/Christ, 16, 106, 218, 293; *also see* Eucharist, *Koinonia*

Comunidades eclesiales de base, 212

Concordism, 118

Cone, James, 213f., 219

Conferences of Roman Catholic Bishops, 251, 268, 270, 272; Canada, 268f.; England and Wales, 269; India, 269; Latin America, xxiii, 106; New Zealand 269; Nigeria, 269; South Africa, 269; United States, xxiii, xxiv, xxv, 251, 253, 269, 275; *also see* Co-Workers in the Vineyard of the Lord, National Catholic Welfare Conference, *Preaching the Mystery of Faith*

Confession, general, 80; of faith, 164, 227, 245; sacrament of, 76, 79, 88, 111, 148; *also see* Penance (Rite of), Sacrament

Confessiones, see Augustine, St.

Confirmation, sacrament of, 112, 120, 141, 147f., 268, 293; *also see* Sacraments of Initiation

Confraternity of Christian Doctrine, 86

Congar, Yves, xi, 5, 6, 13, 264

Consecration to Virginity, 150f.

Context, contextualization, ix, xiiif., xvi, 21ff., 36, 41, 90, 106, 107, 110ff., 124, 134, 138, 142, 156, 172, 176, 185, 195, 204, 211ff., 233ff., 265, 274, 293; Christian, 23, 95, 105, 126, 130, 214; contemporary, xiiff., 15, 17, 20, 24, 41, 96, 117, 122, 143, 169, 175, 186, 247, 254ff.; contextual preaching, xii, 8, 15, 17, 26, 35, 48ff. (of Paul), 95, 98, 99, 127, 148, 161, 171, 205f., 212ff., 225, 233ff., 251, 280f., 283; contextual theology, 100, 180, 233ff.; decontextualization/recontextualization, 224; liturgical-sacramental, 113, 119f., 124, 128, 130f., 135, 147ff., 155, 162, 240, 264, 271, 294; of

Scripture, 41ff., 287ff.; *also see* Culture, Inculturation

Convents, preaching in, 67, 68, 83

Conversation, conversational, xiv, xviff., 112, 238, 245, 259; about preaching, 23, 132, 216, 260; homily/preaching as, xvii, 22f., 52, 53, 52, 98, 99, 112, 132, 157, 161, 163, 238, 273; *also see* Dialogue

Conversion, 70, 82, 106, 109, 155, 226; convert, xvi, 78, 82, 105f., 164; of Augustine, 69, 191, 200, 202f.; of McLuhan, 256; of the preacher, 16, 20; preaching as call to, 75, 85, 107, 109, 112, 113, 114, 130, 132

Coptic, *see* Languages for preaching

Correlation of biblical text, 118

Coughlin, Charles, 91

Councils, *see* Baltimore, Chalcedon, Lateran IV, Lateran V, Nicea, Tours, Trent, Vaison, Vatican II

Court preaching, 80ff., 205

Co-Workers in the Vineyard of the Lord, xxiii, 267

Craddock, Fred, xiv, xxi, 101, 102, 170, 196, 199, 209

Creation, xx, 9, 44, 126, 165, 171, 181f., 187, 189, 194, 215, 277ff., 282, 284, 285; baptism as a new creation, 120, 171; goodness of, 187, 188; *also see* Ecological crisis

Creative, creativity, 3, 12, 21, 110, 123, 191, 196, 205, 215, 226, 258, 259, 262, 274; in hermeneutical methods, 51, 222; in preaching, 8ff., 41, 50, 60, 177, 192, 193, 198, 214, 237

Creed, 53, 58, 69, 124, 125, 126f., 139, 140, 187; Nicene-Constantinopolitan Creed, 126

Crites, Stephen, 171

Cross, 66, 68, 80; feasts of, 69; preaching/teaching about, 91, 289; sign of the, 129; Stations of the, 123; veneration of, 69; *also see* Good Friday

Cross-cultural, *see* Culture

Crowley, Eileen, 258, 263

Culture, cultural, xiiif., 50, 98, 99, 110, 138, 141, 148, 155, 172, 180f., 182, 185f., 187, 195, 206, 221, 233ff., 254, 258, 293f.; African American, 214; Asian American, 235; Catholic/Christian, 54, 85, 87, 89, 197; Chinese, 235; contemporary, xiii, 41, 100; cross-cultural preaching, 41, 41ff., 98; counter-cultural, xiii, 138; Greek, 47ff., 138; Hispanic/Latinoa, 216, 217f., 235; Italian, 76; Jewish, 236, 238; Korean, 235; Mexican, 235; multicultural, 117, 138, 244, 247f.; of encounter, 12; Peruvian, 235; U.S., 84, 90ff., 96; Western, xiii; *also see* Context, Digital age, Inculturation

Cupich, Blase Archbishop, 239f.

Cyprian of Carthage, St., 14, 54, 56, 57

Cyril of Alexandria, St., 59, 135

Cyril of Jerusalem, St., 58f., 135ff.

Davis, H. Grady, 193, 199

De Doctrina Christiana, see Augustine, St.

Deacon, 98, 147, 149, 150, 152, 157, 159, 183, 268ff.

Death penalty, 278, 281

Death, *see* Funeral, Vigil for the deceased

Deductive preaching, 96, 99, 170

Dei Verbum, xx, xxiii, 27f., 60, 96, 124, 130

Delivery, 23, 57, 88f., 96, 192, 198, 208; *also see Pronuntiatio*

Demosthenes, 76, 202

Demythologizing, 84, 222, 228

Devotions, 5, 18, 76, 77, 82, 92, 122f., 146, 158; *also see* Cross, Eucharistic, Forty Hours, Novenas

Dewey, John, 97
Diakonia, 188
Diakrisis, 52f.
Dialogue, dialogical, xvii, 21, 52, 57, 59, 79, 95, 143, 161, 224f., 233f., 237, 239f., 256, 273; interfaith, 245ff.; liturgy as, 96; preaching as, xvi, 15, 33f., 98f., 101, 120, 132, 162, 210, 218, 236; sermons, 170
Dickinson, Emily, 10
Digital age, ix, 17, 41, 100, 164, 254ff.; *also see* Communication
Dignity, 29, 293; human, 165, 188, 278, 280, 282, 283, 284; of God's Word, 60; of wedded love, 151; of work, 279
Dilthey, Wilhelm, 221f., 224, 227
Disasters, preaching in time of, xx; natural disasters, 56, 58, 81, 281; threat of heresy, 64; *see also* Civil unrest, Terrorism
Discipleship, 111, 212, 267, 293, 295; and evangelization, 107, 109f., 112, 114; cost of, 186
Discipline, 3, 6, 10, 11, 178; rhetorical, 57, 60; spiritual, 292
Dispositio, 202
Distanciation, 224f., 228
Diversity, 17, 20, 147, 175f., 247, 249, 281, 291; of assemblies, 98, 100; of liturgy, 143; of preaching styles, 74; *also see* Context, Culture
Doctrinal preaching, xvi, 18, 26, 34, 60, 76, 124ff., 170, 280, 290; doctrine, xvi, 56, 57, 58, 68, 74, 77, 158; social doctrine, 276, 278; *also see* Trinity
Documents on preaching, 26ff.; *also see Evangelii Gaudium*, Fulfilled in Your Hearing
Dodd, C.H., 97
Dolan, Jay, 85, 93, 111, 114
Dominic de Guzmán, St., 64
Dominicans, xi, xv, xvi, 63, 64, 65, 67, 68, 70, 74; *also see* Yves Congar, Dominic, Mendicant, Thomas Aquinas
Dramatic preaching/speaking, 8, 46, 66, 76, 82, 88, 91, 182, 211; dramatizing biblical stories, 57, 59; *also see* Entertainment, Theater
Drexel, Jeremias, 81
DuBois, W. E. B., 213, 219
Dulles, Avery Cardinal, 127, 133

Easter, 58, 91, 141, 254, 282; Easter Vigil, 147
Ebeling, Gerhard, 222ff.
Eck, John, 77
Ecological crisis, xx, 236
Ecumenical preaching, 106, 185, 244ff.; ecumenism, 268, 287ff.; *also see* Interfaith preaching
Education, xiii, 22, 87, 97, 152, 262; Catholic/Christian, 268, 270; educated preachers, 57, 65; for preaching/speaking, 53, 204, 267, 273; of clergy, 70, 77, 88, 89; preaching as, 26, 84, 89, 157; religious, 89, 107, 130, 148, 268; uneducated clergy, 60; *also see* Catechesis, Formation, Seminary, Teaching preaching
Edwards, Jonathan, 183
Eisengrein, Martin, 78
Elliott, Walter, 88
Ellis, John Tracy, 87, 93
Elocutio, 202
Emerson, Ralph Waldo, 10
Emmaus, xivff., 42, 52, 226, 289
Empathy, empathic, 12, 17, 175, 178, 196, 210f., 218, 241, 250, 259
Empereur, James, 211, 219
Enlightenment, preaching during, 74ff.
Entertainment, xii, xiii, age of; preaching as, 55, 110; worship as, 261; *also see* Dramatic preaching/speaking, Theater

Ephrem, St., xii, 51, 57
Epimenides of Knossos, 48, 238
Erasmus, 75
Eschatology, eschatological, 126, 135, 136, 214
Ethos, 60, 92, 117, 201, 206f.
Eucharist, ix, xix, 19, 31 36, 54, 60, 96, 97, 109, 112, 120, 121, 123, 129, 131, 134, 141, 233, 276, 283, 289, 292, 293; eucharistic bread, 141; eucharistic devotion, 76, 123, 146; eucharistic prayer, 36, 113; preaching during, xi, 15, 26f., 29, 34, 52, 113, 119f., 131, 147ff., 156ff., 264, 269, 271ff., 288, 291, 295; synod on, 31; table of, 60, 126, 264; *also see* Communion, Homily, Sacraments
Eudists, 79; also see John Eudes, St.
Eusebio Nieremberg, 82f.
Evangelii Gaudium, xxiv, 6, 19, 32f., 98, 107, 119, 132, 162, 184, 210, 234, 272f., 276, 290
Evangelii Nuntiandi, xiii, xxiv, 6, 28f., 105, 293
Evangelization, evangelizing, 9, 15, 28, 33, 46, 63, 82, 83, 84ff., 89f., 95, 98ff., 105ff., 126,130, 153, 155, 164, 184, 239, 242, 258, 283; and media, 259ff.; as encounter, xiii, 106f., 110, 114; catechesis and, 293ff.; new evangelization, 96, 98, 101, 106, 294; pre-evangelization, 130
Evidence Guilds, 86, 87; *also see* Apologetics
Exegesis, 21, 52, 132, 139, 163, 178, 207, 221, 223ff., 260; exegetes, 224, 290f.; exegetical preaching, 51, 54, 58f., 65f.; exegeting the congregation, 206
Exhortation, ix, 49, 54f., 75, 83, 122, 130, 161, 185, 290; moral, 52, 63, 130
Exordium, 48, 75

Facebook, 100, 254, 254, 259f., *also see* Communication

Facetime, 236
Faculty, 191ff.; canonical, 268, 272; teaching, 85; *also see* Authority to preach, Canon Law, Jurisdiction, Magisterium
Fagan, Harry, 282
Felton, Dan, 5
Feminism, 141; preaching, 214ff.; theology, 239; *also see* Prophetic preaching, Women, Womanist
Festal, festivals, xii; preaching, 55; *also see,* Annunciation, Cross, Easter, Good Friday, Holy (Maundy) Thursday, Liturgical Year, Pentecost, Saints
Fieschi, Tommasina, 67, 72
Film, filmmaking, xiii, 21, 92, 192, 235, 254, 256; *also see* Hollywood, Media
Form criticism, 142
Formation, 107, 139, 140, 282; doctrine as, 133; for/of preaching, 14f., 20, 84, 267, 269, 273, 276; liturgical, 141f.; preaching as, 62, 71, 178; theological, 6; *also see* Education, Seminary, Teaching preaching, Transformation
Forty Hours, 77, 122, 123; *also see* Benediction, Devotions
Fosdick, Harry Emerson, 90
Francis of Assisi, St., 14, 63f., 70, 284; Rule of, 74
Francis, Pope, xi, xxi, 6, 9, 12, 19, 32f., 34, 98, 100f., 107f., 109f., 113, 119f., 132, 162, 164f., 184, 188, 208, 210, 218, 234, 242, 245ff., 252, 259, 266, 272f., 275f., 277, 280ff., 290ff., 295; *also see Evangelii Gaudium, Laudato Si*
Franciscan Order, xii, 62, 63ff., 74, 76, 83; *also see* Bernardino of Siena, Bonaventure, Francis, Mendicant
French, *see* Languages for Preaching
Froelicher, Helene, 87, 93
Fuchs, Ernst, 222ff., 227f.

Fulfilled in Your Hearing, xxiv, 3, 17, 22, 24, 27, 87, 96f., 99f., 113, 116, 130, 159ff., 205f., 288ff.; scriptural text (Luke 4:21), 116, 123, 182, 277
Funerals, preaching at, 80f., 121, 152, 153ff., 164, 271, 283; *also see* Vigil

Galacian, *see* Languages for Preaching
Gallagher, Michael Paul, xviii, 5f., 13
Gaudium et Spes, xxiv, 6, 95, 99, 141, 184, 187, 188, 293
Geertz, Clifford, 235, 243
Gender, *see* social location
General Instruction on the Roman Missal, *see Institutio Generalis Missalis Romani*
Generation, generational, 187, 255, 259; baby boomers, 92, 236; iGeneration, 259; millennials, 236, 259, 263, 279; multigenerational, 117, 244; "now" xx; visual; X, 236; Z, 259
Gerkin, Charles, 172, 179
Gillis, James, 91
Gilroy, Paul, 6
Giovanni Dominici, 70
Globalization, 236
Gloss, preaching as, 53, 65
Goizueta, Roberto, 218, 219
Good Friday, 66, 69, 282; *also see* Cross
Gospel Wagon, 86
Gothic, *see* Languages for preaching
Greek, *see* Languages for Preaching
Gregory Nazianzus, St., 51, 55f., 59
Gregory the Great, St., 51, 59, 65, 157
Gueranger, Prosper, 140

Habitus for preaching, 17, 19ff., 173, 178; preaching as, 19
Hail Mary, *see Ave Maria*
Hall, Tom, 62
Henry of Lausanne, 67
Henry, Hugh T., 89
Herbert, George, 4
Heresy, 78; preaching against, 64

Hermeneutical, hermeneutics, 142, 221ff.; Christ-centered, 289; creed as hermeneutical key, 126; circle, 217; critical, 216; liberating hermeneutic, 212; new hermeneutics, 221ff.; of early Christian preachers, 51; of otherness, 218; of suspicion, 213, 219; of women's experience, 215; preacher as hermeneut, 15; principles, 30, 222; *also see* Interpretation, Paul Ricoeur, Friedrich Schleiermacher
Heschel, Abraham, 4, 13, 210, 219
Hilaritas, xvf.
Hildegard of Bingen, xii, 64, 67
Hilkert, Mary Catherine, xxi, 7, 13, 35, 37, 194, 199, 215, 219, 226, 229
Hill, William, xix
Hillel, Rabbi, 221
Hispanic, 216ff., 281; *also see* Latinoa
Historical criticism, 117, 142, 221, 224f., 291
Hoefler, Richard Carl, 22, 25
Hollywood, 91, 92, 97; *also see* Film
Holmes, Urban, 173, 179
Holy Orders, *see* Ordination
Holy Saturday, *see* Easter Vigil
Holy Spirit, 14, 127, 265, 274, 287; gifts of, 46, 148; inspiration for preaching, 3, 8, 11, 23, 114, 120, 127, 203f., 214f., 291f.; prayer to, 5, 9, 288; *also see* Charism, Jacob of Serug, Trinity
Holy (Maundy) Thursday, 67; *also see* Holy Week, Triduum
Holy Week, 246, 288; *also see* Triduum
Homiletic Directory, xxiv, 33f., 37
Homiletical plot, 170ff., 177, 179
Homiletics, literature on, 37, 87, 89, 191, 221; methods/models, xix, 36f., 99, 170, 205, 224, 228; "new" 99; teaching, 14ff., 75, 88, 89, 204; *also see De Doctrina Christiana,* Education, *Evangelii Gaudium,* Manuals, Seminary, Teaching preaching

Homiliary, 59f., 65, 67; Euseban *Galli-canus*, 59f.; of Paul the Deacon, 65; *also see* Eusebio Nieremberg, Manuals, *Postils*

Homilist as intermediary, xvii, 33f., 162; as mystagogue, 35; as teacher of faith, 127ff.; master homilists, 59ff.; vocation of, xiv, 29; *also see* Preacher

Homily, 26f., 113, 156ff., 205, 264; and Catholic social teaching, 275f., 281f.; and media, 261f.; as quasi-sacramental, 68, 71, 132; definitions of, 27ff., 52, 62, 95, 97f., 130, 158ff., 205ff., 289; in canon law, 271f.; in early church, ix, xvi, 51ff., 156f.; in middle ages, 76, 83, 157f.; in sacra-ments, 146ff.; narrative, 176ff.; of Archbishop Cupich, 239f.; of Pope Francis, 242, 247ff.; poetic, xii, 58; preparation, 12, 33, 37; Sunday, 33, 85, 97f., 131, 146, 238; sung, 57; *also see Fulfilled in Your Hearing*, Hom-iletics, Length of homily/sermon, Sermon

Hopkins, Gerard Manley, 6

House churches, 53

Hudson, Mary Lin, 215, 220

Hughes, Langston, 6

Humanism, humanistic, 67, 75f., 81

Humility of preacher, xvii, 4, 12, 16f., 23, 30, 165, 173; of teachers of preaching, 19

Humility of Faenza, xii, 64

Hymns, 5, 42, 78, 194, 250; hymnic homily, 57; *also see* Breton *cantiques*

Ignatius of Antioch, St., 52, 53

Ignatius of Loyola, St., 79f.

Imagination, 8f., 18, 21, 49, 80, 173, 190ff., 211, 215, 226, 266; and doc-trine, 128; as competency, 197f.; as device, 191ff.; as practice, 193ff.; biblical, 174; catholic, 35; conven-tional, 194ff.; empathetic, 175ff., 196; eschatological, 214; figural, 197f.; Irish, 187; narrative, 175; of Jesus, 8; of assembly, 36, 76; prophetic, 195f., 211, 217; sacramental, 35, 174, 194f.; *also see* Mary Catherine Hilkert

Imitation of Christ, 6, 185f.

Immigration, 84, 98, 217, 236

Incarnational preaching, 174, 187, 194

Incubation process, 22ff.

Inculturation, 30, 234, 291, 295; *also see* Context, Culture

Indigenous people, preaching to, xvi

Inductive method, 96, 99

Initiation, 134, 135ff., 147f., 266, 292, 295; *also see* Baptism, Rite of Chris-tian Initiation of Adults, Sacraments

Innis, Harold, 257, 263

Innocent III, Pope, 68

Instagram, 254

Institutio Generalis Missalis Romani, xxiv, 30f., 154, 271

Integrity, 18, 49, 117, 157, 245, 284

Interfaith preaching, ix, 100, 106, 117, 244ff.; *also see* Ecumenical preaching

Interiority, 12, 16, 20, 67, 105, 255, 291

Internet, 21, 254, 257, 260, 265; *also see* Communication

Interpretation, xiii, 95, 126, 172, 237, 256, 259, 274; community as inter-preter, 96, 98; homily/preaching as, 101, 130, 159ff., 178, 198, 207, 289; of church teaching, 21; of lit-urgy, 141, 207; of Scripture, 3, 15, 18, 27f., 29f., 33f., 59, 77, 116ff., 126, 127, 128, 135ff., 140, 142f., 170, 191, 203, 207, 213, 215f., 219, 221ff., 287, 290f.; public theology as, 180f., 188; Scripture as interpreter of life, 289f.; *also see* Hermeneutics, Prophetic preaching

Inventio, invention, 75, 201f.

Isasi-Díaz, Ada María, 216f., 219

Islam, *see* Muslims

Italian, *see* Language for Preaching
Itinerant preaching, 17, 52, 68, 86

Jacob of Serug, xii, 51, 58
Jacques de Vitry, 65, 69
James, St., 46; Letter of, 181
James of Voragine, 65
Jensen, Richard, 170, 172, 179
Jerome, St., 14, 28, 75
Jesuit Order, xvii, 75, 77ff., 82f., 87, 91, 183; *also see* Charles Borromeo, Ignatius, José de Arriaga, Julian Maunoir, Peter Canisius, Vincent Huby
Jesus Christ, 8, 41ff., 49, 186f., 245, 248, 282, 288f.; as model, 163, 186; as parabler, xv, 14, 41ff., 96, 164, 170, 175f., 223; as preacher, 8, 42ff., 182, 236; as prophet, 42f., 116, 195, 217; as public theologian, 182; as storyteller, 41; as Word of God, xix, 11, 125, 131, 186, 245, 251; commissioning disciples/preachers, 9, 14, 41, 45, 185, 209, 277; death and resurrection, 66, 120, 223, 289; encountering, xviff., 18, 106ff., 153, 164, 174, 176, 186; mystery of, 15; proclaiming, 10, 11, 13, 15, 28, 29, 88, 98, 101, 106, 110, 125, 130, 134, 161, 186f., 227, 240, 260, 266, 295; *also see* Evangelization, Paschal Mystery
John Chrysostom, 14, 51, 53, 56ff., 135, 137f., 183
John Eck, 77
John Eudes, St., 79
John of Capistrano, 68
John Paul II, Pope St., xxiii, 29, 106, 114, 119, 130f., 133, 186, 189, 210, 234, 236, 266, 278, 292, 294, 296
John XXIII, Pope St., 183f., 292
Johnson, Elizabeth, 215, 220
Johnson, Luke Timothy, 50, 125f., 133
Jones, Nasir, 10
José de Arriaga, 83

Journaling, 8, 21, 112
Joy, xv, xviii, xxi, 9, 19, 43, 45f., 49, 107, 147, 153, 171ff., 184, 247, 275, 293; joyful preaching, 19, 24, 33, 100, 164, 242, 276, 295
Julian Maunoir, St., xvii, 79
Jurisdiction, 269, 273; *also see* Canon Law, Faculty
Justice, 15, 43, 96, 175, 183f., 195, 218, 234; Jesus preaching, 43f., 49; preaching, 169, 204, 210, 211ff., 219, 275ff.
Justin Martyr, St., 182

Kant, Immanuel, 240
Kearney, Richard, 175f., 179
Kenosis, 186
Kerygma, 184, 187, 223; kerygmatic dialogue, xvii; preaching, 52, 58, 97, 205
Kiesling, Christopher, 211, 219
King, Jr., Martin Luther, 183, 214, 239, 244, 246; *also see* African American preaching
Kingdom (of God), xx, 14, 96, 283; in Jesus preaching, 43ff., proclaiming, 293; *also see* Reign of God
Koinonia, 189, 212
Kysar, Robert, 221, 223, 229

Laity, 76, 80, 90, 95, 266ff.; apostolate of, 268f.; preaching to, 65, 69f.; *also see* Assembly, Authority, Baptized, Lay Preaching
Language, 3, 62, 100, 110, 125, 172, 200ff., 223, 228, 235ff., 247; for preaching, 10ff., 17, 21, 23, 29f., 33, 37, 57, 65f., 99, 131f., 163, 178, 207f., 249f., 269, 273, 285; local, 66, 129; of doctrine, 127, 187, 195; of encounter, 106; of St. Paul, 48f.; of Scripture, xx, 127, 222, 236; problematic, 157, 159, 208, 216; vernacular, 63, 65, 70, 158, 256

Languages for preaching: Armenian, 54; Breton, 66, 79; Coptic, 54; French, 65, 66, 80f.; German, 65, 77f., 80f.; Gothic, 54; Greek, 54; Latin, 54; Italian, 66, 76; Punic, 54; Romance languages, 65; Syriac, 54, 57f.; *also see* Bilingual preaching, Multilingual preaching, Trilingual preaching

Lateran Council IV, 68; Lateran Council V, 74

Latin America, 106, 212f., 217, 239, 294

Latin, *see* Languages for preaching

Latinoa, 217f., 235; *also see* Hispanic, Latin American

Laudato Si, 277

Lay preaching, xi, 63, 84ff., 96, 265ff.; of monarchs, 63f.; *also see* Authority, Evidence Guilds, Laity

Lectio continua, 54, 62, 225

Lectio divina, 3, 20, 32, 35, 225, 291

Lectionary, xixff., 18, 21, 34ff., 54, 96, 113, 120, 126, 129ff., 160ff., 207, 275, 281, 288f.; Common, 163; interpretation of, 35, 119f., 162, 288f.; Introduction to, 29, 154; narrative, 163; revised Common, 288

Leitourgia, 188

Length of homily/preaching, 10, 30, 78, 81, 82, 83, 100, 112, 113

Lenten preaching, 56, 58, 70, 74ff., 78, 80, 82f.

Leo the Great, St., 51, 59, 157

Leo VI, Emperor, 64, 71

Leo XIII, Pope, 277

Levada, William Cardinal, 127, 132, 133

Liberation theologies, 141f., 211ff., 239; *also see* Feminist, Hermeneutics, Prophetic preaching, Womanist

Literary criticism, 117, 142

Liturgical Bible, 36

Liturgical movement, 85, 293

Liturgical reform, 35, 51, 85, 96, 111, 129, 140, 256, 293

Liturgical year, xx, 131, 158f., 162f., 206, 288f.; *also see* Annunciation, Easter, Exaltation/invention of the Cross, Good Friday, Feasts, Holy (Maundy) Thursday, Lent, Pentecost

Liturgy of the Hours, 121, 151, 161; *also see* Office for the dead

Liturgy of the Word, 31, 113, 119, 121, 160, 264, 269

Logos, 53, 60, 181, 201, 206, 210

Lonergan, Bernard, 6, 20, 25, 132, 133, 180, 182, 189

Long, Thomas, 114, 204, 209

Lord, Daniel A., 91

Louis of Granada, 75, 82

Love, 18f., 110, 113; Christian, 181; God's/Christ's, xx, 5, 8, 10, 13, 28, 81, 100f., 110, 120, 127, 148, 152, 153, 173, 186, 194, 196, 210, 215, 218, 242, 276; human, 120, 255; kenotic, 186; kingdom of, 96; of God, 28, 178, 208f., 291; of language, 3, 12, 208; of neighbor/people, 110, 184, 186, 208, 212, 279, 293; of Scripture, 208; wedded, 151f., 283

Lowry, Eugene, 170, 176ff., 179

Lumen Gentium, xxiv, 6, 85, 95f., 268

Luther, Martin, 77f., 249

Lutheran, ix, 82, 246, 290; *also see* Dietrich Bonhoeffer, Martin Luther, Krister Stendahl

Madrashe, 57

Magisterium, 7, 26ff., 85, 128, 245ff.; *also see* Canon Law, Teaching

Manuals, preaching, 26, 66, 86, 88; *also see* Homiletics (literature on), Homiliary

Marconi, Guglielmo, 254

Marriage, 235, 278; preaching at/on, 77, 81, 113, 120, 151ff., 161, 271, 283; preparation, 233; Rite of; *also see* Love (wedded), Sacraments

Martin, Hervé, 64, 72

Marty, Martin, 180, 189

Martyria, 55, 188; *also see* Architecture

Mary, Blessed Virgin, 20, 86; preaching about, 67; *also see,* Annunciation, *Ave Maria*

Mazzei, Ser Lapo, 70, 72

McGann, Mary E., 241, 243

McLuhan, Marshall, 255ff., 263

Media, xiii, 100, 254ff.; and evangelization, 259ff.; in preaching, 261f.; *also see* Communication, Facebook, Film, Internet, McLuhan, Radio, Technology, Television, Twitter, Video

Megerle, Johann Ulrich, 81

Memoria, 202

Mendicants, 64, 68, 70, 78; *also see* Dominicans, Franciscans

Mercy, 33; of God, 8, 78, 81, 100f., 148f., 154, 169, 178, 276; works of, 69

Methods, contextual, 237ff.; deductive, 99; feminist, 214ff.; for evangelization, 106, 294; for homily preparation, 36f., 88f., 108, 159, 170f., 205, 207f.; inductive, 99; mystagogical, 135ff.; of biblical interpretation, 27, 117f., 135ff., 142, 225; of Joseph Cardijn, 212ff.; of Vincent de Paul, 78; scholastic, 157; see-judge-act, 212ff.; storytelling, 43; theological, 25, 140; *also see* Feminism, Hermeneutics, Historical criticism, Literary criticism, Narrative preaching

Michael, Virgil, 85, 158, 165

Millennials, *see* Generations

Mimesis, 226

Mission, xvi, xvii, 9, 26, 28, 32, 63f., 97, 105, 106, 110, 120, 126, 140, 210, 212, 266, 289, 290, 293, 293, 295; church as missionary, 95, 184, 185, 268, 294; missiological preaching, 41f., 46, 52, 58, 85; missionary disciples, xi, 98, 107, 110, 295; of Jesus

Christ, xvi, 42, 44, 49, 185, 266, 267; Paul as missionary, 47ff.; social mission of church, 275, 276ff.; *also see* Baptized, Evangelization, Missions (preached), Paul

Missions (preached), xvii, 34, 70, 78ff., 82f., 87ff., 96, 100, 105, 107, 108, 111f., 113, 114, 122, 185, 271

Moltmann, Jürgen, 181

Monarchs, preaching by, 63f.; *also see* Lay preaching, Charles IV, Leo VI, Radegund of Poitiers, Robert of Naples

Monastic preaching, xii, 60, 63f., 67ff.

Moral, morality, 17, 90, 119, 277ff., 284; character of the preacher, 9f.; obligation to prepare, 36; preaching, 26, 34, 52, 60, 62f., 74f., 80ff., 97, 128, 130, 132, 137, 290; theology, 181; *also see* Catholic Social Teaching, Norms of Christian life

Movie, *see* Film

Mujerista, 214, 216f.; *also see* Hispanic, Latinoa, Prophetic preaching

Multilingual preaching, 65; *also see* Bilingual preaching, Trilingual preaching

Murray, John Courtney, 183

Music, 8, 208, 234, 247; church, 85; in preaching, xii, 58; in preaching preparation, 21, 36, 192; musical score, 225; *also see* Homilies (sung), Song

Muslim(s), xvii, 244, 251

Musso, Cornelio, 76

Mystagogy, mystagogical catechesis, 32; Jesus as mystagogue, 15; preaching, 15, 32, 36, 58, 122, 134ff., 146, 162, 290; 35f.; *also see* Mysteries

Mysteries, xv, 127f., 133, 134ff., 250, 262; ancient Greek, 55, 134f.; Jesus preaching, 8, 41; of sacraments, 147ff.; participation in, 85, 96;

preaching, xvi, 5, 9ff., 15, 18, 20, 27, 31f., 35, 37, 120, 128, 131, 158ff., 172ff., 186, 272; Paschal, 10, 34, 114, 134, 141, 147, 153ff., 187, 189; *also see* Mystagogy

Narrative preaching, 169ff.; *also see* Storytelling
National Broadcasting Company, 90f.; *also see* Radio
National Catholic Welfare Conference, xxiv, 86, 93f.
National Council of Catholic Men, 86, 90f.; Women, 86
Nausea, Friedrich, 77
Neophyte, 134, 137, 139, 141ff.; preacher, 15, 22; *also see* Mystagogy, Teaching preaching
New Hermeneutics, 221ff.
New Homiletic, 99, 170
New World, church in, 212; preaching in, 83
New York City, 241, 247ff., 254, 285
Nicea, Council of, 126
Noll, John Archbishop, 86f.
Nones, *see* Unaffiliated
Norms of Christian life, preaching, 31, 131, 159, 271
Nostra Aetate, 245, 251
Novenas, 123; *also see* Devotions
Nuns, 63, 66f., 92; as preachers, xii, 64, 67; *also see* Beguines, Hildegard of Bingen, Caterina Vigri, Tommasina Fieschi, Women

Observant convents, 63, 67; preachers, 66, 68ff.
O'Connor, Flannery, 6
Office for the dead, 121; *also see* Liturgy of the hours
Oliver, Mary, 10
Oral/aural event, preaching as, 22f., 26, 34, 51f., 62, 95, 95, 99, 163f., 125, 223f., 225, 258

Oratory, 4, 17, 55, 80, 88, 92; classical, 14, 48, 99, 191, 202, 207: also *see* Augustine, Cicero, Demosthenes, Paul (St.), Rhetoric
Ordinary of the Mass, 27, 31
Ordination conferring right to preach, 272f.; of women, xx; preaching at, 70, 120, 148ff.;
Origen, 51, 54f., 60, 157
Our Father (*Pater Noster*), 69 139
Outdoor preaching, 67f., 79

Paeth, Scott, 181, 188f.
Panegyric, 56, 58, 80, 89
Panigarola, Francesco, 76
Pape, Lance, 226, 229
Parable, 10, 18, 176; Pope Francis as living parable, 276; *also see* Jesus Christ, Story
Paraclete, *see* Holy Spirit
Paraenesis, 55
Paris, 65f., 80; University of, 64
Paschal Mystery, *see* Mystery (Paschal)
Passionist Order, 87
Pater Noster, see Our Father
Pathos in rhetoric, 60, 201, 206; of God, 169, 195, 210ff.
Patience in preacher, 17f., 19, 251, 291
Patrick, St., 58, 187
Patristic preaching, xix, 51ff., 63, 135ff., 157, 159; *also see* Homiliary
Paul VI, Pope, xiii, xxiv, 6, 28, 29, 105ff., . 184, 279, 292ff.; *also see Evangelii Nuntiandi*
Paul, St., 9, 11, 280; and women's preaching, xi; instructions, xi, xvii, 41, 125, 134, 186; Pauline typology, 136; preaching of, xii, 10, 41, 46ff., 52, 125, 237f.
Paulist Order, 88, 91,
Pedro de Calatayud, 83
Pedro di Cordoba, xvi
Penance, Rite of, 111, 148f.; *also see* Confession, Sacraments

Pentecost, 46

Peroratio, 49, 75

Peter Canisius, St., 78, 82

Peter Chrysologus, St., 59

Peter, St., 46, 236; church of, 66, 76

Peyton, Patrick, 92

Philibert, Paul, 266, 274

Philippe de Vigneulles, 66, 71

Piety, 77, 92; Catholic, 85; female, 69; pietism, 140; popular, 85

Pistoia, Synod of, 82

Pius X, Pope St., x, 84f., 111

Pius XI, Pope, 254

Plato, 192, 221, 227; Neoplatonism, 138

Pneumatology, *see* Holy Spirit

Podcasts, 254, 260; *also see* Communication

Poetry, poetic, 5f., 10, 18, 36, 194, 207, 226; poets, 4, 21, 48, 81, 221, 233, 238; preaching, 17, 36, 57f., 142, 163; *also see* Ephrem of Nisibis, Homily (poetic)

Polemics, polemical preaching, 60, 69; *also see* Anti-Catholic preaching, Anti-Semitism, Apologetics, *Postils*, Prejudice, Boniface Spanke, Violence

Politics, political, politicians, xiii, 21, 91, 117, 126, 138, 141, 170, 173, 181, 186, 191, 198, 200f., 204, 211, 217, 222, 278, 284, 293; African American preachers as, 213f.; preaching about, 56ff., 70, 78, 84, 178, 191, 275ff.; speeches, 46; *also see* Charles Coughlin, Court preaching, Martin Luther King Jr.

Polycarp, St., 53

Pontifical Biblical Commission, xv, 29f., 38, 290f., 296

Postils, 77f., 81; *also see* Apologetics, Polemics

Postmodern, postmodernity, 117, 140, 142, 235, 244

Potter, Thomas J., 88

Power, powerful, 182, 195, 212, 215, 235, 265f., 279; powerlessness, 217, 240; of Catholic social teaching, 279, 281; of God's Word, 5, 11; of Jesus, 41, 117, 182; of liturgy, 292; of narrative/ story, 172, 178; of prayer, 4, 9; of preachers/preaching, xii, 3, 14, 46, 66 68, 71, 81, 92, 100, 120, 133, 160, 211, 236, 241, 275f.; of Scripture, 119, 174, 280; of the Spirit, 9, 144, 214; of text/ words, 10f., 105, 225, 228, 266; *also see* Authority of preacher

Powers, Jessica, 6

Prayer, 32, 53, 80, 112, 122f., 143, 189, 225, 249, 258, 277, 283, 285; bidding, 158; evening, 161; liturgical, 18, 132, 159, 269, 288, 290; morning, 161; night, 79; of the church, 126; profession, 151; preaching and, 3ff., 20, 24, 28, 30, 32, 291f.; services, 121, 185, 274; *also see* Eucharistic Prayer, Holy Spirit (prayer to), *Lectio divina*

Preaching the Mystery of Faith, xxv, 98, 113, 129, 131f., 160

Prejudice, 195, 169, 175, 277; in preaching, 69; of preacher, 16, 207; *also see* Polemics

Probatio, 48

Proclus of Constantinople, 59

Profession, *see* Religions Profession

Projection, digital, 254, 262; vocal, 208, 256

Prokop of Templin, 82

Prone, 158

Pronuntiatio, 202; *also see* Delivery

Proper of the Mass, 27, 31

Prophet, prophetic, 52f., 76, 125, 195f., 210ff., 227, 247f., 266, 277, 289; action, 239; imagination, 195f.; people, 15; preacher as, 15, 76; preaching, ix, 52, 60, 136, 144, 169, 202f., 210ff.; *also see* Jesus Christ

Propositio, proposition, 48, 99, 197; propositional preaching, 48, 96, 99

Public theology, 156, 180ff.; preaching as, 164f., 180ff.

Pulpit, *see* Architecture

Punic, *see* Languages for preaching

Quintilian, 75, 202, 209

Quodvultdeus, 58

Race, *see* Social Location

Radegund of Poitiers, Queen, 67; *also see* Monarchs

Radio, xii, 90ff., 97, 181, 249, 254, 257; *also see* Communication, Media

Rahner, Karl, 6, 141, 144, 163

Ratio studiorum, *see* Teaching preaching

Reader-response theory, 142

Reconciliation, *see* Penance

Redemptionis Sacramentum, xxv, 31, 35

Redemptoris Missio, xxv, 234, 236, 294

Redemptorist Order, 82, 87

Redwood, Vernon, 86

Reformation, 71, 139ff., 258; counter-, 78; post-, 138; *also see* Martin Luther, Postils

Reign of God, 42ff., 134, 143, 293, 295; *also see* Kingdom of God

Religious education, *see* Education

Religious Profession, 150f.

Respect, respectful; attitude of, 4, 18f., 270, 277ff.; for women, 284; listening, 5; preaching, 34, 48, 98, 108, 205; respecting context, 22, 48, 98, 117, 249; respecting homily/liturgy, 131, 272; respecting other religions, 48, 251f.; respecting Scripture, xx, 108; shown by Jesus, xviii

Retreat houses, 80, 112; preaching, 96, 100, 105, 108, 112f., 122, 150, 266, 274

Revised Common Lectionary, *see* Lectionary

Rhetoric, 51, 55, 57f., 75, 78, 83, 88f., 95, 127, 200ff., 211, 255; Aristotle's, 75,

92, 99, 191f., 201, 206f., 209, 255, 263; Augustine's, 60, 95, 191, 200, 202ff.; Cicero's, 14, 24, 57, 60, 75, 191, 201f., 204; Greco-Roman, 46, 48ff., 58, 60, 75, 191ff., 201ff.; homily/preaching as rhetorical event, 110, 156, 163f., 205ff.; humanist, 76; questionable, 14, 148, 157, 193, 200, 204; rhetorical circle, 110f.; rhetorical education, 53, 56, 75, 204; rhetorical skills, 29f., 110f.

Rice, Charles, 160, 154, 170

Ricoeur, Paul, x, 172, 222, 224ff.

Right, *see* Authority (to preach), Canon Law, Faculty, Ordination

Rilke, Rainer Maria, 10, 22, 25

Rite of Christian Initiation of Adults, 120, 134; *also see* Initiation, Sacraments

Robert Bellarmine, St., 76, 78

Robert de Basevorn, 64

Robert of Arbrissel, 67

Robert of Naples, King, 64; *also see* Monarchs

Robinson, James, 221

Rome, 53, 56, 87, 97; preaching in, 75f., 76, 78; retreat houses in, 80; rhetoric in, 201ff.; sack of, 59

Rosary College, xii, 86

Rose of Viterbo, xii, 64, 72

Rupert of Deutz, 63

Rural preaching, 60, 78f., 82f., 85f.

Sacrament(s), ix, xi, 60, 258, 264, 287, 289f., 292f., 295; Blessed, 76, 79f.; church as, 100; of initiation, 134ff.; preaching about/during, 26, 32, 35, 75, 79, 108, 113, 119f., 122, 129, 134ff., 146ff., 160f., 276; preaching as sacramental, 68, 71, 96; sacramentality of the Word, 96; *also see* Baptism, Benediction, Confession, Confirmation, Eucharist, Imagination

(sacramental), Marriage, Ordina-
tion, Penance, Rite of Christian
Initiation of Adults
Sacramentum Caritatis, xxv, 31f., 131
Sacrifice for preaching, 3, 9, 227
Sacrosanctum Concilium, xxv, 18, 27, 34,
    140, 272; and catechumenate, 140;
    and homily, 29, 84f., 95f., 158ff.; and
    laity, 268; and Scripture, xix, 27, 60,
    119, 129f., 264, 287, 292
Saints, 36; communion of, 20; cult/ven-
    eration of, 78; lives of, 66; preaching
    on, 18, 30, 58f., 64, 69, 80f.; *also see*
    Festal preaching
Savonarola, Girolamo, 68
Schleiermacher, Friedrich, 96, 221f.,
    224, 227
Schreiter, Robert, 235, 243
Scripture, 37, 52, 57, 173, 190, 194f.,
    198, 202, 233, 289; alone (*Sola Scrip-
    tura*), 287; and doctrine, 124ff.; and
    evangelization, 108; and tradition,
    35, 37, 76, 142f., 233ff.; as food 69;
    as interpreter, 287ff.; as standard
    for judgment, 53; at Mass, 26, 113;
    centrality of, 35f., 131, 292; Christ's
    presence in, 131; Hebrew, 76, 136f.,
    195, 210, 244; in preaching, ix, xixff.,
    15, 27f., 30f., 35f., 59f., 62, 70, 75f.,
    81f., 95, 99, 108, 129, 151ff., 198,
    203, 213, 244; Jesus and, xiv, xix,
    182, 236, 277; physical copies of, 53;
    praying/reading/studying, 3ff.,
    18, 21, 27ff., 35, 53f., 107, 112, 121,
    126, 131, 198, 281, 290ff.; Protestant
    understanding of, 77, 287ff.; respect
    for, 18; social dimensions of, 276;
    also see Authority, Biblical preach-
    ing, Context, *Dei Verbum, Fulfilled in
    Your Hearing,* Hermeneutics, Hom-
    ily, Interpretation, Lectionary, *Lectio
    divina,* Liturgical bible, Love, Power,
    Sacrosanctum Concilium

Segneri, Paolo, 82; the younger, 82
Segovia, Fernando, 217f., 220
Seminary education, 77, 208; training
    preachers, 88; *see also* Education,
    Teaching preaching
Sequeri, Pierangelo, 6
Sermo, sermon, ixff., 26f., 249ff.; after-
    noon event, 77ff.; and imagination,
    190ff.; and rhetoric, 205ff.; before
    Vatican II, 84ff.; dialogue, 170; dis-
    tinct from homily, 26, 53, 62, 75, 113,
    129, 157, 160; life as, 63; medieval,
    62ff.; mission, 85, 111; of Paul, 41ff.;
    patristic, 51ff.; of Peter, 236; pre–
    Vatican II, 84ff.; post-Tridentine,
    74ff.; reading sermons, 59f., 63, 76;
    sermo humilis, 57; Sunday, 84, 87, 89,
    113; superior to Mass, xi, 68, 71; *also
    see* Homiliary, Homily, Length of
    homily/sermon, Martin Luther
    King Jr., Styles of preaching/speaking
Shakespeare, William, 10
Shaw, George Bernard, 190, 199
Sheed, Frank, 86
Sheen, Fulton J. Archbishop, xii, 8,
    89ff., 254
Shorter, Aylward, 234, 243
Silence, 4f., 20, 288; the silenced, 211ff.
Simon, Paul, 10
Skype, 236, 257, 261; *also see*
    Communication
Smyrna, Church of, 53
Snapchat, 255; *also see* Communication
Social; injustice, 169, 175, 195, 210f.,
    217; location, 42, 55, 98, 100, 118,
    141f., 170, 177, 185, 225, 228, 233ff.;
    location of Christians, 54f., 57, 138,
    185; order, 44, 54, 117; preaching so-
    cial issues, 56, 91, 169f., 211, 213; *also
    see* Catholic social teaching, Media,
    Prophetic preaching
Social sciences, 6; methods/theories,
    142, 181, 213

Social media, *see* Media
Society of Jesus, *see* Jesuit Order
Soelle, Dorothee, 6
Sola Scriptura, see Scripture
Song(s), in preaching, 66; liturgical, 36, 233, 258; popular, 235; Servant, 288; *also see* Hymns
Spanke, Boniface, 86, 93
Speech-event, *see* Oral/aural event
Speeches, 33, 53, 63, 164, 173, 223, 225, 262; in the New Testament, 46ff.; metaphorical, 172; prophetic, 52; theological, 164; types of, 11, 57; *also see* Martin Luther King Jr., Oral/aural, Rhetoric
Spiritual, spirituality, 141, 154, 185, 257, 271; care, 258; church as, 194; direction, 266; in ministry, xxi, 110, 276; in missions/retreats, 111f., 122; in teaching preaching, 16; of Christian life, 106, 126, 137, 258; of motherhood, 151; of the preacher, 18, 28, 30, 292; preaching as spiritual exercise, 3ff., 20, 29, 114, 128, 130, 189, 292; *also see* Charism, Holy Spirit, Ignatius of Loyola
Stations of the Cross, *see* Cross
Stendahl, Krister, 251, 253
Stewart, Carlyle, 214, 220
Stiegler, Bernard, 255f., 263
Story, storytelling, 16, 22, 100, 226f.; biblical, 42, 77, 118, 170ff., 197ff., 238, 288; of liturgical year, xx; preaching as, 115, 194f., 249f.; *also see* Jesus Christ, Narrative preaching, Parable
Street preaching, xii, 86
Study, 238; as preaching; biblical, 27, 117, 130, 287, 290ff.; in preparation for preaching, 3, 5ff., 21, 24, 28f., 32, 35, 107, 208, 238; of preaching, 87ff., 211; *also see* Scripture, Seminary, Teaching of Preaching

Styles of preaching/speaking, 14, 57, 76, 81, 131, 170, 202; conversational, 157; embellished, 57; evangelical, 110; high and low, 57; *mediocritas,* 57; *pedestri sermon,* 57; popular, 75, 157; *sermo humilis,* 57; simple, 57, 76, 83; sophisticated, 157; subtle, 49; theatrical, 82; *also see* Conversation, Dramatic preaching/speaking, Entertainment, Rhetoric
Suffering, 175, 188, 217, 293f.; of God/Jesus Christ, 15, 43, 69, 137, 186, 210, 289; of preacher, 29; preaching in the face of, 17, 149, 210ff.; *also see* Paschal Mystery, Sacrifice
Suenens, Leo Joseph Cardinal, 183f.
Surplus of meaning, 116, 224, 228
Symrna, 53
Synagogue, 51, 53, 181, 244; Jesus in, 116, 182, 185; Paul in, 237
Synods, 77; Carolingian, 69; Roman, 31, 32, 97, 105ff., 294; *see* Baltimore, Pistoia
Syriac, *see* Languages for preaching

Table, 238, 249; early Christian table-talk, 52; Jesus table, 43, 46, 134f., 289; of the Eucharist, 126; of God's Word, xix, 96, 119, 287; two tables, 60, 264; *also see* Eucharist
Tableaux, 79, 173
Targum, 54
Taylor, Barbara Brown, 7, 13, 194, 199
Taylor, Charles, 6
Teach, teacher, teaching, xv, 52f., 56, 59f., 78, 89, 90, 125, 191, 202, 245; doctrinal, 127ff.; Jesus as, 43f., 107, 134f., 223; mystagogical, 135, 139; of baptized, 96; of Paul, 125f.; preacher as, 15, 65, 69, 71, 95, 131, 178, 185; teaching of preaching, x, 14ff.; teaching on preaching, 26ff.; *also see* Bishops, Catholic Social Teaching,

Education, Formation, Magisterium, Seminary

Techne, 255f.

Technology, 23, 91, 100, 169, 222, 236, 254ff.; *also see* Communication, Media

Television, xii, 91f., 97, 181; *also see* Communication, Media

Ten commandments, 26, 69, 82

Terrorism, xx, 188; *also see* Disaster, Violence

Tertullian, 53f., 202, 241

Text, xiii, 141, 244, 256; about preaching, 26ff., 192ff., 260; for preaching, 22, 99ff., 163; non-Scriptural, 131; praying, 20, 24; preaching liturgical, 15, 24, 31, 36, 158; proof texting, xx, 172; "sacred" 27, 31f., 35, 150f., 158ff., 271ff., 288f., 291f., 294; texting, 236, 255; *also see* Hermeneutics, Homiliary, Interpretation, *Lectio divina*, Lectionary, Liturgical bible, Ordinary of the Mass, Paul Ricoeur, Proper of the Mass, Scripture, World before/behind/within

Textweek.com, 260

Theater, xii, 55, 66; *also see* Dramatic preaching

Thematic preaching, 32, 56, 58, 70, 75, 131, 290

Theodore of Mopsuestia, 58, 135ff.

Theologian(s), 6, 37, 57, 129, 204; *also see* listings under individual names, e.g., Alan of Lille

Theology, theological, 129, 163; abstraction, 13; and experience, 141; and imagination, 197f.; and language, 223ff.; controversies, 57; homily as, 57, 162; imagination and, 197ff.; in preparation for preaching, 6, 21, 157; language, 157, 208, 223; liberationist, 141, 211ff.; liturgical-sacramental, 137, 139, 152ff., 160ff.;

medieval, 65, 69, 139; method, 140f.; natural, 190; of *Sacrosanctum Concilium*, 129, 264; of discipleship, 111; of preaching, 24, 26ff., 60, 100, 119, 139, 143; Paris as theological center, 65; preacher/preaching as theologian/theological, xix, 6, 57, 64, 69, 119; reflection, 60, 119, 139, 141, 143, 216; theologian(s) values/virtues, 18f., 206; *also see,* Contextual, Doctrinal preaching, Liberation, Prophetic preaching, Public theology

Theresa of Ávila, St., 16

Thiselton, Anthony, 221ff., 229

Thomas Aquinas, St., xiv, xxv, 11, 205

Thomas Becket, St., 183

Thomas More, St., 183

Thoreau, Henry David, 11

Tisdale, Leonora Tubbs, 196, 199

Tours, Third Council of, 65

Tra le Sollecitudini, 85

Tractatus, 85

Transformation, 188f., 241, 295; cultural, 82, 214, 254, 258; liturgical, 256; of assembly/hearers, 34, 50, 70, 76, 85, 105ff., 119, 133, 174, 176, 181, 185f., 198, 218; of preacher, 16, 20, 185, 235; through (biblical) text, 12, 117; through doctrine, 128; through Jesus, 43; through media, 256, 262; through mystagogy, 137, 143f.; through storytelling, 173, 178; *also see* Formation

Translation; by preacher, 54; hermeneutics as, 221; model of contextual theology, 236ff.; of scriptures, 54

Transparency in preaching, 4, 110

Trent, Council of, xix, 74ff., 84, 95

Triduum, 261; *also see* Easter, Good Friday, Holy (Maundy) Thursday, Holy Week

Trilingual preaching, 66; *also see,* Bilingual preaching, Multilingual preaching

Trinity, xvii, 15, 19, 108, 218; preaching on, 69

Trollope, Anthony, xii, xxii

Turkle, Sherry, 258f., 263

Turn to the subject, 96, 141f.

Turner, Mary Donovan, 215, 220

Twitter, 254, 257, 259f.; *also see* Communication

Typology, typological, 135; imagination, 197; interpretation of Scripture, 59, 135f., 139, 143

Unaffiliated, religiously, 164, 259, 279

Urban preaching, 55, 57, 85, 86, 247ff.; *also see* City

Vaison, Council of, 147

Valerio, Agostino, 75, 78

Vatican II, 26, 105, 111ff., 183, 188, 254; liturgical reforms, 35, 122, 129, 140, 256; preaching after, ix, xiii, 27, 95, 129ff., 207, 264ff., 287ff.; preaching before, xii, 84ff.; *also see* Documents on preaching, *Gaudium et Spes,* Homily, Laity, Lectionary, *Lumen Gentium, Nostra Aetate, Sacrosanctum Concilium, Verbum Domini*

Verbum Domini, xvii, xxv, 32f., 97f., 294

Vernacular preaching, *see* Languages for Preaching

Video, 262; live stream, 254, 257, 260; *also see* Media

Vigil for the deceased, 121, 153ff., 274; *also see* Easter Vigil

Vincent de Paul, St., 78f.

Vincent Ferrer, St., 68

Vincent Huby, 80

Visio divina, 139

Violence, 19, 175, 183, 252, 279; preaching during, 169; preaching violence, 69; *also see* Disasters, Polemics, Terrorism

Vocation, 212; of ordained, 276f.; preaching as, xiv, xviii, xx, 3, 7, 11, 70; *also see* Baptized, Laity

Von Balthasar, Hans Urs, 6

Vorgrimler, Herbert, 185, 189

Wakes, *see* Vigil

Walker, Alice, 6

Ward, Maisie, 86

Watson, Francis, xviif., xxii

Weddings, *see* Marriage

Weil, Simone, 8, 13

William of Auxerre, 65

Williams, Dolores, 216, 220

Womanist theology, 141, 214ff.

Women, ix, xi, xx, 244, 249ff.; ministering to the poor, 79; preaching, x, xif., 64, 98, 204, 264f., 270, 284; missions/retreats for, 80, 111f., 122; religious, 89, 112, 150f.; *also see* Evidence Guilds, Feminism, Hildegard of Bingen, Humility of Faenza, Tommasina Fieschi, Nuns, Rose of Viterbo, Radegund of Poitiers, Caterina Vigri

Wood, Susan, 266, 274

Word of God 30, 124, 212f.; as countercultural, xiii; as fluid concept, 52; central to faith, xiiiff.; in evangelization, 107ff.; in Judaism, 245f., 250; in the life of Christians/Church, xv, xix, 35, 87, 282, 291f.; in Reformation, ix; lectionary as, xixf.; preaching, 28, 32, 54, 56, 81, 149, 153, 238, 269ff., 295; proclaiming, 119, 262; *also see* Dignity, Homily, Jesus Christ, Power, Scripture

Wordsworth, William, 8, 11, 13

World before/behind/within the text, 117, 128, 223, 225

World Council of Churches, 293, 296

World War II, xii, 90ff.

Xenophobia, 217

Year, *see* Liturgical year

YouTube, 254, 260; *also see* Media

Yves de Tréguier, 66